Venice &
the Veneto

"All you've got to do is decide to go
and the hardest part is over.

So go!"

TONY WHEELER, COFOUNDER – LONELY PLANET

THIS EDITION WRITTEN AND RESEARCHED BY

Alison Bing,
Paula Hardy

Contents

Plan Your Trip   4

Explore Venice & the Veneto   52

Understand Venice & the Veneto   225

Survival Guide   277

Venice Maps   306

(left) Restaurants in a Venetian *calle* (lane)

(above) Basilica di San Marco (p58)

(right) Glass in a window display, Murano (p180)

Murano, Burano & the Northern Islands p169

Sestiere di Cannaregio p122

Sestieri di San Polo & Santa Croce p99

Sestiere di San Marco p56

Sestiere di Castello p137

Sestiere di Dorsoduro p82

Giudecca, Lido & the Southern Islands p158

Welcome to Venice

Imagine the audacity of building a city of marble palaces on a lagoon – and that was only the start.

Epic Grandeur

Never was a thoroughfare so aptly named as the Grand Canal, reflecting the glories of Venetian architecture lining its banks. At the end of Venice's signature waterway, Palazzo Ducale and Basilica di San Marco add double exclamation points. But wait until you see what's hiding in narrow backstreets: neighbourhood churches lined with Veroneses and priceless marbles, Tiepolo's glimpses of heaven on homeless-shelter ceilings, and a tiny Titian that mysteriously lights up an entire cathedral.

Venetian Feasts

Garden islands and lagoon aquaculture yield speciality produce and seafood you won't find elsewhere – all highlighted in inventive Venetian cuisine, with tantalising traces of ancient spice routes. The city knows how to put on a royal spread, as France's King Henry III once found out when faced with 1200 dishes and 200 bonbons. Today such feasts are available in miniature at happy hour, when bars mount lavish spreads of *cicheti* (Venetian tapas). Save room and time for a proper sit-down Venetian meal, with lagoon seafood to match views at canalside bistros, and toasts with Veneto's signature bubbly, *prosecco*.

Historic Firsts

The city built on water was never afraid to attempt the impossible. When plague struck, Venice consulted its brain trust of Mediterranean doctors, who recommended a precaution that has saved untold lives since: quarantine. Under attack by Genovese rivals, Venice's Arsenale shipyards innovated the assembly line, producing a new warship every day to defeat Genoa. After Genoa backed Christopher Columbus' venture to the New World, Venice's shipping fortunes began to fade – but Venice wasn't about to relinquish the world stage, going on to become the launching pad for baroque music and modern opera.

Defying Convention

Eyeglasses, platform shoes and uncorseted dresses are outlandish Venetian fashions that continental critics sniffed would never be worn by respectable Europeans. When prolific Ghetto publishing houses circulated Renaissance ideas, Rome banned Venice from publishing books. The city was excommunicated for ignoring such bans – but when savvy Venice withheld tithes, Rome recanted. Venice's artistic triumphs over censorship are now displayed in the Gallerie dell'Accademia.

Why I Love Venice

By Alison Bing, Author

In Italo Calvino's *Invisible Cities*, Venetian explorer Marco Polo describes the cities he's seen to Kublai Khan – only everywhere he describes is actually Venice. From the moment you arrive, you'll understand why. Venice floods the imagination with possibility, launching dreams like ships from its Istrian stone shores. Gothic palaces, art biennials, masquerade parties: every seemingly permanent fixture of this floating landscape is the culmination of a thousand creative efforts, anchored by a thousand years of travellers' tales. Yet the city's glories cannot be exaggerated or repeated enough; Venice makes Marco Polos of us all.

For more about our authors, see p328.

Top: Grand Canal (p68)

Venice's
Top 10

Palazzo Ducale *(p61)*

1 Other cities have government buildings; Venice has the Palazzo Ducale, a monumental propaganda campaign. To reach the halls of power, you must pass the Scala dei Censori (Stairs of the Censors) and Sansovino's staircase lined with 24-carat gold, then wait in a Palladio-designed hall facing Tiepolo's *Venice Receiving Gifts of the Sea from Neptune*. Veronese's *Juno Bestowing her Gifts on Venice* graces the trial chambers of the Consiglio dei Dieci (Council of Ten), Venice's CIA. Upstairs is attic-prison the Piombi, where Casanova was confined in 1756 until his escape.

◉ *Sestiere di San Marco*

Basilica di San Marco *(p58)*

2 Early risers urge you to arrive when morning sunlight bathes millions of tesserae with an otherworldly glow, and jaws drop to semiprecious-stone floors. Sunset romantics lobby you to linger in Piazza San Marco until fading sunlight shatters portal mosaics into golden shards, and the Caffè Florian house band strikes up the tango. Yet no matter how you look at it, the basilica is a marvel. Two eyes may seem insufficient to absorb 800 years of architecture and 8500 sq metres of mosaics – Basilica di San Marco will stretch your sense of wonder.

◉ *Sestiere di San Marco*

Gallerie dell'Accademia (p84)

3 They've been censored and stolen, raised eyebrows and inspired generosity: all the fuss over Venetian paintings becomes clear at the Accademia. The Inquisition did not appreciate Venetian versions of biblical stories – especially Veronese's *Last Supper*, a wild dinner party of drunkards, dwarves, dogs, Turks and Germans alongside apostles. But Napoleon quite enjoyed Venetian paintings, warehousing them here as booty. Wars and floods took their toll, but international donations recently restored Sala Albergo's crowning glory: Titian's *Presentation of the Virgin*, where the young Madonna inspires Venetian merchants to help the needy.

⊙ *Sestiere di Dorsoduro*

Travel by Boat (p30)

4 Traffic never seemed so romantic as at sunset in Venice, when smooching echoes under the Ponte dei Sospiri (Bridge of Sighs) from passing gondolas. Venice's morning rush hour may lull you back to sleep with the gentle sounds of footsteps heading to the *vaporetto* (water bus) and oars slapping canal waters. Road rage is not an issue in a town with no actual roads, though *gondolieri* call 'Ooooooeeee!' around blind corners to avoid collisions. Hop on board, or try your hand at the oar with Row Venice. GONDOLA, SAN MARCO

🏃 *Tours*

Tintoretto's Heaven on Earth (p101, p127)

5 During Venice's darkest days of the Black Death, flashes of genius appeared. Tintoretto's loaded paintbrush streaks across stormy scenes inside the Scuola Grande di San Rocco like a lightning bolt, revealing glimmers of hope in the long shadow of the plague that reduced Venice's population by a third. Angelic rescue squads save lost souls until the very last minute of Tintoretto's *Last Judgment* in Madonna dell'Orto – as long as they hold back that teal tidal wave, even a lowly mortal might witness heaven on earth. TINTORETTO ARTWORK, SCUOLA GRANDE DI SAN ROCCO

⊙ *Sestieri di San Polo & Santa Croce, Sestiere di Cannaregio*

ATLANTIDE PHOTOTRAVEL / CORBIS ©

Padua's Scrovegni Chapel (p187)

6 Squint a little at Giotto's 1303–05 Capella degli Scrovegni frescoes, and you can see the Renaissance coming. Instead of bug-eyed Byzantine saints, Giotto's biblical characters look like people you'd recognise today: a middle-aged mother (Anne) with a miracle baby (Mary), a new father (Joseph) nodding off while watching his baby boy (Jesus), a slippery schemer (Judas) breezily air-kissing a trusting friend (Jesus). Giotto captures human nature in all its flawed glory – it's well worth the detour to Padua, and the plane ticket to Italy besides.

⊙ *Day Trips from Venice*

Opera at Teatro La Fenice (p66)

7 Before the curtain rises, the drama has already begun at La Fenice. Wraps shed in lower-tier boxes reveal jewels, while in top *loggie* (balconies), *loggione* (opera critics) predict which singers will be in good voice, and which understudies may merit promotions. Meanwhile, architecture aficionados debate whether the theatre's faithful reconstruction after its 1998 arson was worth €90 million. But when the overture begins, all voices hush. No one wants to miss a note of performances that could match premieres here by Stravinsky, Rossini, Prokofiev and Britten.

☆ *Sestiere di San Marco*

7

8

Venice Biennale (p46)

8 When Venice dared the world to show off its modern masterpieces, delegations from Australia to Venezuela accepted the challenge – who turns down an invitation to Venice? Today the Venice Biennale is the world's most prestigious creative showcase, featuring art (in odd-numbered years) and architecture (in even-numbered years), and hosting the Venice Film Festival and performing-arts extravaganzas annually. Friendly competition among nationals is obvious in the Giardini's pavilions, which showcase architectural sensibilities ranging from magical thinking (Austro-Hungary) to repurposed industrial cool (Korea). WORK BY EL ANATSUI, 2011 VENICE BIENNALE

✵ *Entertainment*

Venetian Artisans *(p49)*

9 In Venice you're not just in good hands; you're in highly skilled ones. As they have for centuries, artisans here ply esoteric trades that don't involve a computer mouse: glass blowing, paper marbling, oarlock carving. Yet while other craft traditions have fossilised into relics of bygone eras, Venetian artisans have kept their creations current. A modern Murano-glass chandelier morphs into an outer-space octopus, marbled paper makes splendid handbags, and oarlocks custom made for the likes of Mick Jagger are mantelpiece sculptures that outclass marble busts. GLASS BLOWER AT WORK

🛍 *Shopping*

Veneto Wines *(p40)*

10 Toast your arrival in Venice with bubbly local *prosecco*, but don't stop there: the Veneto is overflowing with oenological delights. Head to the source of whites as structured as Palladios in Soave, fall in love with brooding Amarones and rebel Valpolicellas north of Verona, and become an Italian wine connoisseur overnight at Italy's annual wine expo: Verona's Vinitaly. For something completely different, taste test at Verona's Viniveri, Italy's natural-process wine showcase.

🍷 *Drinking*

What's New

Rooftop Mysteries, Revealed

What shoes did a Venetian courtesan wear for streetwalking, how did Casanova escape prison while the doge slept downstairs, and what are those guys doing atop the clocktower naked from the waist down? Venice's highest mysteries are solved with revamped, behind-the-scenes guided visits to the Palazzo Mocenigo's attic closets, Palazzo Ducale's attic prison, and to the top of Torre dell'Orologio, where bronze bell-ringers moon Basilica di San Marco at midnight. (p106) (p61) (p67)

Palazzetto Bru Zane

A multi-year effort has restored the frescoed 17th-century Palazzetto Bru Zane to its original function: delighting pleasure seekers with concerts of romantic music by Europe's leading talents. (p117)

Fondazione Prada

Making waves along the Grand Canal, Fondazione Prada has turned the stately Renaissance palace of Ca' Corner into Venice's newest showcase for cutting-edge art and design. (p107)

Museo di Storia Naturale

Curiosity cabinets can't compare to Museo di Storia Naturale, Venice's treasury of mummies, dinosaurs and other natural wonders, all displayed inside a historic Turkish palace on the Grand Canal. (p106)

Jazz Interludes

Tides slapping canal banks provide a funky backbeat to live jazz interrupting Venice's silent nights – check the program at I Figli delle Stelle, Osteria da Filo and Venice Jazz Club, plus impromptu jam sessions at Ai Postali. (p165) (p116) (p96)

All-Natural Happy Hours

Rebel Veneto vintners are behind Italy's natural-process trend, inviting drinkers to taste pristine Italian wines – no pesticides, no additives, no fuss. Sample two of the best natural-process wine menus in Venice (and Italy) at Al Prosecco and Antica Adelaide. (p115) (p132)

Correr Imperial Apartments

How does an empress sleep at night, when a revolution is coming? After a multi-year restoration of Austrian Empress Sissi's suite inside Museo Correr, now the answer is clear: in blissful ignorance, inside a silk-padded suite frescoed with her favourite flowers. (p73)

Salute Sacristy

Now you can see what all the fuss over Titian is about. After years of restoration and masterpieces on loan, the Basilica di Santa Maria della Salute's sacristy showcases early works by Titian painted with such living colour you'll swear they're blushing. (p88)

Giudecca

Improved *vaporetto* service reveals attractions hiding in plain sight across Giudecca Canal: waterfront bistros, art galleries, Bauer Palladio spa treatments, Skyline Rooftop Bar happy hours, and organic farmers markets run by a women's prison cooperative. (p223) (p167)

For more recommendations and reviews, see **lonelyplanet. com/venice**

Need to Know

For more information, see Survival Guide (p277)

Currency
Euros (€)

Language
Italian, Venet (Venetian dialect).

Visas
Not required for EU citizens. Nationals of Australia, Brazil, Canada, Japan, New Zealand and the USA do not need visas for visits up to 90 days.

Money
ATMs widely available; credit cards accepted at most hotels, B&Bs and stores.

Mobile Phones
GSM and tri-band phones can be used in Italy with a local SIM card.

Time
GMT/UTC plus one hour during winter, GMT/UTC plus two hours during summer daylight saving.

Tourist Information
Azienda di Promozione Turistica (☑041 529 87 11; www.turismo venezia.it; Piazza San Marco 71f; ◷9.45am-3.15pm Mon-Sat) is Venice's tourism office, providing information on events, attractions, day trips, transport and shows.

Daily Costs

Budget:
Less than €120
➡ Dorm beds: €22–€30

➡ Basilica di San Marco: free

➡ *Cicheti* at All'Arco: €5–€15

➡ Chorus Pass: €10

➡ Organ vespers at Chiesa di Santa Maria della Salute: free

➡ *Spritz*: €1.50–€2.50

Midrange:
€120–€250
➡ B&B: €50–€150

➡ Civic Museum Pass: €24

➡ Happy hour in Piazza San Marco: €9–€15

➡ Interpreti Veneziani ticket: €25

➡ Dinner at Al Promessi Sposi: €25–€45

Top End:
More than €250
➡ Boutique hotel: €150-plus

➡ Gondola ride: €80

➡ Palazzo Grassi & Punta della Dogana ticket: €20

➡ Dinner at Anice Stellato: €45–€60

➡ La Fenice ticket: from €40

Advance Planning

Two months before Book accommodation for high season and snap up tickets to La Fenice operas, Venice Film Festival premieres and Biennale openings.

Three weeks before Check special-event calendars at www.aguestinvenice.com and www.veneziadavivere.com, and reserve boat trips.

One week before Make restaurant reservations for a big night out; skip the queues by booking tickets to major attractions and events online at www.venetoinside.com or www.veniceconnected.com.

Useful Websites

Lonely Planet (www.lonelyplan et.com) Expert travel advice.

Venice Comune (http://www.comune.venezia.it) City of Venice official site; event announcements and essential info, including high-water alerts.

Venice Connected (www.venice connected.com) Advance ticket sales to major tourist attractions, facilities info, maps and eco tips.

Venezia da Vivere (www.veneziadavivere.com) Music performances, art openings, nightlife, new designers.

2Venice (www.2venice.it) Updated events listings and info on tourist attractions and new initiatives.

WHEN TO GO

Autumn has warm days, sparse crowds and lower rates. Winter has chilly, serene days and sociable nights. Spring is damp but lovely as ever indoors.

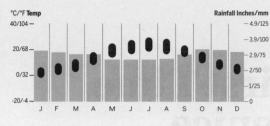

Arriving in Venice

Marco Polo Airport (VCE) Located on the mainland 12km from Venice, east of Mestre. Alilaguna operates a ferry service (€15) to Venice from the airport ferry dock (an eight-minute walk from the terminal); expect it to take 45 to 90 minutes to reach most destinations. Water taxis to Venice from airport docks cost €90 to €110, or €32 for shared taxis with up to eight passengers and 10 bags. ATVO buses (€6) depart from the airport every 30 minutes from 8am to midnight, and reach Venice's Piazzale Roma within 30 minutes, traffic permitting.

Piazzale Roma This car park is the only point within central Venice accessible by car or bus. *Vaporetto* (water-bus) lines to destinations throughout the city depart from Piazzale Roma docks.

Stazione Santa Lucia Venice's train station. *Vaporetto* lines depart from Ferrovia (Station) docks.

Stazione Venezia Mestre Mestre's mainland train station; transfer here to Stazione Santa Lucia.

For much more on **arrival** see p278

Getting Around

➡ **Vaporetto** Slow and scenic, the *vaporetto* is Venice's main public transport. Single rides cost €7; for frequent use, get a timed pass for unlimited travel within a set period (12/24/36/48/72-hour passes cost €18/20/25/30/35). Tickets, passes and maps are available at dockside HelloVenezia ticket booths and www.hellovenezia.com.

➡ **Gondola** Daytime rates run to €80 for 40 minutes (six passengers maximum) or €100 from 7pm to 8am, not including songs (negotiated separately) or tips.

➡ **Traghetto** Locals use this daytime public gondola service (€0.50) to cross the Grand Canal between bridges.

➡ **Water taxi** Sleek teak boats offer taxi service for €8.90 plus €1.80 per minute, plus €6 for hotel service and extra for night-time, luggage and large groups. Flat rates can be negotiated in advance.

For much more on **getting around** see p281

Sleeping

With many Venetians opening historic homes to visitors as B&Bs and rental getaways, you can become a local overnight here. Venice was once known for charmingly decrepit hotels where English poets quietly expired, but new designer-chic boutique hotels are spiffing up historic palaces and attracting a rock-star following. Expect to pay €50 to €150 midrange, plus tourist tax (hostels are exempt). Some upscale hotels offer vouchers for overnight parking in Tronchetto; otherwise it's at least €21 per day. San Marco hotels are ideally located, but the trade-offs are light, space and noise.

Useful Websites

➡ **BB Planet** (www.bbplanet. com) Search Venice B&Bs by neighbourhood, price range and availability.

➡ **APT** (www.turismovenezia. it) Lists hundreds of licensed B&Bs and rental apartments in Venice proper.

➡ **Lonely Planet** (www. lonelyplanet.com) Expert author reviews, user feedback, booking engine.

For much more on **sleeping** see p211

First Time Venice

For more information, see Survival Guide (p284)

Checklist

➡ Ensure your passport is valid for six months after your entry date in Europe

➡ EU citizens do not need visas to visit Venice, and nationals of the US, Canada, Brazil, Japan, Australia and several other countries do not require visas for EU visits up to 90 days. Check current visa requirements at the Italian foreign-ministry website (www.esteri.it)

➡ Check airline baggage restrictions

➡ Inform your debit-/credit-card company that you'll be visiting Italy

➡ Check the public-holiday calendar (p287) to anticipate closures

What to Pack

➡ Walking shoes with traction for flagstones and gondolas

➡ Sunscreen (year-round)

➡ Rain gear for winter and spring visits, including gumboots if staying in low-lying San Marco

Top Tips for Your Trip

➡ Start walking. Venice's extraordinary sights and hidden *bacari* (hole-in-the-wall bars) are worth going that extra mile across footbridges and flagstones for. Bonus: you'll save serious cash on *vaporetto* and water-taxi rides.

➡ Get lost. Venice's ancient crooked *calli* (backstreets) often outwit the latest smartphones and satellite mapping technology. But there are no wrong turns here: unexpected wonders await around every corner in this floating city. To return to major routes, just follow the flow of foot traffic.

What to Wear

Costumes aren't strictly required at Carnevale, but they instantly transform visitors into temporary Venetians – and everything goes with a long-nosed plague doctor's mask.

Gumboots are sometimes necessary in *acque alte*, and sensible flat shoes are always advisable. Resort wear was apparently invented with Venice summers in mind: breezy, yet luxe and vaguely nautical. But to really blend into the Venice scenery, you'll have to get creative. There's no point being shy about colour here – have you seen the paintings?

Venice goes all out for gala arts events, including Venice Film Festival premieres, Biennale art shows and opera opening nights at La Fenice. Dramatic entrances count: think capes and Murano-glass statement necklaces, not cardigans and pearls. Accessories made by Venetian artisans are always appreciated.

Be Forewarned

➡ Mind your step on slippery canal banks and stone footbridges, especially after rains and *acque alte* (high water).

➡ Venice is not childproof. Not all canal banks and bridges have railings, and most Gothic palaces have pointy edges.

➡ You're quite safe in Venice, even alone at night – but watch out for petty theft in and around Venice train station, and crime around the mainland Mestre train station.

Money

Venice built an empire through international trade, and continues to encourage it with ATMs throughout the city. Many eating and drinking establishments are cash only, and some shops may give you a small discount if you pay cash instead of using a credit card and thus avoid vendor service fees.

For more information, see p286.

Taxes & Refunds

If you're staying overnight within Venice, expect to pay €3 to €5 in tourist tax per person for up to five nights (additional nights are free). Children and hostels are exempt from the tax.

VAT (value-added tax) of around 20% is added to purchases over €155 in Italy, but it may be possible to reclaim it – see p287.

Tipping

➡ **Restaurants** Tips of 10% are standard – though check to see that a tip hasn't already been added to your bill, or included in the flat *coperto* (cover) charge. Change is often left on the counter at cafes and *bacari*.

➡ **Hotels** One euro per bag is standard for baggage handling; €1 per night for cleaning service is welcome.

➡ **Transport** Tips may be given for gondolas and water-taxi service graciously provided, especially if singing is involved.

Language

English isn't always widely spoken in Italy, so pick up a few essential phrases before you go. If you have food allergies or dietary restrictions, write down the Italian words for those items, then just point to the word and say 'no' to restaurant servers. Look up the Italian names for any medications you are taking, and write those down in case you have to visit the doctor in Italy.

You may hear the sing-song Venetian dialect spoken. This isn't just an accent. Venetian vocabulary and idioms are so distinct that many Italians can't understand them. Ask a gondolier or bartender to teach you a few words or expressions, and you're bound to win over Venetians – or at least make them laugh.

 What's the local speciality?
Qual'è la specialità di questa regione?
kwa·*le* la spe·cha·lee·*ta* dee *kwes*·ta re·*jo*·ne

A bit like the rivalry between medieval Italian city-states, these days the country's regions compete in speciality foods and wines.

 Which combined tickets do you have?
Quali biglietti cumulativi avete?
kwa·lee bee·*lye*·tee koo·moo·la·*tee*·vee a·ve·te

Make the most of your euro by getting combined tickets to various sights; they are available in all major Italian cities.

 Where can I buy discount designer items?
C'è un outlet in zona? che oon *owt*·let in *zo*·na

Discount fashion outlets are big business in major cities – get bargain-priced seconds, samples and cast-offs for *la bella figura*.

 I'm here with my husband/boyfriend.
Sono qui con il mio marito/ragazzo.
so·no kwee kon eel *mee*·o ma·ree·to/ra·*ga*·tso

Solo women travellers may receive unwanted attention in some parts of Italy; if ignoring fails have a polite rejection ready.

⑤ Let's meet at 6pm for pre-dinner drinks.
Ci vediamo alle sei per un aperitivo.
chee ve·*dya*·mo a·le say per oon a·pe·ree·*tee*·vo

At dusk, watch the main piazza get crowded with people sipping colourful cocktails and snacking the evening away: join your new friends for this authentic Italian ritual!

Etiquette

Venetians are generous about sharing their home with so many visitors – tens of millions annually. But when visitors clog the *calli* (lanes) and block *vaporetto* entrances, Venetians can't get to work and family obligations on time.

To be a gracious guest and help prevent tourist gridlock, keep to the right-hand side of the *calle*, try not to linger on bridges, don't push, and allow passengers to disembark before boarding boats.

Top Itineraries

Day One

San Marco (p56)

 Begin your day in prison on the Secret Passages tour of the **Palazzo Ducale**, then break for espresso at **Caffè Lavena**'s counter before the Byzantine blitz of golden mosaics inside **Basilica di San Marco**. Browse boutique-lined backstreets to **Museo Fortuny**, the palace fashion house whose goddess gowns freed women from corsets.

> **Lunch** Imaginative, bi-coastal Italian seafood at A Beccafico (p76).

Dorsoduro (p82)

Pause atop wooden **Ponte dell'Accademia** for **Grand Canal** photo ops, then discover colourful, timeless drama no camera can convey inside **Gallerie dell'Accademia**. Wander past **Squero di San Trovaso** to glimpse gondolas being built, then bask in the reflected glory of Palladio's **Il Redentore** along waterfront **Zattere**. Stop at tiny **Chiesa di San Sebastian**, packed with Veroneses, then troll artisan boutiques along Calle Lunga San Barnaba until it's '*spritz*' o'clock' (cocktail hour) in **Campo Santa Margherita**.

> **Dinner** Enoteca Ai Artisti (p95) Handmade pasta with perfect pairings.

San Marco (p56)

The hottest ticket in town during opera season is at **La Fenice**, but classical-music fans shouldn't miss Vivaldi played with contemporary verve by **Interpreti Veneziani**.

Day Two

Dorsoduro (p82)

 Discover the modern art that caused uproars and defined the 20th century at the **Peggy Guggenheim Collection**, then confront contemporary art pushing 21st-century buttons inside **Punta della Dogana**. Duck into Baldassare Longhena's domed **Chiesa di Santa Maria della Salute** to witness its legendary curative powers and blushing Titians. Outside, catch the *vaporetto* up the **Grand Canal**.

> **Lunch** Enjoy market-fresh feasts in miniature at All'Arco (p113).

San Polo & Santa Croce (p99)

Experience climate change through masterpieces flanking Campo San Rocco: **I Frari**, featuring Titian's sunny altarpiece, and **Scuola Grande di San Rocco**, lined with stormy Tintorettos. Antique shops and artisan studios line your route to **Campo San Polo** and **Campo San Giacomo dell'Orio**, where the medieval church offers meditative calm – as does the namesake beverage at **Al Prosecco**. Test your orienteering skills on the winding back lanes of the former red-light district, heading across **Ponte delle Tette** (Tits Bridge) towards dinner.

> **Dinner** Fresh seafood and *gnocchi* at hidden Antiche Carampane (p114).

San Marco (p56)

Cross **Ponte di Rialto** to join overflow crowds grooving to DJ sets at **Osteria All'Alba**, or discover your new favourite Veneto vintage at **I Rusteghi**.

Day Three

Castello (p137)

 Stroll **Riva degli Schiavoni** for views across the sparkling lagoon to Palladio's **San Giorgio Maggiore**. See how Carpaccio's sprightly saints light up a room at **Scuola di San Giorgio degli Schiavoni**, then seek out Castello's hidden wonder: **Chiesa di San Francesco della Vigna**. Get stared down by statues atop **Ospedaletto** on your way to brick Gothic **Zanipolo**, where you'll mingle with 25 marble dogi. The Renaissance awaits two bridges away at **Chiesa di Santa Maria dei Miracoli**, a polychrome marble miracle made from Basilica di San Marco's leftovers.

> ✕ **Lunch** Osteria Boccadoro (p133): *crudi* and pasta with fine-dining finesse.

Cannaregio (p122)

Wander serene *fondamente* past statue sentries ringing **Campo dei Mori** to reach **Chiesa della Madonna dell'Orto**, the neighbourhood Gothic church Tintoretto lavished with masterpieces. Tour the Ghetto's rooftop **synagogues** and enjoy quiet reflection in **Ikona Gallery**, until Venice's happiest hours beckon across the bridge at **Al Timon**.

> ✕ **Dinner** Hearty meals to satisfy sailors await at Dalla Marisa (p132).

Cannaregio (p122)

 Take a romantic **gondola** ride through Cannaregio's long canals, which seem purpose-built to maximise moonlight.

Day Four

Murano, Burano & the Northern Islands (p169)

 Make your lagoon getaway on a *vaporetto* bound for rainbow-coloured **Burano** and green-and-gold **Torcello**. Follow the sheep trail to Torcello's Byzantine **Cattedrale di Santa Maria Assunta**, where the apse's golden Madonna calmly stares down the blue devils opposite. Catch the boat back to Burano, to admire extreme home-design colour schemes and handmade lace at **Museo del Merletto**.

> ✕ **Lunch** Venissa (p179): Sunny Mazzorbo vineyards, inspired lagoon cuisine.

Murano, Burano & the Northern Islands (p169)

Witness the fiery passions of glass artisans at Murano's legendary *fornace* (furnaces), and see their finest moments showcased at the **Museo del Vetro** (Glass Museum). After Murano showrooms close, hop on the *vaporetto* all the way to **Giudecca** for one last, long view of San Marco glittering across glassy waters.

> ✕ **Dinner** I Figli delle Stelle (p165): hearty dishes and romantic canalside tables.

San Marco (p56)

 Celebrate your triumphant tour of the lagoon with a *prosecco* toast and tango across Piazza San Marco at **Caffè Florian**; repeat as necessary.

If You Like...

Curiosities

Museo della Follia 'Museum of Madness' is as creepy as it sounds, featuring 'cures' happily no longer in use on the island of San Servolo. (p165)

Museo di Storia Naturale Dinosaurs, mummies and other bizarre specimens brought home by Venetian explorers – all inside a Turkish fortress. (p106)

Mercantino dei Miracoli Cards sent to sweethearts during WWII, talismans worn by sailors for safe passage, offal cookbooks. (p123)

Museo d'Arte Orientale The attic of **Ca' Pesaro** is lined with Japanese samurai gear, thanks to an Italian prince's 1887–89 Asian shopping binge. (p107)

Fondazione Vedova Robots designed by Renzo Piano display Emilio Vedova's abstract canvases, then whisk them back into storage. (p89)

Fashion

Museo Fortuny Glimpse inside the palatial, radical fashion house that freed women from corsets

and innovated bohemian chic. (p67)

Palazzo Mocenigo Find fashion inspiration in this palace packed with Venetian glamour, from bustles and knee-britches to red-carpet gowns. (p106)

Fiorella Gallery Rock subversive Venetian looks, including lilac silk-velvet jackets hand-printed with red rats. (p78)

Godi Fiorenza London-trained Venetian sisters design avant-garde ensembles inspired by *belle epoque* divas and vintage teddy bears. (p79)

Gelato

Giovanna Zanella One-of-a-kind footwear by Venice's most imaginative artisan shoemaker. (p157)

Boats

Arsenale Venice's legendary shipyards built a warship in a day on the world's first assembly line. (p139)

Squero di San Trovaso Witness the making of a gondola, shaped by hand and custom-sized to match the weight and height of the gondolier. (p89)

Museo Storico Navale Four floors of nautical wonders, from the *bucintoro* (ducal barge) to WWII battleships. (p150)

Gilberto Penzo Scale-model gondolas for your bathtub and build-your-own-boat kits from a master artisan. (p118)

Row Venice Learn to row across lagoon waters standing, like *gondolieri* do, from regatta champ Jane Caporal. (p174)

Hidden Gems

Chiesa di San Francesco della Vigna All-star Venetian art showcase and Palladio's first commission, down by Castello's boatyard docks. (p149)

Chiesa di Santa Maria dei Miracoli The little neighbourhood church with big Renaissance ideas and priceless marble, amid a maze of canals. (p130)

Basilica di Santa Maria Assunta Lambs bleat encouragement as you walk through this overgrown island towards golden glory in apse mosaics. (p171)

Ghetto synagogues Climb to rooftop synagogues on tours run by Museo Ebraico. (p124)

Palazzo Contarini del Bovolo A secret spiral staircase in an ancient hidden courtyard sets the scene for a clandestine smooch. (p72)

Dessert

Alaska Gelateria Organic gelato in gourmet flavours invented on site, including cardamom, white peach and artichoke. (p113)

VizioVirtù Artisan hot chocolate slurped from chocolate spoons through a chocolate plague doctor mask: Venetian decadence at its best. (p118)

Pasticceria Da Bonifacio Almond *curasan* (croissants), *zaleti* (cornmeal biscuits) and other Venetian treats rich enough to delight a doge. (p151)

Gelateria Ca' d'Oro Venetian artisan gelato made daily in seasonal flavours like Sorrento lemon and Sicilian pistachio. (p131)

Pasticceria Tonolo Flakey apple strudel and mini-profiteroles bursting with hazelnut-choc mousse provide energy to take on Titian at I Frari. (p91)

Backstreet Bars

I Rusteghi Gourmets search the world over for the prestigious wines popped open nightly in this secret courtyard watering hole. (p76)

All'Arco Creative *cicheti* (Venetian tapas) invented daily with Rialto Market's freshest finds, plus perfect wine pairings – all for the price of a pizza. (p113)

Bacaro Risorto This corner *bacaro* (bar) the size of a newsstand overflows with *cicheti* and good spirits, whenever they feel like opening. (p154)

For more top Venice spots, see the following:
➡ Eating (p32)
➡ Drinking & Nightlife (p38)
➡ Entertainment (p43)
➡ Shopping (p48)

Osteria Alla Vedova Upholds hallowed Venetian happy-hour traditions, including meaty €1 *polpette* (meatballs) and dainty *ombre* (glasses of wine). (p132)

Bacaro Da Fiore Hiding in the heart of expensive, touristy San Marco are affordable wines and authentic *cicheti*, including Venetian tripe. (p75)

Local Hangouts

Lido Beaches When temperatures nudge upwards of 29°C, Venice races to the Lido-bound *vaporetto* to claim sandy beachfront. (p163)

Campo San Giacomo dell'Orio bars Kids tear through the *campo*, while parents watch through the bottom of glasses of natural-process *prosecco*. (p115)

Rialto Market Grandmothers drive hard bargains with joking grocers while photographers shoot heaps of glistening purple lagoon octopus. (p108)

Giudecca Artists sketch views along the canalfront until it's time for organic farmers-market picnics or happy hour at **Skyline Rooftop Bar**. (p167)

Lido di Jesolo Partiers take the bus to Lido di Jesolo clubs, and recover on Adriatic beaches the next day. (p181)

PLAN YOUR TRIP IF YOU LIKE...

Month by Month

February

Snow does occasionally fall in Venice, blanketing gondolas. Velvet costumes and wine fountains warm February nights, when revellers party like it's 1699 at masked balls until wigs itch and livers twitch – in its baroque heyday, Carnevale lasted three months.

Carnevale

Masqueraders party in the streets for two weeks preceding Lent. Tickets to La Fenice's masked balls run up to €230, but there's a free-flowing wine fountain to commence Carnevale (www.carnevale.venezia.it), public costume parties in every *campo* (square), and a Grand Canal flotilla marking the end.

April

The winning springtime combination of relaxed sightseeing, optimal walking weather and reasonable room rates lasts until Easter, when art-history classes on holiday briefly flood the city.

Vinitaly

Good spirits abound at Italy's premier expo of wine and spirits, drawing 150,000 visitors to Verona's VeronaFiere pavilions. The three-day expo starts in sober earnest, with expert-guided tastings of rare vintages, and Slow Food and wine pairings – but by the final afternoon it's a proper bacchanal, with singing erupting at midday over the dregs of more than a million bottles of wine. (www.vinitaly.com)

Su e Zo Per I Ponti

'Up and Down the Bridges' is a 13km non-competitive race through Venice, with 10,000 to 15,000 participants crossing 55 bridges to raise funds for charity – usually a clean-water initiative in developing nations – and enjoying free concerts at the finish line. (www.suezo.it)

Festa di San Marco

Join the celebration of Venice's patron saint on 25 April, when Venetian men carry a *bocolo* (rosebud) in processions through Piazza San Marco, then bestow them on the women they love.

May

Summer is better known in Venice as regatta season, when Venetians limber up and row standing across the sun-dazzled lagoon for glory and *prosecco*.

Vogalonga

Not a race so much as a show of endurance, this 32km 'long row' starts with 1000 boats in front of the Palazzo Ducale, loops past Burano and Murano, and ends with cheers, *prosecco* and enormous blisters at Punta della Dogana. (www.turismovenezia.it)

June

Festivals kick off all month, from millennium-old mystical seafaring celebrations to freaky

(Top) Carnevale costume

(Bottom) Biennale di Venezia: *Amanuensis* (installation detail) by Elizabeth Hoak-Doering (www.ehdoering.com) © 2011

JULIET COOMBE / GETTY IMAGES ©

GETTY IMAGES ©

performance-art marathons.

★★ Festa della Sensa

If Venice loves the sea so much, why don't they get married? Consider it done. Vows have been professed annually since AD 1000 in the Sposalito del Mar (Wedding to the Sea), with celebrations including regattas, outdoor markets and Mass on the Lido. (www.sensavenezia.it)

★★ Festa di San Pietro di Castello

The Festival of St Peter of Castello (Festa de San Piero de Casteo in Venetian) takes place the last week of June at the steps of the church that was once the city's cathedral, with Mass, games, puppetry, hearty rustic fare and rock tribute bands. (www.sanpiero decasteo.org)

☆ Biennale di Venezia (Venice Biennale)

In odd years the Art Biennale usually runs June to November, and in even years the Architecture Biennale kicks off in September – but every summer, the Biennale also features avant-garde dance, theatre, cinema and music. (www.labiennale.org)

July

Fireworks over Giudecca and occasional summer lightning illuminate balmy summer nights on the lagoon, and performances by jazz greats end sunny days on a sultry note.

✨ Festa del Redentore

Walk on water across the Giudecca Canal to Il Redentore via a bobbing, wobbly pontoon bridge the third Saturday and Sunday in July. Join the massive floating picnic along the Zattere, and don't miss the fireworks. (www.turismo venezia.it)

☆ Venice Jazz Festival

International legends from Wynton Marsalis to Buena Vista Social Club bring down the house at La Fenice, while crowd-favourite acts like Sting and Paolo Conte play Piazza San Marco with a full orchestra. Check the calendar for shows in Vicenza, Verona and Treviso year-round. (www.venetojazz.com)

September

Movie stars bask in Venice's golden autumnal light along Venice Film Festival red carpets on the Lido, and musical interludes, island picnics and regattas make the most of optimal weather on the lagoon.

☆ Venice International Film Festival

The only thing hotter than Lido beaches in summer is the red carpet at this star-studded event, which runs the last weekend in August through the first week of September. (www.labien nale.org/en/cinema)

🏃 Regata Storica

Never mind who's winning, check out the gear: 16th-century costumes,

eight-oared gondolas and ceremonial barks re-enact the Venice arrival of the Queen of Cyprus. A floating parade is followed by four races, where kids and male and female rowers compete for boating bragging rights. (www.regatas toricavenezia.it)

☆ Amore e Musica in Spiaggia

The Lido encourages love and music on the beach with Amore e Musica in Spiaggia, a free concert series held on Lido beaches from July through August and culminating in an international battle of the bands mid-September.

✨ Burano Regata

Fishing island Burano angles for attention with Venice's only mixed men's and women's rowing regatta – since this is the last serious match of regatta season, rowers are out to win. Victors are celebrated or at least forgiven at the Burano after-party over fish, polenta and *prosecco*. (www.comune.venezia.it)

✨ Riviera Fiorita

Relive the glory days of 1627 along the Brenta River with a flotilla of antique boats, baroque costume balls at Villa Widmann Rezzonico Foscari and Villa Pisani Nazionale, historically correct country fairs, period music and even gelato in baroque-era flavours; held the second Sunday in September.

October

When the high tourism season ends, festival crowds disperse and

hotel rates come back down to earth. Venice unwinds with a glass of Sant'Erasmo wine and a brisk jog from the Brenta.

✨ Festa del Mosto

A genuine country fair on 'garden isle' Sant'Erasmo, held on the first Sunday in October. The wine-grape harvest is celebrated with a parade, farmers market, gourmet food stalls, live music and free-flowing *vino*.

🏃 Venice Marathon

Six thousand runners work up a sweat over 42km of spectacular scenery, dashing along the Brenta River past Palladian villas before crossing into Venice and heading to Piazza San Marco via a 160m floating bridge. Mind your step... (www.venicemarathon.it)

November

Venice takes a breather from its usual antics to give thanks for its miraculous survival against all odds, and to carbo-load before kicking off another year of revelry, art and inspiration on 1 January.

✨ Festa della Madonna della Salute

If you'd survived plague and Austrian invasion, you'd throw a party too. Every 21 November since the 17th century, Venetians have crossed a pontoon bridge across the Grand Canal to light a candle in thanks at Santa Maria della Salute and splurge on sweets.

With Kids

Adults think Venice is for them; kids know better. This is where every fairy tale comes to life, where prisoners escape through the roof of a palace, Murano glass blowers breathe life into pocket-sized sea dragons, and Pescaria fish balance on their tails as though spellbound. Top that, JK Rowling.

Artworks become playthings during the Venice Biennale

Attractions

Venice is the ultimate for any kid who has ever believed in pirates and princesses: they really did sleep in Grand Canal palaces – possibly on peas – and launched swashbuckling adventures from these shores. Visit Ca' Rezzonico (p90) to see where Venetian nobles danced until dawn at masked balls, see the ballgowns they wore at Palazzo Mocenigo (p106), and enter the royal quarters where Empress Sissi snored inside Museo Correr (p73). Explorers' ships are displayed at Museo Storico Navale (p150), and the samurai swords and armour they brought all the way from Asia are lined up ready for battle in the attic of Ca' Pesaro (p107). When kids refuse another church, savvy parents can play the trump card: Museo di Storia Naturale (p106), a fortress palace with dinosaurs, mummies and a two-headed goat.

Outdoor Activities

Beach Picnics

Lido beaches let the whole family relax in the sun, with the option of umbrellas and cabanas. Kids can pick out their own picnic ingredients at the Rialto Market, and squeal over the squishy lagoon seafood.

Rowing & Sailing

Glide across the teal-blue waters to desert islands on a customised sailing tour from **Laguna Eco Adventures** (☎329 722 62 89; www.lagunaecoadventures.com; 2-8hr trips per person €40-150), or learn to row standing up like *gondolieri* do with Row Venice (p174), with an optional stop on the cemetery island of San Michele for a picnic.

Biking

Explore the Lido by tandem bicycle, and pedal all the way to Malamocco to discover a shrunken, kid-sized version of Venice.

Rainy-Day Activities

Arts & Crafts

Kids inspired by watching Venetian artists at work can make their own Carnevale masks at **Ca' Macana** (Map p312; ☎041 522 97 49; www.camacana.com; Calle delle Botteghe 3172; workshops about €60; ⊙workshops 3pm

NEED TO KNOW

➡ **Change facilities** Available in public restrooms.

➡ **Emergency care** Venice's main hospital offers emergency care and boat-ambulance service.

➡ **Babysitting** Available at several hotels and B&Bs.

➡ **Strollers** Bring your own.

➡ **Nappies (diapers) & formula** Available at groceries citywide.

Wed & Fri ; ⊞Ca' Rezzonico), assemble their own Murano-glass necklaces at Campagnol & Salvadore (p180), paint their own Venetian masterpieces with supplies from Arcobaleno (p80), and build their own gondolas with scale-model kits from Gilberto Penzo (p118).

Secret Passageways Tour

Duck through hidden doorways to explore the secret attic prison hidden in the doge's pretty pink palace on the Itinerari Segreti tour of the Palazzo Ducale (p61).

Transport

Gondolas provide scenic ways to get around Venice once kids get worn out, and timed *vaporetto* tickets allow riders to hop on and off for bathroom breaks. Adventurous kids might want to try the ultimate dare: riding a *traghetto*, an oversized gondola that transports riders across the Grand Canal, standing up. Strollers are helpful with toddlers, but bear in mind that they'll have to be lifted over bridges.

Food

When spirits and feet begin to drag, there's pizza and pasta galore to pick them back up – though if your kids are anything like the Brangelina brood when they stay in Venice, they may demand nothing less than a double scoop of gelato. For tea parties and comfort food, Tearoom Caffè Orientale (p113) offers soups, sandwiches and house-baked cakes. Discerning young diners will want to sample *cicheti*, which are conveniently kid-sized and made to eat with your hands at Dai

Zemei (p113) and Cantina Do Spade (p116). Picky eaters and vegetarians will appreciate the fruit smoothies and lightly fried veggies at Fritto e Frutta (p114). For a culinary challenge, try the freaky gelato flavours such as asparagus at Alaska Gelateria (p113) and chocolates in gourmet flavours like blueberry and olive oil at VizioVirtù (p118).

Toys & Gifts

As certain Venetian dogi and most parents know, a little bribery goes a long way. Wooden puzzles of the Rialto bridge inspire budding architects at Signor Bloom (p98); Fairtrade chocolate and Ferrari racecars made from recycled cans are crowd-pleasers at Le Botteghe della Solidarietà (p81); and vintage bears are found and lovingly repaired at Il Baule Blu (p121). Treasure-hunting is best at outdoor markets, where antique toys and costumes surface from palace attics. Giunti Al Punto (p136) stocks books for kids and young adults in multiple languages.

Kid Hang-outs

Campo San Giacomo dell'Orio

Marathon games of tag in this *campo* probably started around the time its namesake medieval church was built, and kids can jump in any time. Better still, the *campo* is ringed with bar tables where parents can keep an eye on kids through the bottom of a *prosecco* flute.

Giardini

Parents are wowed by the sweeping lagoon views and backdrop of Biennale pavilions, but kids know they've found paradise when they spot the swings, slides and sandlots of this island playground.

Ghetto

Venice's past meets its future in this historic Jewish island: once school lets out, the silent neighbourhood *campo* turns into a lively football pitch.

Campo San Polo

One of the biggest squares in Venice, this *campo* has plenty of room to run around, occasional puppet shows and carnival rides in summer, and pizza to please the whole family at Antica Birraria della Corte (p114).

For Free

Despite its centuries-old reputation as a playground for Europe's elite, Venice's finest moments are freebies. Golden glimpses of heaven in Basilica di San Marco are gratis, Carnevale is best celebrated in the streets, and floating palaces are most extraordinary from outside, reflected in the Grand Canal.

Fruit and vegetables for sale at the Rialto Market (p108)

Venice's Best Bargains

Glamorous Venice is known as a luxury destination, with five-star hotels, five-course meals and plush gondolas – but savvy visitors can live the *bea vita* (beautiful life) for less. B&Bs offer palatial settings and personal service for three figures, and Venice's best meals are gourmet *cicheti* (Venetian tapas) for €1 to €4 per dish, served at lunch and 6pm to 8pm daily. Splurge on an €80 gondola ride, or experience cheap thrills standing on the *traghetto* (public gondola) as you cross the Grand Canal (€0.50 per ride).

Discount Passes

Church and art aficionados can access some of Venice's finest masterpieces in 16 churches with a Chorus Pass. It costs €10 (for a total saving of €35), and includes such spectacular sights as I Frari, Chiesa di Santa Maria dei Miracoli, Chiesa di San Sebastiano and Chiesa della Madonna dell'Orto.

The St Mark's Square Museum Ticket covers both the Palazzo Ducale and the Museo Correr, which includes the newly opened imperial apartments, the Museo Archeologico Nazionale and Biblioteca Nazionale Marciana. Get more history for your money: for €5 extra, buy the Civic Museum Pass, which is valid for six months and gives access to 10 civic museums.

Historical Sites

Four of the most pivotal sites in Venetian history have free entry: Rialto Market, where an empire sprang up around fishmongers; Basilica di Santa Maria della Salute, the domed church built as thanks for Venice's salvation from plague, which also offers free afternoon organ vespers concerts; and the Ghetto, provider of funds and ideas to keep Venice afloat after its shipping empire declined. Best of all is Basilica di San Marco, the apotheosis of Venice's millennium of brilliant self-invention. Besides free entry, free guided tours of the basilica's mosaics are offered by the diocese.

JOY SKIPPER / GETTY IMAGES ©

Arts & Architecture

To defray substantial costs to the city, there's an entry fee to the main art and architecture Biennale shows and Venice film festival premieres – but many dance, music, cinema and ancillary arts programs are free of charge citywide, from summer through autumn. Free admission is offered at Murano glass showrooms and art galleries on your **San Marco Gallery Hop** (p79). The entire city is an architecture showcase year-round, and you can discover hidden gems like Palazzo Contarini del Bovolo on your San Marco walking tour.

Festivals & Events

Festivals fill Venetian *calli* (lanes) with revelry all year, from Carnevale masquerades to raucous regattas. Eternally grateful for being spared the plague, Venice gives thanks at Festa del Redentore (p24) and **Festa della Madonna della Salute** (www.turismovenezia.it) with fireworks, wobbly pontoon bridges and *prosecco*. Free movies and theatre illuminate nights in the Summer Arena (p117), and several bars in Venice now have year-round schedules of free jazz concerts to accompany your *ombra* (half-glass of wine). During regatta season from summer through autumn, join crowds along canal banks from Cannaregio to Burano cheering on rowers.

Island Getaways

A timed *vaporetto* ticket lets you do laps of lagoon hot spots without paying extra. First stop in summer is the Lido, which has three **beaches** (p163) with free access, a miniature version of Venice at Malamocco, and a free summer beach concert series. Escape from tourist flocks with stunning Venice views in Giudecca, wandering past Palladio facades to art galleries, a 14th-century church, the Fortuny showroom, and the organic farmers market (p161) run by the women's prison. Visit the haunting cemetery isle of San Michele on your way to Murano, where you can glimpse glassmakers at work, spot dragon's bones among the Byzantine mosaics of San Donato, and learn trade secrets inside the Museo del Vetro (Glass Museum; free with Museum pass). Take a photography expedition to Burano, and while you're in this colourful neighbourhood, spot masterpieces inside Chiesa di San Martino and watch Buranese women work wonders with a spindle at the new Museo del Merletto (Lace Museum; also free with your Museum Pass). After days pounding the pavements of Venice, Torcello, Mazzorbo and Sant'Erasmo offer welcome stretches of green and prime picnic possibilities.

Like a Local

Venexianarse (making yourself Venetian) is easy to do, even by accident. Slip under an archway into a less-travelled backstreet, order adventurously at the cicheti (Venetian tapas) counter, duck into bacari (hole-in-the-wall bar) for happy hour, and òstrega! (wow!) – you're venexian already.

Haunts & Hangouts

On breaks from class, hotel desks, artisan studios and gondola duty, Venetians take a breather in *campi* (squares) and on *fondamente* (canal banks). Bright spots in Venetian days can always be found in sunny, spacious *campi* such as Campo San Giacomo dell'Orio, Campo Bandiera e Mori, Campo San Polo and Campo Santa Maria Formosa. On weekends, favourite *fondamente* strolls lead along the Zattere to Punta della Dogana, down the Riva degli Schiavoni to Giardini Pubblici, and along Giudecca's sunny waterfront to canalside dinner concerts at I Figli delle Stelle or panoramic drinks at Skyline Rooftop Bar.

Backstreet Routes

On average, Venetians get asked once daily for directions to tourist destinations like Piazza San Marco, Rialto, Accademia and Ferrovia (the train station) – and if you stay awhile and walk confidently, you'll be asked too. Dodge the day-tripper crowds by taking alternative routes to your destination along minor *calli* (lanes) that wiggle through quieter Venetian neighbourhoods, often in approximate parallel with major thoroughfares like **Strada Nuova** (Rialto–Ferrovia), **Marzaria** (San Marco–Rialto) and **Calle Larga XXII Marzo** (San Marco–Accademia). Favourite local bypass routes are the **Fondamenta della Misericordia** (Rialto–Ferrovia, near the Ghetto), **Calle dei Fabbri** (San Marco–Rialto, behind Caffè Quadri) and **Piscina Frezzeria** (San Marco–Accademia, near **La Fenice**).

Favourite Dishes

Lagoon seafood is the pride of Venice, and flies off *cicheti* (Venetian tapas) counters at lunch and happy hour. Arrive by noon or 6pm for today's catch, or your options may be down to the classics: *bacala mantecato* (creamed cod) or *sarde in saor* (sardines in tangy onion marinade). But Venetians also love traditional meat dishes, including *sopressa* (soft salami), *cotechino* (boiled sausage) and *trippa* (tripe). *Fegato Veneziano* (Venetian calf's liver) gets mixed reviews, even from Venetians – but don't miss creative *cicheti* versions, such as velvety fig-and-liver mousse.

Hidden Happy Hours

Campo Santa Margherita and Campo Cesare Battista attract happy-hour throngs of students, tourists and locals alike – but for a drink in local company, track down hidden *bacari* (watering holes). Duck behind the Rialto Market to All'Arco and Cantina Do Spade, drink the good stuff at I Rusteghi and Bacaro Da Fiore in San Marco, seek out Al Timon and Ai Promessi Sposi in Cannaregio, and detour to Bacaro Risorto in Castello.

Tours

To get to know Venice from the inside out, first you have to see the lagoon city as Venetians have for a millennium – by water – then dive into the calli (lanes) and ascend secret staircases for glimpses of Venetian life behind the scenes and above the fray.

Canalside home

Tours on Water

The following outings offer maritime adventures on traditional Venetian boats. Reserve ahead, bring sunscreen and check weather forecasts, since trips are subject to climatic conditions.

Rowing

Learn to row, row, row your boat as *gondolieri* do with Row Venice (p174). Find your footing on the sparkling lagoon as Olympic-trained rowing coach Jane Caporal and her team of women rowers show you how to propel a handcrafted Venetian *sandolo* (flat-bottomed boat) standing up, using a single oar. Glide past Venice's island cemetery, pause for a picnic (book ahead), and hop up on the *poppa* (stern) to row standing and singing, gondolier-style.

Sailing

Laguna Eco Adventures (p25) lets you sail away into the lagoon blue in a traditional Venetian sailing *bragozzo* (barge) or a slim *sanpierota* (twin-sail boat), small enough to slip into canals. Many of their traditional wooden boats accommodate five people maximum, so it's just you, the lagoon birds and the wind at your backs. Itineraries range from a circuit of outlying lagoon desert islands or Lido beaches to a slow drift from the Grand Canal through Venice's maze of canals at sunset.

Vento di Venezia (p178) offers sailing classes for the day or longer, plus stays at the hotel near the Isola di Certosa marina.

Boating

Terra e Acqua (p172) offers wild rides to the outer edges of the lagoon with skipper Cristina della Toffola. Itineraries are customised, and can cover abandoned plague-quarantine islands, fishing and birdwatching hot spots, Burano and Torcello. Cristina serves fish-stew lunches and cocktails on board at picturesque island mooring spots, and takes the utmost care to preserve the fragile lagoon ecosystem en route. Trips accommodate up to 10 people on a sunny, sturdy motorised *bragozzo*, which makes trips sociable and easy-going for those not accustomed to boats.

Natura Venezia (www.natura-venezia.it; 🚶) 🌿 organizes longer sustainable travel circuits of the lagoon with trained environmental guides. The four-day 'Invisible Venice' circuit covers untouristed corners of Cannaregio, a bike-ride excursion on Sant'Erasmo, a *cicheti* (Venetian tapas) tour, and a visit to the wild islands of Torcello and San Francesco del Deserto. Week-long family-oriented trips are also available.

Eolo Cruises (☑049 807 80 32; Via Mantegna 11, Brugine) covers the lagoon on a double-masted 1946 fishing *bragozzo* for one- to eight-day trips (per person from €2000 for six to 10 people), including onboard cooking tours. Guests sleep in selected villas and *palazzi* in Venice or around the lagoon, spend the day sailing and eat seafood lunches on board.

Rendez-Vous Fantasia (☑041 551 04 00; www.rendez-vous-fantasia.com; weekend from €528, week from €924) lets you literally live on the lagoon by renting out houseboats; moorings are in Chioggia.

Tours on Land

Guided Tours of Major Sights

Many major sights offer guided tours, especially Venice's civic museums. Basilica di San Marco offers free mosaic tours run by the diocese; the Itinerari Segreti (Secret Passages) tour of the Palazzo Ducale leads through hidden doorways to the attic prison inside the doge's pretty pink palace; Palazzo Mocenigo offers monthly guided visits to see fragile 300- to 400-year-old fashions inside the palace's walk-in closet attic (p107); and Museo del Vetro offers tours that reveal Murano's glass-making trade secrets, including glass-blowing demonstrations. The only way to visit the Torre dell'Orologio (Clocktower) and see the ancient clockworks in action is by prearranged tour. For additional tours offered by Venetian churches and sights, consult the Tourism/Guided Tours listings on the official website of the **Venice Comune** (www.comune.venezia.it), or the free publication *Un Ospite di Venezia* (A Guest in Venice), distributed in most hotels.

Walking Tours

During Carnevale, check the official schedule for lantern-lit storytelling walking tours created by Venetian historian Alberto Toso Fei and acted by a Venetian

troupe, and special museum tours on Venetian Carnevale themes, such as colour and disguises.

Venice Urban Adventures (p116) offers year-round *cicheti* tours, covering five backstreet *bacari* on a local-guided Venetian bar crawl.

Venicescapes (☑041 520 63 61; www.venicescapes.org; 4-6hr tour incl book 2 adults US$250-290, additional adult US$60, under 18yr US$30) Intriguing walking tours run by a nonprofit historical society (proceeds support ongoing Venetian historical research) with themes such as 'A City of Nations', exploring multiethnic Venice through the ages; and 'A Most Serene Republic', revealing how Venice kept the peace through politics and espionage.

Walks Inside Venice (☑041 524 17 06; www.walksinsidevenice.com; per hr €75, for groups up to 6 people; ⊕) Spirited tours run by three local women lead groups of up to six people on afternoon treks through the city's hidden backstreets to major monuments via paintings that show the Venetian love of colour, following the path of the plague through Venice, on a family-friendly circuit, or on grand tours of Venice with detours to Murano and San Michele.

Azienda di Promozione Turistica (APT; ☑041 529 87 11; www.turismovenezia.it) Guided tours ranging from an introduction to the greatest hits: around San Marco (per person €21); a gondola serenade circuit (per person €40); and a four-hour circuit of Murano, Burano and Torcello (per person €20). Also provides an updated list of authorised guides who lead private walking tours of the city.

Snack stall on the Rialto bridge

 **Eating**

The visual blitz that is Venice tends to leave visitors bug-eyed, weak-kneed and grasping for the nearest panino (sandwich). But there's more to La Serenissima than simple carb-loading. For centuries Venice has gone far beyond the call of dietary duty, and has lavished visitors with wildly inventive feasts. Today visitors enjoy impressive cicheti (Venetian tapas), decadent pastries and a lagoon's worth of fresh seafood.

Venetian Cuisine

'Local food!' is the latest foodie credo, but it's nothing new in Venice. Surrounded by garden islands and a seafood-rich lagoon, Venice offers local specialities that never make it to the mainland, because they're served fresh the same day in Venetian *bacari* (hole-in-the-wall bars) and *osterie* (taverns). A strong sea breeze wafts over the kitchens of the lagoon city, with the occasional meaty dish from the Veneto mainland and traditional local options of rice and polenta in addition to classic Italian pastas and gnocchi. But side dishes of Veneto vegetables often steal the show, and early risers will notice Venetians risking faceplants in canals to grab *violetti di Sant'Erasmo* (tender purple baby artichokes), *radicchio trevisano* (ruffled red bitter chicory) and prized Bassano del Grappa white asparagus from produce-laden barges.

Venice's cosmopolitan outlook makes local cuisine anything but predictable. Cross-cultural fusion fare isn't some new fad in Venice, but dates back to Marco Polo's heyday – 13th-century Venetian cookbooks include recipes for fish with galangal, saffron and ginger. Don't be surprised if some Venetian dishes taste vaguely Turkish or Greek rather than strictly Italian, reflecting Venice's preferred trading partners for over a millennium. Spice-route flavours from the Mediterranean and beyond can be savoured in signature Venetian recipes such as *sarde in saor,* traditionally made with sardines in a tangy onion marinade with pine nuts and sultanas.

Exceptional ingredients from other parts of Italy sneak into Venetian cuisine, such as Tuscan steaks, white truffles from Alba, aromatic Amalfi lemons and Sicilian pistachios and blood oranges. Just don't ask for pesto: the garlicky basil spread hails from Genoa, Venice's chief trade-route rival for 300 years, and some Venetians still hold culinary grudges.

Cicheti

Even in unpretentious Venetian *osterie* and *bacari*, most dishes cost a couple of euros more than they might elsewhere in Italy – not a bad mark-up, considering all that fresh seafood and produce brought in by boat. But *cicheti* are some of the best foodie finds in Italy, served at lunch and from around 6pm to 8pm with sensational Veneto wines by the glass. *Cicheti* range from basic bar snacks (spicy meatballs, fresh tomato and basil bruschetta) to wildly inventive small plates: think white Bassano asparagus and plump lagoon shrimp wrapped in pancetta at All'Arco (p113); fennel and octopus salad fresh from the Pescaria at ProntoPesce (p113); or *crostini* (open-face sandwiches) piled with *sopressa* (soft local salami) with marinated radicchio at Dai Zemei (p113).

Prices start at €1 for tasty meatballs and range from €3 to €6 for gourmet fantasias with fancy ingredients, typically devoured standing up or perched atop stools at the bar. Filling *cicheti* such as *crostini, panini* and *tramezzini* (sandwiches on soft bread, often with mayo-based condiments) cost €1.50 to €6. Many *bacari* and *enoteche* (wine bars) also offer nightly *cicheti* spreads that could easily pass as dinner.

For *cicheti* with ultrafresh ingredients at manageable prices, seek out *osterie* and *bacari* in Venice's backstreets, especially in these *cicheti* hot spots:

Cannaregio Along Fondamenta degli Ormesini and off Strada Nuova.

NEED TO KNOW

Prices

With some notable exceptions in Venice (eg *cicheti* (bar snacks), sandwiches, pizza and gelato), a meal typically consists of two courses, a glass of house wine, and *pane e coperto* (bread and cover charge). In this book, meal prices are defined as follows:

€	less than €25
€€	€25 to €45
€€€	more than €45

Opening Hours

Cafe-bars generally open from 8am to 8pm, although some stay open later and morph into drinking hangouts. Pubs and wine bars are mostly shut by 1am to 2am.

Reservations

Call ahead to book a table at restaurants and *osterie* (taverns) whenever possible, especially at lunch in high season. You may get a table when you walk in off the street, but some restaurants buy ingredients according to how many bookings they've got, and when the food runs low, they stop seating. *Cicheti* are a handy alternative.

Pane e Coperto

'Bread and cover' charges range from €1 to €6 for sit-down meals at most restaurants.

Service Charges

Service may be included in *pane e coperto* (especially at basic *osterie*) or added onto the bill (at upscale bistros and for large parties). Read the fine print before you leave an additional tip.

San Polo & Santa Croce Around the Rialto Market and Campo San Giacomo dell'Orio.

Castello Via Garibaldi and Calle Lunga Santa Maria Formosa.

San Marco Around Campo San Bartolomeo, Campo Santo Stefano and Campo della Guerra.

The Menu

Cicheti are fresh alternatives to fast food worth planning your day around, but you'll also want to treat yourself to a leisurely sit-down meal while you're in Venice, whether it's in a back-alley *osteria* or canalside restaurant. If you stick to tourist menus you're bound to be disappointed, but adventurous diners who order seasonal specialities are richly rewarded, and often spend less too.

PIATTI (COURSES)

No one expects you to soldier through three courses plus antipasti and dessert, but no one would blame you for trying either, given the many tempting *piatti* on the local menu. Consider your à la carte options:

Antipasti (appetisers) vary from lightly fried *moeche* (tiny soft-shell crabs) to lagoon-fresh *crudi* (Venetian sushi) such as sweet mantis prawns, or a traditional platter of cured meats and cheeses.

Primi (first courses) usually include the classic Italian pasta or risotto; one Venetian speciality pasta you might try is *bigoli*, a thick wheat pasta. Many Venetian restaurants have adopted a hearty Verona speciality: gnocchi. Another traditional Venetian option is polenta, white or yellow cornmeal formed into a cake and grilled, or served semisoft and steaming hot. As the Venetian saying goes, '*Xe non xe pan, xe poenta*' (If there's no bread, there's still polenta), a charming way of expressing a Zen-like lack of anxiety or concern.

Secondi (second or main courses) are usually seafood or meat dishes. Adventurous eaters will appreciate a traditional Venetian *secondo* of *trippa* (tripe) or *fegato alla veneziana* (liver lightly pan-roasted in strips with browned onion and a splash of red wine). If you're not an offal fan, you can find standard cuts of *manzo* (beef), *agnello* (lamb) and *vitello* (veal) on most menus. Committed carnivores might also try *carpaccio* (a dish of finely sliced raw beef served with a sauce of crushed tomato, cream, mustard and Worcestershire sauce dreamed up by Harry's Bar (p77) and named for the Venetian painter Vittore Carpaccio, famous for his liberal use of blood-red paint).

Contorni (vegetable dishes) are more substantial offerings of *verdure* (vegetables). For vegetarians, this may be the first place to look on a menu – and meat-eaters may want to check them out too, since *secondi* don't always come with a vegetable side dish. Go with whatever's fresh and seasonal.

Dolci (desserts) are often *fatti in casa* (house-made) in Venice, especially Veneto-invented *tiramisu*, Vienna-influenced *bigne* (cream puffs) and *strudel*, and safffron-

scented Burano *esse* (S-shaped cookies). Otherwise, *gelaterie* (ice-cream shops) offer tempting options for €1.50 to €2.50.

DAILY SPECIALS

Here's one foolproof way to distinguish a serious Venetian *osteria* from an imposter: lasagne, spaghetti Bolognese and pizza are not Venetian specialities, and when all three appear on a menu, avoid that tourist trap. Look instead for places where there's no menu at all, or one hastily scrawled on a chalkboard or laser-printed in Italian only, preferably with typos. This is a sign that your chef reinvents the menu daily, according to market offerings.

Although fish and seafood are increasingly imported, many Venetian restaurant owners pride themselves on using only fresh, local ingredients, even if that means getting up at the crack of dawn to get to the Pescaria (fish market). Lagoon tides and changing seasons on the nearby garden island of Sant'Erasmo bring a year-round bounty to Venetian tables at the Rialto Market (p108).

Beware any menu dotted with asterisks, indicating that several items are *surgelati* (frozen) – seafood flown in from afar is likely to be unsustainable, and indigestible besides.

DRINK MENU

No Venetian feast would be complete without at least one *ombra* (glass of wine) – and that includes lunch. Fishmongers at the Pescaria get a head start on landlubbers, celebrating the day's haul at 9am by popping a cork on some *prosecco* (sparkling white wine), the Veneto's beloved bubbly. By noon, you already have some catching up to do: start working your way methodically through the extensive seafood menu of tender octopus salad, black squid-ink risotto, and *granseola* (spider crab), paired with appropriate *ombre*.

Many Venetian dishes are designed with local wines specifically in mind to round out the flavours – especially delicate lagoon seafood, whose texture may be changed by the powerful acidity of lemon juice. Some *enoteche* and *osterie* have wine selections that run into the hundreds of labels, so don't be shy about soliciting suggestions from your server or bartender.

Vegetarians & Vegans

Even in a city known for seafood, vegetarians need not despair: with a little advance savvy, vegetarian visitors in Venice can enjoy an even wider range of food choices than they might at home. Island-grown produce is a point of pride for many Venetian restaurants, and *primi* such as polenta, pasta and risotto *contorni* make the most of such local specialities as asparagus, artichokes, raddichio and *bruscandoli* (wild hops). Venetian *contorni* include grilled local vegetables and salads, and *cicheti* feature marinated vegetables and Veneto cheeses.

There are eateries that serve a good range of meat-free dishes at all price points. Meat-free and cheese-free pizza is widely available, and *gelaterie* offer milk-free *sorbetto* (sorbet) and gelato with *latte di soia* (soy milk). Self-catering is always an option for vegans and others with restricted diets, but if you call ahead, specific dietary restrictions can usually be accommodated at restaurants and *osterie*.

Self-Catering

Picnicking isn't allowed in most *campi* (squares) – Venice tries to keep a lid on its clean-up duties, since all refuse needs to be taken out by barge – but you can assemble quite a feast to enjoy at your B&B, rental apartment or hotel. For lunch with sweeping lagoon views, pack a picnic and head to the Lido beaches, the Biennale gardens or the northern lagoon islands of Mazzorbo, Torcello, Le Vignole and Sant'Erasmo.

FARMERS MARKETS

The Rialto Market (p108) offers superb local produce and lagoon seafood at the legendary Pescaria. For produce fresh from prison, head to Giudecca on Thursday morning for its organic farmers market (p161), where sales of fruit, vegetables and herbs grown by a cooperative in Giudecca's prison fund job-retraining programs. In fair weather, there's also a produce barge pulled up alongside Campo San Barnaba in Dorsoduro, near Ponte dei Pugni – but a half-kilo is the minimum purchase, so you may need to hit a supermarket for that single peach.

GROCERIES

The area around Rialto Market has gourmet delis and speciality shops, including an organic grocery. **Billa Supermarket** (Map p318; Strada Nova 3660; ◷8.30am-9pm Mon-Sat, 9am-9pm Sun) meets most grocery needs, but the deli selection is better at **Coop** (Map p317; ✆041 296 06 21; Piazzale Roma, Santa

Croce; ◷9am-1pm & 4-7.30pm Mon-Sat; ⊜Piazzale Roma), an agricultural cooperative grocery with branches at Campo San Giacomo dell'Orio and on Salizada San Lio. For a wider range of fresh-baked bread options, check out the pastry purveyors in the Rialto listings (p115).

Mealtimes

Restaurants and bars are generally closed one day each week, usually Sunday or Monday. If your stomach growls between official mealtimes, cafes and bars generally open from 7.30am to 8pm and serve snacks all day.

Prima colazione (breakfast) is eaten between 8am and 10am. Venetians rarely eat a sit-down breakfast, but instead bolt down a cappuccino with a *brioche* (sweet bread) or other type of pastry (generically known as *pastine*) at a coffee bar before heading to work.

Pranzo (lunch) is served from noon to 2.30pm. Few restaurants take orders for lunch after 2pm. Traditionally, lunch is the main meal of the day, and some shops and businesses close for two or three hours to accommodate it. Relax and enjoy a proper sit-down lunch, and you may be satisfied with *cicheti* for dinner. Bear in mind that restaurant lunch menus often cost the same as dinner in Venice, as most day-trippers make a mad dash for lunch places but clear out before dinner.

Cena (dinner) is served between 7pm and 10pm. Opening hours vary, but many places begin filling up by 7.30pm and few take orders after 10pm.

Dining Etiquette

With thousands of visitors trooping though Venice daily demanding to be fed, service can be slow, harried or indifferent. By showing an interest in what Venice brings to the table, you'll get more attentive service, better advice and a more memorable meal. You'll win over your server and the chef with these four gestures that prove your mettle as *una buona forchetta* ('a good fork', or good eater):

Ignore the menu. Solicit your server's advice about seasonal treats and house specials, pick two options that sound interesting, and ask your server to recommend one over the other. When that's done, snap the menu shut and say, '*Allora, facciamo cosi, per favore!*' (Well then, let's do that, please!) You have just won over your server, and flattered the chef – promising omens for a memorable meal to come.

Drink well. Bottled water is entirely optional; *acqua del rubinetto* (tap water) is perfectly potable and highly recommended as an environment-saving measure. But fine meals call for wine, often available by the glass or half-bottle. Never mind that you don't recognise the label: the best small-production local wineries don't advertise or export (even to other parts of Italy), because their yield is snapped up by Venetian *osterie* and *enoteche*.

Try primi without condiments. Your server's relief and delight will be obvious. Venetian seafood risotto and pasta are rich and flavourful enough without being smothered in Parmesan or hot sauce.

Enjoy lagoon seafood. No one expects you to order an appetiser or *secondo*, but if you do, the tests of any Venetian chef are seasonal seafood antipasti and *frittura* (seafood fry). Try yours *senza limone* (without lemon) first: Venetians believe the delicate flavours of lagoon seafood are best complemented by salt, pepper and subtle trade-route spices like star anise. Instead, try washing down seafood with citrusy Veneto white wines that highlight instead of overwhelm subtle briny flavours.

Gourmet Hot Spots

Bad advice has circulated for decades about how it's impossible to eat well and economically in Venice, which has misinformed day-trippers clinging defensively to congealed, reheated pizza slices in San Marco. Little do they realise that for the same price a bridge away, they could be dining on *crostini* topped with scampi and grilled baby artichoke, or tuna tartare with wild strawberries and balsamic reduction. Luckily for you, there's still room at the bar to score the best *cicheti* and reservations

are almost always available at phenomenal eateries – especially at dinner, after the day-trippers depart.

To find the best Venetian food, dodge restaurants immediately around San Marco, near the train station and along main thoroughfares. If you haven't made reservations, try restaurants along these gourmet trails in hidden *campi* and backstreets:

Cannaregio Along Fondamenta Savorgnan, Fondamenta della Sensa and Calle Larga Doge Priulli.

San Polo & Santa Croce Around the Rialto Market, Campo San Polo, Campo San Giacomo dell'Orio and Calle Larga dei Bari.

Castello Around Campo Bandiera e Moro, Zanipolo and Via Garibaldi.

San Marco Along Calle delle Botteghe, Calle Spezier and Frezzeria.

Dorsoduro Along Calle Lunga San Barnaba, Calle della Toletta and Calle Crosera.

Giudecca Along Fondamenta delle Zitelle.

Eating by Neighbourhood

➡ **San Marco** Backstreet *osterie*, Slow Food *cicheti* and *panini*. (p75)

➡ **Dorsoduro** Meat-based cuisine and light bites. (p90)

➡ **San Polo & Santa Croce** Market-inspired cuisine, creative *cicheti*, pizza and vegetarian cuisine. (p113)

➡ **Cannaregio** Traditional *cicheti*, authentic *osterie* and canalside dining. (p131)

➡ **Castello** Daring creative cuisine, pizza and bargain *cicheti*. (p151)

➡ **Giudecca, Lido & the Southern Islands** Traditional seafood and waterfront dining. (p165)

➡ **Murano, Burano & Northern Islands** Just-caught lagoon seafood and garden dining. (p178)

Lonely Planet's Top Choices

All'Arco (p113) *Panini* are decoys for day-trippers; stick around and let Venice's *cicheti maestri* ply you with market-fresh fantasias.

A Beccafico (p76) All-star Italian coastal cuisine, featuring Venetian lagoon seafood, Sardinian specialties and Sicilian zing.

Anice Stellato (p133) Venice redefines the neighbourhood bistro with sustainable seafood, a canalside location and spice-route flair.

Osteria alla Staffa (p153) Artisically inclined Venetian cuisine, inspired by Rialto-fresh fish, organic ingredients and artisan cheeses.

Antiche Carampane (p114) Decadent Venetian pastas and legendary *crudi* in a shady courtesans' courtyard.

Best by Budget

€

All'Arco (p113)

ProntoPesce (p113)

Dai Zemei (p113)

Bacaro Da Fiore (p75)

Zenzero (p151)

€€

A Beccafico (p76)

Ai Promessi Sposi (p131)

I Figli delle Stelle (p165)

Osteria alla Staffa (p153)

Antiche Carampane (p114)

€€€

Anice Stellato (p133)

Trattoria Corte Sconta (p153)

Venissa (p179)

Al Covo (p154)

Best for Cicheti

All'Arco (p113)

ProntoPesce (p113)

I Rusteghi (p76)

La Cantina (p132)

Dai Zemei (p113)

Best for Date Nights

Osteria Boccadoro (p133)

Al Covo (p154)

I Figli delle Stelle (p165)

A Beccafico (p76)

Trattoria Corte Sconta (p153)

Best for Waterfront Dining

Al Pesador (p115)

Osteria l'Orto dei Mori (p132)

I Figli delle Stelle (p165)

La Palanca (p165)

Dalla Marisa (p132)

Best for Vegetarians

Le Spighe (p153)

Tearoom Caffè Orientale (p113)

Osteria La Zucca (p114)

Fritto e Frutta (p114)

Antica Adelaide (p132)

Best for Sustainable Food

Le Garzette (p166)

Anice Stellato (p133)

Alaska Gelateria (p113)

Vecio Fritolin (p115)

Grom (p90)

Best for Garden Dining

Trattoria Corte Sconta (p153)

Trattoria da Ignazio (p115)

Venissa (p179)

La Favorita (p166)

Locanda Cipriani (p179)

Best for Classic Venetian

Dalla Marisa (p132)

Antiche Carampane (p114)

Al Pontil Dea Giudecca (p165)

Enoteca al Volto (p75)

Best for Inventive Venetian

Venissa (p179)

Trattoria Corte Sconta (p153)

Osteria alla Staffa (p153)

Al Pesador (p115)

Al Covo (p154)

Caffè Florian, Piazza San Marco (p76)

🍷 Drinking & Nightlife

When the siren sounds for acque alte (high tide), Venetians dutifully close up shop and head home to put up their flood barriers – then pull on their boots and head right back out again. Why let floods disrupt your evening's entertainment? It's not just a turn of phrase: come hell or high water, Venetians will find a way to have a good time.

Happy Hour(s)

The happiest hour (or two) in Venice begins around 6pm at boozing and *cicheti* (Venetian tapas) hot spots. If you're prompt, you might beat the crowds to the bar for *un ombra* (a 'shade'; a small glass of wine) for as little as €1.50 and get *cicheti* while they're fresh. *Osterie* (taverns), *enoteche* (wine bars) and *bacari* (hole-in-the-wall bars) are also renowned for their food.

Giro d'Ombra

An authentic Venetian *giro d'ombra* (pub crawl) begins around the Pescaria by 9am, drinking *prosecco* with fishermen toasting a hard day's work that began at 3am. For layabouts, Venice offers a second-chance *giro d'ombra* with *cicheti* at *bacari* ringing the Rialto Market around noon. Afterwards, it's a long four-hour dry spell until the next *giro d'ombra* begins in hot spots around Campo Santa Margherita in Dorsoduro, Campo Bella Vienna in San Polo, Fondamenta degli

Ormesini in Cannaregio, and Campo Maria Formosa in Castello. Some bars encourage drinkers to linger with occasional live music acts.

What to Order

No rules seem to apply to drinking in Venice. No mixing spirits and wine? Venice's classic cocktails suggest otherwise; try a *spritz*, made with *prosecco*, soda water and bittersweet Aperol or bitter Campari. No girly drinks? Tell that to burly boat-builders enjoying frothy *prosecco*.

This makes knowing what to order and where tricky. Price is not an indicator of quality – you can pay €2 for a respectable *spritz*, or live to regret that €16 bellini tomorrow (ouch). If you're not pleased with your drink, leave it and move on to the next *bacaro*. Venice is too small and life too short to make do with ho-hum hooch. Don't be shy about asking fellow drinkers what they recommend; happy hour is highly sociable here.

LOCAL FAVOURITES

Prosecco The sparkling white that's the life of any Venetian party, from €1.50 nonvintage to €3.50 DOCG Conegliano Prosecco Superiore.

Spritz A stiff drink at an easy price (€1.50 to €3), this *prosecco* cocktail is a cross-generational hit with students and pensioners at bars across Venice – except *enoteche* (wine bars).

Soave A well-balanced white wine made with Veneto Garganega grapes, ideal with seafood in refreshing young versions (€2 to €5) or as a conversation piece in complex Classico versions (€2.50 to €6).

Amarone The Titian of wines: a profound, voluptuous red blended from Valpollicella Corvina grapes. Complex and costly (€6 to €18 per glass), but utterly captivating while it lasts, like a stormy love affair in a bottle.

Ribolla Gialla A weighty white with all the right curves from Friuli-Venezia Giulia, this wine gets more voluptuous with age; irresistible with buttery fish, gnocchi and cheese.

Valpolicella A versatile grape that's come into its own with a bright young DOC namesake red wine that's more food-friendly than Amarone, a structured, aged version called DOG Valpolicella Ripasso, and the DOCG sweet late-harvest Recioto della Valpolicella.

PLAN YOUR TRIP DRINKING & NIGHTLIFE

NEED TO KNOW

Opening Hours

Cafe-bars generally open from 8am to 8pm, although some stay open later and morph into drinking hangouts. Pubs and wine bars are mostly shut by 1am to 2am.

Events Calendars

Check listings in free mags distributed citywide and online: **VeNews** (www.venezianews.it), **Venezia da Vivere** (www.veneziadavivere.com), and **2Venice** (www.2venice.it). For events in Lido di Jesolo and around the lagoon, see www.turismovenezia.it.

Noise Regulations

Keep it down to a dull roar after 10pm: sound travels in Venice, and worse than a police bust for noise infractions is a scolding from a Venetian *nonna* (grandmother).

Lugana A mineral-rich, well-structured white worthy of Palladio from Trebbiano grapes grown at the border of Veneto and Lombardy; a foodie favourite.

Refosco dal Peduncolo Rosso Intense and brooding, a Goth rocker that hits the right notes. This order is guaranteed to raise your sommelier's eyebrow, and probably your bill.

Morgana beer A worthy Venetian craft beer from the owners of La Cantina: unpasteurised, unfiltered and undeniably appealing on hot days.

Cafes

To line your stomach with coffee and pastry before your next *giro d'ombra*, check out Venice's legendary cafe-bars, and skip milky cappuccino for a stronger, local-favourite espresso drink: *macchiatone* (espresso with a 'big stain' of hot milk). For local flavour, try the Torrefazione Marchi (p133) *noxea*: coffee beans are roasted in small batches with hazelnuts in the roaster behind the bar, then ground and brewed into a nutty espresso.

Historic baroque cafes around Piazza San Marco like Caffè Florian (p76) and Caffè Quadri (p77) serve coffee and hot chocolate to the sound of live orchestras – though your heart might beat a different rhythm once you get the bill. Hint: Caffè Lavena (p77) offers a €1 espresso at the counter. But this is Venice, and decadence is always in order – might as well order *caffe correto* (espresso 'corrected' with liquor), and tango with a stranger.

Enoteche

Request *qualcosa di particolare* (something interesting), and your sommelier will accept the challenge to reach behind the bar for one of Veneto's obscure varietals or innovative wine. Even ordinary varietals take on extraordinary characteristics in Veneto growing regions that range from marshy to mountainous, so a merlot or soave could be the most adventurous choice on the menu. Ask for *un ombra* for starters, or you might end up with a very interesting bill.

Speciality *enoteche* like I Rusteghi (p76), **Enoteca Mascareta** (Map p320; ☎041 523 07 44; Calle Lunga Santa Maria Formosa 5138; meals €30-45; ☯7pm-2am Fri-Tue; ☲Ospedale) and Al Prosecco (p115) uphold Venice's time-honoured tradition of selling good stuff by the glass, so you can discover new favourites without committing to a bottle. To dive deeper into Veneto wines, sign up for a tasting session with **Venetian Vine** (p133),or join a *cicheti* crawl led by Venice Urban Adventures (p116).

Drinking & Nightlife by Neighbourhood

➜ **San Marco** High-end cocktails and DOC wines with DJs. (p76)

➜ **Dorsoduro** Bargain booze and rivers of *spritz*. (p95)

➜ **San Polo & Santa Croce** Inspired *ombre* (half-glasses of wine) and *cicheti* (Venetian tapas) at historic *bacari* (hole-in-the-wall bars). (p115)

➜ **Cannaregio** Happy hours behind the Ghetto with live music. (p133)

➜ **Castello** Drink like a sailor at local *bacari*, or join artistes for pre-Biennale cocktails. (p154)

➜ **Giudecca, Lido & the Southern Islands** Fall film festivals, summer beach clubbing and year-round happy hours. (p167)

➜ **Murano, Burano & the Northern Islands** A quiet drink with a local crowd. (p181)

DOC Versus IGT

In Italy, the official DOC *(denominazione d'origine controllata)* and elite DOCG (DOC *garantita* – guaranteed) designations are usually assurances of top-notch vino, and the Veneto has more DOCG-designated wines than any other Italian region besides Piedmont. Taste the DOC wines that put the Veneto on the world wine-tasting map at select wineries in **Soave** (Soave Superiore and Recioto di Soave), **Conegliano** *(prosecco)*, and **Valpolicella** (Amarone).

But successful as its wines are, the Veneto also bucks the DOC/DOCG system. Many small-production Veneto wineries can't be bothered with such external validation, because they already sell out to Venetian *osterie* and *enoteche*. Some top Veneto producers prefer the IGT designation, which guarantees grapes typical of the region but leaves winemakers room to experiment with non-traditional blends and methods (such as natural-yeast fermentation).

Once you get a taste for local wines, don't miss Verona's annual **Vinitaly** (p22) in March or April, Italy's largest wine expo,

---

DRINKING COMES NATURALLY HERE

Detour through the Veneto's glorious wine country for a day, and you'll see why the region is setting Italy's trend for natural-process wines – an umbrella term describing wines made with organic, biodynamic, natural-fermentation and other unconventional methods. With speciality grapes thriving on the Veneto's unspoilt volcanic hills, who needs pesticides, additives or industrial processing? Instead, growing numbers of Veneto vintners are doing what comes naturally, and experimenting with low-intervention, natural-process approaches.

Taste their results for yourself at **ViniVeri** (www.viniveri.net), the natural-process wine showcase held in Verona every April as an alternative to major label–focused Vinitaly. Between ViniVeri tastings, you can sample excellent selections of natural-process wines at **Antica Adelaide** (p132), **Al Prosecco** (p115) and **Enoteca Mascareta** (above). *Salute* – here's to your health, and the Veneto's, too.

featuring 80,000 wines, including Veneto's finest IGTs and DOCGs.

Nightlife

In central Venice, every footstep reverberates along the *calli* (alleyways), and noise restrictions nix dance-club scenes. Things look up in summer, when beach clubs open on the Lido, and at Lido di Jesolo, about an hour's drive northeast of Venice along the Adriatic Coast. Padua also has a happening club scene, including gay and lesbian venues.

Lonely Planet's Top Choices

I Rusteghi (p76) Gondoliers sing gratis after fourth-generation sommelier Giovanni d'Este's pairings of cult wines with boar salami.

Al Prosecco (p115) Organic grapes, wild-yeast fermentation, biodynamic methods: with Italy's finest natural-process wines, toasts come naturally.

Al Mercà (p116) Top-notch DOC wines, cheeses and *cicheti* enjoyed by the Grand Canal docks.

Cantinone Già Schiavi (p95) Tiny bottles of beer and outsized neighbourhood personalities keep this historic canalside joint hopping.

Al Timon (p133) Canalside tables, *crostini* (open-face sandwiches), carafes of good house wine and occasional live music: idyllic.

Best Specialty Beverages

VizioVirtu (p118) Artisan hot chocolate.

Torrefazione Marchi (p133) *Noxea.*

Alaska Gelateria (p113) *Granita di fragole.*

La Serra (p154) Herbal tisane.

Fritto e Frutta (p114) Smoothie.

Best Happy-Hour Hot Spots

Al Mercà (p116)

Al Timon (p133)

Il Caffe Rosso (p95)

Cantinone Già Schiavi (p95)

Osteria Alla Vedova (p132)

Best for Beer

La Cantina (p132)

Agli Ormesini (p134)

Il Santo Bevitore (p133)

Cantinone Già Schiavi (p95)

Antica Birraria Della Corte (p114)

Best for Vino

Vinitaly (p22)

ViniVeri (p40)

I Rusteghi (p76)

Al Prosecco (p115)

Enoteca Mascareta (p40)

Drogheria Mascari (p119)

Best Signature Cocktails

Danieli at **Bar Terazza Danieli** (p154)

Spritz with olive at **Ai Postali** (p116)

Martini (no olive) at **Harry's Bar** (p77)

White-peach bellini at **Locanda Cipriani** (p179)

Pear bellini at **La Serra** (p154)

Best for Coffee & Tea

Caffè Florian (p76)

Caffè Lavena (p77)

Torrefazione Marchi (p133)

Tearoom Orientale (p113)

Tea Room Beatrice (p95)

Caffè dei Frari (p116)

Best Clubs

Terrazzamare (p181)

B.each (p167)

Lion's Bar (p167)

Il Muretto (p181)

Marina Club (p181)

Best Wine-Tasting Destinations

Vinitaly (p22)

ViniVeri (p40)

La Strada di Prosecco (p200)

Soave (p209)

Valpollicella (p209)

Venetian Vine (p133)

I Rusteghi (p76)

Best for Drinks with a View

Skyline Rooftop Bar (p167)

Bar Terazza Danieli (p154)

Caffè Florian (p76)

Algiubagio (p134)

Harry's Dolci (p165)

Musicians entertaining diners

☆ Entertainment

After the fall of Venice's shipping empire, the curtain rose on the city's music scene. A magnet for classical-music fans for four centuries, Venice today supplies its own soundtrack of opera, baroque music and jazz. Given limited turf in this city of canals, sports events and rock concerts are understandably constrained – but Venice has earned a global reputation for regattas and cinema.

Opera

Venice is the home of modern opera and the legendary, incendiary Teatro La Fenice, one of the world's top opera houses since its founding in 1792 and host to Giuseppe Verdi's premieres of *Rigoletto* and *La Traviata*. But the music doesn't stop when La Fenice takes its summer break: opera divas from around the world perform under the stars from June to August at Verona's Roman Arena, Italy's top summer opera festival.

Today you can see opera as Venetians did centuries ago, inside a frescoed pleasure-palace music room at Palazetto Bru Zane, in Grand Canal palace salons with Musica a Palazzo, among heavenly frescoes at Scuola Grande di San Giovanni Evangelista, and in period costume at Scuola Grande dei Carmini.

Classical Music

Venice is the place to hear baroque music in its original and intended venues, with notes soaring to Sebastiano Ricco–frescoed ceilings

NEED TO KNOW

Advance Tickets

Shows regularly sell out in summer, so purchase tickets online at the venue website, www.veniceconnected.com or www.musicinvenice.com. Tickets may also be available at the venue box-office or from **HelloVenezia ticket outlets** (☎041 24 24; www.hellovenezia.it), located near key *vaporetto* stops and ACTV public-transport ticket points.

Business Hours

Event start times vary, with doors at evening concerts typically opening from 7pm to 8.30pm. Due to noise regulations in this small city with big echoes, live-music venues are limited, and shows typically end by 11pm.

Music Calendar

For schedules of upcoming performances, Venetian discographies and online ticket sales, see www.musicinvenice.com. For upcoming openings, concerts, performances and other cultural events, check listings at www.veneziadavivere.com (mostly in Italian) and www.turismovenezia.it (in Italian, English and German).

Cover

Entry is often free at bars, but the cover runs from €10 to €25 for shows in established venues; pay in advance or at the door.

Free Shows

In summer, don't miss Venice Jazz Festival outdoor events, plus free beach concerts on the Lido and on Lido di Jesolo. Year-round in good weather, you might luck into outdoor happy-hour shows around Campo San Giacomo dell'Orio and Fondamenta degli Ormesini.

at Palazzetto Bru Zan, filling Ca' Rezzonico's vast baroque ballroom, sweeping through the salons at Palazzo Querini Stampalia and reverberating through La Pietà, the original Vivaldi venue. Between opera seasons, summer symphonies are performed by **La Fenice's Philharmonic Orchestra** (www.filarmonica-fenice.it) at the opera house or affiliated Teatro Malibran.

Interpreti Veneziani plays Vivaldi and other baroque classics on original instruments with radical verve, in a style known in Italy as 'baroque-n-roll' or 'ba-rock'. Tickets can be purchased on site or at Museo della Musica, an informative museum of baroque music and instruments with free admission provided by Interpreti Veneziani.

Music becomes a religious experience surrounded by Venetian art masterpieces during organ vespers at Basilica di Santa Maria delle Salute and occasional sacred music concerts at other Venetian churches.

Jazz

July's Venice Jazz Festival features international stars like Cesaria Evora and Omar Sosa, but tributes to Miles Davis, Chet Baker and Charles Mingus continue year-round at Venice Jazz Club and you might catch free-form jazz jams at I Figli delle Stelle, Ostreria da Filo or Ai Postali.

Rock & Pop

A handful of other bars sporadically host live music acts, usually rock, reggae, folk and *leggera* (pop). For all-ages alt-rock and punk, check events at Laboratorio Occupato Morion. Bars with regular musical interludes include Paradiso Perduto, Al Timon, Bagolo, Torino@Notte, Il Santo Bevitore and Antica Osteria Ruga Rialto. But don't expect to roll in late and still catch the show: according to local noise regulations, bars are supposed to end concerts at 11pm.

Summer concerts are held on beaches on the Lido and on Lido di Jesolo – watch the local press in July and August, when international acts like Franz Ferdinand sometimes play Lido di Jesolo for free.

Cinema

International star power and Italian fashion storm Lido red carpets during the Venice International Film Festival, where films are shown in their original language. But the most cinematic crowd scenes are at free summer movies dubbed into Italian at Campo San Polo's Summer Arena, and on Lido sands during the summer open-air movie series at B.each (p167).

Between film festivals and summer screenings, catch award-winning films (sometimes subtitled) and blockbusters (usually dubbed) at Multisala Rossini, a new three-screen venue with digital sound in the heart of San Marco. For revivals and rare cuts in the original language, try the screening room at Casa del Cinema, Venice's video and film library. Check Venice Comune (www.comune.venezia.it) for upcoming movie-screening schedules.

Theatre & Dance

Dance performances are staged year-round in Venice, but especially in summer, during the Venice Biennale's International Festival of Contemporary Dance, usually held the first two weeks in June. For more modern movement, check the schedule at Teatro Fondamenta Nuove; ballet performances are usually staged at Teatro Goldoni, which also shows contemporary theatre and Shakespeare, usually in Italian.

Workshops Learn the art of mask-acting, costuming and pantomime at *commedia dell'arte* classes at Teatro Junghans.

Biennale venues International dance performances are often held inside the historic boatyards of the Arsenale and at Teatro Fondamenta Nuove.

Carnevale street theatre Don't miss roaming street-theatre performances in Italian, French and English created by Venetian historian, storyteller and playwright Alberto Toso Fei.

Sports & Activities

Boating is the sport of choice in Venice, with the Italian passion for football falling a distant second. The great Italian sport of **cycling** is actually banned in central Venice, though the Lido is a prime stretch of waterfront cycling turf and tandem bicycle rentals are available. To see the autumn colours of Sant'Erasmo's vineyards, Il Lato Azzuro offers Bicicheti, an afternoon bike-ride across the garden isle followed by wine and *cicheti* (snacks). The mainland Veneto countryside offers easy routes through patchwork flatlands and tougher challenges into the Dolomite foothills.

Running is gaining popularity in Venice, and though most locals stick to jogs through the Giardini and along the Zattere, sure-footed runners attempt the mad dash from the Brenta riverbanks to San Marco via pontoon bridges during the Venice Marathon.

ROWING

If this improbably floating city has one standing lesson to offer, it's that imagination makes anything possible – including rowing standing up *(voga alla veneta)*,

which is the closest non-Messiahs may get to walking on water. Regattas run from spring's ambitious 32km Vogalonga through autumn's costumed Regata Storica.

Lessons Learn to row from regatta champ Jane Caporal of Row Venice, and you'll be hopping up on the *poppa* (rear oarlock footing) with the best of them.

Style Pied á Terre makes original *fur-lane* (rubber-soled boat shoes) in fashion-forward shades.

Gondolas Get your seaworthy scale model for the bathtub at Gilberto Penzo or sign up on the waiting list at Squero Di San Trovaso, where gondolas are still painstakingly hand-shaped and repaired.

Forcole *Forcola* (oarlock) artisans Saverio Pastor, Franco Furlanetto and Paolo Brandolisio will custom-carve your wooden oarlock to suit your height and weight to propel your boat forward with minimum effort and maximum style – or at least make a compelling conversation piece.

SAILING

Sailing is a year-round passion, especially *vela al terzo*, in traditional, shallow-hulled lagoon vessels with triangular main sails. To get your feet wet in Venice's nautical scene, look into sailing tours of the Venice lagoon and boating trips up the Riviera Brenta. You might try bringing your own boat to the lagoon, but be advised that navigation is tricky for newcomers to this treacherously shallow lagoon – even Napoleon was kept at bay by this daunting system of channels.

Sailing classes are available at Isola di Certosa.

Navigational maps can be purchased at Mare di Carta, which is an excellent source of information about lagoon boating routes and conditions.

Moorings may be available at Chioggia and Isola di Certosa.

FOOTBALL (SOCCER)

Football is a comparatively lesser passion here than in landlocked regions of Italy, although Venetian kids learn to aim carefully so balls kicked around the *campo* don't end up in the canal. Known as the *arancioneroverde* (orange, black and greens), **AC Venezia** (☑041 520 68 99; www.veneziacalcio.it) was founded in 1907 and won major championships during WWII. Since then Venezia has shifted into Serie C (third division), where the team won a championship. Venezia plays at an island stadium, Stadio

VENICE BIENNALE

Europe's premier arts showcase since 1907 is something of a misnomer: the Venice **Biennale** (www.labiennale.org) is actually held every year, but the spotlight alternates between art (odd-numbered years, eg 2013, 2015, 2017) and architecture (even-numbered years, eg 2012, 2014, 2016). The summer art biennial is the biggest draw, with some 300,000 visitors viewing contemporary-art showcases in 30 national pavilions in the Giardini, with additional exhibitions in venues across town. The architecture biennial is usually held in autumn (fall), with architects filling the vast boat sheds of the Arsenale with avant-garde conceptual structures.

But the Biennale doesn't stop there. The city-backed organisation also organises an International Festival of Contemporary Dance and concert series every summer, and runs the Venice International Film Festival each September. For upcoming event listings, venues and tickets, check the Biennale website (www.labiennale.org).

Penzo, on Isola di Sant'Elena, an island on the back side of Castello.

Tickets Match tickets are available at Stadio Penzo and from **HelloVenezia ticket outlets** (☑041 24 24; www.hellovenezia.it; tickets €15-20). Getting a ticket on the day is rarely a problem.

Transport to matches On match days, special ferry services run between Isola del Tronchetto's car parks and Sant'Elena, and all buses arriving in Venice stop at Tronchetto.

Footy on TV On big game nights, Venetians and visitors converge to watch the match at Il Santo Bevitore.

Casino

Fortunes have been won and entire empires lost for centuries in Venice's *ridotti* (gambling houses). Try your luck if you dare at Casinò di Venezia, as long as you're at least 18 years old – they do check identification – and dressed to impress the bouncers (men are expected to wear jackets). Slot machines are less formal and open earlier, but lack the high-stakes drama of the poker and blackjack tables. Ask your hotel for a free-casino-entry coupon, which may also entitle you to a few euros' worth of free gaming.

Entertainment by Neighbourhood

➡ **San Marco** Opera, classical music, dance, theatre, cinema, DJs. (p78)

➡ **Dorsoduro** Jazz. (p96)

➡ **San Polo & Santa Croce** Cinema, outdoor theatre, live-music nights. (p117)

➡ **Cannaregio** Dance, live-music nights, cinema, casino. (p134)

➡ **Castello** Classical music, dance, live-music nights. (p155)

➡ **Giudecca, Lido & the Southern Islands** Lido, cinema. (p167)

➡ **Murano, Burano & the Northern Islands** Lido di Jesolo – live music, DJs. (p181)

Lonely Planet's Top Choices

Venice Biennale (p46) Europe's signature art and architecture biennials draw international crowds in alternate years, while musicians and dancers perform annually in Biennale summer showcases.

Teatro La Fenice (p66) Divas hit new highs in this historic jewel-box theatre for under 1000 lucky ticket-holders.

Venice International Film Festival (p24) Movie stars align along the Lido's red carpet, and thoughtful, stylish films earn top honours.

Verona's Roman Arena (p204) Larger-than-life tenors rock the Roman amphitheatre June to August, to choruses of *Bravo!* from 30,000 fans.

Interpreti Veneziani (p78) Venice's breakthrough classical talents play baroque with such bravado, you'll fear for their antique instruments.

Best Outdoor Activities

Carnevale (p22) Dancing in the streets.

Row Venice (p174) Rowing.

Su e Zo Per I Ponti (p22) Crossing 55 bridges for charity.

Lido (p168) Tandem-biking to Malamocco.

Festa del Redentore (p24) Crossing the Giudecca Canal via pontoon bridge.

Il Lato Azzuro (p175) Bicicheti (cycling plus *cicheti*).

Best Modern Music Events

Venice Jazz Festival (p23)

Carnevale (p22)

Venice Biennale (p46)

Teatro Fondamenta Nuove (p134)

Laboratorio Occupato Morion (p155)

Best for Opera

Teatro La Fenice (p66)

Verona's Roman Arena (p204)

Musica a Palazzo (p78)

Scuola Grande di San Giovanni Evangelista (p108)

Scuola Grande dei Carmini (p89)

Best for Classical Music

Interpreti Veneziani (p78)

Palazzetto Bru Zane (p117)

La Pietà (p143)
Ca' Rezzonico (p90)

Teatro La Fenice (p66)

Palazzo Querini Stampalia (p145)

Best Free Entertainment

Carnevale (p22)

Lido di Jesolo (p181) Free summer beach concerts.

Basilica di Santa Maria della Salute (p88) Organ vespers.

Caffè Florian (p76)

Caffè Lavena (p77)

Summer Arena (p117)

Best for Theatre & Dance

Biennale (p46) International Festival of Contemporary Dance.

Teatro Goldoni (p78)

Teatro Junghans (p167)

Teatro Fondamenta Nuove (p134)

Il Lato Azzurro (p224)

Best for Cinema

Venice International Film Festival (p24)

Casa del Cinema (p117)

Summer Arena (p117)

Multisala Rossini (p78)

B.each (p167)

Best Live Music Nights

Laboratorio Occupato Morion (p155)

Paradiso Perduto (p134)

Venice Jazz Club (p96)

Il Santo Bevitore (p133)

Osteria Da Filo (p116)

I Figli delle Stelle (p165)

Carlo Moretti glassware

 # Shopping

Between world-famous museums and architecture, many visitors miss Venice's best-kept secret: the shopping. No illustrious shopping career is complete without trolling Venice for one-of-a-kind, artisan-made finds. All those kiosks hawking porcelain masks and souvenir tees are just there to throw less dedicated shoppers off the scent of major scores (though striped gondolier shirts look hip out of context).

Artisan Specialities

Your Venice souvenirs may be hard to describe back home without sounding like you're bragging. 'It's an original', you'll say, 'and I met the artisan'. Venice has kept its artisan traditions alive and vital for centuries, especially glass, paper, textiles and woodworking.

Shopping by Neighbourhood

➡ **San Marco** Art galleries, international designers and backstreet artisan showcases. (p78)

➡ **Dorsoduro** Antique shops and fashion-forward boutiques. (p96)

➡ **San Polo & Santa Croce** Artisan studios galore: glass, paper, fashion, gondolas. (p117)

➡ **Cannaregio** High-street retail and artisan bargains. (p135)

➡ **Castello** Cutting-edge artisans and quirky curios. (p155)

➡ **Giudecca, Lido & the Southern Islands** Farmers markets and bikinis. (p161)

➡ **Murano, Burano & the Northern Islands** Handmade lace and the world's finest art glass. (p179)

Studio Visits

For your travelling companions who aren't sold on shopping, here's a convincing argument: in Venice, it really is an educational experience. In backstreet artisans' studios, you can watch ancient techniques used to make strikingly modern *carta memorizzata* (marbled-paper) travel journals (from €12) and Murano glass waterfalls worn as necklaces (from €30). Studios cluster together, so to find unique pieces, just wander key artisan areas: San Polo around Calle dei Saoneri; Santa Croce around Calle Lunga and Calle del Tentor; San Marco along Frezzeria; Dorsoduro around the Peggy Guggenheim Collection; and Murano.

Glass showrooms and shelves of fragile handicrafts may be labelled *'non toccare'* (don't touch) – instead of chancing breakage, just ask to see any piece. The person who shows it to you may be the artisan who made it, so don't be shy about saying *'Complimenti!'* (My compliments!) on impressive pieces. In a world of designer knockoffs and cookie-cutter culture, your support for handicrafts is a vote for Venice's enduring originality.

Venetian Style Signatures

Italian style earns its international reputation for impeccable proportions, eye-catching details, luxe textures and vibrant colours – but Venice goes one step further, with original fashion statements, artisan-made accessories and limited-edition sunglasses.

CLOTHING

Venice has the standard Italian designer brands you can find back home, from Armani to Zegna, along Largo XXII Marzo and Marzaria in San Marco – but for original fashion and better value, venture into Venice's backstreets. The odds of an office mate back home showing up to the holiday party in the same locally designed Spilli (p136) tunic, Venetia Studium (p81) goddess dress, hand-printed Fiorella Gallery (p78)

NEED TO KNOW

Business Hours

Most shops open around 10am to 1pm and 3.30pm to 7pm Monday to Saturday. Some shops in tourist areas stay open 10am to 7pm daily, while shops off the main thoroughfares may remain closed on Monday morning. Most Murano glass showrooms close by 6pm. Many shops close for major Italian holidays, and for all or part of August.

Shipping

Never mind arbitrary airline luggage limits: most home decor and Murano glass showrooms offer shipping services at reasonable costs, especially within Europe. On new merchandise, customs duties may apply in your home country – check before you buy.

Taxes

Visitors from outside the EU may be entitled to VAT sales tax refunds on major purchases (see p287).

---

smoking jacket or Arnoldo & Battois (p80) sculpted silk frock are infinitesimal. Pocket the difference in price between Venetian couture and mass-market logo merchandise, and you could get a return ticket to Venice.

ACCESSORIES

Don't call Venetian artisans designers: their highly skilled handicrafts can't be mass produced, and stand out in a globalised fashion crowd. Paris's latest it bags seem uninspired compared to purses made of marbled paper at Cárte (p117), and Tiffany seems ho-hum once you've glimpsed the glass-ring selection in Murano. When it comes to Godi Fiorenza (p79) hand-beaded belle epoque collars or custom-fit shoes with leather heels sculpted like gondola prows from Giovanna Zanella (p157), there really is no point of comparison.

EYEWEAR

Centuries before geek chic, the first eyeglasses known to Europe were worn in the Veneto c 1348, and Venetian opticians have been hand-grinding lenses and stylish frames ever since. Bring your prescription to Ottica Carraro (p79) or Ottica Vascellari (p121), or snap up a replica of Peggy

Guggenheim's outrageous frames at the Peggy Guggenheim Collection (p87) gift shop.

Bargains

Venetian treasures cost less than you'd think. From Murano blown-glass beads that make sensational pendants (€1 to €15) to custom chandeliers (€400-plus), Venice's handcrafted goods are quite reasonably priced for the highly specialised labour involved. For the record, Murano glass isn't necessarily less expensive in Murano than in Venice proper, but Murano's selection of original art-glass is truly dazzling.

Like the rest of Italy, Venice does have some January and July sales. The sweetest deals can be found in the low-season months of November, March and July.

OUTDOOR MARKETS

From March through to October and around Christmas, treasures hidden in *palazzo* attics turn up at Venice's open-air markets. Upcoming dates are listed at www.turismovenezia.it (search for markets) for these not-to-be-missed events.

Shopping Hot Spots

Mall shopping can't compare to the thrill of treasure hunting in Venice. Here's where to find Venetian specialities:

➡ **Contemporary art** Between Biennales, Venice's contemporary-art galleries make passers-by stop and stare around Campo San Maurizio in San Marco and along Fondamenta San Biagio on Giudecca.

➡ **Gourmet supplies** Depending on your airplane's luggage limitations and home country's customs regulations, Venetian edibles and wines make tasty souvenirs from gourmet shops such as Drogheria Mascari, Aliani and Casa del Parmigiano near the Rialto Market.

➡ **Antiques** Hidden gems surface in open-air markets and the backstreet shops of Cannaregio around the Ghetto and Dorsoduro along Calle delle Bottege.

Lonely Planet's Top Choices

ElleElle (p180) Murano art glass balancing modernity and tradition, with essential shapes and dramatic colours.

Cárte (p117) Marble endpaper breaks free of books and turns into handbags, cocktail rings and jewellery boxes.

Marina e Susanna Sent (p96) Minimalist Murano glass jewellery with vivid colours and architectural impact.

Sigfrido Cipollato (p155) Venetian pirate-king skull rings and enamelled baroque diadems in gold and gems, exquisitely hand-crafted.

Chiarastella Cattana (p78) Locally loomed linens as plush as velvet, in history-inspired modern designs and Venetian colours.

Best Non-Touristy Venice Souvenirs

Gilberto Penzo (p118) Scale-model *gondole*.

I Vetri a Lume di Amadi (p118) Glass mosquitoes.

Pied à Terre Shoes (p118) Gondolier shoes.
Gianni Basso (p135) Calling cards with lion of San Marco.

Paolo Brandolisio miniature forcole (p157) Carved gondola oarlocks.

Best Venetian Home Decor

Fortuny Tessuti Artistici (p161)

Chiarastella Cattana (p78)

Cartavenezia (p118)

Caigo Da Mar (p80)

Bevilacqua Fabrics (p79)

Danghyra (p97)

Best Venetian Fashion

Fiorella Gallery (p78)

Godi Fiorenza (p79)

Arnoldo & Battois (p80)

Spilli Lab & Shop (p136)

Malefatte (p79)

Best for Antiques

Mercantino dei Miracoli (p123)

Ballarin (p157)

Antichità al Ghetto (p136)

Il Baule Blu (p121)

Campiello Ca' Zen (p121)

Best for Art

Caterina Tognon (p79)

Galleria van der Koelen (p79)

Jarach Gallery (p79)

Galleria Traghetto (p79)

Ikona Gallery (p131)

Arcobaleno (p80)

Best Mementos for Musicians

Museo della Musica (p73) CDs.

Mille e Una Nota (p121) Instruments.

Libreria Studium (p81) Vivaldi biographies.

Banco Lotto 10 (p157) Diva-worthy opera wraps.

Music in Venice Concert gift card from www.musicinvenice.com.

Best Gifts for Gourmets

Drogheria Mascari (p119)

Aliani (p115)

VizioVirtù (p118)

Atelier Alessandro Merlin (p157)

Madera (p97)

Este Ceramiche Porcellane (p190)

Best Jewellery

Sigfrido Cipolato (p155)

Marina e Susanna Sent (p96)

Cárte (p117)

Laberintho (p120)

Campagnol & Salvadore (p180)

Venetian Dreams (p80)

Best Leather Goods

Daniela Ghezzo (p80)

Giovanna Zanella (p157)

Arnoldo & Battois (p80)

Pagine e Cuoio (p80)

Kalimala Cuoieria (p156)

Gmeiner (p119)

Explore Venice & the Veneto

VENICE'S
TOP SIGHTS

Neighbourhoods at a Glance

❶ Sestiere di San Marco p56

So many world-class attractions are packed into San Marco, some visitors never leave – and others are loath to visit, fearing crowds. But why deny yourself the pleasures of La Fenice, Basilica di San Marco, Palazzo Ducale and Museo Correr? Judge for yourself whether they earn their reputations – but don't stop there. The backstreets are packed with galleries, boutiques and *enoteche* (wine bars).

❷ Sestiere di Dorsoduro p82

Dorsoduro covers prime Grand Canal waterfront with Ca' Rezzonico's gilded splendour, Peggy Guggenheim Collection's modern edge, Gallerie dell'Accademia's Renaissance beauty and Punta della Dogana's contemporary installation art. The neighbourhood lazes its days away on the Zattere, and convenes in Campo Santa Margherita for cocktails.

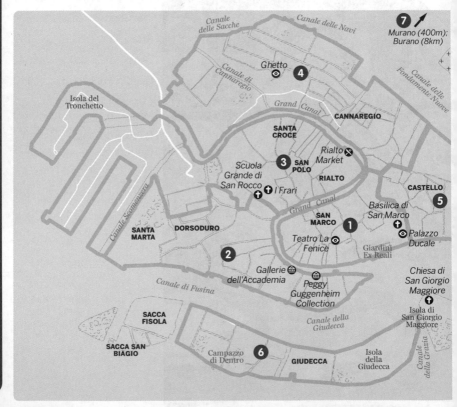

❸ Sestieri di San Polo & Santa Croce p99

Heavenly devotion and earthly delights are neighbours in San Polo and Santa Croce, featuring divine art alongside the ancient red-light district, now home to artisans' workshops and excellent *osterie* (taverns). Don't miss fraternal-twin masterpieces: Titian's glowing Madonna at I Frari and turbulent Tintorettos at Scuola Grande di San Rocco. Quirky museums fill Grand Canal *palazzi* with fashion, video art and scientific oddities, while vendors sing the praises of the Rialto Market's island-grown produce.

❹ Sestiere di Cannaregio p122

Anyone could adore Venice on looks alone, but in Cannaregio you'll fall for its personality. A few streets over from bustling Strada Nuova, footsteps echo along moody

Fondamenta Misericordia without a T-shirt kiosk in sight. Between the Gothic wonder of Madonna dell'Orto and the Renaissance miracle of Santa Maria dei Miracoli are Venice's top *osterie* and the tiny island Ghetto, a living monument to the outsized contributions of Venice's resilient Jewish community.

❺ Sestiere di Castello p137

Sailors, saints and artists made Castello what it is today: home to seafood restaurants, ethereal icons and the Biennale. Some 5000 shipbuilders once worked at the Arsenale, and their output is showcased at Museo Storico Navale. Byzantine churches are gilt to the hilt, luxury hotels sprawl along the waterfront, and Vivaldi echoes from the orphanage where he worked – but Castello slips into something more comfortable to hit the Giardini, *campo* cafes and *bacari* (bars).

❻ Giudecca, Lido & the Southern Islands p158

Architecture binges have brought visitors here for centuries, and no wonder: have you seen the Palladios on Isola di San Giorgio Maggiore? Giudecca was an elite garden getaway before it became an industrial outpost; there's still a women's prison here alongside luxe spas, art galleries and romantic restaurants. Lido is Venice's 12km island escape, with sandy beaches, an A-list film festival and Liberty villas. Resorts ring the Lido, alongside quarantine islands and San Servolo's Museum of Madness.

❼ Murano, Burano & the Northern Islands p169

Other cities have suburban sprawl; Venice has a teal-blue northern lagoon dotted with blown-glass sculptures and rare wildlife. Serious shoppers head to Murano for one-of-a-kind art glass. Escapists prefer lazy days boating on the lagoon, mooring for seafood feasts on the colourful fishing isle of Burano and glimpses of heaven in Torcello's golden mosaics.

Isola di San Michele
Canale delle Navi
0 — 1 km
0 — 0.5 miles
Darsena Grande
Isola San Pietro
LA TANA
Canale di San Marco
Darsena di Sant'Elena
SANT'ELENA
Laguna Veneta
Parco delle Rimembranze
Isola di Sant'Elena
❻ Lido di Venezia (1km)

Sestiere di San Marco

Neighbourhood Top Five

① Joining the chorus of gasps rippling through the crowd as you enter the **Basilica di San Marco** (p58) and look up to discover angels dancing across 8500 sq m of glittering golden mosaics.

② Shouting *Brava!* for encore performances at **La Fenice** (p66), Venice's jewel-box opera house.

③ Discovering dark secrets lurking in the attic behind the rosy facade of **Palazzo Ducale** (p61).

④ Adopting a philosopher painted by Veronese, Titian or Tintoretto as your personal mentor at the Libreria Marciana in **Museo Correr** (p73).

⑤ Tangoing across Piazza San Marco at sunset to the tune of the **Caffè Florian** (p76) orchestra.

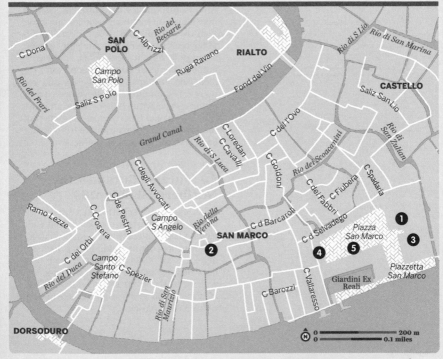

For more detail of this area see Map p308 ➡

Explore Sestiere di San Marco

Discover Venice's golden glories in the basilica and its dark secrets on the Palazzo Ducale Itinerari Segreti tour, then dive into backstreets to find artisan studios, contemporary art galleries and tasty *cicheti* (bar snacks). Detour for fashion and art shows at Museo Fortuny and sunset cocktails at Harry's Bar, but don't miss the overture at La Fenice. Return to moonlit Piazza San Marco for a tango across the square, and watch the Moors strike midnight atop Torre dell'Orlogio, heralding another day in the life of San Marco's charmed existence.

Local Life

➡ **Cheap eats and fancy drinks** Skip sad congealed pizza slices around San Marco and trawl backstreets for bargain *cicheti* and top-notch Veneto wines at I Rusteghi (p76), Bacaro Da Fiore (p75) and Cavatappi (p76).

➡ **Musical stylings** Start on a high note at La Fenice (p66), go for baroque at Interpreti Veneziani (p78), tango at Caffè Florian (p76), tarantella at Caffè Lavena (p77) and hang on to your wine glass through soaring arias at Musica a Palazzo (p78).

➡ **Galleries** In the shadows of historic Santa Maria del Giglio and La Fenice are Venice's best contemporary art galleries, where international and Italian artists supply steady inspiration between Biennales.

➡ **Artisan finds** Mass-market designers line thoroughfares from the Rialto and Accademia to Piazza San Marco – but along the backstreets between, Venetian artisans still hand craft handbags, travel journals and glass jewellery.

Getting There & Away

➡ **Vaporetto** *Vaporetti* 1 and N stop along the Grand Canal at several points in San Marco, including Rialto, Sant'Angelo, San Samuele, Santa Maria del Giglio and San Marco.

➡ **Walking** Follow yellow-signed shortcuts from the Rialto, through shop-lined Marzarie, to Piazza San Marco.

Lonely Planet's Top Tip

In San Marco, the price of a sit-down cappuccino seems more like rent. Take your coffee standing at a bar for just €1 to €2.50, spend a couple more euros for sunshine and people-watching at a *campo* table, or luxuriate in the baroque cafes of Piazza San Marco. There's usually a €6 music surcharge for outdoor seating in Piazza San Marco, so you may as well get your money's worth and tango.

Best Places to Eat

➡ A Beccafico (p76)
➡ Enoteca al Volto (p75)
➡ Bacaro Da Fiore (p75)
➡ Gelateria Suso (p75)
➡ Cavatappi (p76)

For reviews, see p75 ➡

Best Places to Drink

➡ I Rusteghi (p76)
➡ Caffè Florian (p76)
➡ Caffè Lavena (p77)
➡ Harry's Bar (p77)
➡ Osteria all'Alba (p77)

For reviews, see p76 ➡

Best Interior Decor

➡ Museo Correr (p73)
➡ Palazzo Ducale (p61)
➡ Museo Fortuny (p67)
➡ Negozio Olivetti (p72)
➡ Palazzo Grassi (p67)

For reviews, see p67 ➡

TOP SIGHT
BASILICA DI SAN MARCO

Creating Venice's architectural wonder took nearly 800 years and one saintly barrel of lard. In AD 828, wily Venetian merchants allegedly smuggled St Mark's corpse out of Egypt in a barrel of pork fat to avoid inspection by Muslim customs authorities. Venice built a golden basilica around its stolen saint, whose bones were misplaced twice during construction (oops).

Exterior

Church authorities in Rome took a dim view of Venice's tendency to glorify itself and God in the same breath, but Venice defiantly created the official doge's chapel in its own cosmopolitan image, with Byzantine onion-bulb domes, Greek cross layout and Egyptian marble walls. The brick basilica is clad in patchworks of marbles and reliefs from Syria, Egypt and Palestine – priceless trophies from Crusades conquests and battles with Genoa. At the southwestern corner is the **Four Tetrarchs**, an Egyptian porphyry statue supposedly representing four emperors of ancient Rome looted from Constantinople.

Facade

The front of the basilica ripples and crests like a wave, its five niched portals capped with shimmering mosaics and frothy stonework arches. In the far-left portal, lunette mosaics dating from 1270 show St Mark's stolen body arriving at the basilica – a story reprised in 1660 lunette mosaics on the second portal from the right. The far-right portal is another masterpiece of architectural thievery: over Greek columns and a Moorish arch is a lacy screen that might have

DON'T MISS...

➡ Facade lunette mosaics dating from 1270
➡ Dome of Genesis
➡ Dome of the Prophets
➡ Pala d'Oro
➡ Loggia dei Cavalli

PRACTICALITIES

➡ St Mark's Basilica
➡ Map p308
➡ ☏041 270 83 11
➡ www.basilicasan-marco.it
➡ Piazza San Marco
➡ ⊘9.45am-4.45pm Mon-Sat, 2-4pm Sun & holidays, baggage storage 9.30am-5.30pm
➡ ⊠San Marco

been a Turkish sultan's balcony. Grand entrances are made through the central portal, under an ornate triple arch with Egyptian purple porphyry columns and 13th- to 14th-century reliefs of vines, virtues and astrological signs.

Dome Mosaics

Blinking is natural upon your first glimpse of the basilica's glittering mosaics, many made with 24-carat gold leaf fused onto the back of the glass to represent divine light. Just inside the narthex (vestibule) glitter the basilica's oldest mosaics: *Apostles with the Madonna*, standing sentry by the main door for more than 950 years. The atrium's medieval **Dome of Genesis** depicts the separation of sky and water with surprisingly abstract motifs, anticipating modern art by 650 years. *Last Judgment* mosaics cover the atrium vault and the Apocalypse looms large in vault mosaics over the gallery.

Mystical transfusions occur in the **Dome of the Holy Spirit**, where a dove's blood streams onto the heads of saints. In the central 13th-century **Cupola of the Ascension**, angels swirl overhead while dreamy-eyed St Mark rests on the pendentive. Scenes from St Mark's life unfold over the main altar, in vaults flanking the **Dome of the Prophets** (best seen from the Pala d'Oro).

The roped-off circuit of the church interior is free and takes about 15 minutes. Silence is requested, but gasping understandable. For entry, dress modestly (ie knees and shoulders covered) and leave large bags around the corner at Ateneo di San Basso's free one-hour **baggage storage**.

Pala d'Oro

Tucked behind the main altar containing **St Mark's sarcophagus** is the **Pala d'Oro** (Map p308; admission €2; ☺9.45am-5pm Mon-Sat, 2-4.30pm Sun, to 4pm winter), studded with 2000 emeralds, amethysts, sapphires, rubies, pearls and other gemstones. But the most priceless treasures here are biblical figures in vibrant cloisonné, begun in Constantinople in AD 976 and elaborated by Venetian goldsmiths in 1209. The enamelled saints have wild, unkempt beards and wide eyes fixed on Jesus, who glances sideways at a studious St Mark as Mary throws up her hands in wonder – an understandable reaction to such a captivating scene. Look closely to spot touches of Venetian whimsy: falcon-hunting scenes in medallions along the bottom, and the by-now-familiar scene of St Mark's body smuggled out of Egypt on the right.

PLANNING YOUR VISIT

The grandest entrances to the basilica are with a crowd, its polyglot expressions of wonder making a hive-like hum under honey-gold domes. Luckily, the queue moves quickly – waits are rarely more than 15 minutes, even when the queue extends past the Palazzo Ducale's door. Book 'Skip the Line' access online April to October (www.venetoinside. com; €1 booking fee) to bypass queues and head directly into the central portal. Arrive at odd times to avoid tour groups, which tend to arrive on the hour or half-hour. Free guided tours from the diocese explaining the theological messages in the mosaics also enter through the central portal (http://www.ba silicasanmarco.it; tours 11am Monday to Saturday April to October, by prior reservation).

Attending evening vespers allows you to enter the basilica after hours, minus tour groups. Worshippers come in through a side door and are expected to sit quietly for the duration of services; visits beyond the side chapel are not allowed.

BASILICA DI SAN MARCO

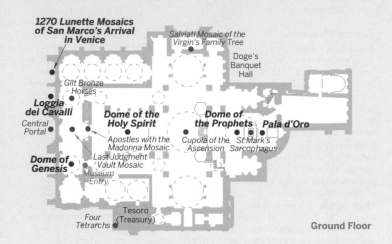

1270 Lunette Mosaics of San Marco's Arrival in Venice

Salviati Mosaic of the Virgin's Family Tree

Doge's Banquet Hall

Gilt Bronze Horses

Loggia dei Cavalli

Central Portal

Dome of the Holy Spirit

Dome of the Prophets

Pala d'Oro

Apostles with the Madonna Mosaic

Cupola of the Ascension

St Mark's Sarcophagus

Dome of Genesis

Last Judgment Vault Mosaic

Museum Entry

Four Tetrarchs

Tesoro (Treasury)

Ground Floor

Museum

San Marco remained the doge's chapel until 1807, and the ducal treasures upstairs in the **Museo** (Basilica di San Marco Museum; Map p308; €5; ☉9.45am-4.45pm Mon-Sat, 2-4pm Sun) put a king's ransom to shame. Gilt bronze horses taken by Venice from Constantinople were stolen in turn by Napoleon but were eventually returned to the basilica and installed in the 1st-floor gallery. Portals lead from the gallery on to the giddiness-inducing **Loggia dei Cavalli**, where reproductions of the horses gallop off the balcony over Piazza San Marco.

In the Museo's displays of restored 13th- to 16th-century mosaic fragments, the Prophet Abraham is all ears and raised eyebrows, as though scandalised by Venetian gossip. On an interior balcony, Salviati's restored 1542–52 mosaic of the Virgin's family tree shows Mary's ancestors perched on branches, alternately chatting and ignoring one another, as families do. Hidden over the altar is the **doge's banquet hall**, where dignitaries wined and dined among lithe stucco figures of Music, Poetry and Peace.

Treasury

Holy bones and booty from the Crusades fill the **Tesoro** (Treasury; Map p308; admission €3; ☉9.45am-5pm Mon-Sat & 2-5pm Sun, to 4pm winter), including a 10th-century rock-crystal ewer with winged feet made for Fatimid Caliph al-'Aziz-bi-llah. Don't miss the bejeweled 12th-century Archangel Michael icon, featuring tiny, feisty enameled saints that look ready to break free of their golden setting and mount a miniature attack on evil. Velvet-padded boxes preserve doges' remains alongside alleged saints' relics, including St Roch's femur, St Mark's thumb, the arm St George used to slay the dragon and even a lock of the Madonna's hair.

TOP SIGHT
PALAZZO DUCALE

Don't be fooled by its genteel Gothic elegance: behind that lacy, pink-chequered facade, the doge's palace shows serious muscle and a steely will to survive. The seat of Venice's government for nearly seven centuries, this powerhouse stood the test of storms, crashes and conspiracies – only to be outwitted by Casanova, the notorious seducer who escaped from the attic prison.

Exterior

After fire gutted the original palace in 1577, Venice considered Palladio's offer to build one of his signature neoclassical temples in its place. Instead, Antonio da Ponte won the commission to restore the palace's Gothic facade with white Istrian stone and Veronese pink marble. Da Ponte's Palazzo effortlessly mixes past with present and business with pleasure, capping a graceful colonnade with medieval capitals depicting key Venetian guilds. The **loggia** along the *piazzetta* (little square) may seem like a fanciful flourish, but it served a solemn purpose: death sentences were read between the ninth and 10th columns from the left. Facing the piazza, Zane and Bartolomeo Bon's 1443 **Porta della Carta** (Paper Door) was an elegant point of entry for dignitaries, and served as a public bulletin board for government decrees.

Courtyard

Entering through the colonnaded courtyard you'll spot Sansovino's brawny statues of Apollo and Neptune flanking Antonio Rizzo's **Scala dei Giganti** (Giants' Staircase). Recent restorations have preserved charming cherubim

DON'T MISS

➡ Scala dei Giganti
➡ Sala del Scudo
➡ Scala d'Oro
➡ Sala delle Quattro Porte
➡ Anticollegio

PRACTICALITIES

➡ Ducal Palace
➡ Map p308
➡ ☏848 08 20 00
➡ www.palazzodu cale.visitmuve.it
➡ Piazzetta San Marco 52
➡ adult/reduced/ child incl Museo Correr €16/8/free or with Museum Pass
➡ ⏰8.30am-7pm Apr-Oct, to 5.30pm Nov-Mar
➡ 🚤San Zaccaria

PALAZZO DUCALE'S TOP FIVE PROPAGANDA PAINTINGS

Veronese's *Juno Bestowing Her Gifts on Venice*, Tiepolo's *Venice Receiving Gifts of the Sea from Neptune*, Titian's *Doge Antonio Grimani Kneeling before Faith*, Tintoretto's *Minerva Dismissing Mars* and Veronese's *Virtues of the Republic* are not to be missed.

propping up the pillars, though slippery incised-marble steps remain off-limits. On the east side of the courtyard arcade were the dreaded **Poggi** (Wells), where prisoners shivered below water level – but now a baggage deposit is installed in their place.

First Floor

Climb the Scala dei Censori (Stairs of the Censors) to the **Doge's Apartments**, where the doge lived under 24-hour guard with a short commute to work up a **secret staircase**. Walk up a couple of steps and turn around to spot Titian's painting of St Christopher wading across troubled lagoon waters over the archway. The 18 roaring lions decorating the doge's **Sala degli Stucchi** are reminders that Venice's most powerful figurehead lived like a caged lion in his gilded suite, which he could not leave without permission. Still, consider the real estate: a terrace garden with private entry to the basilica, and a dozen salons with splendidly restored marble fireplaces carved by Tullio and Antonio Lombardo. The **Sala dello Scudo** (Shield Room) is covered with world maps that reveal the extents of Venetian power (and the limits of its cartographers) c 1483 and 1762. The New World map places California near *Terra Incognita d'Antropofagi* (Unknown Land of the Maneaters), aka Canada, where Cuzco is apparently located.

Second Floor

Head up Sansovino's 24-carat gilt stuccowork **Scala d'Oro** (Golden Staircase) and emerge into rooms covered with gorgeous propaganda. In the Palladio-designed **Sala delle Quattro Porte** (Hall of the Four Doors), ambassadors awaited ducal audiences under a lavish display of Venice's virtues by Giovanni Cambi, whose over-the-top stuccowork earns him the nickname Bombarda. Other convincing shows of Venetian superiority include Titian's 1576 *Doge Antonio Grimani Kneeling Before Faith* amid approving cherubs and Tiepolo's 1740s *Venice Receiving Gifts of the Sea from Neptune,* where Venice is a gorgeous blonde casually leaning on a lion.

Delegations waited in the **Anticollegio** (Council Antechamber), where Tintoretto drew parallels between Roman gods and Venetian government: *Mercury and the Three Graces* reward Venice's industriousness with beauty, and *Minerva Dismissing Mars* is a Venetian triumph of savvy over brute force. The recently restored ceiling is Veronese's 1577 *Venice Distributing Honours*, while on the walls is a vivid reminder of diplomatic behaviour to avoid: Veronese's *Rape of Europe*.

Few were granted an audience in the Palladio-designed **Collegio** (Council Room), where Veronese's

PALAZZO DUCALE

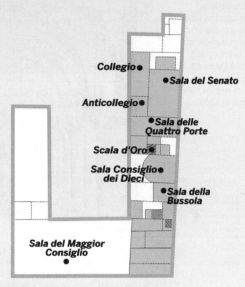

Collegio●

●**Sala del Senato**

Anticollegio●

●**Sala delle Quattro Porte**

Scala d'Oro●

Sala Consiglio ●
dei Dieci

●**Sala della Bussola**

Sala del Maggior Consiglio
●

Second Floor

Secret Staircase ● **Sala degli Stucchi**

Terrace ●

Doge's Apartments ●

Sala dello Scudo ●

Scala dei Censori ●

First Floor

THE MISSING DOGE

In the Sala del Maggior Consiglio the wall frieze depicts the first 76 doges of Venice, but note the black space: Doge Marin Falier would have appeared there had he not lost his head for treason in 1355.

Arcade, Palazzo Ducale

1575–78 *Virtues of the Republic* ceiling shows Venice as a bewitching blonde waving her sceptre like a wand over Justice and Peace. Father-son team Jacopo and Domenico Tintoretto attempt similar flattery, showing Venice keeping company with Apollo, Mars and Mercury in their *Triumph of Venice* ceiling for the **Sala del Senato** (Senate Hall), but frolicking lagoon sea-monsters steal the scene.

Government cover-ups were never so appealing as in the **Sala Consiglio dei Dieci** (Trial Chambers of the Council of Ten; Room 20), where Venice's star chamber plotted under Veronese's *Juno Bestowing her Gifts on Venice*, a glowing goddess strewing gold ducats. Over the slot into which anonymous treason accusations were slipped in the **Sala della Bussola** (Compass Room; Room 21) is his *St Mark in Glory* ceiling.

The cavernous 1419 **Sala del Maggior Consiglio** (Grand Council Hall) features the doge's throne with a 22m-by-7m *Paradise* backdrop (by Tintoretto's son Domenico) that's more politically correct than pretty: heaven is crammed with 500 prominent Venetians, including several Tintoretto patrons. Veronese's political posturing is more elegant in his oval *Apotheosis of Venice* ceiling, where gods marvel at Venice's coronation by angels, with foreign dignitaries and Venetian blondes rubbernecking on the balcony below.

SECRET PASSAGES TOUR

Discover Venice's state secrets in the Palazzo Ducale attic on a fascinating 75-minute guided tour: Itinerari Segreti (see museum website for times). Follow your guide up the Scala d'Oro and through a hidden passageway into the cramped, unadorned Council of Ten Secret Headquarters. Beyond this ominous office suite, the vast Chancellery is lined with drawers of top-secret files, including reports by Venice's far-reaching spy network, accusations by Venetians against their neighbours, and judgements copied in triplicate by clerks. The accused were led into the windowless Interrogation Room, where until 1660 confessions were sometimes extracted from prisoners dangling from a rope. Upstairs lie the Piombi (Leads), the attic prison cells where Casanova was condemned to five years' confinement in 1756 for corrupting nuns and the more serious charge of spreading Freemasonry. As described in his memoirs, Casanova made an ingenious escape through the roof, then convinced a guard he was an official locked into the palace overnight. He would later return to Venice, enlisted as a spy for the Council of Ten.

Prisons

Only visitors on the **Secret Passages** tour can access the secret Council of Ten headquarters and **Piombi** attic prison. Pass through the **Sala del Magistrato alle Leggi** (Hall of the Legal Magistrate), featuring ominous scenes by the master of apocalyptic visions, Hieronymus Bosch. Follow the path of condemned prisoners across the **Ponte dei Sospiri** (Bridge of Sighs) to Venice's 16th-century **Priggione Nove** (New Prisons). Dank cells are covered with graffitied protestations of innocence and paved with marble stolen in a state-sanctioned heist: the sacking of Constantinople.

TOP SIGHT
TEATRO LA FENICE

Once La Serenissima's dominion over the high seas ended, Venice discovered the power of high Cs, hiring as San Marco choirmaster Claudio Monteverdi, the father of modern opera, and opening La Fenice (The Phoenix) opera house to much fanfare in 1792. The building burned down twice, but international reputations are still made on La Fenice's stage.

Fires & Rebuilding

Rossini and Bellini staged operas here, making La Fenice the envy of Europe – until it went up in flames in 1836. Venice without opera was unthinkable, and within a year the opera house was rebuilt. Verdi premiered *Rigoletto* and *La Traviata* at La Fenice, and international greats Stravinsky, Prokofiev and Britten composed for the house. But La Fenice was again reduced to ashes in 1996; two electricians found guilty of arson were apparently behind on repairs. A €90-million replica of the 19th-century opera house reopened in 2003, and though architectural reviews were mixed – critics had lobbied for an avant-garde design by Gae Aulenti – the reprise performance of *La Traviata* was a triumph.

Opera Season

From January to July and September to October, you'll spot opera fans in rustling silks and patched corduroy jackets loitering on La Fenice's steps with glasses of *prosecco* – until the curtains-up signal dings, and the crowd sweeps up the grand stairway in time for the overture. Tours are possible with advance booking (☏041 24 24), but the best way to see La Fenice is in full swing with the *loggione,* opera buffs who pass judgement from on high in the top-tier cheap seats. With limited runs of bravura performances and a snug 900-seat venue, tickets sell out faster than you can say 'Bravo!' Book ahead online for performances and tours.

Off Season

Between operas, the theatre hosts symphonies and lavish events, ranging from gala Carnevale balls to star-studded private events like the 2009 wedding of luxury-fashion magnate François-Henri Pinault to actress Salma Hayek. Check also for chamber-music concerts at La Fenice or operas staged at the charming, diminutive 17th-century Teatro Malibran.

DON'T MISS...

➡ Opera season
➡ *Intermezzo* (intermission) at the baroque bar
➡ Summer symphonies
➡ Carnevale balls
➡ Debating divas with *loggione* critics

PRACTICALITIES

➡ Map p308
➡ ☏041 78 65 11
➡ www.teatrolafenice.it
➡ Campo San Fantin 1965
➡ theatre visits adult/reduced €8.50/6, opera tickets from €40
➡ ⊙tours 9.30am-6pm
➡ ⊠Santa Maria del Giglio

⊙ SIGHTS

BASILICA DI SAN MARCO CHURCH
See p58.

PALAZZO DUCALE MUSEUM
See p61.

TEATRO LA FENICE THEATRE
See p66.

TORRE DELL'OROLOGIO LANDMARK
(Clock Tower; Map p308; ☑041 4273 0892; www.museicivicivenziani.it; Piazza San Marco; adult/reduced with Museum Pass €12/7; ⊙tours in English 10am & 11am Mon-Wed, 2pm & 3pm Thu-Sun, in Italian noon & 4pm daily, in French 2pm & 3pm Mon-Wed, 10am & 11am Thu-Sun; ⧢San Marco) The two hardest-working men in Venice stand duty on a rooftop around the clock, and wear no pants. No need to file workers' complaints: the 'Do Mori' (Two Moors) exposed to the elements atop the Torre dell'Orologio are made of bronze, and their bell-hammering mechanism runs like, well, clockwork. Below the Moors, Venice's gold-leafed 15th-century timepiece tracks lunar phases.

The clock, designed by Zuan Paolo Rainieri and his son Zuan Carlo in 1493–99, had one hitch: the clockworks required constant upkeep by a live-in clockwatcher and his family until 1998. After a nine-year renovation, the clock's works are in independent working order: 132-stroke chimes keep time in tune, moving barrels indicate minutes and hour on the world's first digital clock face (c 1753), and wooden statues of the three kings and angel emerge from side panels annually on Epiphany and the Feast of the Ascension. Tours climb steep four-storey spiral staircases past the clockworks to the roof terrace, for giddy, close-up views of the Moors in action.

MUSEO FORTUNY MUSEUM
(Map p308; ☑041 4273 0892; http://fortuny.visit muve.it/; Campo San Beneto 3758; adult/reduced with Museum Pass €10/8 ; ⊙10am-6pm Wed-Mon; ⧢Sant'Angelo) Find design inspiration at the palatial home-studio of Art Nouveau designer Mariano Fortuny y Madrazo, whose shockingly uncorseted Delphi goddess frocks set the standard for bohemian chic. First-floor salon walls are eclectic mood boards: Fortuny fashions and Isfahan tapestries, family portraits and James Turrell's sublime red-light installation. Look closely: Fortuny's Moorish lanterns illuminate Roberta di Camerino purses and glittering Warhols.

Large-scale art installations in Fortuny's attic warehouse are often overshadowed by the striking architecture and rooftop views, but the downstairs gallery hosts intriguing contemporary art shows. If these salons inspire design schemes, visit Fortuny Tessuti Artistici (p161) in Giudecca, where textiles are still hand-printed according to Fortuny's top-secret methods.

PALAZZO GRASSI MUSEUM
(Map p308; ☑box office 199 13 91 39, 041 523 16 80; www.palazzograssi.it; Campo San Samuele 3231; adult/reduced/child €15/10/free, 72hr ticket incl Punta della Dogana €20/15/free; ⊙10am-7pm Wed-Mon; ⧢San Samuele) Grand Canal gondola riders gasp at their first glimpse of massive sculptures by contemporary artists like Thomas Houseago docked in front of Giorgio Masari's 1749 neoclassical palace. French billionaire François Pinault's provocative art collection overflows Palazzo Grassi, supplying Venice with sensation and scandal aplenty between Biennales – but Tadao Ando's creatively repurposed interior architecture steals the show.

Clever curation and shameless art-star namedropping are the hallmarks of rotating Palazzo Grassi exhibits, showcasing Takashi Murakami's smiling Superflat daisies, Raymond Pettibon's poetically captioned cartoons ('I curse the happy for whom the unhappy is only a spectacle') and Barbara Kruger's provocative maxims ('We are astonishingly lifelike').

Postmodern architect Gae Aulenti peeled back twee rococo decor to highlight Masari's muscular classicism in 1985–86, and minimalist master Ando added stage-set drama in 2003–05 with ethereal backlit scrims and strategic spotlighting. Ando's design directs attention to contemporary art, without detracting from baroque ceiling frescoes. Don't miss the cafe overlooking the Grand Canal, with interiors redesigned by contemporary artists with each new show.

CHIESA DI SANTO STEFANO CHURCH
(Map p308; www.chorusvenezia.org; Campo Santo Stefano; admission €3 or with Chorus Pass; ⊙10am-5pm Mon-Sat; ⧢Accademia) The free-standing **bell tower** behind it leans disconcertingly, but this brick Gothic church has stood tall since 1325. Credit for ship-shape splendour goes to Bartolomeo Bon for the marble entry portal and to Venetian shipbuilders, who constructed the vast wooden *carena di nave*

continued on p72

Grand Canal

The 3.5km route of *vaporetto* (passenger ferry) No 1, which passes some 50 *palazzi* (mansions), six churches and scene-stealing backdrops featured in four James Bond films, is public transport at its most glamorous.

The Grand Canal starts with controversy: **Ponte di Calatrava 1** a luminous glass-and-steel bridge that cost more than triple the original estimate. Ahead are castle-like **Fondaco dei Turchi 2**, the historic Turkish trading-house that now houses Venice's Museum of Natural History; Renaissance **Palazzo Vendramin 3**, housing the city's casino; and double-arcaded **Ca' Pesaro 4**. Don't miss **Ca' d'Oro 5**, a 1430 filigree Gothic marvel.

Points of Venetian pride include the **Pescaria 6**, built in 1907 on the site where fishmongers have been slinging lagoon crab for 600 years, and neighbouring **Rialto Market 7** stalls, overflowing with island-grown produce. Cost overruns for 1592 **Ponte di Rialto 8** rival Calatrava's, but its marble splendour stands the test of time.

The next two canal bends could cause architectural whiplash, with Sanmicheli-designed Renaissance **Palazzo Grimani 9** and Mauro Codussi's **Palazzo Corner-Spinelli 10** followed by Giorgio Masari-designed **Palazzo Grassi 11** and Baldassare Longhena's baroque jewel box, **Ca' Rezzonico 12**.

Wooden **Ponte dell'Accademia 13** was built in 1930 as a temporary bridge, but the beloved landmark was recently reinforced. Stone lions flank **Peggy Guggenheim Collection 14**, where the American heiress collected ideas, lovers and art. You can't miss the dramatic dome of Longhena's **Chiesa di Santa Maria della Salute 15** or **Punta della Dogana 16**, Venice's triangular customs warehouse reinvented as a contemporary art showcase. The Grand Canal's grand finale is pink Gothic **Palazzo Ducale 17** and its adjoining **Ponte dei Sospiri (Bridge of Sighs) 18**.

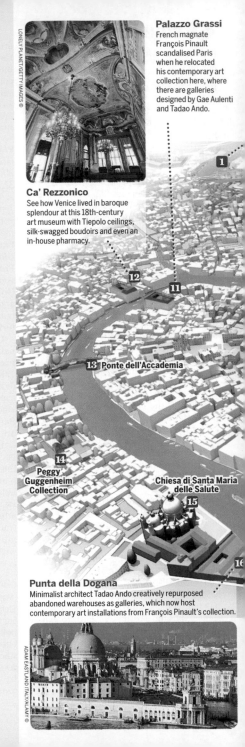

Palazzo Grassi
French magnate François Pinault scandalised Paris when he relocated his contemporary art collection here, where there are galleries designed by Gae Aulenti and Tadao Ando.

Ca' Rezzonico
See how Venice lived in baroque splendour at this 18th-century art museum with Tiepolo ceilings, silk-swagged boudoirs and even an in-house pharmacy.

13 Ponte dell'Accademia

Peggy Guggenheim Collection

Chiesa di Santa Maria delle Salute

Punta della Dogana
Minimalist architect Tadao Ando creatively repurposed abandoned warehouses as galleries, which now host contemporary art installations from François Pinault's collection.

Ponte di Calatrava
With its starkly streamlined fish-fin shape, the 2008 bridge is the first to be built over the Grand Canal in 75 years.

Fondaco dei Turchi
Recognisable by its double colonnade, watchtowers, and dugout canoe parked at the Museo di Storia Naturale's ground-floor loggia.

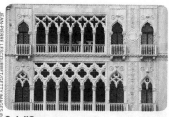

Ca' d'Oro
Behind the triple Gothic arcades are priceless masterpieces: Titians looted by Napoleon, a rare Mantegna and semiprecious stone mosaic floors.

2

3 Palazzo Vendramin

4

5

6 Pescaria

7 Rialto Market

10 Palazzo Corner-Spinelli

Palazzo Grimani

9

8 Ponte di Rialto

Ponte dei Sospiri

18

Palazzo Ducale **17**

Ca' Pesaro
Originally designed by Baldassare Longhena, this palazzo was bequeathed to the city in 1898 to house the Galleria d'Arte Moderna and Museo d'Arte Orientale.

Ponte di Rialto
Antonio da Ponte beat out Palladio for the commission of this bridge, but construction costs spiralled to 250,000 Venetian ducats – about €19 million today.

Building the Dream City

Impossible though it seems, Venetians built their home on 118 small islands connected by some 400 bridges over 159 canals. But if floating marble palaces boggle the mind, consider what's underneath them: an entire forest's worth of wood pylons, rammed through silty *barene* (shoals) into the clay lagoon floor. Some 100,000 petrified pylons support the brick and Istrian stone base of Baldassare Longhena's 1631 Basilica di Santa Maria della Salute.

Ongoing Restoration

Venice's upkeep is constant and painstaking. Venice's canals must be regularly dredged, which involves pumping water out, carefully removing pungent sludge and a ticklish technique Venetians call *scuci-cuci* (patching brickwork by hand).

Highest Tide

Venice is so ingeniously constructed to contend with lagoon tides that even a four-alarm *acque alte* (exceptionally high tide) is rarely cause for panic. But on 4 November 1966, disaster struck. Record floods poured into 16,000 Venetian homes in terrifying waves, and residents were stranded in the wreckage of 1400 years of civilisation. Thanks to Venice's historic cosmopolitan charms, the response was instantaneous: assistance poured in from Mexico to Australia, from millionaires and pensioners alike, and Unesco coordinated 50 private organisations to redress the ravages of the flood.

1. Canalside buildings
2. Chiesa di San Giorgio Maggiore (p160)
3. Grand Canal (p68)

Clean-up Duty

Cleaning up after *acque alte is* a tedious job for Venetians at the best of times, pumping water out of flooded ground floors and preventing corrosion by scrubbing salt residue off surfaces. Venice's historic Pasticceria Rizzardini collects samples of Venice's most extreme *acque alte* from the shop floor, and preserves them in bottles over the bar. The 1966 bottle still dominates the top shelf.

New Challenges

Deep channels dug to accommodate tankers and cruise ships allow more seawater into the lagoon, changing lagoon aquaculture and elevating high tides. The controversial, multi-billion-euro mobile flood barrier known as Mose is intended to limit *acque alte*, but critics question its effectiveness and environmental impact and the diversion of funds critical for Venice's upkeep.

HELP KEEP VENICE AFLOAT

➡ **Take the train to Venice** instead of higher-impact cruise ships

➡ **Pick up litter** to protect Venice's fragile ecosystem

➡ **Enjoy local products** lagoon seafood, island-grown produce and Venetian handicrafts are Venice's pride, joy and livelihood

➡ **Go slowly on motorboats** wakes expose and damage fragile foundations

➡ **Drink tap water** to spare Venice the current burden of recycling 20 to 60 million water bottles annually

continued from p67

(ship's keel) ceiling that resembles an up-turned Noah's Ark.

Enter the cloisters museum to see Canova's 1808 funerary stelae featuring gorgeous women dabbing their eyes with their cloaks, Tullio Lombardo's wide-eyed 1505 saint, and three brooding 1575–80 Tintorettos: *Last Supper,* with a ghostly dog begging for bread; the gathering gloom of *Agony in the Garden;* and the abstract, mostly black *Washing of the Feet.* Observe a moment of silence near the apse, and you may hear the subterranean canal burbling under the choir stalls.

NEGOZIO OLIVETTI   LANDMARK

(Olivetti Store; Map p308; ✆041 522 83 87; www. negoziolivetti.it; Piazza San Marco 101, Procuratie Vecchie; adult/reduced incl audio tour €5/2.50; ⊘11am-6.30pm Tue-Sun Apr-Oct, to 4.30pm Nov-Mar; 🚊San Marco) Like a revolver pulled from a petticoat, ultra-modern Negozio Olivetti was an outright provocation when it first appeared under the frilly arcades of Piazza San Marco in 1958. High-tech pioneer Olivetti comissioned Venetian architect Carlo Scarpa to transform a narrow, dim souvenir shop into a showcase for its sleek typewriters and 'computing machines' (several 1948–54 models are displayed).

Instead of fighting the elements, Scarpa invited them indoors. He sliced away walls to let light flood in, included a huge planter for tall grasses and added a black slab-marble fountain as a wink at *acque alte.* Scarpa enticed visitors to cross primary-coloured Murano glass–tiled floors, scale the floating white-marble stairway, pass satiny Venetian plaster walls and browse the teak-wood balcony. Semicircular port-hole windows resemble eyes open wide to the historic piazza, and the Architecture Biennale's modernist horizons.

PONTE DELL'ACCADEMIA   BRIDGE

(Map p308; btwn Campo di San Vidal & Campo della Carità; 🚊Accademia) The wooden Ponte dell'Accademia was built in 1933 as a temporary replacement for an 1854 iron bridge, but this span, arched like a cat's back, remains a beloved landmark. Engineer Eugenio Miozzi's notable works include the Lido Casino, but none has lasted like this elegant little footbridge – and recent structural improvements have preserved it for decades to come.

CHIESA DI SANTA
MARIA DEL GIGLIO   CHURCH

(Santa Maria Zobenigo; Map p308; www.cho rusvenezia.org; Campo di Santa Maria del Giglio;

admission €3 or with Chorus Pass; ⊘10am-5pm Mon-Sat; 🚊Santa Maria del Giglio) Experience awe through the ages in this compact church with a 10th-century Byzantine layout, charmingly flawed maps of Venice's territories c 1678 on the facade, and three intriguing masterpieces. Veronese's *Madonna with Child* hides behind the altar, Tintoretto's four evangelists flank the organ, and Peter Paul Rubens' *Mary with St John* in the **Molin Chapel** features a characteristically chubby baby Jesus.

Admiral Antonio Barbaro commissioned this reconstruction of the original 9th-century church by Giuseppe Sardi for the glory of the Virgin, Venice, and of course himself – his statue gets prime facade placement. This self-glorifying architectural audacity enraged 19th-century architectural critic John Ruskin, who called it a 'manifestation of insolent atheism'.

CAMPANILE   TOWER

(Bell Tower; Map p308; www.basilicasanmarco. it; Piazza San Marco; admission €8; ⊘9am-9pm Jul-Sep, to 7pm Apr-Jun & Oct, 9.30am-3.45pm Nov-Mar; 🚊San Marco) The basilica's 99m-tall tower has been rebuilt twice since its initial construction in AD 888, and Galileo Galilei found it handy for testing his telescope in 1609. Critics called Bartolomeo Bon's 16th-century tower redesign ungainly, but when this version suddenly collapsed in 1902, Venetians rebuilt the tower as it was, brick by brick.

Visitors head to the tower top for 360-degree lagoon views and close encounters with the Marangona, the booming bronze bell that could be heard in the Arsenale shipyards (bring earplugs on the hour). Sansovino's classical marble loggia at the base of the Campanile is decidedly secular, showcasing bronzes of pagan dieties Minerva, Apollo and Mercury, plus Peace.

PALAZZO CONTARINI DEL BOVOLO   PALACE

(Map p308; Calle Contarini del Bovolo 4299; entry to open courtyard free; 🚊Sant'Angelo) **FREE** No need to wait for San Marco sunsets to inspire a snog: this romantic Renaissance 15th-century *palazzo* with an external spiral *bovolo* (snail-shell) stairwell is closed for restoration, but its shady courtyard offers stirring views and privacy.

CHIESA DI SAN MOISÈ   CHURCH

(Map p308; ✆041 528 58 40; Campo di San Moisè; ⊘9.30am-12.30pm Mon-Sat; 🚊San Marco) **FREE** Icing flourishes of carved-stone ornament across the 1660s facade make this church appear positively lickable, although 19th-century architecture critic John Ruskin found its wedding-cake appearance indigestible. From an engineering perspective, Ruskin had a point: several statues had to be removed in the 19th century to prevent the facade from collapsing under their combined weight.

The remaining statuary by Flemish sculptor Heinrich Meyring (aka Merengo in Italian) includes scant devotional works but a sycophantic number of tributes to church patrons. Among the scene-stealing works inside are Tintoretto's *Washing of the Feet*, in the chapel to the left of the altar, and Palma il Giovane's *The Supper*, on the right side of the chapel.

MUSEO DELLA MUSICA   MUSEUM
(Map p308; ☑041 241 18 40; http://www.interpreti veneziani.com/en/museo-della-musica.php; Campo San Maurizio 2761; ⊙10am-7pm; ⬚Santa Maria del Giglio) FREE Housed in the restored neoclassical Chiesa di San Maurizio, this collection of rare 17th- to 19th-century instruments is accompanied by informative panels on the life and times of Venice's Antonio Vivaldi. To hear these instruments in action, check out the kiosk with CDs and concert tickets for Interpreti Veneziani (p78), which funds this museum.

CHIESA DI SAN ZULIAN   CHURCH
(Map p308; ☑041 523 53 83; Campo San Zulian; ⊙9am-6.30pm Mon-Sat, to 7.30pm Sun; ⬚San Marco) FREE Founded in 829, San Zulian got a Sansovino makeover funded by physician Tomasso Rangone, who made his fortune selling syphilis cures and secrets to living past 100 (he died at 84). The doctor is immortalised in bronze over the portal, holding sarsaparilla – his VD 'miracle cure'. Inside are works by Palma il Giovane and Veronese's *Dead Christ and Saints*.

PALAZZO FRANCHETTI   PALACE
(Istituto Veneto di Scienze Lettere ed Arti; Map p308; ☑041 240 77 11; www.istitutoveneto.it; Campo Santo Stefano 2842; exhibits vary, cafe admission free; ⊙10am-7pm daily; ⬚Accademia) Three Venetian families originally lived at this 16th-century Grand Canal palace, and they didn't agree on decor. When Archduke Frederick of Austria snapped up this Gothic palace in the 19th century, he unified competing styles with a modern makeover. The

---

◉ TOP SIGHT
MUSEO CORRER

Napoleon filled his Piazza San Marco palace with the doges' riches, and took Venice's finest heirlooms back to France. But the greatest treasure here couldn't be lifted: Libreria Nazionale Marciana, arguably Europe's first public library, lavishly painted with larger-than-life philosophers by Veronese, Titian and Tintoretto.

Napoleon lost Venice to Austrian emperor Franz Joseph before completing this palace. The Hapsburgs loved luxury, and after 10 years of restoration, Empress Sissi's suite is newly restored to its original brocade-swagged, 19th-century elegance.

Collection highlights include Jacopo di Barbari's minutely detailed woodblock perspective of Venice; bright-eyed, peach-cheeked Bellini saints (Room 36); Carpaccio's St Peter stabbing himself in the head (Room 38); and a wonderful anonymous 1784 portrait of champion rower Maria Boscola, five-time regatta winner (Room 47). Antonio Canova's 1777 Orpheus and Eurydice are Neoclassical Ballroom scene stealers.

DON'T MISS...

➡ Libreria Nazionale Marciana

➡ Empress Sissi's suite

PRACTICALITIES

➡ Map p308

➡ ☑041 4273 0892

➡ http://correr. visitmuve.it/

➡ Piazza San Marco 52

➡ adult/reduced incl Palazzo Ducale €16/8 or with Museum Pass

➡ ⊙10am-7pm Apr-Oct, to 5pm Nov-Mar

➡ ⬚San Marco

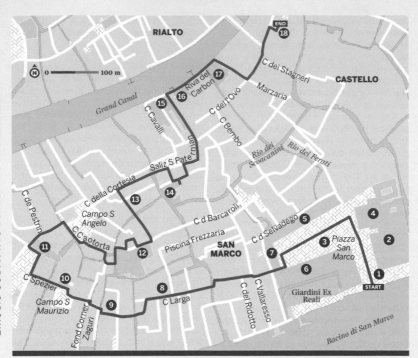

Neighbourhood Walk
San Marco Circuit

START PIAZZETTA SAN MARCO
END I RUSTEGHI
LENGTH 3KM; 1½ HOURS

Venetians still hurry past the granite **①** **Columns of San Marco**, site of public executions for centuries. Past **②** **Palazzo Ducale** (p61) is **③** **Piazza San Marco**, crowned by the **④** **Basilica di San Marco** (p58) and flanked by Mauro Codussi's 16th-century **⑤** **Procuratie Vecchie** and the Scamozzi-designed and Longhena-completed **⑥** **Procuratie Nuove**. Today the Museo Correr occupies the upper storeys of the Procuratie Nuove and **⑦** **Ala Napoleonica**, the palace Napoleon brazenly razed San Geminiano church to build.

Follow **⑧** **Calle Larga XXII Marzo** towards baroque **⑨** **Chiesa di Santa Maria del Giglio** (p72), covered in peculiar maps charting Venetian vassal states c 1678–81. Further west, 15th-century **⑩** **Santo Stefano bell tower** leans 2m from its intended perpendicular stance, as though it's had one *spritz* too many. Nearby, Bartolomeo Bon's

marble Gothic portals grace brick **⑪** **Chiesa di Santo Stefano** (p67).

Follow Calle Caotorta to **⑫** **Teatro La Fenice** (p67), veering left onto **⑬** **C dei Assassini**. Corpses were so frequently found here that in 1128, Venice banned the full beards assassins wore as disguises. Snogging in *campi* is such an established Venetian pastime it's surprising dogi didn't find a way to tax it – but duck into **⑭** **Palazzo Contarini del Bovolo** (p72) courtyard for privacy.

Along Calle del Carbon, wander into city hall weekdays at **⑮** **Palazzo Loredan**. Outside, a plaque honours philosopher Eleonora Lucrezia Corner Piscopia, the first woman to earn a Padua University PhD, in 1678. Along the quay is 14th-century Gothic **⑯** **Palazzo Dandolo**, home of blind doge and erstwhile Crusader Enrico Dandolo, who sacked Constantinople in 1203. Next door is Sansovino-designed **⑰** **Palazzo Dolfin-Manin** (1547), where the last doge, Ludovico Manin, died in seclusion in 1802. End your grand tour at **⑱** **I Rusteghi** (p76).

Franchetti family lived here after independence and restored its Gothic fairy-tale look, including an **art nouveau staircase** dripping with dragons.

The palace was home to a private bank from 1922–99, when the Veneto Institute of Sciences, Letters and Arts moved in and began hosting arts expositions and academic conferences (see website). The Palazzo Franchetti Caffè in the garden cloisters has baroque-patterned window screens for a secluded espresso away from San Marco crowds.

CHIESA DI SAN VIDAL · CHURCH

(Map p308; Campo di San Vidal 2862; ⊙9am-noon & 3.30-6pm Mon-Sat; ⊠Accademia) **FREE** Built by Doge Vitale Falier in the 11th century, Chiesa di San Vidal got a 1706–14 Palladian facelift to comemmorate Doge Francesco Morosoni's victory over Turkish foes. Inside is *St Vitale on Horseback and Eight Saints* by Vittore Carpaccio, featuring his signature traffic light red and miniaturist's attention to detail. The deconsecrated church now serves as a concert venue (p78).

EATING

ENOTECA AL VOLTO · VENETIAN, CICHETI BAR €

(Map p308; ☑041 522 89 45; Calle Cavalli 4081; cicheti €2-4, meals under €25; ⊙10am-3pm & 5.30-10pm Mon-Sat; ⊠Rialto) Join the bar crowd working its way through the vast selection of wine and *cicheti,* or come early for a table outdoors (in summer). Inside the snug backroom that looks like a ship's hold, tuck into seaworthy bowls of pasta with *bottarga* (dried fish roe), steak drizzled with aged balsamic vinegar, and housemade ravioli. Cash only.

BACARO DA FIORE · CICHETI BAR, VENETIAN €

(Map p308; ☑041 523 53 10; www.dafiore.it; Calle delle Botteghe 3461; meals €10-15; ⊙5.30-9pm Wed-Mon; ⊠San Samuele) Attached to a posh trattoria, this *cicheti* counter wins Venetian loyalty with small plates of *baccala mantecato* (creamed cod), octopus-fennel salad, *arancini* (risotto balls) and Venetian *trippa* (tripe) to enjoy on a stool at the bar or in the *calle* (lane). Even with gorgeous DOC soave by the glass, meals cost a fraction of what you'd pay for table seating.

GELATERIA SUSO · GELATO €

(Map p308; ☑348 564 65 45; Calle della Bissa 5453; gelati €2-5; ⊙10am-10pm; ⋈; ⊠Rialto) 🍦

ⓘ ART SMART

To see more of Pinault's collection of more than 2000 artworks, get a **combined ticket** (adult/reduced €20/15) that gives you 72 hours to visit Palazzo Grassi and Punta della Dogana, Venice's ancient customs houses renovated by Ando in 2009 to showcase larger art installations.

Indulge in gelato as rich as a doge, in original seasonal flavors like marscapone cream with fig sauce and walnuts. All Suso's gelati are locally made and free of artificial colours, and even the gluten-free flavors are extra creamy – but a waffle cone with hazelnut and extra-dark chocolate passes as dinner.

OSTERIA DA CARLA · OSTERIA, CICHETI BAR €

(Map p308; ☑041 523 78 55; Frezzaria 1535; meals €20-25; ⊙10am-9pm Mon-Sat; ⊠Vallaresso) For the price of hot chocolate in Piazza San Marco, diners in the know duck into this hidden courtyard to feast on handmade ravioli with poppyseed, pear and sheep's cheese. Expect a wait at lunch and happy hour, when *gondolieri* abandon ship for DOC soave and *sopressa crostini* (soft salami on toast).

CAFFÈ MANDOLA · PANINI €

(Map p308; ☑041 523 76 24; Calle della Mandola 3630; panini €3-7; ⊙9am-7pm Mon-Sat; ⊠Sant'Angelo) Carbo-load before the opera or between museums with fresh focaccia loaded with tangy tuna and capers or lean *bresaola,* rocket and seasoned Grana Padano cheese. On cold days, get your *porchetta* (pork) and gorgonzola cheese panini toasted to gooey perfection. Plan your breaks before 1pm or after 3pm to snag a stool indoors (no extra charge).

ROSA SALVA · BAKERY €

(Map p308; ☑041 522 79 34; www.rosasalva.it; Mercerie 5020; pastries €1.10-2.80; ⊙7.30am-8pm Thu-Tue; ⋈⋈; ⊠Rialto) With just-baked strudel and reliably frothy cappuccino, Rosa Salva has provided Venetians with fresh reasons to roll out of bed for over a century. Cheerfully efficient women working the spotless granite counter ensure that no *curasan* (croissant) order waits for more than a minute, and supply gale-force espresso and turbo-loaded chocolate profiteroles to power you across 30 more bridges.

HOW MANY MOSAIC TILES IN BASILICA DI SAN MARCO?

Good question: mathematicians' estimates range wildly, from a few million into the hundreds of millions. The basilica dazzles with 8500 square metres of *tesserae* (tiles), individually hand cut to fingernail-size and closely set in mortar. Designs that call for fine detail – saints' eyes, for example – may require *tesserae* mere millimetres square. You do the maths...or join the crowd, and observe in awe.

★A BECCAFICO   ITALIAN €€

(Map p308; ☑041 527 48 79; www.abeccafico.com; Campo Santo Stefano 2801; meals €25-45; ☺noon-3pm & 7-11pm; ⛴Accademia) Far from clubby pubs lining Venice's alleyways, A Beccafico basks in the sunshine of Campo Santo Stefano and open Venetian admiration. Instead of cold seafood on toast, Chef Adeli serves Sicily-sized bowls of mussels under a bubbling, flaky crust. He defies Venice's cardinal rule never to mix lagoon seafood with cheese, serving squid-ink pasta with lemon zest and ricotta. Linger over feather-light Pieoropan Soave Classico, and leave with a surprisingly full belly – and wallet.

CAVATAPPI   OSTERIA, CICHETI BAR €€

(Map p308; ☑041 296 02 52; Campo della Guerra 525/526; cicheti €2-4, meals €25-40; ☺10am-9pm Tue-Thu & Sun, to 11pm Fri & Sat; ☑; ⛴San Marco) A casual charmer offering *cicheti* and artisanal cheeses and DOC bubbly by the glass. Get the risotto of the day and an ultrafresh salad with toasted hazlenuts – and if your dinner date is exceptionally worthy, share the warm sheep's cheese that's drizzled with Dolomite wildflower honey.

SANGAL   ITALIAN €€

(Map p308; ☑041 319 27 47; http://www.sangalvenicerestaurant.com/; Campo San Gallo 1089; mains €25-45; ☺10am-midnight Wed-Mon; ☑⛴; ⛴Vallaresso) Like a jazz chanteuse singing standards, Sangal covers popular favourites with unexpected grace notes. Dinner standouts include handmade *bigoli* (Venetian wheat pasta) and rosemary-crusted Tuscan chianina steak. Lunch is a less inspired greatest-hits collection of pastas, from Genovese pesto to Rome's bacon-studded *ammatriciana*. Go for chipper

service, excellent wines and a breezy roof terrace right behind Piazza San Marco.

ANONIMO VENEZIANO   ITALIAN €€

(Map p308; ☑041 528 97 30; Calle del Fruttariol 1847; meals €25-35; ☺noon-3pm & 5.30-9pm Mon-Wed & Fri & Sat, 5.30-9pm Sun; ⛴Santa Maria del Giglio) A casual charmer with classic fare at eminently reasonable prices – under €10 for pasta and €4 for a small carafe of house Friulano white – and impeccable social graces. Dapper bow-tied servers may not allow you to leave until you've enjoyed a grappa-filled chocolate, and graciously help ladies don their coats only after return visits are promised.

DA MARIO   VENETIAN €€

(Map p308; ☑041 528 59 68; Fondamenta della Malvasia Vecchia 2614; meals €20-30; ☺Sun-Mon; ☑; ⛴Santa Maria del Giglio) Squeeze in between watercolours on the walls, action figures in the rafters, and gondoliers at the bar, and brace yourself for generous plates of gnocchi and fried calamari. This eccentric *osteria* seems miles from tourist attractions, yet Gallerie dell'Accademia and Palazzo Grassi are minutes away. As your host promises, house wine 'helps you see art more clearly – even minimalism'.

🍷 DRINKING & NIGHTLIFE

★I RUSTEGHI   WINE BAR

(Map p308; ☑041 523 22 05; http://www.osteria irusteghi.com/; Corte del Tentor 5513; mini-panini €2-5; ☺10.30am-3pm & 6-11.30pm Mon-Sat; ⛴Rialto) Honouring centuries of Venetian *enoteca* tradition, fourth-generation sommelier Giovanni d'Este will open any bottle on his shelves to pour you an *ombra* (half-glass of wine) – including collector's wines like Cannubi Barolo. Request *'qualcosa di particolare'* (something exceptional) and Giovanni will reward you with a sensual Ribolla Gialla to pair with truffle-cheese mini-panini and platters of Spanish and Veneto ham.

★CAFFÈ FLORIAN   CAFE

(Map p308; ☑041 520 56 41; www.caffeflorian.com; Piazza San Marco 56/59; drinks €6.50-16; ☺10am-midnight Thu-Tue; ⛴San Marco) Florian maintains rituals established c 1720: white-jacketed waiters serve cappuccino on silver trays, lovers canoodle in plush banquettes and the orchestra strikes up a tango as sunsets illuminate San Marco's mosaics. Piazza seating during concerts costs €6 extra, but dreamy-eyed romantics hardly notice. Among Italy's first bars to welcome women and revolutionaries, Florian maintains its radical-chic reputation with art installations.

CAFFÈ LAVENA
CAFE

(Map p308; ☑041 522 40 70; www.lavena.it; Piazza San Marco 133/4; drinks €1-12; ☺9.30am-11pm; ⛴San Marco) Opera composer Richard Wagner had the right idea: when Venice leaves you weak in the knees, get a pick-me-up at Lavena. The €1 espresso at Lavena's mirrored bar is a baroque bargain – never mind the politically incorrect antique 'Moor's head' chandeliers. Spring for piazza seating to savor *caffè corretto* (coffee 'corrected' with liquor) accompanied by Lavena's nimble violinists.

HARRY'S BAR
BAR

(Map p308; ☑041 528 57 77; Calle Vallaresso 1323; cocktails €12-22; ☺10.30am-11pm; ⛴San Marco) Aspiring auteurs hold court at bistro tables well scuffed by Ernest Hemingway, Charlie Chaplin, Truman Capote and Orson Welles, enjoying the signature €16.50 bellini (Giuseppe Cipriani's original 1948 recipe: white-peach juice and *prosecco*) with a side of reflected glory. Upstairs is one of Italy's most unaccountably expensive restaurants – stick to the bar to save financing for your breakthrough film.

OSTERIA ALL'ALBA
WINE BAR

(Map p308; ☑340 124 56 34; Ramo del Fontego dei Tedeschi 5370; ☺10am-1am; ⛴Rialto) That roar behind the Rialto means the DJ's funk set is kicking in at All'Alba. Squeeze inside to order salami sandwiches (€1 to €2.50) and DOC Veneto wines (€5 to €6), and check out walls festooned with vintage LPs and effusive thanks scrawled in 12 languages.

TEAMO
CAFE, BAR

(Map p308; ☑347 549 90 82; Rio Terà della Mandola 3795; ☺8am-10pm; ⛴Sant'Angelo) Sunny tearoom by day, sleek backlit alabaster bar by night and fabulous full time. Arrive by 6.30pm for first choice of fresh *cicheti* at the bar and lookers in the leather banquettes – this bar swings both ways, so there's something for everyone.

CAFFÈ QUADRI
CAFE, BAR

(Map p308; ☑041 522 21 05; http://www.alajmo. it; Piazza San Marco 120; drinks €6-25; ☺9am-11.30pm; ⛴San Marco) Powdered wigs seem appropriate in this baroque cafe, serving royal happy hours since 1638. The upstairs restaurant charges a king's ransom for finicky fare upstaged by Piazza San Marco views, but the gilded downstairs cafe serves a princely €12 hot chocolate with *panna* (whipped cream). Reserve ahead during Carnevale, when costumed Quadri revellers party like it's 1699.

CAFFÈ CENTRALE
LOUNGE

(Map p308; ☑041 296 06 64; www.caffeecent ralevenezia.com; Piscina Frezzaria 1659b; drinks €3.50-15; ☺7pm-2am Wed-Mon; ⛴San Marco) Under moody Murano-chandelier lighting, you might spot Salma Hayek, Spike Lee and sundry America's Cup sailors within these exposed-brick walls. Meals are pricey and canalside VIP tables chilly, but Centrale draws La Fenice post-opera crowds with signature foamy *spritz* cocktails, midnight snacks, chill-out DJ sets and occasional live jazz.

TORINO@NOTTE
BAR

(Map p308; ☑041 522 39 14; Campo San Luca 4592; ☺7pm-1am Tue-Sat; ⛴Rialto) Freeform, eclectic and loud, Torino adds an element of the unexpected to otherwise staid San Marco. By day it's a cafe, but after 7pm locals roll in for €2 to €5 drinks and marathon DJ sessions of vintage reggae and soul on vinyl. Stop by Friday and Saturday after 9pm for a late bite or nightcap with live jazz, blues or rock.

OSTERIA SAN MARCO
WINE BAR

(Map p308; ☑041 528 52 42; www.osteriasan marco.it; Frezzaria 1610; drinks €3-7; ☺12.30-11pm Mon-Sat; ⛴Vallaresso) Romance is in the air in Venice – but the top-notch wines lining these exposed-brick walls surely

---

LOCAL KNOWLEDGE

A DRINK WITH A VIEW

Eating options in San Marco boil down to a simple choice: good food or a view. Getting both is nearly impossible, especially at reasonable prices – but you can always enjoy Piazza San Marco panoramas over coffee or *aperitivi*, then spelunk into the *sestiere*'s narrow alleyways for *cicheti* or pasta at hidden *osterie*. For scenic canalside dining at more down-to-earth prices, try Cannaregio, Giudecca or San Polo.

help. From 6.30pm till 8pm locals crowd the bar for prime selections from the chalkboard list of wines available by the glass. Starters and mains here are variable, costly and occasionally microwaved, but cheese plates and a book-size wine list make this a post-concert destination.

 # ENTERTAINMENT

★ INTERPRETI VENEZIANI   CLASSICAL MUSIC

(Map p308; ☎041 277 05 61; www.interpretiven eziani.com; Chiesa San Vidal, Campo di San Vidal 2862; adult/reduced €25/20; ⊘doors open 8.30pm; 🛳Accademia) Everything you've heard of Vivaldi from weddings and mobile ring tones is proved fantastically wrong by Interpreti Veneziani, which plays Vivaldi on 18th-century instruments as a soundtrack for living in this city of intrigue – you'll never listen to *The Four Seasons* again without hearing summer storms erupting over the lagoon, or snow-muffled footsteps hurrying over footbridges in winter's-night intrigues.

MUSICA A PALAZZO   OPERA

(Map p308; ☎340 971 72 72; www.musicapalazzo. com; Palazzo Barbarigo-Minotto, Fondamenta Barbarigo o Duodo 2504; tickets incl beverage €60; ⊘doors open 8pm; 🛳Santa Maria del Giglio) Hang onto your *prosecco* and brace for impact: in palace salons, the soprano's high notes imperil glassware, and thundering baritones reverberate through inlaid floors. During 1½ hours of selected arias from Verdi or Rossini, the drama progresses from receiving-room overtures to parlour duets overlooking the Grand Canal, followed by

second acts in the Tiepolo-ceilinged dining room and bedroom grand finales.

TEATRO GOLDONI   THEATRE

(Map p308; ☎041 240 20 14; www.teatrostabi leveneto.it; Calle Teatro Goldoni 4650b; tickets €8-29; ⊘box office 10am-1pm & 3-7.30pm Mon-Fri; 🛳Rialto) Named after the city's great playwright, Venice's main theatre has an impressive dramatic range that runs from Goldoni's comedy to Shakespearean tragedy (mostly in Italian), plus ballets and concerts. Don't be fooled by the huge modern Brutalist bronze doors: this venerable theatre dates from 1622, and the jewel-box interior seats just 800.

MULTISALA ROSSINI   CINEMA

(Map p308; ☎041 241 72 74; Calle San Benedetto 3997a; adult/reduced €7.50/6, 3D films €10/9; ⊘shows Tue-Sun; 🚻; 🛳Rialto) Film buffs who miss the proverbial boat to the annual Venice Film Festival on the Lido, rejoice: award-winning films and blockbusters screen year-round at the city's newest and largest cinema. Sala 1 is the largest of three screening rooms, with seating for 300 and excellent sound. Some films are screened in the original language, but most are dubbed in Italian.

🛍 SHOPPING

★ CHIARASTELLA
CATTANA   ARTISANAL, HOME & GARDEN

(Map p308; ☎041 522 43 69; www.chiarastella cattana.it; Salizada San Samuele 3357; ⊘10am-1pm & 3-7pm Mon-Sat; 🛳San Samuele) Transform any home into a thoroughly modern *palazzo* with these locally woven, strikingly original Venetian linens. Whimsical cushions feature a chubby purple rhinoceros and grumpy scarlet elephants straight out of Pietro Longhi paintings, and hand-tasseled Venetian jacquard hand towels will dry your royal guests in style. Decorators and design aficionados, save an afternoon to consider dizzying woven-to-order napkin and curtain options here.

FIORELLA GALLERY   FASHION

(Map p308; ☎041 520 92 28; www.fiorellagallery. com; Campo Santo Stefano 2806; ⊘9.30am-1.30pm & 3.30-7pm Tue-Sat, 3-7pm Mon; 🛳Accademia) Groupies are the only accessory needed to go with Fiorella's silk-velvet smoking jackets in louche lavender and

GALLERY-HOP SAN MARCO

For all its splendours of bygone eras, San Marco is not just a museum piece. Slip into the backstreets behind Santa Maria del Giglio and you'll jump ahead of the art curve in galleries showcasing contemporary works ranging from painting to video installation. Inspiration is abundant at the following exhibition spaces.

Galleria van der Koelen (Map p308; ✆041 520 74 15; www.galerie.vanderkoelen.de; Ramo Primo dei Calegheri 2566; ◷10am-12.30pm & 3.30-6.30pm Mon-Sat; ⬚Santa Maria del Giglio) Hidden behind thundering Teatro La Fenice, this conceptual art gallery makes bold statements with Ai Weiwei's 'Fairytale', a line-up of Qing dynasty chairs waiting for the next imperious politicians to fill them, and Lore Bert's heraldic symbols made from ruffled plastic.

Caterina Tognon Arte Contemporanea (Map p308; ✆041 520 78 59; www.caterinatognon.com; Palazzo da Ponte, Calle delle Dose 2746; ◷10am-1pm & 3-7.30pm Tue-Sat; ⬚Santa Maria del Giglio) Press the brass doorbell for 'stART' on this 17th-century palace to be buzzed up to the 2nd-storey gallery, where guest artists experiment with Venetian materials and ideas: Maurizio Donzelli tiled the floor with watery drawings, while Maria Morganti covered the walls with high-watermark paintings in vivid colours.

Galleria Traghetto (Map p308; ✆041 522 11 88; www.galleriatraghetto.it; Campo Santa Maria del Giglio 2543; ◷3-7pm Mon-Sat; ⬚Santa Maria del Giglio) Gutsy shows of young Italian artists on the brink of international breakthroughs, including Serafino Maiorano's blurred digital photographs with bleeding reds evoking Carpaccio and Mirco Marchelli's tattered, patchworked Italian flag paintings.

Jarach Gallery (Map p308; ✆041 522 19 38; www.jarachgallery.com; Campo San Fantin 1997; ◷10am-1pm & 2.30-7.30pm Tue-Sat; ⬚Santa Maria del Giglio) Contemporary photography and video art waits in the wings near La Fenice, with the quiet drama of thoughtful shows inspired by the passage of time in Venice and Pink Floyd's *Dark Side of the Moon*.

---

oxblood, printed by hand with skulls, peacocks or a Fiorella signature: wide-eyed rats. Shock frock coats starting in the mid-three figures make Alexander McQueen seem retro – Fiorella's been pioneering rebel couture since 1968. Hours are approximate; as the sign says, 'we open sometime'.

BEVILACQUA FABRICS   ARTISANAL, FABRICS
(Map p308; ✆041 241 06 62; www.bevilacquatessuti.com; Campo di Santa Maria del Giglio 2520; ◷10am-7pm; ⬚Santa Maria del Giglio) TV dens become grand salons with Venetian swagger at Bevilacqua, a purveyor of fine silk-velvet brocades, damasks and tassels to Venice's baroque palaces and Italy's swankiest modern apartments. Master artisans still weave the fabrics in Venice on 18th-century wooden looms, and the front-room display here is just a sample of their artistry; ask about custom cushions and upholstery.

MALEFATTE   ARTISANAL, ACCESSORIES
(Map p308; www.rioteradeipensieri.org; Campo Santo Stefano kiosk; ◷10.30am-5.30pm Tue-Sat; ⬚Accademia) ✐ 'Misdeeds' is the name of this nonprofit initiative by and for incarcerated workers, but its pop-art man-bags made from recycled-vinyl museum banners are clever indeed. T-shirts showing *acque alte* measurements and aprons silk screened with the *spritz* recipe are souvenirs with a difference: all proceeds support training and transitions from jail on Giudecca to new lives and productive careers in Venice.

OTTICA CARRARO   EYEWEAR
(Map p308; ✆041 520 42 58; www.otticacarraro.it; Calle della Mandola 3706; ◷9am-1pm & 3-7.30pm Mon-Sat; ⬚Sant'Angelo) Lost your sunglasses on the Lido? Never fear: Ottica Carraro can make you a custom pair within 24 hours, including the eye exam. The store has its own limited-edition 'Venice' line, ranging from cat-eye shades perfect for facing paparazzi to chunky wood-grain frames that could get you mistaken for an art critic at the Biennale.

GODI FIORENZA   ARTISANAL, FASHION
(Map p308; ✆041 241 08 66; Rio Tera San Paternian 4261; ◷9.30am-6.30pm Mon-Sat; ⬚Rialto) Impeccably tailored midnight-blue silk-satin dresses with exuberant woolly

shoulders showcase the Saville Row skills of sisters Patrizia and Samanta Fiorenza, but also their vivid imaginations – their latest collection was inspired by men's tuxedos and deconstructed teddy bears. They specialise in couture at off-the-rack prices: for under €100, hand-beaded antique-lace collars add turn-of-the-century elegance to modern minimalism.

ARCOBALENO
ART SUPPLIES

(Map p308; ☑041 523 68 18; Calle delle Botteghe 3457; ☺9.30am-1.30pm & 3-7pm Mon-Sat; ☐Accademia) After seeing umpteen Venetian art masterpieces, anyone's fingers will start twitching for a paint brush. Arcobaleno provides all the raw materials needed to start your own Venetian art movement, with shelves fully stocked with jars of all the essential pigments: Titian red, Tiepolo sky-blue, Veronese rose, Bellini peach and Tintoretto teal.

DANIELA GHEZZO
SHOES

(Map p308; ☑041 522 21 15; http://www.danie laghezzo.it; Calle dei Fuseri 4365; ☺10am-1pm & 3-7pm; ☐Vallaresso) A gold chain pulled across this historic atelier doorway means Daniela is already consulting with a client, discussing rare leathers while taking foot measurements. Maestra Ghezzo custom makes every pair, so you'll never see your emerald ostrich-leather boots on another diva, or your dimpled manta-ray brogues on a rival mogul. Each pair costs €700 to €1100 and takes about six weeks for delivery.

ARNOLDO & BATTOIS
FASHION, ACCESSORIES

(Map p308; ☑041 528 59 44; www.arnoldoebat tois.com; Calle dei Fuseri 4271; ☺10am-1pm & 3.30-7pm Mon-Thu & Sat; ☐Rialto) Handbags become heirlooms in the hands of Venetian designers Massimiliano Battois and Silvano Arnoldo, whose handcrafted clutches come in bold, buttery turquoise and magenta leather with baroque closures in laser-cut wood. Artfully draped emerald and graphite silk dresses complete the look for Biennale openings.

PAGINE E CUOIO
ARTISANAL, LEATHER

(Map p308; ☑041 528 65 55; Calle del Fruttariol 1845; ☺9.30am-7pm Mon-Sat; ☐Santa Maria del Giglio) The lion of San Marco looks fashionably fierce embossed upon a turquoise billfold by leather artisan Davide Desanzuane. Unexpected colours update Venetian heraldry for the 21st century on Davide's tablet cases,

smartphone carriers and business-card holders – and since they're all one of a kind, they make singular fashion statements.

CAIGO DA MAR
HOME & GARDEN

(Map p308; ☑041 243 32 38; www.caigodamar. com; Calle delle Botteghe 3131; ☺11am-1pm & 4-7pm Mon-Fri, 11am-7pm Sat; ☐Accademia) Venetian pirates once headed to Constantinople for all their interior-decoration needs, but today they'd need look no further than Caigo da Mar. This tiny treasure trove brims with dramatic black Murano glass candleabras and a designer booty of Fornasetti cushions, plus enough octopus-shaped lamps and nautilus-shell dishes to make any living room look like the lost city of Atlantis.

VENETIAN DREAMS
ARTISANAL, ACCESSORIES

(Map p308; ☑041 523 02 92; http://venetian dreams.altervista.org; Calle della Mandola 3805a; ☺11am-6.30pm Wed-Mon; ☐Sant'Angelo) High fashion meets *acque alte* in Marisa Convento's aquatic accessories. La Fenice divas demand her freshwater pearl–encrusted velvet handbags, while Biennale artistes snap up octopus-tentacle glass-bead necklaces. Between customers, Marisa can be glimpsed at her desk, painstakingly weaving coral-branch collars from antique Murano *conterie* (seed beads). To wow Carnevale crowds, ask about custom costume orders.

ESPERIENZE
GLASS, JEWELLERY

(Map p308; ☑041 521 29 45; www.esperienzeven ezia.com; Calle degli Specchieri 473b; ☺10am-noon & 3-7pm; ☐San Marco) When an Italian minimalist falls in love with a Murano glassblower, the result is spare, spirited glass jewellery. Esperienze is a collaborative effort for husband-wife team Graziano and Sara: he breathes life into her designs, including matte-glass teardrop pendants and cracked-ice earrings. Their mutual admiration for Guggenheim Collection modernists shows in colourful necklaces that resemble Calder moblies and Kandinsky paintings.

ARTIGIANCARTA DI
MASSIMO DORETTO
ARTISANAL, PAPER, LEATHER

(Map p308; ☑041 522 56 06; Frezzaria 1797; ☺10am-7pm Mon-Sat; ☐Vallaresso) Conquer writer's block in style with one-of-a-kind hand-marbled notecards, linen-bound composer's notebooks, travel journals emblazoned with vintage Venice postcards and gilt leather albums fit for a royal wedding. The hand-tanned leather must be handled with care, but Massimo is delighted to pull down any pieces for you – he made them all.

LE BOTTEGHE DELLA SOLIDARIETÀ
GIFTS, HOMEWARES

(Map p308; ☑041 522 75 45; www.coopfilo.it; Salizada Pio X 5164; ☉10am-7pm Mon-Sat; ⊠Rialto) Italian design sensibilities meet Venetian trading smarts at this fair-trade boutique on the steps of the Rialto. Gondola rides call for straw hats woven by a Bangladeshi collective and refreshing Libera Terra wine from vineyards reclaimed from the mafia, while kids are placated by organic chocolate and recycled cans fashioned into toy Vespas.

LIBRERIA STUDIUM
BOOKS

(Map p308; ☑041 522 23 82; Calle di Canonica 337; ☉9am-7.30pm Mon-Sat, 9.30am-1.30pm & 2-6pm Sun; ⊠San Zaccaria) Consult bibliophile staff for worthy vacation reads, page-turning Venetian history or top picks from shelves groaning under the weight of Italian cookbooks. Many titles are available in English and French, and there's a respectably vast Lonely Planet section (not that we're biased). Don't miss conversation-starting 'Eye on Venice' pamphlets addressing current Venetian issues, from lagoon acquaculture to palace preservation.

MATERIALMENTE
JEWELLERY, DECOR

(Map p308; ☑041 528 68 81; www.materialmente. it; Mercerie San Salvador 4850; ☉10am-7pm Mon-Sat; ⊠Rialto) Prolific sibling artisans Maddelena Venier and Alessandro Salvadori pack their tiny boutique with modern Venetian luxuries, casting skull signet rings fit for Johnny Depp, hand-silkscreening mirrors with baroque ballgown patterns, and weaving fish-skeleton chandeliers from wire. They also stock whimsical, affordable works by young Italian designers, including free-form porcelain earrings and anime-inspired mobiles.

CHARTA
ARTISANAL, BOOKS

(Map p308; ☑041 522 98 01; www.chartaonline. com; 831 Calle del Fabbri; ☉10am-12:30pm & 4-7.30pm; ⊠Vallaresso) Even pulp fiction becomes high art at Charta, where favourite books are custom bound: *Twilight* has vampire bitemarks, Dostoyevsky's *Brothers Karamozov* is emblazoned with three brothers joined at the beard, and a manual of Freemason's rites is enshrined in a gilt temple. Limited editions start around €30, while customised antique books run €150 to €850.

CAMUFFO
ARTISANAL, GLASS

(Map p308; Calle delle Acque 4992; ☉10am-12.30pm & 1-5pm Mon-Sat; ⊠Rialto) Kids, entomologists and glass collectors seek out Signor Camuffo in this cabinet of miniature natural wonders. Expect to find him wielding a blowtorch, fusing metallic foils and molten glass into shimmering wings for the city's finest lampworked glass beetles and dragonflies. Between bugs, he'll chat about his work and sell you strands of Murano glass beads at excellent prices.

EPICENTRO
HOMEWARES

(Map p308; ☑041 523 34 92; www.epicentros tore.com; Frezzaria 1728a; ☉9.30am-1.30pm & 3-7pm Tue-Sat, 3-7pm Mon; ⊠San Marco) For the price of a couple of cappuccinos in Piazza San Marco, you could load up on Italian coffee-break essentials here: stove-top espresso makers, rechargeable milk frothers, cups in futurist shapes and architect-designed spoons. For the gourmet who's got it all, the back gallery stocks an entire Alessi catalogue of bunny-eared sugar bowls and salt-and-pepper trolls.

GLORIA ASTOLFO
JEWELLERY

(Map p308; ☑041 520 68 27; www.gloriastolfo. com; Frezzaria 1581; ☉10am-7pm; ⊠San Marco) Take your fashion cues from Venetian painting masterpieces at this Venetian bead artisan's showcase. Garlands of beaded tiger lilies make open-necked T-shirts instantly glamorous, and those baroque pearl earrings would gently tickle your shoulders if you started to nod off at La Fenice. Prices starting at €35 are surprisingly down-to-earth for jewellery this original.

VENETIA STUDIUM
ACCESSORIES, FASHION

(Map p308; ☑041 523 69 53; www.venetiastu dium.com; Palazzo Zuccato 2425; ☉10am-7.40pm Mon-Sat, 10.30am-6.30pm Sun; ⊠Santa Maria del Giglio) Get that 'just got in from Monaco for my art opening' look beloved of bohemians who marry well. The high-drama Delphos tunic dresses make anyone look like a high-maintenance modern dancer or heiress (Isadora Duncan and Peggy Guggenheim were both fans) and the hand-stamped silk-velvet bags are more arty than ostentatious (prices from €40).

Sestiere di Dorsoduro

Neighbourhood Top Five

1 Finding out what all the fuss is about Venetian painting at **Gallerie dell'Accademia** (p84), a former convent that is now positively blushing with masterpieces of glowing colours, censored subjects and a newly restored dramatic finale.

2 Hanging out with modern sculpture worth millions on the Grand Canal dock of the **Peggy Guggenheim Collection** (p87).

3 Waltzing through baroque palace boudoirs filled with social graces and sharp wits at **Ca' Rezzonico** (p90).

4 Comparing, contrasting and debating fearless contemporary art and boldly repurposed architecture at **Punta della Dogana** (p91).

5 Testing the curative powers of Longhena's mystical marbles, and finding hidden Titian wonders inside **Chiesa di Santa Maria della Salute** (p88).

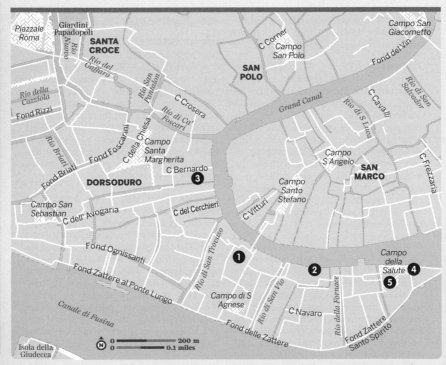

For more detail of this area see Map p312 ➡

Explore Sestiere di Dorsoduro

After sprinting through centuries of masterpiece paintings at Gallerie dell'Accademia, recover the use of your senses over canalside *panini* at Cantinone Gia Schiavi, in the company of gondola builders from Squero di San Trovaso. Next, see how Pollock splatter-paintings and Calder mobiles make a splash along the Grand Canal at the Peggy Guggenheim Collection, then argue the merits of Jeff Koons and other controversial installations at Punta della Dogana. Give your eyes a chance to refocus with a stroll along the Zattere, before they're boggled again by Vedova's robotic art at Magazzini del Sale and Veronese's floor-to-ceiling masterpieces at San Sebastian. Mingle with witty Venetian socialites of yore at baroque Ca' Rezzonico, then raise a toast to Venice in Campo Santa Margherita. Dine near Campo San Barnaba, but don't be late for a concert at one of Dorsoduro's historic venues – ideally Ca' Rezzonico's frescoed ballroom or Tiepolo-ceilinged Scuola Grande dei Carmini.

Local Life

→ **Spritz o'clock** The best place to be when the clock strikes six *(spritz)* o'clock is Campo Santa Margherita, Venice's nightlife hub.

→ **Antique & avant-garde** Rummage through relics from Venice's past at Antiquariato Claudia Canestrelli (p98) and L'Angolo del Passato (p97), then fast forward to cutting-edge Venetian style at Marina e Susanna Sent (p96), Danghyra (p97) and Papuni Art (p97).

→ **Rush-hour detour** Dodge pedestrian traffic shuttling between Ponte dell'Accademia and Campo Santa Margherita in peak season and take the Zattere (p98) instead to bask in the late-afternoon sun.

→ **Concert scene** Choose your music and your scene: chamber music in the grand ballroom at Ca' Rezzonico (p90), costume-drama arias at baroque Scuola Grande dei Carmini (p89), or swinging canalside tributes at Venice Jazz Club (p96).

Getting There & Away

→ **Vaporetto** Grand Canal 1, 2 and N lines stop at Accademia; line 1 also calls at Ca' Rezzonico and Salute. Lines 51, 52, 61, 62 and the N night *vaporetto* (small passenger ferry) call at the Zattere and/or San Basilio.

→ **Traghetto** The San Marco *traghetto* (ferry) heads directly to Salute, saving you a 40-minute walk. For a shortcut between Ca' Rezzonico and Palazzo Grassi, hop the Ca' Rezzonico *traghetto* across the Grand Canal to the San Samuele stop.

Lonely Planet's Top Tip

Dorsoduro points into the lagoon like a slightly dinged gondola prow, and sites are spread out. Museums are along the Grand Canal on the east side, while boisterous bars and upbeat eateries are clumped around Campo Santa Margherita and Campo San Barnaba to the northwest – a 20-minute walk from the Guggenheim or Punta della Dogana. Head south along Zattere for quiet churches and sunshine.

✖ Best Places to Eat

→ Ristorante La Bitta (p94)
→ Enoteca Ai Artisti (p95)
→ Grom (p90)
→ Antica Trattoria La Furatola (p95)

For reviews, see p90 →

🍷 Best Places to Drink

→ Cantinone Giá Schiavi (p95)
→ Il Caffè Rosso (p95)
→ Osteria alla Bifora (p95)
→ Tea Room Beatrice (p95)

For reviews, see p95 →

◉ Best Venetian Views

→ *Feast in the House of Levi*, Accademia (p84)
→ Grand Canal alongside *Angel of the City*, Guggenheim (p87)
→ Ando's water-gate windows, Punta della Dogana (p91)
→ Vedutisti Gallery, Ca' Rezzonico (p90)

For reviews, see p88 →

SESTIERE DI DORSODURO

XIANPIX / CORBIS ©

TOP SIGHT
GALLERIE DELL'ACCADEMIA

Hardly academic, these galleries contain more murderous intrigue, forbidden romance and shameless politicking than the most outrageous Venetian parties. The former Santa Maria della Carità convent complex maintained its serene composure for centuries, but ever since Napoleon installed his haul of Venetian art trophies in 1807, there's been nonstop visual drama inside these walls.

Rooms 1–5

To guide you through the ocular onslaught, the gallery layout is loosely organised by style and theme from the 14th to 18th centuries, though recent restorations and works on loan have shuffled around some masterpieces. The grand gallery you enter upstairs features vivid early works that show Venice's precocious flair for colour and drama. Case in point: Jacobello Alberegno's late-14th-century *Apocalypse* (Room 1) shows the whore of Babylon riding a hydra, babbling rivers of blood from her mouth. At the opposite end of the emotional spectrum is Paolo Veneziano's 1553–59 *Coronation of Mary* (Room 1), where Jesus bestows the crown on his mother with a gentle pat on the head to the tune of an angelic orchestra.

UFO arrivals seem imminent in the eerie, glowing skies of Carpaccio's *Crucifixion and Glorification of the Ten Thousand Martyrs of Mount Ararat* (Room 2) – Harry's Bar was apt in naming its shimmering, raw-beef dish after him. But Giovanni Bellini's **Pala di San Giobbe** (Room 2) shows hope on the horizon, in the form of a sweet-faced Madonna and Child emerging from a dark niche, as angels

➡ Veronese's *Feast in the House of Levi*
➡ Titian's *Presentation of the Virgin*
➡ Sala dell'Albergo
➡ Tintoretto's *Creation of the Animals*

PRACTICALITIES

➡ Map p312
➡ 🕿041 520 03 45
➡ www.gallerieac cademia.org
➡ Campo della Carità 1050
➡ ticket incl Palazzo Grimani adult/ reduced/EU child & senior €14/11/free
➡ ⏲8.15am-2pm Mon, to 7.15pm Tue-Sun, last admission 45min before closing
➡ ⛴Accademia

tune their instruments. The martyrs surrounding them include St Roch and St Sebastian, suggesting that this luminous, uplifting work dates from the dark days of Venice's second plague in 1478.

Lock eyes with fascinating strangers across the portrait-filled Room 4. Hans Memling captures youthful stubble and angst with the exacting detail of a Freudian miniaturist in *Portrait of a Young Man*, while Giorgione's sad-eyed *La Vecchia* (Old Woman) points to herself as the words 'with time' unfurl ominously in the background.

Rooms 6–10

Venice's Renaissance awaits around the corner in Room 6, featuring Titian and Tintoretto. Tintoretto's *Creation of the Animals* is a fantastical bestiary suggesting God put forth his best efforts inventing Venetian seafood (no argument here). Tintoretto's 1562 *St Mark Saving a Saracen from Shipwreck* is an action-packed blockbuster, with fearless Venetian merchants and an improbably muscular, long-armed saint rescuing a turbaned sailor.

Titian's 1576 *Pietà* was possibly finished posthumously by Palma il Giovane, but notice the smears of paint Titian applied with his bare hands and the column-base self-portrait, foreshadowing Titian's own funeral monument.

Artistic triumph over censorship dominates Room 10: Paolo Veronese's freshly restored *Feast in the House of Levi,* originally called *Last Supper* until Inquisition leaders condemned him for showing dogs, drunkards, dwarves, Muslims and Reformation-minded Germans cavorting with Apostles. He refused to change a thing, besides the title, and Venice stood by this act of defiance against Rome. Follow the exchanges, gestures and eye contact among the characters, and you'll concede that not one Turkish trader, clumsy server, gambler or bright-eyed lapdog could have been painted over without losing an essential piece of the Venetian puzzle.

Rooms 11–19

Now that you've reached the halfway mark of Venice's contributions to art history, you'll notice a lighter baroque touch and more down-to-earth subject matter. As you enter Room 11, you may feel observed by the gossipy Venetian socialties hanging over balconies in 1743–45 lunettes by Tiepolo. These charming ceiling details originally hung in the Scalzi Church, and were narrowly salvaged after 1915 Austrian bombings.

Rooms 12 to 18 are currently undergoing restoration to showcase Canaletto's sweeping views of Venice and Giorgione's highly charged *La Tempesta*

THE ACCADEMIA'S STAR ARCHITECTS

The Accademia represents Venice's single most important art collection – and the work of several of its finest architects.

➡ **Bartolomeo Bon** completed the spare, Gothic-edged Santa Maria della Carità facade in 1448.

➡ In 1561, **Palladio** took a classical approach to the Convento dei Canonici Lateranensi, which was absorbed into the Accademia.

➡ From 1949 to 1954, modernist **Carlo Scarpa** took a minimalist approach to restorations, taking care not to upset the delicate symmetries achieved between architects over the centuries.

SESTIERE DI DORSODURO GALLERIE DELL'ACCADEMIA

SKIP THE QUEUE & SAVE MONEY

To skip ahead of the Accademia queue in high season, book tickets ahead online (booking fee €1.50). Otherwise, queues tend to be shorter in the afternoon, after school groups depart and day-trippers begin their treks back to mainland hotels. Still, don't put off joining the queue too long: the last entry is 45 minutes before closing, and proper visits take at least 90 minutes.

To save a few euro during your visit:

➡ Leave any large items behind, or you'll have to drop them off at the baggage depot (€0.50 per piece).

➡ The Accademia offers an audio guide (€5) that is mostly descriptive and largely unnecessary – better to avoid the wait and just follow your bliss and explanatory wall tags.

➡ The Accademia bathrooms are elegantly restored in spotless marble, so there's no need to pay €1 for iffy public restrooms outside.

(The Storm). Art historians still debate the meaning of the mysterious nursing mother and passing soldier with a bolt of summer lightning: is this an expulsion from Eden, an allegory for alchemy, or a reference to Venice conquering Padua in the War of Cambria?

Restored portrait galleries will feature larger-than-life Venetian characters: Lorenzo Lotto's soul-searching *Portrait of a Young Scholar;* Rosalba Carriera's brutally honest self-portrait; Pietro Longhi's lovestruck violinist watching a twirling debutante in *The Dance Lesson*; and a saucy, fate-tempting socialite in Giambattista Piazzetta's *Fortune-Teller.*

Rooms 20–24

Finales don't come any grander than the Accademia's final suite of rooms. Room 20 is currently undergoing restorations to accommodate Gentile Bellini and Vittore Carpaccio's Venetian versions of *Miracles of the True Cross,* thronged with multicultural merchant crowds. After careful restoration, the original convent **chapel** (Room 23) is a serene showstopper fronted by a **Bellini altarpiece**, with temporary shows in the center.

Ornamental splendours were reserved for the Scuola della Carita's boardroom, the newly restored **Sala dell'Albergo**. Board meetings would not have been boring here, under a lavishly carved ceiling and facing Antonio Vivarini's wraparound 1441–50 masterpiece, filled with fluffy-bearded saints keeping a watchful eye on boardroom proceedings.

Titian closes the Accademia with his touching 1534–39 *Presentation of the Virgin.* Here, a young, tiny Madonna trudges up an intimidating staircase while a distinctly Venetian crowd of onlookers point to her example – yet few of the velvet- and pearl-clad merchants offer alms to the destitute mother, or even feed the begging dog.

TOP SIGHT
PEGGY GUGGENHEIM COLLECTION

After tragically losing her father on the Titanic, heiress Peggy Guggenheim befriended Dadaists, dodged Nazis and changed art history at her palatial home on the Grand Canal. Peggy's Palazzo Venier dei Leoni is a showcase for surrealism, futurism and abstract expressionism by some 200 breakthrough modern artists, including Peggy's ex-husband Max Ernst and Jackson Pollock (among her many rumoured lovers).

Collection

Peggy collected according to her own convictions rather than for prestige or style, so her collection includes inspired folk art and lesser-known artists alongside Kandinsky, Picasso, Man Ray, Rothko, Mondrian, Joseph Cornell and Dalí. Major modernists also contributed custom interior decor, including the Calder silver bedstead hanging in the former bedroom. In the corners of the main galleries, you'll find photos of the rooms as they appeared when Peggy lived here, in fabulously eccentric style.

For this champion of modern art who'd witnessed the dangers of censorship and party-line dictates, serious artwork deserved to be seen and judged on its merits. The Jewish American collector narrowly escaped Paris two days before the Nazis marched into the city, and arrived in Venice in 1948 to find the city's historically buoyant spirits broken by war. More than a mere tastemaker, Peggy became a spirited advocate for contemporary Italian art, which had largely gone out of favour with the rise of Mussolini and the partisan politics of WWII.

Peggy sparked renewed interest in postwar Italian art and resurrected the reputation of key Italian Futurists, whose dynamic style had been co-opted to make Fascism more visually palatable. Her support led to reappraisals of Umberto Boccioni, Giorgio Morandi, Giacomo Balla, Giuseppe Capogrossi and Giorgio de Chirico, and aided Venice's own Emilio Vedova and Giuseppe Santomaso. Never afraid to make a splash, Peggy gave passing gondoliers an eyeful on her Grand Canal quay: Marino Marini's 1948 *Angel of the City*, a bronze male nude on horseback visibly excited by the possibilities on the horizon.

Garden & Pavilion

The Palazzo Venier dei Leoni was never finished, but that didn't stop Peggy Guggenheim from filling every available space indoors and out with art. Wander past bronzes by Moore, Giacometti and Brancusci, Yoko Ono's *Wish Tree* and a shiny black-granite lump by Anish Kapoor in the **sculpture garden**, where the city of Venice granted Peggy an honorary dispensation to be buried beneath the Giacometti sculptures and alongside her dearly departed lapdogs in 1979. Through the gardens is a **pavilion** housing a sunny cafe, a bookshop, bathrooms, and temporary exhibits highlighting underappreciated modernist rebels. Around the corner from the museum on Fondamenta Venier dei Leoni is a larger **museum shop**, selling art books in several languages and replicas of Peggy's signature glasses – winged, like the lion of San Marco.

DON'T MISS...

➡ Rotating permanent collection
➡ Calder silver bedstead
➡ *Angel of the City*
➡ Sculpture garden
➡ Temporary pavilion shows

PRACTICALITIES

➡ Map p312
➡ ☎041 240 54 11
➡ www.guggenheim
-venice.it
➡ Palazzo Venier dei Leoni 704
➡ adult/senior/reduced €14/11/8
➡ ◷10am-6pm Wed-Mon
➡ 🚤Accademia

⊙ SIGHTS

GALLERIE DELL'ACCADEMIA GALLERY
See p84.

PEGGY GUGGENHEIM COLLECTION MUSEUM
See p87.

**BASILICA DI SANTA
MARIA DELLA SALUTE** CHURCH
(La Salute; Map p312; ☑041 241 10 18; www.semi
nariovenezia.it; Campo della Salute 1b; admission
free, sacristy adult/reduced €3/1.50; ⊙9am-
noon & 3-5.30pm; ⛴Salute) A monumental
sigh of relief, this splendid domed church
was commissioned by Venice's plague sur-
vivors as thanks for salvation. Baldassare
Longhena's uplifting design is an engineering feat that defies simple logic, and in fact
the church is said to have mystical curative
properties. Titian eluded the plague until
age 94, leaving a legacy of masterpieces
now in Salute's sacristy.

Longhena's marvel makes good on an official appeal by the Venetian Senate directly
to the Madonna in 1630, after 80,000 Venetians had been killed by plague brought in by
a carpenter working on Venice's quarantine
island, the Lazzaretto Vecchio. The Senate
promised the Madonna a church in exchange
for her intervention on behalf of Venice – no
expense or effort spared. Before 'La Salute'
could even be started, at least 100,000 pylons
had to be driven deep into the *barene* (mud
banks) to shore up the tip of Dorsoduro.

The Madonna provided essential inspiration, but La Salute draws its structural
strength from a range of architectural and
spiritual traditions. Architectural scholars
note striking similarities between Longhena's unusual domed octagon structure and
both Greco-Roman goddess temples and
Jewish cabbala diagrams. The lines of the
building ingeniously converge beneath the
dome to form a vortex on the inlaid marble

ⓘ PERKS FOR NEWCOMERS

New in town? Save a few euro on
admission to the Peggy Guggenheim
Collection by bringing your Trenitalia
or Alitalia ticket to the museum. Don't
dawdle: the offer is good for new arrivals with train tickets no more than
three days old, and Alitalia airline
passengers with tickets up to seven
days old.

---

floors, and the black dot at the centre is said
to radiate healing energy.

The newly restored sacristy is a wonder
within a wonder, featuring 12 key works by
Titian – including a vivid self-portrait in the
guise of St Matthew and his earliest known
work from 1510, *Saint Mark on the Throne*.
Salute's most charming allegory for Venice's
miraculous survival from plague is Palma Il
Giovane's painting of Jonah emerging from
the mouth of the whale, where the survivor
stomps down the sea creature's tongue like
an action hero walking the red carpet. Life
in a time of plague is a miracle worth celebrating in Tintoretto's upbeat 1561 *Wedding Feast of Cana*, featuring a Venetian
throng of multi-culti musicians, busy wine
pourers, and Tintoretto himself in the pink,
gently schooling a young, thin-bearded
Paolo Veronese.

Thousands still observe the annual pilgrimage on Festa della Madonna della
Salute, heading across a pontoon bridge
from Piazzetta Santa Maria del Giglio to
the church, where Venetians light candles
for the continued health of their families
and their extraordinary city. Unlike many
Venetian churches, Salute remains an active place of prayer and reflection; out of
respect for worshippers, no flash photography is allowed. Want to hear the organ
played? See p89.

CHIESA DI SAN SEBASTIAN CHURCH
(Map p312; www.chorusvenezia.org; Campo San
Sebastiano 1687; admission €3, or with Chorus
Pass; ⊙10am-5pm Mon-Sat; ⛴San Basilio) A
hidden treasure of Venetian art in the
heart of Dorsoduro, this otherwise humble
neighbourhood church was embellished
with floor-to-ceiling masterpieces by Paolo
Veronese over three decades. Antonio Scar-
pignano's relatively austere 1508–48 facade
creates a sense of false modesty from the
outside, because inside, the restored interior decor goes wild.

According to popular local legend, Veronese found sanctuary at San Sebastian in
1555 after fleeing murder charges in Verona, and his works in this church deliver lavish thanks to the parish and an especially
brilliant poke in the eye of his accusers. Veronese's virtuosity is everywhere here, from
the horses rearing on the coffered ceiling to
organ doors covered with his *Presentation
of the Virgin*. In Veronese's *Martyrdom of
Saint Sebastian* near the altar, the bound
saint defiantly stares down his tormen-

SACRED MUSIC AT SALUTE

If you think Longhena's dome looks magnificent, wait until you hear how it sounds. Weekdays at 3.30pm, vespers are played on the basilica's original 1782–83 organ. These musical interludes are free, and the acoustics are suitably heavenly.

tors amid a Venetian crowd of socialites, turbaned traders and Veronese's signature frisky spaniel. St Sebastian was the fearless patron saint of Venice's plague victims, and Veronese suggests that, though sticks and stones may break his bones, Venetian gossip couldn't kill him.

Pay respects to Veronese, who chose to be buried here underneath his masterpieces – his memorial plaque is to the right of the organ – but don't miss Titian's 1563 *San Niccolo* to the right of the entry. Peek into the **sacristy** to glimpse Veronese's 1555 *Coronation of the Virgin* on the ceiling – it's recently been restored with American funds, and is positively glowing.

SCUOLA GRANDE
DEI CARMINI   HISTORICAL BUILDING
(Map p312; ☎041 528 94 20; www.scuolagrande carmini.it; Campo Santa Margherita 2617; adult/reduced €5/4; ⊙11am-4pm; ⛴Ca' Rezzonico) Eighteenth-century backpackers must have thought they'd died and gone to heaven at Scuola Grande dei Carmini, with its lavish interiors by Giambattista Tiepolo and Baldassare Longhena. Longhena designed the gold-leafed stucco **stairway to heaven**, glimpsed upstairs in Tiepolo's **nine-panel ceiling** of a rosy *Virgin in Glory*. The adjoining hostel room is bedecked in *boiserie* (wood carving).

This *scuola* was the first formed by women in the 13th century. It was also Venice's first known order of Battuti (Flagellants), who practiced self-mortification with a wooden rod – a practice since discredited. The Carmini continued to extend hospitality to destitute and wayward travellers from the 13th century right through to the time of Napoleon's occupation of Venice. Sadly, cots are no longer available in this jewel-box building, but evening concerts are held here (p96), and members of the Carmini continue to organise charitable works to this day.

MAGAZZINI DEL SALE   ART GALLERY
(Map p312; ☎041 522 66 26; www.fondazioneve dova.org; Zattere 266; donation suggested during shows; ⊙during shows 10.30am-6pm Wed-Mon; ⛴Zattere) A recent retrofit designed by Pritzker Prize–winning architect Renzo Piano transformed Venice's historic **salt warehouses** into **Fondazione Vedova** art galleries, commemorating pioneering Venetian abstract painter Emilio Vedova. Fondazione Vedova shows are often literally moving and rotating: powered by renewable energy sources, 10 robotic arms designed by Vedova and Piano move major modern artworks in and out of storage slots.

Although their facade is a neoclassical job from the 1830s, these nine salt warehouses were established in the 14th century, when the all-important salt monopoly made Venice's fortune. Before fridges and electricity, the only way to preserve foodstuffs was to cure or pack them in salt – and since preserved foods were essential for ocean voyages, salt was crucial to maritime commerce. By controlling the salt trade, Venice effectively controlled the seas for centuries.

Today's creatively repurposed salt warehouses are only fitting, now that Venice's most precious commodity is art, not salt. Neighbouring **Spazio Vedova** (at Zattere 50) includes a public art and performance space. Zattere warehouses not used for exhibitions are used by the Bucintoro rowing club for storage, and serve the city as environmental initiative labs.

CHIESA DEI GESUATI   CHURCH
(Church of Santa Maria del Rosario; Map p312; www. chorusvenezia.org; Fondamenta delle Zattere 918;

SQUERO DI SAN TROVASO

The **wood cabin** (Map p312; Campo San Trovaso 1097; ⛴Zattere) along Rio di San Trovaso may look like a stray ski chalet, but it's one of Venice's three working *squeri* (shipyards), with refinished gondolas drying in the yard. When the door's open, you can peek inside in exchange for a donation left in the can by the door. To avoid startling gondola-builders working with sharp tools, no flash photography is allowed.

admission €3 or Chorus Pass; ⊙10am-5pm Mon-Sat; 🚊Zattere) Venice's forecast calls for year-round sunshine inside Giorgio Massari's baroque church. Luminous afternoon skies surrounding St Dominic in Tiepolo's 1737–39 **ceiling frescoes** are so convincing, you'll wonder whether you're wearing enough sunscreen. Tintoretto's sombre 1565 *Crucifixion* shows Mary fainting with grief – but Sebastiano Ricci's cherubs perform comical celestial tumbling routines in the 1730–33 *Saints Peter and Thomas with Pope Pius V.*

CA' DARIO
PALACE

(Map p312; Ramo Ca' Dario 352; 🚊Salute) Grand Canal palaces rank among the world's most desirable real estate, and multi-coloured marble Gothic marvel Ca' Dario casts a mesmerising reflection painted by no less than Claude Monet – but there's a catch. Starting with the daughter of its original owner, Giovanni Dario, an unusual number of Ca' Dario occupants have met untimely deaths.

Local legend associates this palace with at least seven deaths, which gossips claim effectively dissuaded Woody Allen from buying the place in the 1990s. The former manager of The Who, Kit Lambert, moved out after complaints of being hounded by the palace's ghosts, and was found dead shortly thereafter. One week after renting the place for a holiday in 2002, The Who's bass player, John Entwhistle, died of a heart attack. At this writing, Ca' Dario is for sale; any takers?

PALAZZO ZENOBIO
PALACE

(Map p312; ☎041 522 87 70; www.collegioarmeno.com; Fondamenta del Soccorso 2597; entry fees vary; ⊙10am-5pm Mon-Sat; 🚊Ca' Rezzonico) A gilded 1690 palace that formerly housed a school for Venice's Armenian community recently opened its doors to visitors, who may recognise its frescoed, mirrored salon as the setting for Madonna's 1984 'Like a Virgin' video. The palace's *trompe l'œil* frescoed ceilings by Louis Dorigny are splendid, and its overgrown formal garden is among Venice's largest and loveliest.

 **EATING**

GROM
GELATERIA €

(Map p312; ☎041 099 17 51; www.grom.it; Campo San Barnaba 2461; gelati €2.50-4; ⊙11am-midnight Sun-Thu, to 1am Fri & Sat; 👪; 🚊Ca' Rezzon-

---

 TOP SIGHT
CA' REZZONICO

Baroque dreams come true at Baldassare Longhena's Grand Canal palace. Giambattista Tiepolo's **Throne Room ceiling** is a masterpiece of elegant social climbing, showing gorgeous Merit ascending to the Temple of Glory clutching the Golden Book of Venetian nobles' names – including Tiepolo's patrons, the Rezzonico family.

In the **Pietro Longhi Salon**, sweeping Grand Canal views are upstaged by the artist's winsome satires of society antics observed by disapproving lapdogs. **Sala Rosalba Carriera** features Carriera's wry, unvarnished pastel portraits of socialites that aren't conventionally pretty but look like they'd be the life of any party. Giandomenico Tiepolo's swinging court jesters and preening parrots add cheeky humour to the reassembled **Zianigo Villa frescoes.**

On the top floor, don't miss Emma Ciardi's moody Venice canal views in the **Vedutisti gallery**, and an **antique pharmacy** with 183 majolica ceramic jars of 18th-century remedies.

Check the schedule downstairs for **chamber-music concerts**.

DON'T MISS...

➡ Tiepolo's *trompe l'oeil* ceilings
➡ Pietro Longhi Salon

PRACTICALITIES

➡ Museum of the 18th Century
➡ Map p312
➡ ☎041 241 01 00
➡ www.visitmuve.it
➡ Fondamenta Rezzonico 3136
➡ adult/reduced €8/5.50 or Museum Pass
➡ ⊙10am-6pm Wed-Mon Apr-Oct, to 5pm Nov-Mar
➡ 🚊Ca' Rezzonico

TOP SIGHT
PUNTA DELLA DOGANA

Fortuna, the weathervane atop Punta della Dogana, swung Venice's way in 2005, when bureaucratic hassles in Paris convinced art collector François Pinault to showcase his works in Venice's long-abandoned customs warehouses. Here massive installations include Chen Zhen's pure crystal versions of his diseased internal organs and Abdel Abdessemed's drawings of Molotov-cocktail throwers propped on concert stands to create orchestrated violence.

The warehouses were built by Giuseppe Benoni in 1677 to ensure no ship entered the Grand Canal without paying duties. Re-opened in 2009 after a three-year reinvention by architect Tadao Ando, Venice's splashiest art space pays its dues to the city's seafaring history and its changing architecture. Ando cut windows in Benoni's ancient water gates to reveal cutaway views of passing ships, while his floating concrete staircases honour the innovations of Venetian modernist Carlo Scarpa.

Upstairs, don't miss Maurizio Cattelan's haunting *All*: nine shrouded marble figures laid out on the floor, like ghosts of Venice's plagued past.

DON'T MISS...

➡ Fortuna
➡ Tadao Ando interiors
➡ Rotating art installations

PRACTICALITIES

➡ Map p312
➡ ☏041 271 90 39
➡ www.palazzograssi.it
➡ adult/reduced/child €15/10/free, incl Palazzo Grassi €20/15/free
➡ ⏱10am-7pm Wed-Mon
➡ 🚤Salute

---

ico) Lick the landscape at Grom, featuring Slow Food ingredients from across Italy: lemon from the Amalfi Coast, pistachio from Sicily, hazelnuts from Piedmont. Fairtrade chocolate and coffee sourcing helped win the Turin-based Grom chain a 'Master of Slow Food' designation, but with seasonal flavours ranging from chestnut cream to apricot sorbet, you might award it another honorary title: lunch.

PASTICCERIA TONOLO
PASTRIES & CAKES €

(Map p312; ☏041 532 72 09; Calle dei Preti 3764; pastries €1-3; ⏱7.45am-8pm Tue-Sat, 8am-1pm Sun; 🚤Ca' Rezzonico) Dire B&B breakfasts with packaged croissants are corrected at Tonolo, which serves flaky *apfelstrudel* (apple pastry), velvety *bignè al zabaione* (marsala cream pastry) and oozing *pain au chocolat* (chocolate croissants). Chocolate-topped beignets are filled with rich hazelnut mousse.

IMPRONTA CAFÉ
ITALIAN €

(Map p312; ☏041 275 03 86; Calle Crosera 3815; meals €8-15; ⏱7am-2am Mon-Sat; 🍴; 🚤San Tomà) Join Venice's value-minded jet set for *prosecco* and bargain polenta-salami combos, surrounded by witty architectural diagrams of cooking pots. When other restaurants close, Impronta stays open to accommodate late lunches, teatime with a wide tea selection, and midnight snacks of club sandwiches – yet somehow, the staff remains chipper and the bathroom spotless.

BAR ALLA TOLETTA
SANDWICHES €

(Map p312; ☏041 520 01 96; Calle la Toletta 1192; sandwiches €1.50-6; ⏱8am-8pm Mon-Sat; 🍴🖶; 🚤Accademia) Midway through museum crawls from Accademia to Ca' Rezzonico, Bar Toletta satisfies starving artists with creative, grilled-to-order *panini*, including ham with fresh porcini and daily vegetarian options. *Tramezzini* (sandwiches) are tasty, too – Bar Toletta goes easy on mayonnaise in favour of more flavourful toppings like olive tapenade. Have a seat for €0.50 extra per sandwich, or get yours to go.

PIZZA AL VOLO
PIZZERIA €

(Map p312; ☏041 522 54 30; Campo Santa Margherita 2944; pizza slices from €2, small pizzas €4.50-7; ⏱noon-11.30pm; 🚤Ca' Rezzonico) Peckish night owls run out of options fast in Venice once restaurants start to close at

ARVED GINTENREITER / DPA / CORBIS ©

TATIANA BRZOZOWSKA / GETTY IMAGES ©

DAVID C TOMLINSON / GETTY IMAGES ©

1. I Frari (p104)
Antonio Canova's marble pyramid mausoleum.

2. Chiesa del Santissimo Redentore (p161)
Palladio's masterpiece was built to celebrate the city's deliverance from the Black Death.

3. I Frari (p104)
Bellini's *Madonna with Child* triptych dominates the sacristy.

4. Chiesa di San Giorgio Maggiore (p160)
Stunning from across the water, and bright and serene within.

10pm – but slices here are cheap and tasty, with a thin yet sturdy crust that won't collapse on your bar-hopping outfit.

RISTORANTE LA BITTA
RISTORANTE €€

(Map p312; ☑041 523 05 31; Calle Lunga San Barnaba 2753a; meals €30-40; ☉dinner Mon-Sat; ☱Ca' Rezzonico) The daily menu arrives on an artist's easel, and the hearty rustic fare looks like a still life and tastes like a carnivore's dream: steak comes snugly wrapped in bacon, and roast rabbit tops marinated rocket. This bistro focuses on local meats and seats only 35 – 'bitta' means 'mooring post'. Reservations essential; cash only.

DO FARAI
SEAFOOD, VENETIAN €€

(Map p312; ☑041 277 03 69; Calle del Cappeller 3278; meals €25-35; ☉11am-3pm & 7-10pm Mon-Sat; ☱Ca' Rezzonico) Venetian regulars pack this hidden wood-panelled room, hung with football-championship scarves and fragrant with mouthwatering seafood: pasta with shellfish and sweet prawns; herb-laced, grilled *orata* (bream); and Venetian *tris di saor sarde, scampi e sogliole* (sardines, prawns and sole in tangy Venetian *saor* marinade). Service is leisurely; bide your time with a Negroni *aperitivo*, or postprandial *sgropin* (prosecco-lemon sorbet).

PANE VINO E SAN DANIELE
ITALIAN €€

(Map p312; ☑041 243 98 65; www.panevinovenice. com; Calle Lunga San Barnaba 2861; meals €15-30; ☉10am-2pm Tue-Sun; ☱Ca' Rezzonico) Artists can't claim they're starving any more after a meal in this wood-beamed trattoria, a favourite of art students and professors alike. Settle in to generous plates of gnocchi laced with truffle cheese, Veneto game such as roast rabbit and duck, lavish appetisers featuring the namesake San Daniele cured ham, and Friulian house wines made by the Fantinel family owners.

RISTORANTE SAN TROVASO
VENETIAN €€

(Map p312; ☑041 523 08 35; Rio Terà Carità 967; meals €15-30; ☉noon-3.30pm & 7-11pm Fri-Wed; ☱Accademia) After the Accademia leaves you delirious with visual overload, come to your senses with fried calamari, polenta, *sarde in saor* and a carafe of the house soave. Hidden behind the museum, this sensibly priced rustic restaurant hastens recovery with brisk service, sunny garden seating and an airy, wood-beamed dining room.

CASIN DEI NOBILI
ITALIAN €€

(Map p312; ☑041 241 18 41; Calle Lunga San Barnaba 2765; meals €25-40; ☉Fri-Wed; ☱Ca'

WORTH A DETOUR

CHIESA DI SAN NICOLÒ DEI MENDICOLI

Other churches in town are grander, but none is more quintessentially Venetian. This striking brick Veneto-Gothic **church** (Map p312; ☑041 528 45 65; Campo San Nicolò 1907; ☉10am-noon & 4-6pm Mon-Sat; ☱San Basilio) dedicated to serving the poor hasn't changed much since the 12th century, when its cloisters functioned as a women's refuge and its **portico** sheltered *mendicoli* (beggars). The tiny, picturesque *campo* out front is Venice in miniature, surrounded on three sides by canals and featuring a pylon bearing the winged lion of St Mark – one of the few in Venice to escape target practice by Napoleon's troops.

Dim interiors are illuminated by an **18th-century golden arcade** and a profusion of clerestory paintings, including a Palma Il Giovane masterpiece. His *Resurrection* shows onlookers cowering in terror and awe, as Jesus leaps from his tomb in a blaze of golden light. The right-hand **chapel** is a typically Venetian response to persistent orders from Rome to limit music in Venetian churches: Madonna in glory, thoroughly enjoying a concert by angels on flutes, lutes and violins. The parish's seafaring livelihood is honoured in Leonardo Corona's **16th-century ceiling panel** *San Nicolo Guiding Sailors Through a Storm,* which shows the saint as a beacon guiding sailors rowing furiously through a storm.

Film buffs might recognise church interiors from the 1973 Julie Christie thriller *Don't Look Now* as the church Donald Sutherland was assigned to restore. Though the movie cast Venice in a spooky light, the publicity apparently helped San Nicolò: the British Venice in Peril Fund underwrote extensive church renovations, completed in 1977.

Rezzonico) A historic bordello now serves dinner on a charming patio packed with curios and tables. The wide menu selection ranging from pizza to steak is a boon for families and indecisive diners, but quality does vary – housemade gnocchi, seafood pastas and chocolate soufflés are the strong points. Book ahead, or join the wait list.

ENOTECA AI ARTISTI RISTORANTE €€€

(Map p312; 📞041 523 89 44; www.enotecaartisti. com; Fondamenta della Toletta 1169a; meals €40-50; ⊗noon-4pm & 6.30-10pm Mon-Sat; 🚤Ca' Rezzonico) Indulgent cheeses, exceptional *nero di seppia* (cuttlefish ink) pasta, and tender *tagliata* (sliced steak) drizzled with aged balsamic vinegar atop arugula are paired with exceptional wines by the glass by your oenophile hosts. Sidewalk tables for two make great people-watching, but book ahead for indoor tables for groups; space is limited.

ANTICA TRATTORIA LA FURATOLA VENETIAN, SEAFOOD €€€

(Map p312; 📞041 520 85 94; Calle Lunga San Barnaba 2870a; meals €40-60; ⊗12.30-2.30pm & 7.30-10.30pm Tue-Wed & Fri-Sun, 7.30-10.30pm Thu; 🚤Ca' Rezzonico) Before becoming museum central, Dorsoduro was a fishermen's neighbourhood where the *furatola* (provisioner) offered simple, honest fare. La Furatola has gone upscale but still dishes seafood to Venetian fishermen's standards, fresh from the Pescaria. Seafood appetisers are main events with *canoce* (mantis prawn), followed by handmade pastas – go Sunday for ravioli *alla busara* (with prawn sauce). Cash only.

🍷 DRINKING & NIGHTLIFE

★CANTINONE GIÀ SCHIAVI BAR

(Map p312; 📞041 523 95 77; Fondamenta Nani 992; ⊗8.30am-8.30pm Mon-Sat; 🚤Zattere) Regulars gamely pass along orders to timid newcomers, who might otherwise miss out on tuna-leek *cicheti* with top-notch house soave, or *pallottoline* (mini-bottles of beer) with generous *sopressa* (soft salami) *panini*. Chaos cheerfully prevails at this legendary canalside spot, where Accademia art historians rub shoulders with San Trovaso gondola builders without spilling a drop.

CAMPO SANTA MARGHERITA

Even in the dead of winter and the heat of summer, you can count on action here in Venice's nightlife hub. The oblong, unruly square features a bevy of beverage temptations – including Imagina Café, Osteria alla Bifora, Ai Do Draghi and Cantina di Millevini – but it also hosts a regular weekday fish market, the odd flea market and periodic political protests. The nightly happy-hour scene unfolds like a live-action, 21st-century Veronese painting, with an animated, eclectic crowd of Italian architecture and foreign exchange students, gay and straight international hipsters, wise-cracking Venetian grandmothers and their knitwear-clad pugs.

IL CAFFÈ ROSSO CAFE, BAR

(Map p312; 📞041 528 79 98; Campo Santa Margherita 2963; ⊗7am-1am Mon-Sat; 🚤Ca' Rezzonico) Sunny piazza seating speeds recovery from last night's revelry, with espresso that opens eyes like a rip-cord on Venetian blinds – until the cycle begins again at 6pm, with standing-room-only happy-hour crowds. Locals affectionately call this red storefront *'al rosso'*, and its inexpensive *spritz* generously splashed with scarlet Aperol gives visitors and locals alike an instant flush of Venetian colour.

OSTERIA ALLA BIFORA BAR

(Map p312; 📞041 523 61 19; Campo Santa Margherita 2930; ⊗noon-3pm & 6pm-1am Wed-Mon; 🚤Ca' Rezzonico) Other bars around this *campo* cater to *spritz*-pounding students, but this chandelier-lit medieval wine cave sets the scene for gentle flirting over big-hearted Veneto merlot. Cured-meat platters are carved to order on that Ferrari-red meat slicer behind the bar, and there are placemats to doodle on and new-found friends aplenty at communal tables.

TEA ROOM BEATRICE TEA ROOM

(Map p312; 📞041 724 10 42; Calle Lunga San Barnaba 2727a; ⊗3-10pm; 🚤Ca' Rezzonico) After long museum days, Beatrice offers a relaxing alternative to espresso bolted at a bar. Rainy days call for iron pots of green tea and almond cake, and sunshine brings iced drinks and salty pistachios to the garden patio. Gossip is a given in this discreet spot with Venice's best eavesdropping (overheard: 'But I'm old enough to be your grandmother...')

CAFÉ NOIR
CAFE, BAR

(Map p312; ☎041 71 09 25; Calle dei Preti 3805; ⊙7am-2am Mon-Fri, 5pm-2am Sat, 9am-2am Sun; ⊠San Tomà) Shocking but true: sometimes even Venetians need a break from the usual *spritz*, and crave a fortifying Guinness or minty mojito instead. Café Noir obliges at strictly fair prices – no drink costs over €6, service included, even when there's live music. This cosy wood-beamed, exposed-brick bar entices afternoon coffee drinkers to stick around for flatbreads, drinks and conversation until late.

IMAGINA CAFÉ
BAR

(Map p312; ☎041 241 06 25; www.imaginacafe. it; Rio Terà Canal 3126; ⊙8am-2am Mon-Sat; ⊠; ⊠Ca' Rezzonico) Emerging artists on the walls, comfortable seating and a wall of beverage options behind the backlit bar attract a steady creative, chatty and gay-friendly crowd that should probably start paying rent. Piazza tables are usually nabbed by regulars and their little dogs, who bask in the sun and the admiration of passers-by.

CANTINA DI MILLEVINI
WINE BAR

(Millevini in Campo; Map p312; ☎041 522 34 36; www.millevini.it; Campo Santa Margherita 3026; ⊙3pm-midnight Mon-Sat; ⊠Ca' Rezzonico) This respected Venetian wine merchant broadens happy-hour options on Campo Santa Margherita with bottle-lined brick walls, a select menu of DOC, biodynamic and organic Veneto vintages by the glass, and the occasional tasting class (see website). Grab a table indoors on on the piazza for soothing soups, salads and fish carpaccio of the day (€6.50 to €10).

CAFFÈ BAR AI ARTISTI
CAFE, BAR

(Map p312; ☎393 968 01 35; Campo San Barnaba 2771; ⊙7am-midnight Mon-Sat, from 9am Sun; ⊠Ca' Rezzonico) The cast of characters who sweep into this tiny cafe throughout the day seem borrowed from Pietro Longhi's paintings at neighboring Ca' Rezzonico. Cheerful bartenders aren't the least fazed by dashing caped strangers swilling double espresso, spaniels tucked underarm jealously eying the pastries, and Ca' Macana shoppers requesting straws to sip DOC *prosecco* through long-beaked plague-doctor masks.

AI DO DRAGHI
BAR

(Map p312; ☎041 528 97 31; Calle della Chiesa 3665; ⊙7.30am-10pm Fri-Wed; ⊠Ca' Rezzonico) '*Permesso!*' (Pardon!) is the chorus inside this historic *bacaro* (bar), where the crowd spills onto the sidewalk and tries not to spill drinks in the process. Approach the tiny wooden bar to choose from 45-plus wines by the glass and respectable *tramezzini* (sandwiches). Hold on tight to your order, and let the crowd carry you outside to a *campo* corner table.

☆ ENTERTAINMENT

VENICE JAZZ CLUB
LIVE MUSIC

(Map p312; ☎041 523 20 56; www.venicejazzclub. com; Ponte dei Pugni 3102; admission incl 1st drink €20; ⊙doors 7pm, set begins 9pm, closed Aug; ⊠Ca' Rezzonico) Jazz is alive and swinging in Dorsoduro, where the resident Venice Jazz Club Quartet pays regular respects to Miles Davis and John Coltrane, heats up on Latin Friday, and grooves to bossa nova and chanteuse standards. Drinks are steep, so starving artists booze beforehand and arrive by 8pm to pounce on complimentary cold-cut platters.

🛍 SHOPPING

★MARINA E SUSANNA SENT
ARTISANAL, GLASS

(Map p312; ☎041 520 81 36; www.marinaesusannasent.com; Campo San Vio 669; ⊙10am-1pm & 3-6.30pm Tue-Sat, 3-6.30pm Mon; ⊠Accademia) Wearable waterfalls and unpoppable soap-bubble necklaces are Venice style signatures, thanks to the Murano-born Sent sisters. Defying centuries-old beliefs that women can't

---

SOIREES IN THE SCUOLA

Music and dancing in a religious institution? Rome tried to forbid it for centuries, but the Venetian tradition continues today at the Scuola Grande dei Carmini with **Musica in Maschera** (Musical Masquerade; ☎347 912 24 50; www.musicainmaschera.it; tickets €20-50; ⊙9pm Sep-Jul), concerts performed in 1700s costume with opera singers and a ballet corps. Tickets are available downstairs at the Scuola.

handle molten glass, their minimalist art-glass statement jewellery is featured in museum stores worldwide, from Palazzo Grassi to MoMA. See new collections at this flagship, their Murano studio, or the San Marco branch (at Ponte San Moise 2090).

DANGHYRA
ARTISANAL, CERAMICS

(Map p312; ☑041 522 41 95; www.danghyra.com; Calle delle Botteghe 3220; ☺10am-1pm & 3-7pm Tue-Sun; ⛴San Tomà) Spare white bisque cups seem perfect for a Zen tea ceremony, but look inside: that iridescent lilac glaze is pure Carnevale. Danghyra's striking ceramics are hand-thrown in Venice with a magic touch – her platinum-glazed bowls make the simplest pasta dish appear fit for a modern doge.

LAURETTA VISTOSI
ARTISAN, ACCESSORIES

(Map p312; ☑041 528 65 30; www.laurettavistosi.org; Calle Lunga San Barnaba 2866b; ☺10am-1pm & 3-7pm Tue-Sat; ⛴Ca' Rezzonico) Murano-born Renaissance artisan Lauretta Vistosi hand-crafted shoes, stationery and dresses before inventing her own signature craft: handmade handbags, eyeglass cases and journals, emblazoned with Murano-glass bullseyes. Each piece strikes a balance between playful and architectural, with hand-finished flourishes like contrasting orange outstitching and grid patterns in green ribbon. Prices are surprisingly reasonable for one-of-a-kind finds, starting at €18.

MADERA
DESIGN STORE

(Map p312; ☑041 522 41 81; www.shopmadera venezia.it; Campo San Barnaba 2762; ☺10am-1pm & 4.30-7.30pm Tue-Sat; ⛴Ca' Rezzonico) Double-takes are a given at this modern design showcase, where iron witches' cauldrons are reinvented as must-have kitchenware, sleek gold tote bags are woven from reclaimed plastic bags, and sleek teapots dress casually in denim tea cosies. Owner-designer Francesca Meratti stocks a well-curated selection of Italian and Scandinavian designs that are original, portable and affordable, starting at €14.

LE FORCOLE DI SAVERIO PASTOR
FORCOLE

(Map p312; ☑041 522 56 99; www.forcole.com; Fondamenta Soranzo detta Fornace 341; ☺8.30am-12.30pm & 2.30-6pm Mon-Sat; ⛴Salute) Only one thing in the world actually moves like Jagger: Mick Jagger's bespoke *forcola*, hand-carved by Saverio Pastor. Each forked wooden gondola oarlock is individually designed to match a gondolier's height, weight and movement, so the gondola doesn't rock too hard when the gondolier hits a groove. Pastor's *forcole* twist elegantly, striking an easy balance on gondolas and mantelpieces alike.

ARRAS
ARTISANAL, ACCESSORIES

(Map p312; ☑041 522 64 60; http://arrastes suti.wordpress.com; Campiello dei Squelini 3235; ☺10am-1pm & 3-7.30pm Mon-Sat; ⛴Ca' Rezzonico) 🏷 The plush, handwoven silk and wool wraps piled high on Arras' shelves represent the combined efforts of this weaving cooperative, which offers vocational workshops for people with disabilities. Shimmering scarlet shawls deserve at least one summer sunset gondola ride, and cleverly draped wool jackets reduce Venice's winter chill factor even better than *prosecco*.

L'ANGOLO DEL PASSATO
ANTIQUES, HOME & GARDEN

(Map p312; ☑041 528 78 96; Campiello dei Squelini 3276; ☺10am-1pm & 3-7pm Mon-Sat; ⛴Ca' Rezzonico) The 19th century bumps into the 21st on this hidden corner showcase of rare Murano glass, ranging from spun-gold chandeliers beloved of royal decorators to sultry smoked-glass sconces that serve Hollywood stars better than Botox. Contemporary art glass lines the back shelves, including blown-glass vases with graffiti-graphic squiggles.

PAPUNI ART
ARTISANAL, JEWELLERY

(Map p312; ☑041 241 04 34; www.papuniart.it; Ponte dei Pugni 2834a; ☺11am-1pm & 3-7pm Mon & Wed-Sat, 11am-1pm Tue; ⛴Ca' Rezzonico) Handmade industrial chic isn't what you'd expect to find across the footbridge from baroque Ca' Rezzonico, but Ninfa Salerno's clients delight in the unexpected. The Venetian artisan gives staid pearl strands a sense of humour with bouncy black rubber, weaves fuschia rubber discs into glowing UFO necklaces, and embeds Murano glass beads in rubber daisy cocktail rings.

GUALTI
JEWELLERY, ACCESSORIES

(Map p312; ☑041 520 17 31; www.gualti.it; Rio Terà Canal 3111; ☺10am-7.30pm Mon-Sat; ⛴Ca' Rezzonico) Either a shooting star just landed on your shoulder, or you've been to Gualti, where iridescent orange glass bursts from clear resin stems on a supernova brooch. Pleated-silk evening wraps unfurl like jellyfish tendrils, and mirrored sea-urchin cocktail rings evoke an underwater disco. One-off designs start at €45.

A HEALTHY STROLL: THE ZATTERE

On sunny days, the leisurely stretch of Dorsoduro's **Giudecca Canal** waterfront known as the Zattere becomes an idyllic seaside holiday resort, the perfect spot for a lazy stroll or sunbathing dockside – but a few centuries back, the Zattere was the absolute last resort for many Venetians. The imposing building at 423 Zattere was once better known as **Ospedale degli Incurabili** (Hospital of the Incurables), built in the 16th century to address a problem spreading rapidly through Europe's nether regions. Euphemistically called the 'French sickness', syphilis quickly became a Venetian problem, passing from the ranks of its 12,000 registered prostitutes to the general populace.

With no known cure for syphilis at the time, and blindness and insanity its common side effects, Venetians petitioned the state to create a hospice for the afflicted and the orphans they left behind. Venetian women were outspoken lobbyists for this forward-thinking effort, and funds were pledged early on by prostitutes and madams with a particular interest in the problem. Venice was ahead of its time in dedicating public funds to this public health crisis, though at times even this large building was sometimes overcrowded. When penicillin provided a cure, the facility was happily rendered obsolete, and since 2003 the building has housed the **Accademia delle Belle Arti** (Fine Arts School), formerly located in the Gallerie dell'Accademia building.

Nearby you'll spot a new plaque dedicated to Nobel Prize–winning Russian American poet **Joseph Brodsky**, a sometime local resident who named his 1989 book *Fondamenta degli Incurabili* after this infamous canalbank. He is fondly remembered internationally for his book *Watermark*, which captures Venice's ebbs and flows, its murky tragedies and crystalline graces. As the plaque says in Russian and Italian: 'He loved and sang this place'. Brodsky died in New York in 1996, but by his request and the city's exceptional permission, his body was buried in Venice's cemetery at Isola di San Michele.

ANTIQUARIATO CLAUDIA CANESTRELLI
ANTIQUES, JEWELLERY

(Map p312; ☑340 577 60 89; Campiello Barbaro 364a; ☺10.30am-1pm & 3-5pm Mon & Wed-Sat, 10.30am-1pm Tue; ☒Salute) Hand-coloured lithographs of fanciful lagoon fish and 19th-century miniatures of cats dressed as generals are charming souvenirs of Venice's past in this walk-in curio cabinet. Collector-artisan Claudia Canestrelli is bringing back bygone elegance with her repurposed antique earrings, including free-form baroque pearls dangling from tiny silver pigs.

AQUA ALTRA
HOME & GARDEN

(Map p312; ☑041 521 12 59; www.aquaaltra.it; Campo Santa Margherita 2898; ☺9.30am-12.30pm & 4-7.30pm Tue-Sat, 4-7.30pm Mon; ☒Ca' Rezzonico) 🖊 Globally oriented but with Italian tastes firmly in mind, this volunteer-run fair-trade co-op sells single-origin drinking chocolate from Sierra Leone growers' collectives, anti-aging argan-nut oil from Moroccan women's cooperatives, and match-standard footballs made by a Pakistani cooperative.

CA' MACANA
MASKS, COSTUMES

(Map p312; ☑041 277 61 42; www.camacana.com; Calle delle Botteghe 3172; mask-making workshops from €60; ☺10am-6.30pm Sun-Fri, 10am-8pm Sat, mask-making workshops 11am-1pm & 2-6pm Mon-Fri; ☒Ca' Rezzonico) Glimpse the talents behind the Venetian Carnevale masks that so impressed Stanley Kubrick, he ordered several for his final film *Eyes Wide Shut*. Choose your papier-mâché persona from the selection of coquettish courtesan's eye-shades, chequered Casanova disguises and long-nosed plague doctors' masks – or invent your own alter ego at Ca' Macana's one- to two-hour **mask-making workshops** for individuals and families.

SIGNOR BLOOM
ARTISANAL, TOYS

(Map p312; ☑041 522 63 67; Campo San Barnaba 2840; ☺10am-6.30pm Mon-Sat; ☒Ca' Rezzonico) Kids may have to drag adults away from these 2D wooden puzzles of the Rialto bridge and grinning wooden duckies before these clever handmade toys induce acute cases of nostalgia. Calder-esque mobiles made of carved red gondola prows would seem equally at home in an arty foyer and a nursery.

Sestieri di San Polo & Santa Croce

Neighbourhood Top Five

❶ Seeing lightning strike indoors at the **Scuola Grande di San Rocco** (p101), where Tintoretto's streaky brushwork illuminates hope in a time of plague.

❷ Watching Titian's red-hot Madonna light up the room in *Assunta* at **I Frari** (p104).

❸ Hearing fishermen and island farmers sing the praises of lagoon ingredients at **Rialto Market** (p108).

❹ Following the trail of Venetian explorers through a world of natural wonders at the **Museo di Storia Naturale** (p106).

❺ Posing like a Venetian with fashion hints from **Palazzo Mocenigo** (p106), from 18th-century Venetian platform shoes through to Madonna's Venice Film Festival couture.

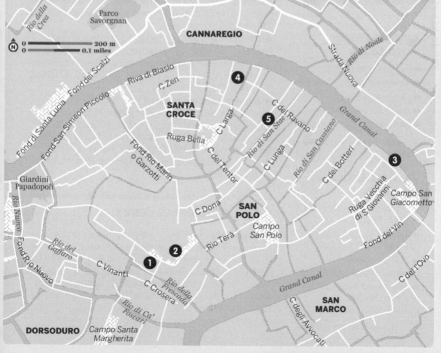

For more detail of this area see Map p314 and p317 ➡

Lonely Planet's Top Tip

Many of Venice's best restaurants, artisans' studios and *bacari* are in the backstreets of San Polo and Santa Croce: if you can find them. This is the easiest area in which to get lost, so allow extra time if you have dinner reservations or a powerful thirst. If totally lost, follow the flow of foot traffic toward yellow Rialto or Ferrovia signs or red-and-white Scuola Grande di San Rocco signs, or head to central Campo San Polo.

✗ Best Places to Eat

➡ All'Arco (p113)

➡ Antiche Carampane (p114)

➡ Alaska Gelateria (p113)

➡ ProntoPesce (p113)

➡ Al Pesador (p115)

For reviews, see p113 ➡

🍷 Best Places to Drink

➡ Al Prosecco (p115)

➡ Al Mercà (p116)

➡ Osteria da Filo (p116)

➡ Caffè Dei Frari (p116)

➡ Muro Vino e Cucina (p116)

For reviews, see p115 ➡

🔒 Best Artisanal Finds

➡ Marbled-paper handbags at Cárte (p117)

➡ Pocket gondola kits at Gilberto Penzo (p118)

➡ Glass dragon goblets at Schantalle Vetri d'Arte (p118)

➡ Embossed San Marco lion sketchbooks at Cartavenezia (p118)

For reviews, see p117 ➡

Explore Sestieri di San Polo & Santa Croce

Start the morning among masterpieces at Scuola Grande di San Rocco, then bask in the glow of Titian's Madonna at I Frari. Shop backstreet artisans' boutiques all the way to the Rialto Market, where glistening purple octopus and feathery red *radicchio treviso* (chicory) present culinary photo-ops. Stop at All'Arco for *cicheti* (Venetian tapas) before breezing through four centuries of avant-garde fashion at Fondazione Prada and Palazzo Mocenigo, then swing by Alaska to celebrate freedom from corsetry with adventurous gelato. Head to medieval San Giacomo dell'Orio for happy hour at Al Prosecco, and wander the maze of Venice's former red-light district to Antiche Carampane for dinner.

Local Life

➡ **Shopping obsessions** Museum collections are built around Venetian shopping habits at Ca' Pesaro, Museo di Storia Naturale and Palazzo Mocenigo – and you can see how that might happen, with museum-quality works at local artisans' studios.

➡ **Hideouts** When Venetians shirk work, they bask in the sun at Campo San Giacomo dell'Orio, play board games at Osteria da Filo, take the kids to Museo di Storia Naturale or watch movie marathons at Casa del Cinema.

➡ **Cicheti central** Ringing the Rialto are authentic *bacari* (bars) offering inventive Venetian bites, best devoured standing with top-notch *ombre* (half-glasses of wine) at All'Arco, ProntoPesce, Dai Zemei, Al Mercà, Al Pesador and Muro.

➡ **Musical accompaniment** Listen to romantic music in an actual pleasure palace at Palazetto Bru Zane, opera among Tiepolos at Scuola Grande di San Giovanni Evangelista, live folk-rock acts around Campo San Giacomo dell'Orio, Gregorian chants at Scuola Grande di San Rocco and summertime concerts at the Summer Arena.

Getting There & Away

➡ **Vaporetto** Most *vaporetti* call at Piazzale Roma or Ferrovia at the northwest corner of Santa Croce. In San Polo, the Rialto stop is serviced by lines 1, 4 and N. Line 1 also calls at Riva de Biasio, San Stae (the N stops here too), San Silvestro and San Tomà (the N stops here as well). The Rialto-Mercato stop (line 1) is in use during the day only.

TOP SIGHT
SCUOLA GRANDE DI SAN ROCCO

You'll swear the paint is still fresh on the 50 action-packed Tintorettos completed from 1575 and 1587 for the Scuola Grande di San Rocco, dedicated to the patron saint of the plague-stricken. While the 1575–77 plague claimed one-third of Venice's residents, Tintoretto painted nail-biting scenes of looming despair and last-minute redemption, illuminating a survivor's struggle with breathtaking urgency.

Assembly Hall

Downstairs, the assembly hall contains a handful of works on easels by Venetian A-list artists including Titian, Giorgione and Tiepolo. But Tintoretto steals the scene with the story of the Virgin Mary, starting on the left wall with *Annunciation* (pictured), where the angel sneaks up on Mary at her sewing through a broken door. Tintoretto shows a light touch in *Presentation at the Temple*, where the infant Mary is steadied on her feet by a cheerleading cherub.

Tintoretto's Virgin cycle ends with *Ascension* opposite; it's a dark and cataclysmic work, compared with Titian's glowing version at I Frari. **Gregorian chant concerts** are occasionally performed here (ask at the counter), and you can practically hear their echoes in Tintoretto's haunting paintings.

Sala Grande Superiore

Take the grand **Scarpagnino staircase** to the Sala Grande Superiore, where you may be seized with a powerful instinct to duck, given all the action in the **Old Testament ceiling scenes** – you can almost hear the *swoop!* overhead

DON'T MISS...

➡ *Ascension*
➡ Scarpagnino staircase
➡ *Elijah Fed by an Angel*
➡ New Testament wall scenes
➡ Francesco Pianta's sculpture of Tintoretto
➡ *St Roch in Glory* ceiling

PRACTICALITIES

➡ Map p314
➡ ☎041 523 48 64
➡ www.scuolagrande sanrocco.it
➡ Campo San Rocco 3052, San Polo
➡ adult €8, incl Scuola Grande dei Carmini €12
➡ ⊙9.30am-5.30pm, Tesoro to 5.15pm
➡ ⍌San Tomà

AN INTERFAITH EFFORT AGAINST THE PLAGUE

While the Black Death ravaged the rest of Europe, Venice mounted an interfaith effort against it. The city dedicated a church and *scuola* (religious confraternity) to San Rocco where Venetians could pray for deliverance from the disease, while also consulting resident Jewish and Muslim doctors about prevention measures. Venice established the world's first quarantine, with inspections and 40-day waiting periods for incoming ships at Lazaretto. Venice's forward-thinking, inclusive approach created artistic masterpieces that provide comfort to the afflicted and bereaved to this day, and set a public-health standard that has saved countless lives down the centuries.

as an angel dives to feed ailing Elijah. Grab a mirror to avoid the otherwise inevitable neck strain as you follow dramatic, super-heroic gestures through these ceiling panels. Mercy from above is a recurring theme, with Daniel's salvation by angels, the miraculous fall of manna in the desert, and Elisha distributing bread to the hungry.

Tintoretto's **New Testament wall scenes** read like a modern graphic novel, with eerie lightning-bolt illumination striking his protagonists against the backdrop of the Black Death. Scenes from Christ's life aren't in chronological order: birth and baptism are followed by resurrection. The drama builds as background characters disappear into increasingly dark canvases, until an X-shaped black void looms at the centre of *Agony in the Garden* – a painting marked like a house doomed by plague contamination, with only a glimmer of light on a still-distant horizon.

When Tintoretto painted these scenes, Venice's outlook was grim indeed: the plague had just taken 50,000 Venetians, including the great colourist Titian, and the cause of and cure for the bubonic plague would not be discovered for centuries. By focusing his talents on dynamic lines instead of Titianesque colour, Tintoretto creates a shockingly modern, moving parable for epidemics through the ages. A portrait of the artist with his paintbrushes is captured in Francesco Pianta's recently restored 17th-century carved-wood sculpture, third from the right beneath Tintoretto's New Testament masterpieces.

Sala Albergo

The New Testament cycle ends with the *Crucifixion* in the Sala Albergo, where things suddenly begin to look up – literally. Every Venetian artist who'd survived the plague wanted the commission to paint this building, so Tintoretto cheated a little: instead of producing sketches like his rival Paolo Veronese, he painted a magnificent *tondo* (ceiling panel) and dedicated it to the saint, knowing that such a gift couldn't be refused, or matched by other artists.

The Sala Albergo is crowned by Tintoretto's newly restored *St Roch in Glory*, surrounded by representations of the four seasons and the saving graces of Felicity, Generosity, Faith and Hope. The angels are panting from their efforts at salvation, and feeble Hope is propped up on one elbow – still reeling from the tragedy of the Black Death, but miraculously alive. Now you see why no other artist stood a chance.

Tesoro

After a century of closure, the Scuola's Tesoro (Treasury) is open to visitors. Through a side door

SESTIERI DI SAN POLO & SANTA CROCE SCUOLA GRANDE DI SAN ROCCO

> ### SAN ROCCO: PATRON SAINT OF THE PLAGUE-STRICKEN
>
> In 1315, 20-year-old St Roch (aka San Rocco) began wandering southern France and northern Italy helping plague victims. Despite frequent exposure to contagion, he miraculously survived to continue his humanitarian work until his death at age 32. His body was transferred to Venice as a plague-prevention talisman in 1485.

in the Sala Superiore, climb to the landing to see unexpected multicultural marvels, including 13th-century lustreware from Iran and a 1720–27 chinoiserie tea set. Upstairs, pass through heavy bolted doors to see the jewel of San Rocco: an enchanting candlestick made from a branch of coral.

Architecture

Tintoretto's indoor fireworks are a near-impossible act to follow, but Scarpagnino's uplifting, proto-baroque facade puts a brave face on the confraternity. Veined marble frames the windows and doors, figures lean out from atop the capitals to greet visitors, and flowering garlands around pillars provided welcome signs of life after the plague. Bartolomeo Bon began the *scuola* in 1517, and at least three other architects were called in to finish the work by 1588.

TOP SIGHT I FRARI (CHIESA DI SANTA MARIA GLORIOSA DEI FRARI)

As you've no doubt heard, there's a Titian – make that *the* Titian – altarpiece at I Frari. But the 14th-century Italian-brick Gothic cathedral is itself a towering achievement, with intricate marquetry choir stalls, a rare Bellini, and a creepy Longhena funeral monument. While Canova's white-marble tomb seems permanently moonlit, Titian's *Assunta* seems to shed its own sunlight.

Assunta

Like moths to an eternal flame, visitors are inexorably drawn to the front of this cavernous, dimly lit Gothic church by a small altarpiece that seems to glow from within. This is Titian's 1518 *Assunta* (Ascension), capturing the split second the radiant Madonna reaches heavenward, finds her footing on a cloud, and escapes this mortal coil in a dramatic swirl of Titian-red robes. According to local lore, a glimpse of the Madonna's wrist slipping from her cloak has led monks to recant their vows over the centuries.

Both inside and outside the painting, onlookers gasp and point at the sight: with careful 2012 restoration by Save Venice, the Assunta Madonna is positively glowing. Titian outdid himself here, upstaging his own **1526 Pesaro altarpiece** – a dreamlike composite family portrait of the Holy Family with the Venetian Pesaro family.

Other Masterpieces

As though this weren't quite enough artistic achievement for one church or planet, there's puzzlework marquetry worthy of MC Escher in the **coro** (choir stalls), Bellini's

DON'T MISS...

→ Titian's *Assunta*
→ Titian's Pesaro altarpiece
→ Coro
→ Bellini's *Madonna with Child*
→ Vivarini's *St Mark Enthroned*

PRACTICALITIES

→ Basilica di Santa Maria Gloriosa dei Frari
→ Map p314
→ www.chorusvenezia.org
→ Campo dei Frari 3004, San Polo
→ adult/reduced €3/1.50
→ ⊘9am-6pm Mon-Sat, 1-6pm Sun, last admittance 5.30pm
→ 🚤San Tomà

achingly sweet and startlingly 3D *Madonna with Child* triptych in the **sacristy**, and Bartolomeo's *St Mark Enthroned*, showing the fluffy-bearded saint serenaded by an angelic orchestra in the **Capella Corner**.

In the middle of the nave, Baldassare Longhena's eerie **Doge Pesaro funereal monument** is hoisted by four burly, black-marble figures bursting from ragged white clothes like Invisible Hulks. Bringing up the rear are disconsolate mourners dabbing at their eyes with the hems of their cloaks on Canova's marble **pyramid mausoleum**, which he originally intended as a monument to Titian. The great painter was lost to the plague at 90 in 1576, but legend has it that, in light of his contributions here, Venice's strict rules of quarantine were bent to allow Titian's burial near his masterpiece.

Architecture

Built for the Franciscans in the 14th and 15th centuries, of modest brick rather than stone, the Frari has none of the flying buttresses, pinnacles and gargoyles typical of international Gothic – but its vaulted ceilings and broad, triple-nave, Latin-cross floor plan give this cathedral a grandeur befitting its art masterpieces.

The facade facing the canal has delicate scalloping under the roofline, contrasting red-and-white mouldings around windows and arches, and a repeating circle motif of *oculi* (porthole windows) around a high rosette window. The tall bell tower has managed to remain upright since 1386 – a rare feat, given the shifting *barene* (shoals) of Venice – and its bell-ringer still takes to the task with zeal when it's time for Mass.

NOT ALLOWED

....

Note that no phones, cameras or food are allowed in the church, and appropriate dress is required.

SESTIERI DI SAN POLO & SANTA CROCE | FRARI

⊙ SIGHTS

SCUOLA GRANDE DI SAN ROCCO   MUSEUM
See p101.

I FRARI (CHIESA DI SANTA
MARIA GLORIOSA DEO FRARI)   CHURCH
See p104.

MUSEO DI STORIA
NATURALE DI VENEZIA   MUSEUM
(Fondaco dei Turchi; Map p314; ✆041 275 02 06; http://msn.visitmuve.it; Salizada del Fontego dei Turchi 1730, Santa Croce; adult/reduced €8/5.50, or with Museum Pass; ☺10am-6pm Tue-Sun, to 5pm Tue-Fri Nov-May; ⛴San Stae) Never mind the doge: insatiable curiosity rules Venice, and inside the Museo di Storia Naturale (Museum of Natural History) it runs wild. The adventure begins upstairs with dinosaurs, then dashes through evolution to Venice's great age of exploration, when adventurers like Marco Polo fetched peculiar specimens from distant lands. Around every turn, scientific marvels await discovery in luminous new exhibits.

The obvious stars of the *museo* are the spotlit dinosaurs, including a terrifying ouransaurus from the Sahara and a psittacosaurus mongoliensis, a 120-million-year-old baby-dinosaur skeleton from the Gobi Desert. But the curators and designers of the museum's stunning new exhibits steal the show, leading visitors through evolution with a trail of dinosaur footprints and into galleries that follow the tracks of Venetian explorers. In hot pursuit of ancient legends from mummies to headhunters, macabre colonial trophies like elephant's feet, and circus-sideshow curiosities including a two-headed goat, Venetian explorers like Giuseppe Reali and Giancarlo Ligabue stumbled across wondrous scientific specimens.

As you might expect from this lagoon city, the marine-biology exhibits are especially breathtaking. The most startling ceiling in Venice isn't a salon Tiepolo fresco but the *museo*'s 19th-century *wunderkammer* (cabinet of curiosities), covered with shark jaws, poisonous blowfish and other outrageous sea creatures. Corals and starfish fill glass columns in the glowing tidepool chamber, leading into a marine-blue room with deep-sea specimens encased in glass bubbles. This undersea journey is accompanied by a spooky soundtrack that brings to mind whale-song recordings and Philip Glass.

The museum's grand finale downstairs is comparatively anti-climatic: a fish tank of Venetian coastal specimens bubbling for attention. Still, don't miss a close-up glimpse of the enormous dugout canoe moored at the water door – an unexpected sight for *vaporetto* riders along the Grand Canal.

Alongside the exit staircase you'll notice charming marble heraldic symbols of kissing doves and knotted-tail dogs, dating from the building's history as a ducal palace and international trading house. The dukes of Ferrara had the run of this 12th-century mansion until they were elbowed aside in 1621 to make room for Venice's most important trading partner: Turkey. Turkish merchants were a constant in Venice throughout the maritime powers' rocky romance, celebrated with favoured-nation trading status and inter-Adriatic weddings, and tested by periodic acts of piracy, invasion and looting.

Dubbed the Fondaco dei Turchi (Turkish Trading House), this building remained rented out to the Turks until 1858. Afterwards, a disastrous renovation indulged 19th-century architectural fancies, including odd crenellations that made the gracious Gothic building resemble a prison. Luckily, the renovation spared the courtyard and charming back garden, which is open during museum hours and ideal for picnics.

PALAZZO MOCENIGO   MUSEUM
(Map p314; ✆041 72 17 98; http://mocenigo.visitmuve.it; Salizada di San Stae 1992, Santa Croce; adult/reduced €5/3.50, or with Museum Pass; ☺10am-5pm Tue-Sun Apr-Oct, to 4pm Nov-Mar; ⛴San Stae) Hello, gorgeous: from 18th-century duchess *andrienne* (hip-extending dresses) to Anne Hathaway's mega-ruffled Versace Venice Film Festival ballgown, Palazzo Mocenigo's historic, head-turning fashion will leave you feeling glamorous by association, if a tad underdressed. Necklines plunge in the **Red Living Room**, lethal corsets come undone in the **Contessa's Bedroom** and men's paisley knee-breeches reveal leg in the **Dining Room**.

Costume dramas unfold across the piano nobile of the Mocenigo family's swanky Grand Canal palace, much as they did at 18th-century A-list Venetian parties held here. Yet even when flirting shamelessly under Jacopo Guarana's 1787 *Allegory of Nuptial Bliss* ceiling in the Green Living Room, wise guests minded their tongues:

the Mocenigos reported philosopher and sometime houseguest Giordano Bruno for heresy to the Inquisition, who subsequently tortured and burned the betrayed philosopher at the stake in Rome.

PONTE DI RIALTO · BRIDGE
(Map p314; ⛴Rialto-Mercato) A superb feat of engineering, Antonio da Ponte's 1592 Istrian stone span cost 250,000 gold ducats to construct – a staggering sum that puts Calatrava Bridge cost overruns into perspective. When crowds of shutterbugs clear out around sunset, the bridge's south side offers a romantic view of black gondolas pulling up to golden Grand Canal *palazzi* at striped moorings.

FONDAZIONE PRADA · MUSEUM
(Ca' Corner; Map p314; ☎041 810 91 61; www.fondazioneprada.org; Calle de Ca' Corner 2215, Santa Croce; adult/reduced €10/free; ◷10am-6pm Wed-Mon during exhibitions; ⛴San Stae) This stately Grand Canal palace has been commandeered by Fondazione Prada, but you won't necessarily find handbags here. Instead Ca' Corner showcases the art and avant-garde design that have shaped modern visual sensibilities, from Fortunato Depero's fragmented Futurist suits to Andy Warhol's Brillo boxes. Rotating multimedia shows are imaginative and exhaustive, though one visiting dachshund critic yawned audibly at early video art.

CA' PESARO · MUSEUM
(Galleria Internazionale d'Arte Moderna e Museo d'Arte Orientale; Map p314; ☎041 72 11 27; www.visitmuve.it; Fondamenta di Ca' Pesaro 2070, Santa Croce; adult/reduced €8/5.50, or with Museum Pass; ◷10am-6pm Tue-Sun Apr-Oct, to 5pm Nov-Mar; ⛴San Stae) Like a Carnevale costume built for two, the stately exterior of this Baldassare Longhena–designed 1710 *palazzo* hides two quirky museums: **Galleria Internazionale d'Arte Moderna** and **Museo d'Arte Orientale**. Galleria d'Arte Moderna covers three floors and highlights Venice's role in modern-art history, while the attic holds treasures from Prince Enrico di Borbone's epic 1887–89 souvenir-shopping spree across Asia.

Galleria Internazionale d'Arte Moderna begins with flag-waving early Biennales, showcasing Venetian landscapes and Venetian socialites by Venetian painters (notably Giacomo Favretto) and Luigi Nono's Italian social realism. Savvy Venice Biennale

TOUR THE ULTIMATE WALK-IN CLOSET

Fashion alert: by popular demand, Palazzo Mocenigo (p106) now opens its secret attic storeroom the last Friday of every month for fascinating tours through fashion history. Costume historians lead up to 15 people into the ultimate walk-in closet, and open cupboards to reveal 1700s cleavage-revealing, nude-coloured silk gowns, men's 1600s embroidered peacock frock-coats with exaggerated hips, and other daring fashions too delicate for permanent display. Reserve ahead for 11am and 2pm tours in Italian and English (☎041 270 03 70; admission €12).

organisers soon diversified, showcasing Gustav Klimt's 1909 *Judith II (Salome)* and Marc Chagall's *Rabbi of Vitebsk* (1914–22). The 1961 De Lisi Bequest added Kandinskys and Morandis to the modernist mix of de Chiricos, Mirós and Moores, plus radical abstracts by postwar Venetian artists Giuseppe Santomaso and Emilio Vedova. Second-floor temporary exhibits are variable but often upstaged by sweeping Grand Canal views.

Climb the creaky attic stairs of the Museo d'Arte Orientale past a phalanx of samurai warriors, guarding a princely collection of Asian travel souvenirs. Prince Enrico di Borbone reached Japan when Edo art was discounted in favour of modern Meiji, and Edo-era netsukes, screens and a lacquerware palanquin are standouts in his collection of 30,000 objets d'art. The collection has been left much as it was organised in 1928, with a rotating selection of vintage curio cabinet displays covered to prevent light damage.

CHIESA DI SAN GIACOMO DELL'ORIO · CHURCH
(Map p314; www.chorusvenezia.org; Campo San Giacomo dell'Orio 1457, Santa Croce; admission €3, or with Chorus Pass; ◷10am-5pm Mon-Sat; ⛴Riva de Biasio) La Serenissima seems serene as ever inside the cool gloom of this Romanesque church, founded in the 9th to 10th centuries and completed in Latin-cross form by 1225 with chapels bubbling along the edges. Notable 14th- to 18th-century

artworks include luminous **sacristy paintings** by Palma Il Giovane, a rare Lorenzo Lotto *Madonna with Child and Saints*, and an exceptional Veronese crucifix (currently undergoing restoration).

Don't miss Gaetano Zompini's macabre *Miracle of the Virgin*, which shows a rabble-rouser rudely interrupting the Virgin's funeral procession, only to have his hands miraculously fall off when he touches her coffin. Architectural quirks include decorative pillars, a 14th-century **carena di nave (ship's keel) ceiling** and a Lombard pulpit perched atop a 6th-century Byzantine green-marble column.

CHIESA DI SAN GIOVANNI ELEMOSINARIO
CHURCH

(Map p314; Ruga Vecchia di San Giovanni 477, San Polo; admission €3, or with Chorus Pass; ◷10am-5pm Mon-Sat, 1-5pm Sun; ◉Rialto-Mercato) Hunkering modestly behind skimpy T-shirt kiosks is this soaring Renaissance brick church, built by Scarpagnino after a disastrous fire in 1514 destroyed much of the Rialto area. Cross the darkened threshold to witness flashes of Renaissance genius: Titian's tender *St John the Almsgiver*

(freshly restored and returned from the Accademia) and gloriously restored dome frescoes of frolicking angels by Pordenone.

IL GOBBO
MONUMENT

(Map p314; ◉Rialto-Mercato) Rubbed for luck for centuries, the 1541 statue *Il Gobbo* (The Hunchback) is now protected by an iron railing. *Il Gobbo* served as a podium for official proclamations and punishments: those guilty of misdemeanours were forced to run a gauntlet of jeering citizens from Piazza San Marco to the Rialto. The minute they touched *Il Gobbo*, their punishment was complete.

SCUOLA GRANDE DI SAN GIOVANNI EVANGELISTA
HISTORIC BUILDING

(Map p314; ☏041 71 82 34; www.scuolasangio vanni.it; Campiello della Scuola 2454, San Polo; admission €5; ◷vary, check website; ◉Ferrovia) Flagellants founded this confraternity in 1261, and it served as social club to the Council of Ten, Venice's dreaded secret service. Political power had obvious perks: Pietro Lombardo's 1481 triumphal entry arch, a Codussi-designed double staircase, and a 1729 1st-floor meeting hall designed by Giorgio Massari and decorated by Gian-

---

TOP SIGHT
RIALTO MARKET

Restaurants worldwide are catching on to a secret that this market has loudly touted for 700 years: food tastes better when it's fresh, seasonal and local. Before there was a bridge at the Rialto or palaces along the Grand Canal, there was a Pescaria (fish market) and a produce market. So loyal are locals to their market that recent talk of opening a larger, more convenient mainland fish market was swiftly crushed.

More vital to Venetian cuisine than any top chef are Pescaria fishmongers, calling out today's catch: glistening mountains of *moscardini* (baby octopus), crabs ranging from tiny *moeche* (soft-shell crabs) to *granseole* (spider crabs) and inky *seppie* (cuttlefish) of all sizes. Sustainable fishing practices are not a new idea at the Pescaria; marble plaques show regulations set centuries ago for the minimum allowable sizes for lagoon fish. Note the line-caught lagoon seafood here, and you'll recognise tasty, sustainable options on dinner menus.

Compared with supermarket specimens, Veneto veggies look like they landed from another planet. Tiny purplish Sant'Erasmo *castraure* (baby artichokes) look like alien heads and white Bassano asparagus seems to have sprouted on the moon. *Buon appetito!*

DON'T MISS...

➡ Lagoon seafood displays

➡ Chanted boasts about local produce at bargain prices

➡ Produce barges by Grand Canal docks

➡ Veneto speciality produce

➡ Seasonal fruit

PRACTICALITIES

➡ Map p314

➡ ☏041 296 06 58

➡ ◷7am-2pm, Pescaria closed Mon

➡ ◉Rialto-Mercato

THE OTHER RIALTO MARKET: PONTE DELLE TETTE

No one remembers the original name of **Ponte delle Tette** (Map p314; ♿San Silvestro), known since the 15th century as 'Tits Bridge'. Back in those days, shadowy porticos around this bridge sheltered a designated red-light zone where neighbourhood prostitutes were encouraged to display their wares in windows instead of taking their marketing campaigns to the streets in their platform shoes. Between clients, the most ambitious working girls might be found studying: for educated conversation, *cortigiane* (courtesans) might charge 60 times the going rates for basic services from average prostitutes.

Church authorities and French dignitaries repeatedly professed dismay at Venice's lax attitudes towards prostitution, but Venice's idea of a crackdown was to prevent women prostitutes from luring clients by cross-dressing (aka false advertising) and to ban prostitutes from riding in two-oared boats – lucky that gondolas only require one oar. Fees were set by the state and posted in Rialto brothels (soap cost extra), and the rates of high-end *cortigiane* were published In catalogues extolling their various merits. The height of platform shoes was limited to a staggering 30cm by sumptuary laws intended to distinguish socialites from *cortigiane*, with little success.

domenico Tiepolo, who was obliged to finish contracts begun by his father.

Bellini and Titian turned out world-class works for the *scuola* that have since been moved to the Gallerie dell'Accademia – but Palma Il Giovane's works still illuminate the Sala d'Albergo, and Pietro Longhi's wriggling baby Jesus is magnetic in *Adoration of the Wise Men*. The confraternity was suppressed by Napoleon, and today the *scuola* hosts conferences and concerts, and opens occasionally to the public during the day.

If you get the chance to visit, ask at the front desk to look inside the chapel across the street. The deconsecrated Chiesa di San Giovanni Evangelista has a Tintoretto *Crucifixion*, and the adjoining private chapel founded by the Badoer family in 970 features Pietro Vecchia's painting of St John the Evangelist holding a pen, eagerly awaiting dictation from God.

CHIESA DI SAN POLO
CHURCH

(Map p314; www.chorusvenezia.org; Campo San Polo 2118, San Polo; admission €3, or with Chorus Pass; ⊙10am-5pm Mon-Sat; ♿San Tomà) Travellers pass this modest 9th-century Byzantine brick church without guessing that major dramas unfold inside. Under the **carena di nave ceiling**, Tintoretto's *Last Supper* shows apostles alarmed by Jesus' announcement that one of them will betray him. Giandomenico Tiepolo's *Stations of the Cross* **sacristy** cycle shows onlookers tormenting Jesus, who leaps triumphantly from his tomb in the ceiling panel.

CHIESA DI SAN STAE
CHURCH

(Map p314; www.chorusvenezia.org; Campo San Stae 1981, Santa Croce; admission €3, or with Chorus Pass; ⊙2-5pm Mon-Sat; ♿San Stae) English painter William Turner painted San Stae obsessively, capturing early-morning Grand Canal mists swirling around the angels gracing its Palladian facade. The church was founded in 966 but finished in 1709, and though the interiors are surprisingly spare for a baroque edifice, Giambattista Tiepolo's *The Martyrdom of St Bartholomew* and Sebastiano Ricci's *The Liberation of St Peter* are grace notes.

CHIESA DI SAN ROCCO
CHURCH

(Map p314; ☎041 523 48 64; Campo San Rocco 3053, San Polo; ⊙8am-12.30pm & 3-5.30pm Mon-Sat; ♿San Tomà) **FREE** Originally built by Bartolomeo Bon in 1489–1508, this church got a baroque facelift in 1765–71 with a grand portal flanked by Giovanni Marchiori statues. Bon's rose window was moved to the side of the church, near Bon's original side door. Inside the church's Sala dell'Albergo are a couple of comparatively quiet Tintorettos, including *San Rocco Healing the Animals*.

CASA DI GOLDONI
MUSEUM

(Map p314; ☎041 275 93 25; www.visitmuve.it; Calle dei Nomboli 2794, San Polo; adult/reduced €5/3.50, or with Museum Pass; ⊙10am-5pm Thu-Tue Apr-Oct, to 4pm Nov-Mar; ♿San Tomà) Venetian playwright Carlo Goldoni (1707–93) mastered second and third acts: he was a doctor's apprentice before switching to law, which proved handy when an *opera buffa*

Secrets of the Calli

Yellow signs point the way to major sights, but the secret to any Venetian adventure is: *ignore them*. That *calle* (backstreet) behind the thoroughfare leads to a world of artisan studios, backstreet *bacari* (bars) and hidden *campi* (squares).

Campo San Polo to San Giacomo dell'Orio

Take Calle del Scalater past artisan studios to hidden Campiello Sant'Agostin for draught beer and dramatic glass jewellery; cross the bridge to join happy hour and tag games alongside medieval San Giacomo dell'Orio.

San Zaccaria to Chiesa di Santa Maria dei Miracoli

Head north of San Marco past chatty Campo Santa Maria Formosa for *cicheti* (Venetian tapas) in Campo Santa Marina, or Venetian designers and antiques alongside the chapel.

Rialto Market to Museo di Storia Naturale

Gather picnic supplies at Rialto Market, then *campo*-hop from nearby Campo delle Beccarie through sunny Campo San Cassian to artisan studio–ringed Campo Santa Maria Domini; then follow wiggling, sometimes shoulder-width *calli* to Museo di Storia Naturale for your garden picnic.

Chiesa della Madonna dell'Orto to the Ghetto

Cannaregio calm restores overloaded senses as you pass sculptures flanking Campo dei Mori, stroll sunny Fondamente della Misericordia and Ormesini, and reach bridges leading into the historic Ghetto.

Chiesa di San Sebastian to I Frari

Follow bargain *osterie* (taverns) along Calle Lunga San Barnaba to its bustling namesake *campo*, where Calle delle Botteghe leads past antiques, ceramics, shawls and chocolates to Titian's masterpiece.

1. Sestiere di Castello laneway 2. Calle Larga, Sestiere di Santa Croce 3. Campo Santa Maria Formosa

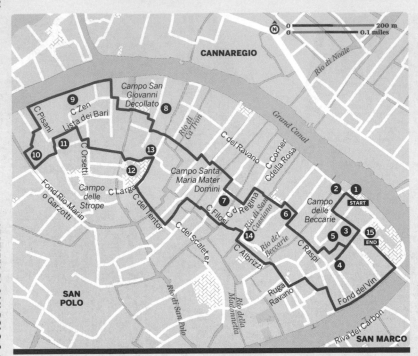

🏃 Neighbourhood Walk
Venice Gourmet Crawl

START RIALTO MARKET
END AL MERCÀ
DISTANCE 3.5KM
DURATION TWO HOURS, NOT INCLUDING STOPS

A trip through gourmet history starts where great Venetian meals have begun for centuries: **1 Rialto Market** (p108). Under the roof of the **2 Pescaria**, fishmongers artfully arrange the day's catch atop hillocks of ice.

Around the corner, glimpse the trade-route treasures that made Venice's fortune at **3 Drogheria Mascari** (p119), with pyramids of spices filling shop windows. Down the road, the tantalising displays of *sopressa* (soft salami), San Daniele hams, and Taleggio cheese-wheels at **4 Aliani** (p115) remind you that Veneto's culinary fame wasn't built on seafood and imported spices alone. Duck into **5 All'Arco** (p113) for the city's best *cicheti* – ask for *una fantasia* (a fantasy), and father-son chefs Francesco and Matteo will invent a dish with ingredients you just saw at the market.

WAnder northwest to **6 Cárte** (p117) to browse recipe albums and cocktail rings in lagoon-rippled marble paper, and over a couple of bridges until you smell the ink drying on letterpress menus (also sold blank for dinner parties) at **7 Veneziastampa** (p119).

Continue to **8 Museo di Storia Naturale** (p106). Walk a sunny stretch of Grand Canal along **9 Riva de Biasio**, allegedly named for 16th-century butcher Biagio (Biasio) Cargnio, whose sausages contained a special ingredient: children. When found out, Biasio was drawn and quartered.

You'll be glad to hear there's a restaurant nearby, **10 Tearoom Caffè Orientale** (p113), where speciality teas are served with excellent inhouse pastries. Leave room for organic roasted-pistachio gelato at **11 Alaska** (p113). Over in **12 Campo San Giacomo dell'Orio**, natural-process *prosecco* awaits at **13 Al Prosecco** (p115) – but don't be late for dinner at **14 Antiche Carampane** (p114). The end of your tour deserves a toast along the Grand Canal with DOC wines from **15 Al Mercà** (p116).

(comic opera) didn't sell. But as the 1st-floor display at his birthplace explains (in Italian), Goldoni had the last laugh with his social satires. Highlights include an **18th-century puppet theatre** and occasional **performances** on site.

EATING

ALL'ARCO
VENETIAN €

(Map p314; ☑041 520 56 66; Calle dell'Ochialer 436; cicheti €1.50-4; ☺8am-3.30pm Mon-Sat, plus 6-9pm Apr-Oct, closed Jul & Aug; ☒Rialto-Mercato) Father-son *maestri* Francesco and Matteo invent Venice's best *cicheti* daily with Rialto Market finds. Behind the marble counters, Francesco wraps poached Bassano white asparagus with seasoned pancetta, while Matteo creates *otrega* (butterfish) *crudo* (Venetian-style sushi) with mint–olive oil marinade and Hawaiian red-clay salt. Be patient: even with copious *prosecco,* hardly any meal here tops €20 or falls short of five stars.

★ALASKA GELATERIA
GELATO €

(Map p314; ☑041 71 52 11; Calle Larga dei Bari 1159, Santa Croce; gelati €1-2; ☺noon-8pm; 🖪; ☒Riva de Biasio) 🍴 Outlandish organic artisanal gelato: enjoy a Slow Food scoop of house-roasted local pistachio, or two of the tangy Sicilian lemon with vaguely minty Sant'Erasmo *carciofi*. Even vegans are spoiled for choice of flavours, including watermelon and rose. Kids who choose strawberry *granita* (shaved ice) can top the confection with a leaf plucked from the basil plant on the counter.

PRONTOPESCE
SEAFOOD, CICHETI BAR €

(Map p314; ☑041 822 02 98; www.prontopesce. it; Rialto Pescheria 319, San Polo; cicheti €3-8; ☺9am-2.45pm & 7-11.30pm Tue-Sat; ☒Rialto-Mercato) Alongside Venice's fish market, this designer deli serves artfully composed *crudi*, well-dressed seafood salads, legendary Saturday-only fish risotto (served at 1pm exactly) and superb shellfish stews in winter. Grab a stool and a (unfortunately) plastic glass of DOC soave with *folpetti* (baby octopus) salad and plump prawn *crudi*, or enjoy yours dockside along the Grand Canal.

DAI ZEMEI
VENETIAN, CICHETI BAR €

(Map p314; ☑041 520 85 46; www.ostariadaize mei.it; Ruga Vecchia San Giovanni 1045, San Polo;

cicheti €1.50-4; ☺9am-8pm Wed-Mon; ☒San Silvestro) The *zemei* (twins) who run this closet-sized *cicheti* counter serve loyal regulars and well-informed foodie tourists small meals with outsized imagination: octopus salad with marinated rocket, duck breast drizzled with truffle oil, or *crostini* (toast) loaded with tuna-leek salad. A gourmet bargain for inspired bites and DOC/IGT wine pairings – try floral Ribolla Gialla or sophisticated Valpolicella.

SACRO E PROFANO
ITALIAN €

(Map p314; ☑041 523 79 24; Ramo Terzo del Parangon 502, San Polo; meals €15-25; ☺11.30am-1pm & 6.30pm-1am Mon-Tue & Thu-Sat, 11.30am-2pm Sun; ☒Rialto-Mercato) Musicians, artists and philosophising regulars make this hideaway under the Rialto exceptionally good for eavesdropping – but once that handmade gnocchi or spaghetti *alla búsara* (Venetian prawn sauce) arrives, all talk is reduced to satisfied murmurs. The place is run by a Venetian ska-band leader, which explains the trumpets on the wall and the upbeat, arty scene.

SNACK BAR AI NOMBOLI
PANINI €

(Map p314; ☑041 523 09 95; Rio Terà dei Nomboli 271c, San Polo; sandwiches €2-6; ☺9am-8.30pm Mon-Sat; ☒San Tomà) A snappy Venetian comeback to McDonald's: crusty rolls packed with local cheeses, fresh greens, roast vegetables, salami, prosciutto and roast beef, served at an antique marble lunch counter. Beyond standard mayo, condiments range from spicy mustard to wild nettle sauce. Two panini make a filling, tasty lunch for €4 to €5; three is a feast deserving of a glass of Brunello.

PASTICCERIA RIZZARDINI
PASTRIES & CAKES €

(Map p314; ☑041 522 38 35; Campiello dei Meloni 1415, San Polo; pastries €1-3.50; ☺7.30am-8pm Wed-Mon; ☒San Silvestro) 'From 1742' boasts this corner bakery, whose reputation for *krapfen* (cream puffs), strudel and doughnuts has survived many an *acqua alta* – waters bailed from the store are preserved in bottles above the bar. Stop by any time for reliable espresso, *spritz* and *pallone di Casanova* (Casanova's balls) biscuits – but act fast if you want that last slice of tiramisu.

TEAROOM CAFFÈ ORIENTALE
VEGETARIAN, PASTRIES & CAKES €

(Map p317; ☑041 520 17 89; Rio Marin 888, Santa Croce; meals €6-12; ☺noon-9pm Fri-Wed; 🖊;

Riva de Biasio) Detour from tourist-trail espresso bars and seafood restaurants to this art-filled canalside tearoom, which offers vegetarian delights ranging from asparagus-studded quiches to hearty bean soups. Baked goods are made in-house with extra-fluffy, high-protein Italian '00' flour, so after that whisper-light apple crumble, you'll be raring to tackle the museums.

FRITTO E FRUTTA   SNACKS, JUICE BAR €

(Map p317; 041 524 68 52; Fondamenta dei Tolentini 220, Santa Croce; noon-10pm Mon-Sat; Piazzale Roma) Venice offers indulgence and redemption at Fritto e Frutta, a juice bar with an infrared deep fryer. Strict vegans, picky kids, commuters and barflies converge at this counter for Venice's lightest *fritture* – flash-fried bites of fresh seafood and/or vegetables – and smoothies custom-frothed into liquid meals. *Fritture* are served in paper cones ranging from dainty to family size (€3.50 to €6).

OSTERIA MOCENIGO   VENETIAN €

(Map p314; 041 523 17 03; Salizada San Stae 1919, Santa Croce; meals €15-25; noon-2.30pm & 7-10pm Tue-Sun; San Stae) Times and dining habits have changed since dogi strained waistcoat buttons at neighbouring Palazzo Mocenigo: Osteria Mocenigo offers light meals of *cicheti* at the bar (including upstanding *sarde in saor*), casual lunches of homemade ravioli with radicchio and whitefish and grilled meats for dinner. A single dish here makes a satisfying meal with Veneto wine by the glass.

ANTICA BIRRARIA DELLA CORTE   PIZZERIA €

(Map p314; 041 275 05 70; Campo San Polo 2168, San Polo; pizzas €8-13; noon-2.30pm & 6-10.30pm Mon-Fri; San Tomà) This former bullfight pen became a brewery in the 19th century to keep Venice's Austrian occupiers occupied, and beer and heritage beef remain reliable bets here. Perennial favourites include *bresaola* and rocket and buffalo-mozzarella pizzas, with German beer on tap or Italian artisan bottled brews. There's seldom a wait for indoor seating, though piazza seating is prime in summer.

LA RIVETTA   CICHETI €

(Map p317; 041 71 84 98; Calle Sechera 637a, Santa Croce; cicheti €1-3.50; 9am-9.30pm Mon-Sat; Ferrovia) Cabernet Franc comes out of a hose and platters of hearty fare are passed around at this *bacaro* (hole-in-the-

wall bar), a favourite of salty sailors and neighbourhood eccentrics. Go for mixed plates with salami, *carciofini* (marinated artichokes) and *porchetta* (roast pork) with crusty bread. Angle for canalside spots, or get comfortable inside amid bicycle parts and pre-war English gin bottles.

ANTICO PANIFICIO   PIZZERIA €

(Map p314; 041 277 09 67; Campiello del Sol 929, San Polo; pizzas €8-10; 7-11pm Wed-Mon; San Silvestro) Most Venetian pizzerias pander to tourists, but this historic spot is packed with a neighbourhood crowd – be prepared to lunge at open tables when you get the nod, or get yours to go. Basic options like pizza with sausage and/or *mozzarella di bufala* are reliably tasty, but adventurous foodies pile on anchovies, squash blossoms and other seasonal speciality toppings.

PASTICCERIA TREVISAN   PASTRIES & CAKES €

(Map p317; 041 71 85 23; Calle Sechera 636, Santa Croce; pastries €1-3; 7am-6.30pm Mon-Sat; Ferrovia) Mini-profiteroles bursting with dark-chocolate mousse and flaky croissants laced with apricot jam are perfect pick-me-ups after train rides or packaged B&B breakfasts, especially with a proper, scorching-hot Venetian *macchiatone* (an espresso liberally 'stained' with milk).

★ANTICHE CARAMPANE   VENETIAN €€

(Map p314; 041 524 01 65; www.antichecarampane.com; Rio Terà delle Carampane 1911, San Polo; meals €30-45; noon-2.30pm & 7-11pm Tue-Sat; San Stae) Hidden in the once-shady lanes behind Ponte delle Tette, this culinary indulgence is a trick to find. The sign proudly announcing 'no tourist menu' signals a welcome change: say goodbye to soggy lasagne and hello to silky, lagoon-fresh *crudi*, asparagus and *granseola* (lagoon crab) salad, cloudlike gnocchi, and San Pietro (whitefish) atop grilled *radicchio trevisano*.

OSTERIA LA ZUCCA   MODERN ITALIAN €€

(Map p314; 041 524 15 70; www.lazucca.it; Calle del Tintor 1762, Santa Croce; meals €30-45; 12.30-2.30pm & 7-10.30pm Mon-Sat; San Stae) Vegetable-centric, seasonal small plates bring Venetian spice-trade influences to local produce: zucchini with ginger zing, cinnamon-tinged pumpkin flan, and raspberry spice cake. Herbed roast lamb is respectable here too, but the island-grown produce is the breakout star. The snug

VENICE'S GOURMET CENTRAL: THE RIALTO DISTRICT

Rialto Market (p108) offers superb local produce next to the legendary **Pescaria**, Venice's 600-year-old fish market. Nearby, backstreets are lined with bakeries, *bacari* (hole-in-the-wall bars) and notable gourmet shops. Don't miss **Aliani** (Map p314; ☑041 522 49 13; Ruga Vecchia di San Giovanni, San Polo 654; ⊗8.30am-1pm & 5-7.30pm Tue-Sat; ⓢRialto Mercato), with gourmet specialities from balsamic vinegar (aged 40 years) to *bottarga* (dried fish-roe paste); **Casa del Parmigiano** (Map p314; ☑041 520 6 525; www.aliani-casadelparmigiano.it; Campo Cesare Battisti 214; ⊗8am-1.30pm Mon-Wed, to 7.30pm Thu-Sat; ⓢRialto), with cheeses ranging from fresh Dolomite goat's-milk *tomino* to potent *parmigiano reggiano* aged 18 months; and Drogheria Mascari (p119), a historic emporium lined with spices, sweets and truffles galore, with a backroom stash of speciality Italian wines. For organic edibles from baby food to biscuits plus sustainably produced wines, visit **Rialto Biocenter** (Map p314; ☑041 523 95 15; www.rialtobiocenter.it; Calle della Regina, Santa Croce 2264; ⊗8.30am-1pm & 4.30-8pm Mon-Thu, 8.30am-8pm Fri & Sat; ⓢSan Stae).

wood-panelled interior gets toasty, so reserve canalside seats in summer.

TRATTORIA DA IGNAZIO
VENETIAN, SEAFOOD €€

(Map p314; ☑041 523 48 52; www.trattoriadaignazio.com; Calle dei Saoneri 2749, San Polo; meals €25-30; ⊗noon-3pm & 7-11pm Mon-Sat; 🖪; ⓢSan Tomà) Dapper white-jacketed waiters serve pristine grilled lagoon fish, fresh pasta and desserts made in-house ('of course') with a proud flourish, on tables bedecked with yellow linens and orchids. On cloudy days, homemade crab pasta with a bright Lugana white wine make a fine substitute for sunshine. On sunny days and warm nights, the neighbourhood converges beneath the garden's grape arbour.

AL NONO RISORTO
ITALIAN, PIZZERIA €€

(Map p314; ☑041 524 11 69; Sottoportego della Siora Bettina 2338, Santa Croce; pizzas €7-9, meals €20-30; ⊗7-11pm Thu-Tue; 🖪; ⓢSan Stae) Manifesto or menu? At Al Nono Risorto, pizzas are listed alongside urgent action alerts: 'No abandoning animals!', 'More rights for gays and domestic partners!' Prices are left of centre, radical-chic servers graciously indulge petty-bourgeois pizza orders, and on sunny days, all of Venice converges on the garden for *frittura mista* (seafood fry), the bargain house *prosecco*, and cross-partisan bonding.

AL PESADOR
MODERN ITALIAN €€€

(Map p314; ☑041 523 94 92; www.alpesador.it; Campo San Giacometto 125, San Polo; cicheti €1.50-5, meals €40-55; ⊗noon-3pm & 7-11pm Mon-Sat; ⓢRialto-Mercato) Watch the world drift down the Grand Canal outside or canoodle indoors, but prepare to sit up and

pay attention once the food arrives. Pesador reinvents Venetian cuisine with culinary finesse: *cicheti* feature mackerel with balsamic-vinegar *saor* marinade and paperthin *lardo* crostini with mint oil, while *primi* (mains) include red-footed scallops kicking wild herbs across squid-ink gnocchi.

VECIO FRITOLIN
VENETIAN €€€

(Map p314; ☑041 522 28 81; www.veciofritolin.it; Calle della Regina 2262, Santa Croce; mains €45-55, tasting menu €55; ⊗noon-2.30pm & 7-10.30pm Wed-Sun, 7-10.30pm Tue; ⓢSan Stae) 🖉 Order handmade langoustine tortelloni like Italian Slow Foodies, or choose today's special with confidence – all seafood and produce here is hand selected daily from the Rialto Market, and breads and desserts are made in-house. Thursday, don't miss creative gnocchi, such as beetroot with blue cheese and nutmeg; for Rialto quayside picnics, call ahead for €10 *frittura* takeaway.

🍷 DRINKING & NIGHTLIFE

★ AL PROSECCO
WINE BAR

(Map p314; ☑041 524 02 22; www.alprosecco.com; Campo San Giacomo dell'Orio, Santa Croce 1503; ⊗9am-10.30pm Mon-Sat, to 8pm winter; ⓢSan Stae) 🖉 The urge to toast sunsets in Venice's loveliest *campo* is only natural – and so is the wine at Al Prosecco. This forward-thinking bar specialises in *vini naturi* (natural-process wines) – organic, biodynamic, wild yeast fermented – from the €3.50 unfiltered 'cloudy' *prosecco* to the silky €5 Veneto Venegazzú that

❶ GUIDED BAR CRAWLS

Why drink alone? To help visitors navigate Venice's vast *cicheti* menu and confusing backstreets, **Venice Urban Adventures** (www.urbanadvantures. com; cicheti tour €52) offers intimate tours of happy-hour hot spots led by knowledgable, enthusiastic, English-speaking local foodies. Tours cost €52 per person (with up to 12 participants), covering *ombre* and *cicheti* in five (yes, five) *bacari* and a tipsy Rialto gondola ride. Departure points vary seasonally; consult website.

trails across the tongue and lingers in the imagination.

AL MERCÀ
WINE BAR

(Map p314; ☑393 992 47 81; Campo Cesare Battisti 213, San Polo; ☉9.30am-2.30pm & 6-9pm Mon-Sat; ☒Rialto) Discerning drinkers throng this cupboard-sized bar crammed with *cicheti* and 60 different wines, including top-notch *prosecco* and DOC wines by the glass (€2 to €3.50). Arrive by 6.30pm for meatballs and mini-*panini* (€1 to €2) and easy bar access, or mingle with crowds stretching to the Grand Canal docks – there's no seating, and it's elbow room only at Venice's friendliest bar counter.

OSTERIA DA FILO
CAFE, BAR

(Hosteria alla Poppa; Map p314; ☑041 524 65 54; Calle delle Oche, Santa Croce; ☉11am-midnight Wed-Sun, from 5pm Mon & Tue; ☎; ☒Riva de Biasio) A living room where drinks are served, Hosteria alla Poppa comes complete with creaky sofas, free wi-fi, abandoned novels, and board games for marathon sessions mastering the Italian version of Risk. Service is brusque, but drinks are cheap and Mediterranean tapas tasty. Wednesday is live-music night starting around 8pm – usually it's jazz, with the owner on the drums.

CAFFÈ DEI FRARI
CAFE, BAR

(Map p314; ☑041 524 18 77; Fondamenta dei Frari 2564, San Polo; ☉8am-9pm Mon-Sat; ☒San Tomà) Take your espresso with a heaping of history at this century-old carved wooden bar, or recover from the sensory overload of I Frari with a sandwich, a glass of wine and easy conversation at the dinky indoor cafe tables downstairs or on the Liberty-style wrought-iron balcony upstairs.

MURO VINO E CUCINA
BAR

(Map p314; ☑041 241 23 39; www.murovenezia. com; Campo Bello Vienna 222, San Polo; ☉9am-3pm & 5pm-2am Mon-Sat; ☒Rialto) No velvet rope here, though it's the kind of buzzing, urban-chic place at which you'd expect to find one. The throng at Muro's sleek aluminum *cicheti* counter are on to something – no one wants to miss *sopressa* with porcini cream, or smoked goose and arugula crostini. Prices are friendly too, with wines by the glass starting at €2 and *cicheti* from €1.50 to €3.50.

★CANTINA DO SPADE
PUB

(Map p314; ☑041 521 05 83; www.cantinadospade. it; Calle delle Do Spade 860, San Polo; ☉10am-3pm & 6-10pm; ☒Rialto) Since 1488 this bar has kept Venice in good spirits, and the laid-back young management extends warm welcomes to *spritz*-sipping Venetian regulars and visiting connoisseurs drinking double-malt Dolomite beer and bargain Venetian DOC cab franc. Come early for market-fresh *fritture* (batter-fried seafood; €2 to €6) and stick around for local gossip (free).

TAVERNA DA BAFFO
OSTERIA

(Map p314; ☑041 524 20 61; www.tavernada baffo.com; Campiello Sant'Agostin 2346, Santa Croce; ☉7am-2am; ☒San Tomà) This *osteria* named for Casanova's licentious poet pal Giorgio Baffo is actually a converted chapel, stripped to its naked brick walls. With strong *spritz,* draught beer and tasty house wines, there may be impromptu poetry from the *campo* crowd by night's end. Arrive early at summer happy hours to claim outdoor tables, *bruschetta* orders and the bartender's attention.

BARCOLLO
BAR

(Map p314; ☑041 522 81 58; Campo Cesare Battista 219, San Polo; ☉5pm-midnight; ☒Rialto) Consider permission to get happy granted: *barcollo* means stagger. DJs and sass from the handlebar-mustachoied bartender put the crowd in a party mood, especially on Wednesday buffet nights that draw university students by the dozen. Prices aren't staggering – an *ombra* (half glass) of DOC wine plus snacks of *polpette* (meatballs) or fried calamari runs under €5.

AI POSTALI
BAR

(Map p314; ☑041 71 51 76; Fondamenta Rio Marin 821, Santa Croce; ☉6pm-2am Mon-Sat; ☒Ferrovia) Jazz provides a backbeat to buzzing conversation until the wee hours, and local musicians have been known to break into jam sessions around midnight. Off-duty mailmen once had the run of the marble bar – hence the name – but now the hipper half of Santa Croce vies for seats along the canal and the unconventional *spritz* served with an olive.

ANTICA OSTERIA RUGA RIALTO PUB
(Map p314; ☎041 521 12 43; Ruga Rialto 692, San Polo; ⊙6.30pm-midnight; ⛴Rialto) Seafood salads and classic *fritto misto e pattatine* (fried lagoon seafood and potatoes; Venice's answer to fish and chips) earn this *osteria* (pub) a loyal following, but drink is the common bond by night's end. The back room doubles as a gallery for local artists, and the occasional live-music set fills the narrow alleyway with revellers.

BAGOLO BAR
(Map p314; ☎041 71 75 84; Campo San Giacomo dell'Orio 584, Santa Croce; ⊙7am-midnight; ⛴Riva de Biasio) Leave it to Venice to invent a family-friendly happy-hour spot: kids play tag in the medieval *campo*, while parents recover over house *prosecco* and feed tots from big bowls of not-too-fancy pasta. Mood lighting indoors and candlelit tables outside on the *campo* rekindle the romance, with *cicheti*, cocktails and occasional live folk-rock and jazz acts.

CAFFÈ DEL DOGE CAFE
(Map p314; ☎041 522 77 87; www.caffedeldoge. com; Calle dei Cinque 609, San Polo; ⊙8.30am-8pm Mon-Sat, 9am-1pm Sun; ⛴San Silvestro) Sniff your way to the Doge, where dedicated drinkers slurp their way through the menu of speciality imported coffees from Ethiopia to Guatemala, all roasted on the premises. The decor is more laboratory than classic Venetian cafe and the looped video ad seems like hype, but these beans have earned an international following.

☆ ENTERTAINMENT

★PALAZZETTO BRU ZANE CLASSICAL MUSIC
(Centre du Musique Romantique Française; Map p314; ☎041 521 10 05; www.bru-zane.com; Palazzetto Bru Zane 2368, San Polo; adult/reduced €25/15; ⊙box office 2.30-5.30pm Mon-Fri; ⛴San Tomà) Pleasure palaces don't get more romantic than Palazzetto Bru Zane on concert nights, when exquisite harmonies tickle Se-

bastiano Ricci angels tumbling across stucco-frosted ceilings. Multi-year restorations returned the 1695–97 Casino Zane's 100-seat music room to its original function, attracting world-class musicians to enjoy its acoustics. By day the palace hosts academic music conferences, but its concerts are pure pleasure.

CASA DEL CINEMA CINEMA
(Videoteca Pasinetti; Map p314; ☎041 524 13 20; www.comune.venezia.it/cinema; Salizada San Stae 1990, Santa Croce; adult/reduced €6/5; ⊙shows afternoon Mon-Sat; ⛴San Stae) Venice's public film archive shows art films in a new 50-seat, wood-beamed screening room inside Palazzo Mocenigo. Original-language classics are shown Monday and first-run independent films on Friday night and Saturday afternoon; check online for pre-release previews and revivals with introductions by directors, actors and scholars. Show up early for prime seating.

SUMMER ARENA CINEMA, THEATRE
(Map p314; Campo San Polo, San Polo; ⊙Jul & Aug; ⛴San Silvestro) Where bullfights were once held by rowdy Austrians, the city now hosts open-air movies, concerts and theatre performances from July to September – but watch this space year-round for kiddie carousels, food kiosks, political rallies and street musicians.

OPERA AT SCUOLA GRANDE DI SAN GIOVANNI EVANGELISTA OPERA
(Map p314; ☎041 426 65 59; www.scuolasangiovanni.it; Campiello della Scuola 2454, Santa Croce; adult/reduced from €30/25; ⊙concerts 8.30pm; ⛴Ferrovia) Drama comes with the scenery when Italian opera favourites – Puccini's *Tosca*, Verdi's *La Traviata*, Rossini's *Il Barbiere di Seviglia* – are performed in the lavish hall where Venice's secretive Council of Ten socialised. Stage sets can't compare to the Scuola: sweep up Mauro Codussi's 15th-century staircase into Giorgio Massari's 1729 hall, and take your seat amid Giandomenico Tiepolo paintings.

SHOPPING

★CÁRTE ARTISANAL, PAPER GOODS
(Map p314; ☎320 024 87 76; www.cartevenezia. it; Calle dei Cristi 1731, San Polo; ⊙11am-5pm Mon-Sat, to 3pm Nov-Mar; ⛴Rialto-Mercato) Lagoon

ripples swirl across marbled-paper statement necklaces and artist's portfolios, thanks to the steady hands and restless imagination of *carta marmorizzata* (marbled-paper) *maestra* Rosanna Corrò. After years restoring ancient Venetian books, Rosanna began creating her original, bookish beauties: aquatic marbled-paper cocktail rings, op-art jewellery boxes and hypnotically swirled handbags. Wall panels, wedding albums and even chairs can be custom ordered.

★SCHANTALLE
VETRI D'ARTE   ARTISANAL, GLASS
(Map p314; ☑041 522 61 00; Campo Santa Maria Mater Domini 2115, Santa Croce; ⊗9am-12.30pm & 2-7pm Mon-Sat; ⊠San Stae) Murano must be jealous: Santa Croce boasts the new studio-showroom of glass-making power couple Schantalle Menegus and Igor Balbi. Homes become castles with Igor's gossamer dragon goblets, poised for flight before you even finish your magic potion. Christmas arrives in Venice when Schantalle twists Babbo Natale (Father Christmas) off her torch, Santa hat pulled low and nose rosy from *spritz*.

★GILBERTO PENZO   ARTISANAL, CRAFTS
(Map p314; ☑041 71 93 72; www.veniceboats. com; Calle 2 dei Saoneri 2681, San Polo; ⊗9am-12.30pm & 3-6pm Mon-Sat; 🚻; ⊠San Tomà) Yes, you actually can take a gondola home in your pocket. Anyone fascinated by the models at Museo Storico Navale will go wild here, amid handmade wooden models of all kinds of Venetian boats, including some that are seaworthy (or at least bathtub worthy). Signor Penzo also creates kits so crafty types and kids can have a crack at it themselves.

VIZIOVIRTÙ   ARTISANAL, CHOCOLATE
(Map p314; ☑041 275 01 49; www.viziovirtu.com; Calle del Campaniel 2898a, San Polo; ⊗10am-7.30pm; ⊠Ca' Rezzonico) Work your way through Venice's most decadent vices and tasty virtues at this Willy Wonka–esque chocolatier, from the hot-chocolate fountain to the dark-chocolate plague-doctor's masks. Ganache-filled chocolates come in a five-course meal of flavours: barolo wine, pink pepper, ginger curry, chestnut honey and mimosa flower. A second location on Campo San Tomá offers more cupcakes, mousses, pralines and upscale gift-wrapped treats.

I VETRI A LUME DI AMADI   ARTISANAL, GLASS
(Map p314; ☑041 523 80 89; Calle Saoneri 2747, San Polo; ⊗9am-12.30pm & 3-6pm Mon-Sat; ⊠San Silvestro) Glass menageries don't get more fascinating than the one created before your eyes by Signor Amadi. Fierce little glass crabs approach pink-tipped sea anemones, and glass peas spill from a speckled pea pod. You might be tempted to swat at eerily lifelike glass mosquitoes, and the outlines of galloping horses in blue glass would do Picasso proud.

CARTAVENEZIA   ARTISANAL, PAPER GOODS
(Map p314; ☑041 524 12 83; www.cartavenezia. it; Calle Lunga 2125, Santa Croce; ⊗11am-1pm & 3.30-7.30pm Tue-Sat, 3.30-7.30pm Mon; ⊠San Stae) Paper is anything but two-dimensional here: paper maestro Fernando di Masone embosses and sculpts handmade cotton paper into seamless raw-edged lampshades, hand-bound sketchbooks, and paper versions of marble friezes that would seem equally at home in a Greek temple or a modern loft. White gloves are handy for easy, worry-free browsing; paper-sculpting courses are available by prior request.

PIED À TERRE SHOES   ARTISANAL, SHOES
(Map p314; ☑041 528 55 13; www.piedaterre -venice.com; Sotoportego degli Oresi 60, San Polo; ⊗10am-1pm & 3-7pm Tue-Sat, 3-7pm Mon; ⊠Rialto) Rialto courtesans and their 30cm-high heels are long gone, but Venetian slippers stay stylish. Pied à Terre's colourful *furlane* (slippers) are handcrafted with recycled bicycle-tyre treads, ideal for finding your footing on a gondola. Choose from velvet, brocade or raw silk in vibrant shades of lemon and ruby, with optional piping. Don't see your size? Shoes can be custom made and shipped.

ALBERTO SARRIA MASKS   ARTISANAL, MASKS
(Map p314; ☑041 520 72 78; www.masksvenice. com; Calle del Tintor 1807, Santa Croce; ⊗10am-7pm; ⊠San Stae) Go Gaga or channel Casanova at this atelier dedicated to the art of masquerade for more than 30 years. Sarria's *commedia dell'arte* masks are worn by theatre companies from Argentina to Osaka – ominous burnished black leather for dramatic leads, or harlequin-checquered *cartapesta* (papier-mâché) for comic foils, starting from €30. Watch as masks are hand-cast, and one-of-a-kind marionettes take their first steps.

DROGHERIA MASCARI
FOOD, WINE

(Map p314; ☑041 522 97 62; www.imascari.com; Ruga degli Spezieri 381, San Polo; ◷8am-1pm & 4-7.30pm Mon, Tue & Thu-Sat, 8am-1pm Wed; ◸Rialto) Ziggurats of cayenne, leaning towers of star anise and chorus lines of olive oils draw awestruck foodies to Drogheria Mascari's windows. Indoors, chefs clutch truffle jars like holy relics, kids ogle candy in copper-lidded jars and dazed gourmands confront 50 different aromatic honeys. For small-production Italian wines – including Veneto cult producers like Quintarelli – don't miss the backroom *cantina*.

DIETRO L'ANGOLO
DESIGN STORE

(Map p314; ☑041 524 30 71; www.dietrolango lo2657.com; Calle Seconda dei Saoneri 2657, San Polo; ◸San Tomà) A totally Venetian concept store: modern Italian design finds hidden on a backstreet behind I Frari, with affordable, original pieces by young local and international designers. Blue pigeon earrings bring back San Marco memories, charming rat puppets made of upcycled clothing support a local shelter, and herringbone-tweed cocktail rings with Murano-glass centres remind you it's time for a *spritz*.

FRANCO FURLANETTO
ARTISANAL, CRAFTS

(Map p314; ☑045 209 544; Calle delle Nomboli 2768, San Polo; ◷10am-6.30pm Mon-Sat; ◸San Tomà) Masks and violins inspire maestro Franco's sleek, original designs for *forcole* (gondola oarlocks), hand-carved on site from blocks of walnut, cherry and pear wood. There's a science to each *forcole*, perfectly weighted and angled to propel a gondola forward, but also a delicate art: for its sculptural finesse, Franco's work has been shown in New York's Metropolitan Museum of Art.

ANATEMA
FASHION, ACCESSORIES

(Map p314; ☑041 524 22 21; www.anatema.it; Rio Terà 2603, San Polo; ◷10am-2pm & 3-7pm; ◸San Tomà) Add a Venetian eye for colour to a Japanese flair for sculptural fashion, and here you have it: teal Italian mohair tube scarves that float around the collarbone like clouds, and pleated Thai silk shawls in neon-yellow shades worthy of Milan runways. Venetian-Japanese design duo Anatema brings out new collections each season, from sunhats to wool-felt brooches.

GMEINER
ARTISANAL, SHOES

(Map p314; ☑338 896 21 89; www.gabrielegmein er.com; Campiello del Sol 951, San Polo; ◷by appointment 10am-1pm & 3-7pm; ◸Rialto-Mercato) Paris, London, Venice: Gabriele Gmeiner honed her shoemaking craft at Hermès and John Lobb, and today jet-setters fly to Venice just for her ultrasleek Oxfords with hidden 'bent' seams and minutely handstiched brogues, made to measure for men and women (around €3000, including hand-carved wooden last). If Gabriele's not on site, she's probably at Guidecca women's prison, leading shoe-design job-training programs.

HIBISCUS
FASHION

(Map p314; ☑041 520 89 89; Ruga Ravano 1061, San Polo; ◷10am-7.30pm; ◸San Silvestro) Blend in at the Biennale with Venice's creative crossroads style, layered piece by distinctive piece at Hibiscus: easygoing Italian linen swing dresses, Okinawan indigo wrap jackets, ombre violet Kashmiri cashmere shawls, French watercolour-patterned socks and Maria Calderara pop-art resin necklaces. As original as ready-to-wear gets and priced accordingly, but sales are fabulous.

VENEZIASTAMPA
ARTISANAL, PAPER GOODS

(Map p314; ☑041 71 54 55; www.veneziastampa. com; Campo Santa Maria Mater Domini 2173, Santa Croce; ◷8.30am-7.30pm Mon-Fri, 9am-12.30pm Sat; ◸San Stae) Mornings are best to catch the 1930s Heidelberg machine in action – but whenever you arrive, you'll find mementos hot off the proverbial press. Veneziastampa recalls more elegant times, when postcards were gorgeously lithographed and Casanovas invited dates upstairs to 'look at my etchings'. Pick your signature symbols – meteors, faucets, trapeze artists – for original stationery, menus and bookplates.

NERODISEPPIA
ARTISANAL, DESIGN STORE

(Map p314; ☑041 865 18 89; www.nerodisep piavenezia.com; Calle Larga dei Bari 968, Santa Croce; ◷noon-7pm Mon-Sat; ◸Ferrovia) In the indie heart of Venice's student quarter, this collective gallery replaces Venetian baroque glitz with handmade organic originality: gondola-prowed bisque teacups, driftwood earrings, handwoven shawls in soft mossy and violet tweed and blankets made of natural black sheep's wool. Nerodiseppia doubles as an alt-culture hub, hosting art openings, CD release parties and local zine launches – and you're invited.

LABERINTHO
ARTISANAL, JEWELLERY

(Map p314; ☎041 71 00 17; www.laberintho.it; Calle del Scaleter 2236, San Polo; ⊗10am-12.30pm & 3-7pm Tue-Sat; 🚤San Stae) A token jewel in the window is a tantalising hint of the custom jewellery this versatile goldsmiths' atelier can create for you, with original designs that nod at Venice's seafaring, Byzantine past: a nautilus-inspired ring inset with opal and turquoise mosaic, a square gold bracelet inlaid with ebony, or a necklace of Murano glass seascapes that float on the collarbone like islands.

SAN POLO VETRO
ARTISANAL, GLASS

(di Viviana Toso; Map p314; ☎041 71 46 88; Campo San Agostin 2309, San Polo; ⊗10.30am-6.30pm Mon-Sat; 🚤San Tomà) Leaving a fine Veneto vintage unfinished is usually unforgiveable in Venice, unless you save the remainder with a wine-bottle stopper of lampworked glass by Viviana Toso. The artisan can be found at her torch, spinning molten glass into red devils, pink-lipped conch shells, polka-dotted perfume bottles and her signature stoppers in psychedelic shades of orange, sky blue and acid green.

SABBIE E NEBBIE
HOME & GARDEN, ACCESSORIES

(Map p314; ☎041 71 90 73; www.sabbienebbie. com; Calle dei Nomboli 2768a, San Polo; ⊗10am-12.30pm & 4-7.30pm Mon-Sat; 🚤San Tomà) East-West trade-route trends begin here, with Rina Menardi's Japanese-inspired deep-purple ceramics, opera wraps that are saffron on one side and paprika on the other, and handmade books from Bologna made with Turkish paper-marbling techniques.

MARE DI CARTA
BOOKS, BOATING

(Map p317; ☎041 71 63 04; www.maredicarta. com; Fondamenta dei Tolentini 222, Santa Croce; ⊗9am-1pm & 2.30-7.30pm Tue-Sat; 🚤Ferrovia) Sailors, pirates and armchair seafarers should navigate to this canalside storefront, which stocks every maritime map and sailor's-knot manual needed for lagoon exploration, boat upkeep and sealife spotting. If you're considering rowing lessons or a sailboat excursion – who doesn't after a few days on the lagoon? – stop here to check out the schedule of boating classes and trips.

IL PAVONE DI
PAOLO PELOSIN
ARTISANAL, PAPER GOODS

(Map p314; ☎041 522 42 96; Campiello dei Meoni 1478, San Polo; ⊗10am-7pm Tue-Sun; 🚤San Silvestro) Consider Paolo's hand-bound marbled-paper journals and photo albums a challenge: now it's up to you to create Venice memories worthy of such inspired workmanship. Recipe books are covered in violet and gold feather patterns, rippled blue sketchbooks inspire seascapes, and paper-wrapped pens seem to catch fire with flickers of orange and red.

TOP FOUR VENETIAN FASHIONS, THEN & NOW

Platform shoes *Then*: Worn by women working the shady end of Ponte delle Tette (p109), often hovering around 30cm high. *Now*: Lady Gaga's stagewear can't compare to the original 18th-century *zampe* (elephant's foot) platforms in the Palazzo Mocenigo (p106) collection. For more footwear that's stylish yet sensible for crossing footbridges, try on handmade *furlane* at Pied à Terre (p118) or have brogues custommade at Gmeiner (p119).

Jewels *Then*: Sumptuary laws attempted to limit conspicuous displays of diamonds and pearls on Venetian socialites, to no avail. *Now*: Statement necklaces have gone creative, in marble-paper at Cárte (p117) and Murano glass at La Pedrera (p121).

Eyeglasses *Then*: A jaw-dropping, monocle-popping invention, the first modern eyeglasses were worn in Venice around 1300. *Now*: Eco-friendly resin glasses are still hand-finished at Ottica Vascellari (p121), and vintage '60s sunglasses regularly surface at Il Baule Blu (p121).

Outerwear *Then*: Sumptuous *piviale* (capes) were worn as rain ponchos in Venice, though velvet brocade wasn't exactly water-repellent. *Now*: Brocade *piviale* are still worn by priests during mass, but Anatema (p119) mohair tube-scarves and Hibiscus (p119) ombre shawls offer hipper ways to keep damp chills off Venetian necks.

MILLE E UNA NOTA
MUSICAL INSTRUMENTS

(Map p314; ☑041 523 18 22; Calle di Mezzo 1235, San Polo; ⊙9.30am-1pm & 3.30-7.30pm Mon-Sat; ⬛San Tomà) The same thought occurs to almost everyone after hearing a concert in Venice: is it too late to take up an instrument? The easiest would be harmonica or recorder, and Mille e Una Nota has impressive vintage and modern ones from the Italian Alps. If you're feeling ambitious, you can pick up Albinoni sheet music and a lute too.

IL BAULE BLU
TOYS, VINTAGE

(Map p314; ☑041 71 94 48; www.ilbaeleblu.com; Campo San Tomà 2916a, San Polo; ⊙10.30am-12.30pm & 4-7.30pm Mon-Sat; ⬛; ⬛San Tomà) A curiosity cabinet of elusive treasures, which on recent inspection included antique Steiff teddy bears, 1970s bubble sunglasses, vintage Murano *murrine* (glass beads) and a striped green Marni garden-party dress. If travel has proved tough on your kid's favourite toy, first aid and kind words will be administered at the in-house teddy hospital.

LA PEDRERA
ARTISANAL, JEWELLERY

(Map p314; ☑041 244 01 44; www.lapedrera.it; Campo Sant'Agostin 2279a, San Polo; ⊙10am-6pm Mon-Sat, 10am-1pm Sun; ⬛San Stae) Made you look: these Murano glass jewels in bold colours and essential shapes have the attention-getting powers of traffic lights, and merit a detour between Campo San Polo and Campo San Giacomo dell'Orio. Cascades of lilac beads cluster around the collarbone like wisteria, and a 1920s flapper-inspired drop necklace made with antique scarlet beads demands a Venetian jazz concert.

IL GUFO ARTIGIANO
ARTISANAL, LEATHERWORK

(Map p314; ☑041 523 40 30; Ruga degli Speziali 299, San Polo; ⊙10am-3.30pm Mon-Sat; ⬛Rialto-Mercato) Hot copper and extremely careful handling are the secrets to the embossed leather designs gracing journals, handbags and wallets in this artisan's atelier. Ancient ironwork patterns in Venetian windows inspire the swirling designs on saffron albums and green journals, while the winged lion of St Mark roars with high-fashion fierceness on scarlet handbags and tawny satchels.

OTTICA VASCELLARI
EYEWEAR

(Map p314; ☑041 522 93 88; www.otticavascellari. it; Ruga Rialto 1030, San Polo; ⊙9am-12.30pm & 3-7.30pm Mon-Sat, closed Mon Oct-Mar; ⬛San Silvestro) ✐ Second-generation opticians and first-class stylists, Vascellari family opticians intuit eyewear needs with a glance at your prescription and a long look to assess your face shape and personal style. Angular features demand Vascellari's architectural eyewear with hand-finished two-tone laminates, while delicate features are set off with sleek specs of eco-friendly cotton-resin – all for less than mass-market brands.

CAMPIELLO CA' ZEN
ANTIQUES, GLASS

(Map p314; ☑041 71 48 71; www.campiellocazen. com; Campiello Zen 2581, San Polo; ⊙9am-1pm & 3-7pm Mon-Sat; ⬛San Tomà) Antique Murano glass lamps are the last thing you'd want to cram into your luggage – or so you thought before you saw the 1940s Salviati silver chandelier and the rare ultra-mod red Seguso lamp. That golden Venini goblet seems safe to admire, but here's a dangerous thought: they ship.

LA MARGHERITA
ARTISANAL, CERAMICS

(Map p314; ☑393 210 02 72; lamargheritavenezia.com; Campo San Cassian 2345, Santa Croce; ⊙10am-7pm Mon-Fri, to 2pm Sat; ⬛Rialto-Mercato) The charm of Venice is captured in a squiggle of Gothic archways by Margherita Rossetto, a cartoonist who also applies her graphic talents to ceramics at this studio. Hand-drawn cards feature Venetian signoras leaning over ironwork balconies, kitchen tiles feature cats sunning on Gothic windowsills, and grinning fish greet diners with a knowing wink on oval fish platters.

GIUSEPPE TINTI
ARTISANAL, GLASS

(Map p314; ☑041 524 12 57; www.tintimuranoglass.com; Campo San Cassian 2343, Santa Croce; ⊙9am-1pm & 3-7pm Mon-Sat; ⬛Rialto-Mercato) Watch Giuseppe turn molten glass into a colourful, cartoony fish with a blowtorch and very steady hands. The results are all around you in this tiny, packed corner shop: highly portable, affordable souvenirs, including orange glass earrings with white starbursts (€8 to €12), stackable glass-band rings (three for €8) and Tinti's glass fish magnets (€4 to €8).

Sestiere di Cannaregio

Neighbourhood Top Five

1 Exploring the tiny island that offered refuge from the Inquisition, bailed out the Venetian empire and sparked a Renaissance in thought: the **Ghetto** (p124), historic home of Venice's Jewish community.

2 Discovering the little neighbourhood corner chapel that marked a turn-ing point in art history: **Chiesa di Santa Maria dei Miracoli** (p130).

3 Paying respects to the patron saint of travellers and the genius of Tintoretto at **Chiesa della Madonna dell'Orto** (p127).

4 Finding Grand Canal photo ops, stolen master-pieces and priceless pave-ment at glorious Venetian Gothic **Ca' d'Oro** (p127).

5 Channeling your inner Marco Polo and seeking out far-flung **Anice Stellato** (p133) for Venice's finest trade route–inspired sea-food dishes.

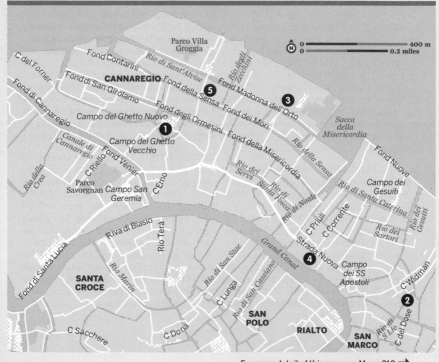

For more detail of this area see Map p318 ➡

Explore Sestiere di Cannaregio

Ignore the Ferrovia signs trying to rush you through Cannaregio, and detour behind the Rialto to tiny, splendid Chiesa di Santa Maria dei Miracoli. Wander up to Fondamenta Nuove, and turn the corner to glimpse bombastic, baroque I Gesuiti. Follow aptly named Fondamenta Zen and misnomer Fondamenta della Misericordia towards Campo dei Mori and Madonna dell'Orto, bedecked with Tintoretto masterpieces. Break for a stellar lunch at Anice Stellato, followed by a fascinating tour of historic Ghetto synagogues. Browse poetry, antiques and Ikona Gallery in the Ghetto before hitting the Cannaregio *cicheti* circuit: Al Timon, La Cantina and Alla Vedova.

Local Life

➡ **Canalside dining** Romance comes naturally to candlelit tables reflected in the canal at Dalla Marisa (p132), Osteria ai Canottieri (p132), Anice Stellato (p133) and Osteria L'Orto dei Mori (p132).

➡ **Shopping secrets** Campo Santa Maria Nova hosts a monthly weekend outdoor antiques market, **Mercanto dei Miracolo** (⊘9am-5pm), from spring to autumn, but you'll also find artisans, fashion, gifts and books galore in this Cannaregio corner.

➡ **Beer here** Thirsty sightseers craving a proper pint will find Venice's best brews at La Cantina (p132), Agli Ormesini (p134) and Il Santo Bevitore (p133).

➡ **Good and loud** Cannaregio's timeless calm is broken at night by modern music acts at Al Timon (p133), Al Parlamento (p133), Paradiso Perduto (p134) and Teatro Fondamenta Nuove (p134).

Getting Around

➡ **Vaporetto** After the busy Ferrovia stop, there are two more Grand Canal stops in Cannaregio: San Marcuola (lines 1, 82 and N) and Ca' d'Oro (1 and N). Lines 41, 42, 51 and 52 head from Ferrovia into the Canale di Cannaregio and onwards to Fondamenta Nuove. Ferries head from Fondamenta Nuove to the northern islands, including San Michele, Murano, Burano, Le Vignole and Sant'Erasmo.

Lonely Planet's Top Tip

Napoleon created the wide pedestrian boulevard that links the train station to the Rialto, and it's a lot like a highway, with rush-hour pedestrian traffic, fast food and chain stores. But one of Venice's most scenic walks runs parallel to it, along the sunny *fondamente* (canal bank) running north of the Ghetto and along the lagoon on the Fondamenta Nuove.

✸ Best Places to Eat

➡ Anice Stellato (p133)
➡ Dalla Marisa (p132)
➡ Ai Promessi Sposi (p131)
➡ Boccadoro (p133)
➡ Gelateria Ca' d'Oro (p131)

For reviews, see p131 ➡

🍷 Best Places to Drink

➡ Al Timon (p133)
➡ Torrefazione Marchi (p133)
➡ Al Parlamento (p133)
➡ Algiubagiò (p134)
➡ Il Santo Bevitore (p133)

For reviews, see p133 ➡

⛫ Best Cannaregio Backstreet Buys

➡ Hand-stamped Venetian-motif calling cards at Gianni Basso (p135)
➡ Biennale-worthy linen dresses from Spilli (p136)
➡ Fisherman's lamps shaped like pumpkins at De Rossi (p135)
➡ Journals embossed with Venetian Gothic flourishes by Paolo Olbi (p135)

For reviews, see p135 ➡

SESTIERE DI CANNAREGIO

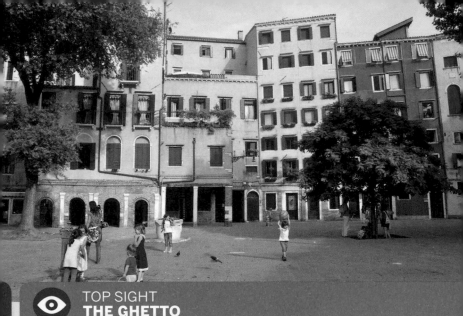

◉ TOP SIGHT
THE GHETTO

This Cannaregio corner once housed Venice's *getto* (foundry) – but its role as Venice's designated Jewish quarter from the 16th to 18th centuries gave the word a whole new meaning. In accordance with the Venetian Republic's 1516 decree, Jewish artisans and lenders stocked and funded Venice's commercial enterprises by day, while at night and on Christian holidays they were restricted to the gated island of Ghetto Nuovo.

Campo del Ghetto Nuovo

Unlike most European cities of the era, pragmatic Venice granted Jewish communities the right to practise certain professions key to the city's livelihood, including medicine, trade, banking, fashion and publishing. When the Inquisition forced Jewish communities out of Spain, many fled to Venice. Around Campo del Ghetto Nuovo, upper storeys were added to house new arrivals, synagogues and publishing houses.

According to official orders c 1516, the island's bridges were closed at midnight. Such laws were abolished under Napoleon in 1797, when some 1626 Ghetto residents gained standing as Venetian citizens. However, Mussolini's 1938 Racial Laws revived 16th-century discrimination, and in 1943 most Jewish Venetians were deported to concentration camps. As a **memorial** on the northeast end of the *campo* notes, only 37 returned. Today few of Venice's 400-person Jewish community actually live in the Ghetto, but their children come to Campo del Ghetto Nuovo to play, surrounded by the Ghetto's living legacy of bookshops, art galleries and religious institutions.

Synagogues

As you enter Campo del Ghetto Nuovo, look up: atop private apartments is the wooden cupola of the 1575 **Schola Italiana** (Italian Synagogue). The Italians were the poorest in

DON'T MISS...

➡ Campo del Ghetto Nuovo
➡ Synagogue tour
➡ Museo Ebraico
➡ 1704 Ghetto decree
➡ 1943 memorial

PRACTICALITIES

➡ Map p318
➡ synagogue tour incl museum admission €10/8
➡ 🚊 Guglie

the Ghetto, and their synagogue is starkly beautiful, with elegantly carved woodwork.

Recognisable from the square by its five long windows, the **Schola Tedesca** (German Synagogue) has been the spiritual home of Venice's Ashkenazi community since 1528. By 16th-century Venetian law, only the German Jewish community could lend money, and the success of this trade shows in the handsome decor. The baroque pulpit and carved benches downstairs are topped by a gilded, elliptical women's gallery, modelled after a Venetian opera balcony.

Above the Schola Tedesca in the corner of the *campo*, you'll spot the wooden cupola of **Schola Canton** (the Corner or French Synagogue), built c 1531 with gilded rococo interiors added in the 18th century. Though European synagogues typically avoid figurative imagery, this little synagogue makes an exception to the rule with eight charming landscapes inspired by Biblical parables.

Over the bridge in **Campo del Ghetto Vecchio**, refugees from Portugal and Spain raised two synagogues considered among the most elegant in northern Italy, with renovated 17th-century interiors often attributed to Baldassare Longhena. The **Schola Levantina** (Levantine Synagogue) has a magnificent 17th-century woodworked pulpit, while the main hall of the **Schola Spagnola** (Spanish Synagogue) is reached by a sweeping staircase. This Sephardic synagogue founded in 1583 shows how Venetian the community had become within a generation or two, with a flair for Venetian architectural flourishes: repeating geometric details, high-arched windows, and exuberant marble and carved-wood baroque interiors.

Hour-long English-language tours of the synagogues leave from Museo Ebraico seven to eight times daily starting at 10.30am, and lead inside three of the Ghetto's synagogues: Schola Tedescha, Schola Canton, and either Schola Italiana or still-active Schola Spagnola. The Schola Levantina is still used for Saturday prayers in winter (it has heating), while the Schola Spagnola is used in summer.

Museo Ebraico

At the Ghetto's heart, **Museo Ebraico** (Jewish Museum; ☏041 71 53 59; www.museoebraico.it; Campo del Ghetto Nuovo 2902b; adult/student €4/3; ⊙10am-7pm Sun-Fri except Jewish holidays Jun-Sep, 10am-5.30pm Sun-Fri Oct-May) explores the history of Venice's Jewish community through everyday artefacts, and showcases its pivotal contributions to Venetian, Italian and world history. Opened in 1955, the museum has a small collection of finely worked silverware and

WARNING

On the wall at No 1131 Calle del Ghetto Vecchio, an official 1704 decree of the Republic forbids Jews converted to Christianity entry into the Ghetto, punishable by 'the rope [hanging], prison, galleys, flogging...and other greater punishments, depending on the judgment of their excellencies (the Executors Against Blasphemy)'.

RENAISSANCE IN THE GHETTO

Despite a 10-year censorship order issued by the church in Rome in 1553, Jewish Venetian publishers contributed hundreds of titles popularising new Renaissance ideas on humanist philosophy, medicine and religion – including the first printed Qur'an. In the 17th century, the Schola Italiana's learned rabbi Leon da Modena was so widely respected as a thinker and scientist that Christians began attending his services, and Modena accommodated them by delivering his sermons in Italian. Ghetto literary salons organised by Modena, bestselling philosopher Sara Copia Sullam and other notable Venetian Jewish intellectuals brought leading thinkers of all faiths to the Ghetto. The Ghetto's literary tradition continues today, with religious study centers ringing the *campo*.

other Judaica art objects used in private prayer and to decorate synagogues, as well as early books published in the Ghetto during the Renaissance. Entry to the museum is included with tickets for guided synagogue tours, and you can also enquire at the museum about guided tours to the Antico Cimitero Israelitico (Old Jewish Cemetery) on the Lido.

⊙ SIGHTS

THE GHETTO &
MUSEO EBRAICO   MUSEUM
See p124.

CA' D'ORO   MUSEUM
(Map p318; ☏041 520 03 45; www.cadoro.org;
Calle di Ca' d'Oro 3932; adult/reduced €6/3;
☺8.15am-7.15pm Mon-Sat, 9am-12.30pm Sun;
⛴Ca' d'Oro) Along the Grand Canal, you
can't miss 15th-century Ca' d'Oro's lacy
arcaded Gothic facade, resplendent even
without the original gold-leaf details that
gave the palace its name (Golden House).
Baron Franchetti donated to Venice this
treasure-box palace packed with masterpieces displayed upstairs in **Galleria Franchetti**, alongside Renaissance wonders
plundered from Veneto churches during
Napoleon's Italy conquest.

Napoleon had excellent taste in souvenirs, including bronzes, tapestries, paintings and sculpture ripped (sometimes
literally) from church altars. Most were
warehoused at Milan's Brera Museum as
Napoleonic war trophies until they were
reclaimed by Venice for display here. Collection highlights include Titian's flushed,
smouldering *Venus at the Mirror* (c 1550;
note the perfect pout and freakishly long
arm); Tintoretto's suitably shadowy portrait of the Consiglio dei Dieci master
spy Nicolo Priuli; and Pietro Lombardo's
chubby-kneed Jesus leaning on his mother,
in glistening Carrara marble that actually
looks soft. Recently restored masterpieces
include Andrea Mantegna's arrow-riddled
St Sebastian and Titian fresco fragments
rescued after Venice's 1967 flood. Restorers
work right in the gallery, so you might get
to witness treasures painstakingly brought
back to life before your eyes.

Yet even Renaissance masters are upstaged by the elegant palace itself, the city's
finest example of Venetian Gothic. Step outside onto Ca' d'Oro's **double-decker loggie** (balconies), where Grand Canal views
framed by Gothic arcades make the city's
most irresistible photo op. When open, galleries off the loggia showcase 12th- to 19th-
century polychrome ceramics. On your way
out, peek into the water-door entry courtyard to admire the intricate **geometric mosaic floors**, puzzled together from a major
Mediterranean haul of semiprecious stone
from Tunisia, Turkey, Greece and Egypt.

SESTIERE DI CANNAREGIO SIGHTS

WORTH A DETOUR

CHIESA DELLA MADONNA DELL'ORTO
•••

Dedicated to the patron saint of *gondolieri*, merchants and travellers – basically, all
of Venice – this sublime 1365 Italian Gothic **cathedral** (Map p318; Campo della Madonna dell'Orto 3520; admission €3 or Chorus Pass; ☺10am-5pm Mon-Sat; ♿; ⛴Madonna
dell'Orto) remains one of Venice's best-kept secrets. Due to its remote location, Madonna dell'Orto was eventually downgraded to a parish church. But just across the
footbridge was the home-studio of Venetian Renaissance master Tintoretto, who
dedicated masterpieces to his neighbourhood church.

Tintoretto and his family were buried in Madonna dell'Orto's corner chapel, and
he saved some of his best work for the apse: *Presentation of the Virgin in the Temple*,
with throngs of star-struck angels and mortals vying for a glimpse of Mary; and his
1546 *Last Judgment*, where lost souls attempt to hold back a teal tidal wave while
an angel rescues one last person from the ultimate *acque alte*. Tintoretto is better
known for dark, brooding works, but these works show he could handle uplifting
technicolour drama with the best Venetian painters.

A side chapel on the left of the nave features a comparatively lightweight Titian:
Archangel Raphael with Tobia (c 1530), where a spaniel helps the angel point the hesi-
tant young boy toward his destiny. Madonna dell'Orto also had a Bellini masterpiece
that was stolen in 1993 – note the empty space in the side chapel.

A red-brick marvel edged in white Istrian stone and statuary, Madonna dell'Orto and
its adjoining monastery were originally intended to honour St Christopher. But when
the Madonna statue parked in neighbouring sculptor Giovanni de Santi's *orto* (garden)
began to work miracles, the statue won pride of place inside the church, and the design
was upgraded to cathedral quality with a doorway designed by Bartolomeo Bon.

Medieval Melting Pot

Gourmet imports in the window of Venice's Drogheria Mascari seem wildly exotic, but nothing could be more Venetian. Before Marco Polo extended Venice's trade routes to China, Venice had already cultivated cosmopolitan tastes.

Egypt

➡ **Then** According to legend, two Venetian merchants smuggled St Mark's body out of Alexandria in 828. Venice built Basilica di San Marco using purple porphyry – also pilfered from Egypt.

➡ **Now** Tintoretto's newly restored 1562 painting *St Mark Saving a Saracen* at the Accademia shows Venice's stolen saint returning to Alexandria's coast to rescue a shipwrecked Egyptian, assisted by Venetian merchants.

Croatia

➡ **Then** Doge Pietro Orseolo took over Dalmatia (including present-day Croatia) in 1000. Dalmatia remained Venice's favourite war trophy, as shown on the 1697 map of Venetian-conquered territories Admiral Antonio Barbaro had carved onto the facade of Santa Maria del Giglio.

➡ **Now** Venice lost Dalmatia to Napoleon, but two Dalmatian landmarks remain: luxury hotel–lined Riva degli Schiavoni, and the 1451 Scuola di San Giorgio degli Schiavoni, with Carpaccio's convincingly detailed Croatian scenery.

Turkey

➡ **Then** Despite Doge Dandolo's 1203–04 sack of Constantinople, Turkey and

1. Palazzo Zenobio (p90) **2.** Riva degli Schiavoni (p143) **3.** Chinoiserie drawing room, Ca'Rezzonico (p90)

Venice maintained close trade relations for 600 years.

➡ **Now** The Turkish art of paper marbling is still practised by Venetian artisans.

Armenia

➡ **Then** Venice's former leper colony of San Lazzaro degli Armeni became a monastery founded by Armenian refugees in 1717 – but Armenian students lived in grander style at frescoed Palazzo Zenobio.

➡ **Now** Palazzo Zenobio remains an Armenian cultural centre and popular venue for concerts and Carnevale.

China

➡ **Then** Since Marco Polo's 1271–95 heyday, no Venetian palace could be complete without Chinese art – hence the chinoiserie drawing room at Ca' Rezzonico, and Ca' Pesaro's Museo d'Arte Orientale, featuring Prince Enrico Borbone's Chinese porcelain hoard.

➡ **Now** Venice awarded an unprecedented two Film Festival Golden Lions to Chinese director Zhang Yimou and prime placement at the Biennale to Chinese artist-provocateur Ai Weiwei.

LONG FRIENDSHIPS

In recognition of longstanding historical ties, Venice's official sister cities include Ragusa (Croatia), Istanbul (Turkey), Yerevan (Armenia), and Suzhou (China). Once again, Alexandria (Egypt) was robbed.

TOP SIGHT
CHIESA DI SANTA MARIA DEI MIRACOLI

When Nicolò di Pietro's Madonna icon started miraculously weeping in its outdoor shrine around 1480, crowd control became impossible. With pooled resources and marble scavenged from San Marco slag-heaps, neighbours built this chapel (1481–89) to house the painting. Pietro and Tullio Lombardo's miraculous design dropped grandiose Gothic in favour of human-scale harmonies, introducing Renaissance architecture to Venice.

The father-son team creatively repurposed **polychrome marbles** plundered from Egypt to Syria from the sides of Basilica di San Marco. Note fine scrollwork capitols, and Venetian fish-scale patterns framing veined-marble panels.

The lofty vaulted interior and domed apse seem effortless, but they're marvels of Renaissance engineering, achieved without the Gothic gimmick of buttressing. Look closely at the **chancel staircase** – there are angels and mermaids carved right into the railings by Tullio Lombardo. In a prime example of Renaissance humanism, Pier Maria Pennacchi filled each of the 50 wooden **coffered ceiling panels** with a bright-eyed portrait of a saint or prophet dressed as a Venetian, like a class photo in a school yearbook.

DON'T MISS...

➡ Pietro Lombardo's Renaissance design

➡ Tullio Lombardo's chancel staircase

➡ Pier Maria Pennacchi's 50 saints on the ceiling

PRACTICALITIES

➡ Map p318

➡ Campo dei Miracoli 6074

➡ admission €3 or with Chorus Pass

➡ ⊙10am-5pm Mon-Sat

➡ 🚤Fondamenta Nuove

I GESUITI   CHURCH
(Santa Maria Assunta; Map p318; ☎041 528 65 79; Salizada dei Specchieri 4880; ⊙10am-noon & 3.30-5.30pm daily; 🚤Fondamenta Nuove) Giddily over the top even by rococo standards, this gaudy, glitzy 18th-century Jesuit church is difficult to take in all at once, with a staggering spaceship of a **pulpit**, white-and-green inlaid marble floors, and undulating marble walls crowned with gilded stucco. Gravity is provided by Titian's uncharacteristically gloomy *Martyrdom of St Lawrence*, on the left as you enter the church.

Also playing against type here is Tintoretto's *Assumption of the Virgin*, in the northern transept. This image is the antithesis of Tintoretto's dark images in the Scuola Grande di San Rocco, showing the Virgin on her merry way to heaven, with the light step of Tiepolo and a rosy glow that nods at Titian. Interior scaffolding for essential structural reinforcements may limit access and church views.

CAMPO DEI MORI   PIAZZA
(Map p318; 🚤Madonna dell'Orto) A gent in an outsized turban called Sior Rioba has been hanging out at the corner of Calle dei Mori since the Middle Ages. This is one of four such figures on building facades ringing the Campo dei Mori (Square of the Moors) – a misnomer, since these statues are believed to represent the Greek Mastelli family, 12th-century merchants from Morea.

The Mastelli brothers became internationally notorious for their shady dealings and eager participation in Doge Dandolo's sacking of Constantinople. According to Venetian legend, Mary Magdalene herself turned them into stone for their hardhearted business dealings.

PONTE DI CALATRAVA   BRIDGE
(Ponte della Costituzione; Map p318; 🚤Piazzale Roma) Avant-garde Spanish architect Santiago Calatrava's 2008 bridge over the Grand Canal has been called many things: a fish tail, a glass tongue, unnecessary, overdue, pleasingly streamlined and displeasingly wheelchair-inaccessible. Some prefer the bridge by night, as a ghostly streak of light reflected in the Grand Canal; others appreciate daylight revealing its red ribbed-steel underbelly.

The bridge's €15-million cost is triple the original estimate, and includes a belatedly tacked-on wheelchair lift. But as the round trip takes an estimated 16 minutes, plus waiting time, *vaporetto* may remain the faster way for travellers with disabilities to cross the canal between Piazzale Roma bus station and the Ferrovia (train station). Judge for yourself whether the time and money has paid off, and join the ongoing debates on the bridge's relative merits at happy hours across Venice.

IKONA GALLERY
ART GALLERY

(Map p318; ✏️041 528 93 87; www.ikonavenezia. com; Campo del Ghetto Nuovo 2909; ⏰during shows 11am-7pm Sun-Fri; 🚏Guglie) **FREE** Art provides the missing link between the Ghetto's history and its contemporary context at Ikona, a showcase for think pieces and themed installations. Recent shows have featured rare 100-year-old photography of Nijinsky dancing a Diaghilev ballet, Eduard Angeli's spare, exquisitely melancholy *Venezia Now* series, and Luigi Viola's powerful *Kaddish* series, commemorating the Ghetto's vanished generation.

SPEZERIA ANTICA
SANTA FOSCA
HISTORICAL SITE

(Map p318; ✏️041 720 600; Campo Santa Fosca 2234a; ⏰9am-12.30pm & 3.30-7.30pm Mon-Fri, 9am-12.45pm Sat; 🚏Ca' d'Oro) **FREE** This perfectly preserved storefront pharmacy illustrates how Venetian medical advice was dispensed three centuries ago, with curatives in ceramic jars lined up on hand-carved shelves, and etchings of wise doctors hanging beneath gilded wood-beam ceilings. An adjoining modern pharmacy and homeopathy centre offers the latest health aids, from condoms and baby formula to orthopaedic insoles.

🍴 EATING

GELATERIA CA' D'ORO
GELATO €

(Map p318; ✏️041 522 89 82; Strada Nuova 4273; gelati €2-4.50; ⏰noon-8pm; 👶; 🚏Ca' d'Oro) Foot traffic stops here for slow-food flavours artisanally made in-house daily. Regional Italian flavours are top choices – especially Sorrento lemon and extra-creamy Bronte pistachio – but *sorbetto* (sorbet) in seasonal fruit flavours like kiwi and canteloupe could turn anyone temporarily vegan. For a summer pick-me-up, try the *granita di caffe con panna* (coffee shaved ice with whipped cream).

OSTERIA DA ALBERTO
VENETIAN €

(Map p318; ✏️041 523 81 53; Calle Larga Giacinto Gallina 5401; meals €15-25; ⏰noon-3pm & 6-11pm Mon-Sat; 🚏Fondamenta Nuove) All the makings of a true Venetian *osteria* – hidden location, casks of wine, chandeliers that look like medieval torture devices – plus fair prices on spaghetti *alla busara* (with shrimp sauce), seasonal *cicheti*, crispy Venetian seafood fry, and silky panna cotta with strawberries. Call ahead, because the kitchen closes early when the joint's not jumping.

RIZZO
SANDWICHES, PASTRIES & CAKES €

(Map p318; ✏️041 71 83 22; www.rizzovenezia.it; Campo San Leonardo 1355; sandwiches €2.20-5; 🚏San Marcuola) Since 1890 Rizzo has been preparing Venetians for train journeys to *terra firma* with grilled *panini* packed with garlic-spiked *sopressa* and top-notch San Daniele prosciutto, plus just-baked Burano *esse* (S-shaped biscotti). *Foccace* and *tramezzini* (sandwiches) are rigorously fresh, and the efficient, cheerful *signore* behind the counter sincerely wish you to *torno subito* (return soon) – though no convincing is necessary.

PASTICCERIA DAL MAS
PASTRIES & CAKES €

(Map p318; ✏️041 71 51 01; Rio Terà Lista di Spagna 150a; pastries €0.90-1.70; ⏰7am-6pm daily; 🚻; 🚏Ferrovia) Early departures and commuter cravings call for flaky pastries near the train station, devoured warm with a *macchiatone* (espresso stained with milk). Reliable bets include apple turnovers, *krapfen* (doughnuts) and the classic *curasan* (croissant).

AL CICHETO
VENETIAN, CICHETI BAR €

(Map p318; ✏️041 71 60 37; Calle della Misericordia 367; meals €6-10; ⏰7.30am-7.30pm Mon-Fri, to 1pm Sat; 🚏Ferrovia) Train-station sandwiches would be an anticlimactic ending to any Venetian culinary adventure, so stop by this *bàcaro* near the station to toast your trip with a glass of *prosecco* and the €6 menu of *primi* of the day – asparagus risotto, *pasta e fagioli* (pasta with beans), or *casarecce* (scroll pasta) with sausage, olives and tomato if you're lucky.

AI PROMESSI SPOSI
VENETIAN €€

(Map p318; ✏️041 241 27 47; Calle d'Oca 4367; meals €25-35; ⏰11.30am-3pm & 6-11pm Thu-Sun

& Tue, 6-11pm Mon & Wed; ⊠Ca' d'Oro) Bantering Venetians thronging the bar are the only permanent fixtures at this newly revived neighbourhood *osteria*, where handwritten menus created daily feature fresh Venetian seafood and Veneto meats at excellent prices. Seasonal standouts include *seppie in umido* (cuttlefish in rich tomato sauce) and housemade tagliatelle with *anatra* (wild duck), but pace yourself for cloudlike tiramisu and elegant chocolate torte.

OSTERIA L'ORTO DEI MORI   MODERN ITALIAN €€

(Map p318; ☑041 524 36 77; www.osteriaortodei mori.com; Campo dei Mori 3386; meals €25-45; ⊗12.30-3.30pm & 7.30pm-midnight Wed-Mon; ⊠Madonna dell'Orto) Not since Tintoretto lived next door has this neighbourhood seen so much action, thanks to this bustling *osteria*. Sicilian chef Lorenzo makes fresh surf-and-turf pasta daily, including squid atop spinach *tagliolini* and pasta with zucchini blossoms and scampi. Upbeat staff and fish-shaped lamps set a playful mood, and you'll be handed *prosecco* to endure waits for tables (book ahead).

WORTH A DETOUR

DALLA MARISA

At **Dalla Marisa** (Map p318; ☑041 72 02 11; Fondamenta di San Giobbe 652b; set menus €15-35; ⊗noon-3pm & 7-11pm Tue & Thu-Sat, noon-3pm Mon & Wed; ⊠Crea), you'll be seated where there's room and get no menu – you'll have whatever Marisa's cooking, and like it. Lunches are a bargain at €15 for a first, main, side, wine, water and coffee – pace yourself through prawn risotto to finish steak and grilled zucchini, or Marisa will jokingly scold you over coffee. For dinner, you will be informed whether the absurdly abundant menu is meat- or fish-based when you book (ample house wine is included in the fixed price). Fish night (usually Tuesday) brings hauls of lagoon seafood grilled, fried and perched atop pasta and arugula, while meaty menus often feature Marisa's *fegato alla veneziana* (Venetian calf's liver) to send Venetian regulars into raptures. Advance reservations and pre-meal fasting advised.

ANTICA ADELAIDE   TRATTORIA €€

(Map p318; ☑041 523 26 29; Calle Priuli 3728; meals €25-40; ⊗7.30-10.30pm; ⊠Ca' d'Oro) ✔ An old *osteria* with inspired new ideas, Antica Adelaide combines hearty lagoon fare served here since the 18th century with one of Italy's most exciting menus of small-production natural wines (eg biodynamic, organic, natural fermentation). Pair lagoon-clam linguine with organic Cantina Filippi DOC soave and *orechiette* (ear-shaped) pasta with almonds and gorgonzola with Castello di Arcano's sulfite-free organic Refosco blend.

LA CANTINA   VENETIAN, CICHETI BAR €€

(Map p318; ☑041 522 82 58; Campo San Felice 3689; cicheti €2.50-5, meals €25-40; ⊗11am-11pm Mon-Sat; ⊠Ca' d'Oro) Talk about slow food: grab a stool and local Morgana beer while you await seasonal *bruschette* made to order and hearty bean soup. Seafood platters require larger appetites and deeper pockets – market price varies, so ask today's rate – but mullet with roast potatoes, *scampi crudi* (Venetian-style sweet-prawn sushi) and corn-breaded fried anchovies are worthy investments.

OSTERIA ALLA VEDOVA   VENETIAN, CICHETI BAR €€

(Map p318; ☑041 528 53 24; Calle del Pistor 3912; cicheti €1-3.50, meals €15-40; ⊗11.30am-2:30pm & 6.30-10.30pm Mon-Wed, Fri & Sat, 6.30-10.30pm Sun; ⊠Ca' d'Oro) Culinary convictions run deep here at one of Venice's oldest *osterie*, so you won't find *spritz* or coffee on the menu or pay more than €1 to snack on a Venetian meatball. Enjoy superior seasonal *cicheti* and *ombre* with the local crowd at the bar, or call ahead for brusque table service and strictly authentic Venetian tripe or clam pasta.

OSTERIA AI CANOTTIERI   VENETIAN €€

(Map p318; ☑041 71 79 99; www.osteriaaicanot tieri.com; Fondamenta del Macello 690; meals €15-35; ⊗11am-11pm; ⊠Crea) Architecture students and professors pack this out-of-the-way *osteria* for the €15 pasta, main and water lunch special, and date-night diners arrive at night for candlelit, canalside seafood dinners featuring exemplary polenta with *schie* (lagoon shrimp) and strictly line-caught Sicilian tuna. Book ahead for canalside seating during regattas, which row furiously past this turning point.

ANICE STELLATO   VENETIAN €€€

(Map p318; ☑041 72 07 44; Fondamenta della Sensa 3272; mains €18-23; ☺noon-2pm & 7.30-11pm Wed-Sun; ☻Madonna dell'Orto) ✔ If finding this obscure corner of Cannaregio seems like an adventure, wait until dinner arrives: pistachio-encrusted lamb chops, succulent house-made prawn ravioli and lightly fried *moeche* (soft-shell crab) gobbled whole. Tin lamps and recycled paper placemats on communal tables keep the focus on local food and local company – all memorable. Book ahead.

OSTERIA BOCCADORO   VENETIAN €€€

(Map p318; ☑041 521 10 21; www.boccadoroven ezia.it; Campiello Widmann 5405a; meals €40-55; ☺noon-3pm & 7-10pm Tue-Sun; ☻Fondamenta Nuove) Birds sweetly singing in this *campo* are probably angling for your leftovers, but they don't stand a chance. Chef-owner Luciano's creative *crudi* (raw seafood) are two-bite delights – tuna with blood orange, sweet prawn atop tart green apple – and cloudlike gnocchi topped with spider crab are gone entirely too soon. Save room for luxuriant mousse with six kinds of chocolate.

BENTIGODI   SEAFOOD €€€

(Map p318; ☑041 822 37 14; Calle Sele 1423; meals €35-50; ☺11.30am-2pm & 6.30-10pm Sun-Wed, to midnight Fri & Sat; ☻San Marcuola) Follow daring seafood devotees to this Ghetto *trattoria*, where seafood with red-onion *saor* (tangy marinade), octopus with *uove di seppia* (cuttlefish eggs), creamy burrata ravioli and tuna tartare with candied orange raise contented murmurs to the wooden rafters. Chef Domenico offers creative twists on classic dishes with speciality ingredients, paired with top Veneto and Friuli wines.

🍷 DRINKING & NIGHTLIFE

⭐**AL TIMON**   WINE BAR

(Map p318; ☑041 524 60 66; Fondamenta degli Ormesini 2754; ☺11am-1am Thu-Tue & 6pm-1am Wed; ☻Guglie) Find a spot on the boat moored out front along the canal and watch the motley parade of drinkers and dreamers arrive for seafood *crostini* (open-face sandwiches) and quality organic and DOC wines by the *ombra* (half-glass) or carafe. Folk singers play sets canalside when the

LOCAL KNOWLEDGE

FURTHER ADVENTURES IN WINE

Prosecco, soave and Amarone aren't the only wines in town, especially in Cannaregio bars. Expand your happy-hour options with an immersion experience in Veneto wines led by an English-speaking professional sommelier from **Venetian Vine** (www. venetianvine.com; tastings per person €70 for up to six people). Tasting sessions are usually held at La Cantina (p132) and cover two flights with *cicheti* pairings over two hours – though participants have been known to keep toasting after class is dismissed.

weather obliges; when it's cold, regulars scoot over to make room for newcomers at indoor tables.

⭐**TORREFAZIONE MARCHI**   CAFE

(Map p318; ☑041 71 63 71; www.torrefazione marchi.it; Rio Terà San Leonardo 1337; ☺7am-7pm; ☻Guglie) Venetians can't catch a train without a pit stop at this aromatic shopfront lined with brass-knobbed coffee bins. Since 1930, Venice's Marchi family has been importing speciality beans, roasted fresh daily in a washtub-size roaster behind the marble bar and ground to order. Connoisseurs who disdain flavoured brews: try *noxea*, espresso made with coffee beans roasted with fresh hazelnuts.

AL PARLAMENTO   CAFE, BAR

(Map p318; ☑041 244 02 14; Fondamenta Savorgnan 511; ☺8am-midnight Mon-Fri, 6pm-midnight Sat & Sun; ☻Crea) Entire university careers and international romances are owed to Al Parlamento's powerful espresso, 6pm-to-9pm happy-hour cocktails and excellent overstuffed *tramezzini*. When they warn you the ham, chicory and pepper-spread *tramezzino* is *picante* (spicy), you'd best pre-order that mojito. Thursday brings live music at 9pm, and weekends you'll be talking over DJ sets unless you claim canalside seating early.

IL SANTO BEVITORE   PUB

(Map p318; ☑335 841 57 71; www.ilsantobevitore pub.com; Calle Zancani 2393a; ☺8am-midnight Mon-Sat; ☻Ca' d'Oro) San Marco has its glittering cathedral, but beer lovers prefer pilgrimages to this shrine of the 'Holy Drinker' for 14 brews on tap, including Trappist ales and seasonal stouts. The faithful receive canalside seating, footy matches on TV, free afternoon internet access, a saintly *spritz*, and the occasional live concert (Irish groups and all-girl rock bands are perennial favourites).

AGLI ORMESINI   PUB
(Da Aldo; Map p318; ☑041 71 58 34; Fondamenta degli Ormesini 2710; ⊙8pm-1am Mon-Sat; ⑤Madonna dell'Orto) While the rest of Venice is awash in wine, Ormesini offers more than 100 brews, including reasonably priced bottles of speciality craft ales and local Birra Venezia. The cheery, beery scene often spills into the street – but keep it down, or the neighbours will get testy.

OSTERIA AI OSTI   BAR
(Map p318; ☑041 520 79 93; Corte dei Pali della Testori 3849; ⊙9.30am-8pm Mon-Sat; ⑤Ca' d'Oro) Behind the old well and between a kebab joint and an Irish pub is this authentic *ombra* outpost, where Venetians stop in throughout the day for friendly glasses of wine at friendly prices. Tasty Friuli whites with a good selection of *sopressa* (Venetian soft salami) and *cicheti* easily pass as lunch or a light dinner.

UN MONDO DI VINO   BAR
(Map p318; ☑041 521 10 93; Salizada San Canciano 5984a; ⊙11am-3pm & 5.30-11pm Tue-Sun; ⑤Rialto) Get there early for first crack at

> **WORTH A DETOUR**
> ## ALGIUBAGIÒ
> Pretty much any other bar in town can claim a more central location than **Algiubagiò** (Map p318; ☑041 523 60 84; www.algiubagio.net; Fondamente Nuove 5039; ⊙9am-midnight Wed-Mon; ⑤Fondamente Nuove), which is really only convenient to Murano shoppers and Burano photographers – but for modern romance, none quite compare. The long indoor bar is a most promising start to date nights, with some 300 wine options and moody spotlighting under the exposed-beam ceiling. Casual drinks may lead to cosy, candlelit tables for two and ambitious (if pricey) meals of goose and truffle ravioli.

marinated artichokes and *sarde in saor* (sardines in tangy onion marinade) and claim a few square inches of ledge for your plate and wineglass. There are 45 wines offered by the glass here, with prices ranging from €1.50 to €5, so take a chance on a freak blend or obscure varietal.

CANTINA VECIA CARBONERA   BAR
(Map p318; ☑041 524 23 88; Ponte Sant'Antonio 2329; ⊙10am-11pm Tue-Sun; ⑤Ca' d'Oro) Wine-barrel tables are rough around the edges in this historic coal-hole-in-the-wall bar, and that suits regulars just fine. *Cicheti* are basic – salami, cheese, meatballs – but the broad wine selection runs €2.50 to €3.50 for an *ombra* of robust Veneto wines. Buy a round and challenge fellow drinkers to a singalong on that scuffed, warped piano.

☆ ENTERTAINMENT

TEATRO FONDAMENTA NUOVE   THEATRE, DANCE
(Map p318; ☑041 522 44 98; www.teatrofondamentanuove.it; Fondamenta Nuove 5013; tickets €2.50-15; ⑤Fondamenta Nuove) Expect the unexpected in Cannaregio's experimental corner: dances inspired by water and arithmetic, new American cellists and long-lost Kyrgyz composers, Egyptian performance-art premieres in collaboration with Palazzo Grassi, and a steady stream of acclaimed artists from Brazil to Finland playing to a full house of 200.

CASINÒ DI VENEZIA   CASINO
(Palazzo Vendramin-Calergi; Map p318; ☑041 529 71 11; www.casinovenezia.it; Palazzo Vendramin-Calergi 2040; admission €5, with €10 gaming-token purchase free; ⊙11am-2.30am Sun-Thu, to 3am Fri & Sat; ⑤San Marcuola) Fortunes have been won and lost inside this palatial casino since the 16th century. Slots open at 11am; to take on gaming tables, arrive after 3.30pm wearing your jacket and poker face. Ask your hotel concierge for free-admission coupons, and take the casino's free water-taxi ride from Piazzale Roma – bargains, unless you count your losses. You must be at least 18 to enter the casino.

PARADISO PERDUTO   LIVE MUSIC
(Map p318; ☑041 72 05 81; Fondamenta della Misericordia 2540; ⊙6pm-1am Mon & Thu, 11am-1am

WAGNER'S CASINO FINALE

Evenings at the casino (p134) can be downright operatic: Richard Wagner survived the 20-year effort of composing his stormy Ring cycle only to expire here in 1883. Wagner's suite has been turned into a museum, with Wagner memorabilia that includes a request from Wagner's wife to deliver Champagne to their favourite gondolier and, in a rather macabre touch, a copy of the sofa on which he had his fatal heart attack. There are also copies of scores Wagner created in the 1830s – since the originals are now worth around €700 a page, keeping them lying around here would be too much of a gamble, even for a casino. The museum offers tours (☑041 276 040; usually 10.30am Tuesday and Saturday and 2.30pm Thursday) by reservation at least 24 hours in advance; check the casino website for occasional concerts.

Fri-Sun; ⌂Madonna dell'Orto) 'Paradise Lost' is a find for anyone craving a cold beer canalside on a hot summer's night, with occasional live-music acts. Over the past 25 years, troubadour Vinicio Capossela, Italian jazz great Massimo Urbani and Keith Richards have played the small stage at the Paradiso. On Sunday, jam sessions hosted by two independent local labels alternate with local art openings.

CINEMA GIORGIONE
MOVIE D'ESSAI   CINEMA

(Map p318; ☑041 522 62 98; Rio Terà di Franceschi 4612; adult/student €7.50/6; ☺films from 5.30pm; ⌂; ⌂Fondamenta Nuove) Screenings of international film-festival winners, recently restored classics and family-friendly animation share top billing at this modern cinema in the heart of Venice. There are two screens (one tiny) and two or three screenings a day (usually 5.30pm and 7.30pm, occasionally also 9.30pm), plus matinees on Sunday (usually at 3.30pm).

🛍 SHOPPING

★GIANNI BASSO   ARTISANAL, STATIONERY

(Map p318; ☑041 523 46 81; Calle del Fumo 5306; ☺9am-1pm & 2-6pm Mon-Fri, 9am-noon Sat; ⌂Fondamenta Nuove) Gianni Basso doesn't advertise his letterpressing services: the clever calling cards crowding his studio window do the trick. Restaurant critic Gale Greene's title is framed by a knife and fork, and Hugh Grant's moniker appears next to a surprisingly tame lion. Bring cash to commission business cards, ex-libris, menus or invitations, and trust Signor Basso to deliver via post.

DE ROSSI   ARTISANAL, IRONWORK

(Map p318; ☑041 520 00 77; www.derossiferro battuto.com; Calle del Fumo 5045; ☺10am-7pm Mon-Fri; ⌂Ca' d'Oro) Set a romantic Venetian mood in your own backyard with De Rossi's authentic fisherman's lanterns, a bubble of Murano glass inside a forged-iron frame. This family workshop is among the last, best Venetian lantern-makers, producing traditional and new styles with coloured and matte glass in shapes that range from classic *zucca* (pumpkin) lanterns to sleek modern wall sconces.

PAOLO OLBI   ARTISANAL, STATIONERY

(Map p318; ☑041 523 76 55; http://olbi.atspace. com; Campo Santa Maria Nova 6061; ☺11.30am-1pm & 3.30-7.30pm; ⌂Fondamenta Nuove) Thoughts worth committing to paper deserve Paolo Olbi's keepsake books, albums and stationery. Ordinary journals can't compare to Olbi originals handmade with heavyweight paper, bound with either hand-tanned or affordable reclaimed leather bindings. Office supplies are upgraded with an embossed winged lion of San Marco, one paw resting on an open book.

LIBRERIA INTERNAZIONALE
MARCO POLO   BOOKS

(Map p318; ☑041 522 63 43; www.libreriamar copolo.com; Calle del Teatro Malibran 5886a; ☺9.30am-1pm & 3.30-7.30pm Mon-Sat; ⌂Rialto) Everything you'd travel the world to find in an indie bookseller is right here in Venice: impassioned book recommendations from writerly staff, book exchanges for credit toward gorgeous limited-edition art books, used and new titles in English, and local manifestos such as Eye on Venice pamphlets *Dear Tourist* and *Bennetown*. Meet here for writing workshops, author readings, and bookish flirtations.

SESTIERE DI CANNAREGIO SHOPPING

SPILLI LAB & SHOP

Glamour comes easily at **Spilli Lab & Shop** (Map p318; ☑340 276 72 96; Ponte dei Miracoli 6091; ☺9.30am-12.30pm & 3.30-7.30pm Tue-Sun, 3.30-7.30pm Mon; ⚓Fondamente Nuove), a Venetian design showcase with embroidered tunic dresses, graphite wool wrap-dresses and broad-brimmed fedoras. Alessia Sopelsa has an eye for luxe textures and original details – yet everything here is surprisingly affordable, with double-digit fashion statements that command attention in five-digit Biennale crowds.

BRANDS
DESIGN STORE, ACCESSORIES

(Fullspot; Map p318; www.fullspot.it; San Geremia 314; ☺10am-7.30pm; ⚓Ferrovia) Right in style and on the money, this Padua-based designer sells affordable, mix-and-match accessories: watch faces with interchangeable rubber wristbands, and sleek silicon totebags with removeable handles. Try tone-on-tone with a lagoon-teal-blue face and band, or a high-contrast yellow-and-grey combo. Switch up totebags seasonally: flocked fuschia with white patent-leather handles works for winter, while orange with sailor's-rope handles says summer.

GIBIGIANA
ARTISANAL, GLASS

(Map p318; ☑041 524 28 97; Lista di Spagna 159; ☺10am-7pm; ⚓Ferrovia) Last-minute gift-buyers, rejoice: this showcase of independent Venetian glass designers right near the train station will save you a hasty trip to Murano. Among the surprisingly affordable, authentic local designs are chiseled glass rings, striped perfume bottles, and two-tone *goti* (water glasses) – each with a price tag under €25.

CARTA & DESIGN
DESIGN STORE

(di Roberta Molin; Map p318; ☑041 720 514; Strada Nuova 2083; ☺10am-7.30pm; ⚓Ca' d'Oro) Venice aficionados will recognise the architectural silhouettes emblazoned on Roberta Molin's original designs: that's the Rialto Bridge on purple travel journals, the Ca' d'Oro on yellow bookmarks, and the Palazzo Ducale on coloured-pencil sets. Daisy cocktail rings made of rubber and Murano glass deserve a Cannaregio canalside *spritz*, and Venice tote bags enable Strada Nuova shopping sprees.

VLADÌ SHOES
SHOES

(Map p318; ☑041 244 00 84; www.vladishoes.it; Rio Terà della Maddalena 2340; ☺10am-1.30pm & 2.30-7.30pm Mon-Sat; ⚓Ca' d'Oro) Step out in stylish, well-heeled and surprisingly practical shoes, made right in Venice. Algae-green high-button boots, oxblood oxfords and strappy citrus sandals turn Cannaregio *fondamente* into your own personal runways at happy hour, without leaving your arches aching for a *vaporetto*.

ANTICHITÀ AL GHETTO
ANTIQUES

(Map p318; ☑041 524 45 92; Calle del Ghetto Vecchio 1133/4; ☺9.30am-noon & 2.30-6pm Wed-Sat, 2.30-6pm Tue, 10am-1pm Sun; ⚓Guglie) Instead of souvenir T-shirts, this antique shop offers mementos of Venetian history: ancient maps of the canals, etchings of Venetian dandies daintily alighting from gondolas, and 18th-century cameos worn by the most fashionable ladies in the Ghetto.

GIUNTI AL PUNTO
BOOKS

(Map p318; ☑041 524 37 28; Rio Terà della Maddalena; ☺9am-8pm Mon-Wed, to midnight Fri & Sat, 10am-10pm Thu & Sun; ⚓Guglie) Late hours, decent paperbacks, kids books in several languages, useful cookbooks and maps of Venice make this a handy outlet for further information and vacation reading.

DOLCEAMARO
FOOD, WINE

(Map p318; ☑041 523 87 08; Campo San Canciano 6051; ☺10am-1pm & 4-7.30pm Mon-Sat, 11.30am-1.30pm & 4.40-7.30pm Sun; ⚓Rialto) For the well-travelled foodie who's been there, eaten that, here's something original: a miniature platter of Italian cheeses and cured meats, made out of artisanal chocolate. Dolceamaro also stocks wines, speciality Veneto grappa (spirits), and other gourmet temptations, including aged balsamic vinegars and whole truffles.

Sestiere di Castello

Neighbourhood Top Five

1 Getting an insider's view during special events at the **Arsenale** (p139), the Venetian Republic's vast honeycomb of a shipyard and once the world's best-kept industrial secret.

2 Gawking at the sheer scale of **Zanipolo** (p141), a 14th-century church packed with master works of painting and sculpture.

3 Taking an early-morning stroll along **Riva degli Schiavoni** (p143), Castello's breathtaking waterfront promenade.

4 Taking a break from brick and marble amid the leafy byways of Napoleon's **Giardini Pubblici.** (p142)

5 Basking in the golden glow of Carpaccio's paintings in the **Scuola di San Giorgio degli Schiavoni** (p144).

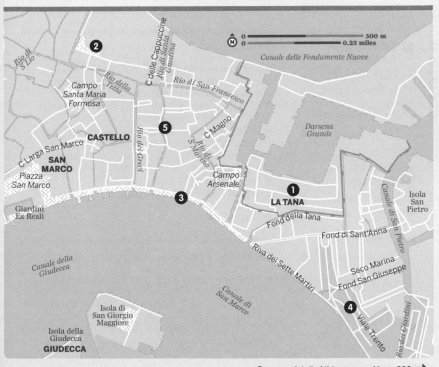

For more detail of this area see Map p320 ➡

Lonely Planet's Top Tip

Venice is always best early in the morning or after the crowds thin in the evening. This is especially true of the Riva degli Schiavoni, which is packed from 9am to 9pm with day-trippers as cruises disgorge their madding crowds. But if you can get yourself out of bed at sunrise, the seafront promenade makes for a magnificent and remarkably solitary morning constitutional – it's also a great chance to get people-free photos.

Best Places to Eat

➡ Trattoria Corte Sconta (p153)

➡ al Covo (p154)

➡ Osteria alla Staffa (p153)

For reviews, see p151 ➡

Best Places to Drink

➡ La Serra (p154)

➡ Bar Terazza Danieli (p154)

➡ Bacaro Risorto (p154)

For reviews, see p154 ➡

🔒 Best Places to Shop

➡ Sigfrido Cipolato (p155)

➡ Atelier Alessandro Merlin (p157)

➡ Al Campanil (p157)

For reviews, see p155 ➡

SESTIERE DI CASTELLO

Explore Sestiere di Castello

Stretching eastwards from San Marco, Castello is the city's most sprawling *sestiere* and exploring its entirety in one day will test walking shoes. Start with its most compelling sites – the masterfully grand Zanipolo church, Negroponte's rose-fringed Madonna in San Francesco della Vigna and Bellini's *Virgin Enthroned* in opulent San Zaccaria. All are within a stone's throw of San Marco and Rialto.

Moving east, you'll reach the engine of the city's seafaring might: the sprawling shipyards known simply as the Arsenale. While the Arsenale is only open for special events, the nearby Museo Storico Navale helps fill in the city's blockbuster maritime history. East of the Arsenale lie working-class neighbourhoods around Via Garibaldi and on the Isola di Sant'Elena. You're most likely to hear the Venetian dialect here, and it's a great place for an *aperitivo* (pre-dinner drink) or a local lunch.

The Napoleonic gardens, the pavilion-dotted Giardini Pubblici and the Parco Sant'Elena skirt the southern shore, the Giardini springing to life in summer months when Biennale events attract artists, architects and curators from around the world. In Castello's easternmost reaches visit Venice's first cathedral on the island of San Pietro del Castello before returning at sunset along the Riva dei Partigiani for sweeping views of San Giorgio Maggiore and the Bacino di San Marco.

Local Life

➡ **Castello craftsmen** Away from the main tourist areas, Castello's artisans are freer to experiment. Don't miss 16th-century enamel work at Sigfrido Cipolato (p155), Alessandro Merlin's (p157) *sgraffito* ceramics and Giovanna Zanella's (p157) surreal shoes.

➡ **Backstreet bacaro** Locals drop in all day for *cicheti* at Bacaro Risorto (p154), Al Portego (p154) and El Rèfolo (p155); while *gondolieri* prefer their breakfast *cornetto* at Pasticceria Da Bonifacio (p151).

➡ **Outdoor living** *Nonne* (grandmothers) gather for afternoon gossip while their young charges kick balls across Campo di Bandiera e Mori, Campo Zanipolo and the Giardini Pubblici (p142).

Getting There & Away

➡ **Vaporetto** Line 1 makes all stops along the Riva degli Schiavoni, linking it with both Grand Canal stops and the Lido. Line 2 also heads up the Grand Canal. Lines 41, 42, 51 and 52 circle the outer perimeter of Venice, including stops along Riva degli Schiavoni and Giudecca.

TOP SIGHT
ARSENALE

Founded in 1104, the Arsenale quickly grew to become Europe's greatest naval installation and the largest productive complex in the world. Sustained by an enormous 10% of the city's income and employing up to 16,000 highly skilled *arsenolotti* (Arsenale workers), it was the very heart of Venice's mercantile and military power. A unique pre-industrial example of mass production, its centralised organisation, standardised processes and stringent quality control all anticipate the modern factory. Not only was the Arsenale capable of turning out a new galley in a single day, its 45-hectare (100-acre) physical footprint occupied 15% of the city. Even today, it is completely surrounded by 3.2km (2 miles) of crenellated walls.

At its peak, the Arsenale must have made an enormous impression, with its boiling black pitch, metalworking and timber cutting. Many streets in Castello are still named after its activities: Calle della Pece (pitch), del Piombo (lead), delle Ancore (anchors) and delle Vele (sails). Indeed, Dante used it as a model scene for hell in his *Divina Commedia* (Divine Comedy; Canto XXI, lines 7 to 21).

Perhaps the most revolutionary aspect of the Arsenale was that it used canals as moving assembly lines. The growing ship would move through the canals from one stage of construction to the next – a system that was not reproduced at such a scale until Henry Ford's 'revolutionary' car factory in the 20th century. As a result of this innovation, as many as 100 galleys could be in production at a single time. In addition, special consultants, such as Galileo, helped the Venetians rationalise production and build ships that could be equipped with increasingly powerful munitions. The treatise he later wrote, drawing on his experience, is considered a seminal text of materials science.

DON'T MISS...

- ➡ Porta Magna
- ➡ Corderia
- ➡ Artigliere
- ➡ Gaggiandre

PRACTICALITIES

- ➡ Map p320
- ➡ ☎ 041 521 88 28
- ➡ www.labiennale.org
- ➡ Campo della Tana
- ➡ adult €20, reduced €12-16
- ➡ ⏱10am-6pm Tue-Sun
- ➡ 🚤Arsenale

BUCINTORO

Seven centuries before *Pimp My Ride*, there was the Bucintoro. The most lavish creation of the Arsenale, it was the doge's official galley. There were four versions of the *Bucintoro*, the first of which was built in 1311. However, the most extravagant was the fourth and last. Completed in 1727, the multistorey floating *palazzo* was clad entirely in gold leaf and had seating for 90 – the main salon alone boasted 48 windows. And it required 168 oarsmen to manoeuvre. You can see a scale model in the Museo Storico Navale, plus a few original details salvaged after Napoleonic troops burned it in 1798.

The Fondazione Bucintoro is now leading an effort to build a life-size recreation of the 1727 *Bucintoro* for an estimated €15 million. Underwritten by the Banco Nazionale del Lavoro in 2012, shares in the golden hull will be sold in order to raise the necessary finance. Completion is expected in 2016.

The physical appearance of the yards was also a matter of prestige and cutting-edge design. At the core of the complex is the **Arsenale Vecchio** (Old Arsenal), which included storage for the *bucintoro*, the doge's ceremonial galley. In 1303–04 came the first expansion, known as **La Tana**. Occupying almost the whole length of the southern side of the Arsenale and performing essential rope-making work, it was refashioned in 1579 by Antonio da Ponte (of Rialto bridge fame). The **Arsenale Nuovo** (New Arsenal) was added in 1325, followed in 1473 by the **Arsenale Nuovissimo** (Very New Arsenal). In the 16th century, production of *galeazze* (large war vessels with a deep draught) required the creation of a deeper Canale delle Galeazze along with further workshops and sheds, such as the **Gaggiandre** (dry dock), which were fashioned from designs attributed to Jacopo Sansovino.

Now, large parts of the Arsenale have been retooled for use as exhibition space during the Art and Architecture Biennales and other special events. Outside of these exhibits the area remains tantalisingly off-limits.

Porta Magna

Capped by the lion of St Mark that somehow eluded destruction by Napoleon's troops, the Arsenale's land gateway is considered by many to be the earliest example of Renaissance architecture in Venice; it was probably executed in 1460. A plaque was installed commemorating the 1571 victory at Lepanto, and the fenced-in terrace was added in 1692. Below the statues is a row of carved lions; the biggest one, regally seated, was taken as booty by Francesco Morosini from the Greek port of Piraeus, which must have taken some doing. On the right flank of the lion, you'll notice some Viking runes, said to be a kind of 11th-century war-trophy inscription left behind by Norwegian mercenaries. They boast of their role in helping Byzantium quell a Greek rebellion – the mercenary equivalent of leaving behind a résumé.

Biennale Exhibition Spaces

Architecture and Art Biennale exhibitions are mounted in the construction sheds of the Arsenale; the Herculaean effort harkens back to earlier times. Unfortunately, the Arsenale is only accessible to the public during these events. Biennale shows do often offer peeks inside, including the former **Corderia** (where ships' cables were made), the **Artiglierie** (gun workshop) and the magnificent arcaded **Gaggiandre**. More creative repurposing lies ahead: ongoing work to transform the entire Arsenale will create modern ship-maintenance areas, shops, restaurants, exhibition spaces, a study centre and more.

TOP SIGHT
ZANIPOLO

When the Dominicans began building Zanipolo in 1333 to rival the Franciscans' Basilica di Santa Maria Gloriosa dei Frari (p104), the church stirred passions more common to Serie A football than architecture. Both structures feature red-brick facades with high-contrast detailing in white stone. But since Zanipolo's facade remains unfinished, the Frari won a decisive early decision with its soaring grace and Titian's *Assunta* altarpiece. Over the centuries, Zanipolo has at least tied the score with its pantheon of ducal funerary monuments and the variety of its masterpieces.

Named after two minor martyrs of early Christian Rome, Santi Giovanni e Paolo – elided to San Zanipolo in Venetian dialect – the structure was designed to make worshippers feel small and reverential. Little can prepare you for its cavernous interior (90m by 38m), suffused by a soft pink glow.

Architecture
Built in classic Italian Gothic style, the basilica could accommodate virtually the entire population of 14th-century Castello. Its 33m-high nave is reinforced by a clever series of cross-beams – necessary because of Venice's waterlogged soil. Typical of Italian Gothic and different from French Gothic, its exteriors and interiors have a barnlike simplicity. Rarest of all is the surviving 15th-century stained glass in the south transept. Created on Murano, it richly illuminates designs by Bartolomeo Vivarini and Girolamo Mocetto.

Tombs of the Dogi
For centuries, Zanipolo was the site of doges' funerals, and the walls are punctuated by 25 of their lavish tombs. From Pietro Lombardo's three-tier monument celebrating the Ages of Man for Pietro Mocenigo (1406–76) to the Gothic tomb of Michele Morosini (1308–82) and Andrea Tirali's bombastic *Tomba dei Valier* (1708), they provide an overview of the stylistic development of Venetian art.

DON'T MISS...

➡ Giovanni Bellini's *SS Vincent Ferrer, Christopher and Sebastian*

➡ Pietro Lombardo's tomb for Pietro Mocenigo

➡ Stained glass in the south transept

➡ Guido Reni's *San Giuseppe*

➡ Giambattista Lorenzetti's *Jesus the Navigator*

PRACTICALITIES

➡ Chiesa dei SS Giovanni e Paolo

➡ Map p320

➡ 041 523 59 13

➡ www.basilicasanti giovanniepaolo.it

➡ Campo Zanipolo

➡ adult/student €2.50/1.25

➡ 9am-6pm Mon-Sat, noon-6pm Sun

➡ Ospedale

Bellini's Triptych
In 1867, a fire destroyed paintings by Tintoretto, Palma di Giovanni, Titian and Bellini. Anti-Catholic arson was suspected, but nothing was proved. A second Bellini polyptych, on the second altar in the right aisle, survived. Depicting *SS Vincent Ferrer, Christopher and Sebastian*, the work has a vivid sensuousness that was to become a hallmark of Venetian painting.

Reni, Lorenzetti & Veronese
Guido Reni's *San Giuseppe* is a rare expression of holy bonding, with Joseph exchanging adoring looks with baby Jesus. The dome on the southwest end of the nave boasts Giambattista Lorenzetti's *Jesus the Navigator* – Jesus scans the skies like an anxious Venetian sea captain. In the **Cappella del Rosario**, Paolo Veronese's *Assunta* ceiling depicts the rosy Virgin ascending a staggering staircase to be crowned by cherubs.

TOP SIGHT
GIARDINI PUBBLICI

Venice's public gardens were laid out between 1808 and 1812 on the orders of Napoleon, who decided the city needed a little breathing space. Never mind that an entire residential district had to be demolished or acres of swampland reclaimed. A winning combination of formal gardens and winding pathways, the park now stretches from Via Garibaldi, past the Garibaldi monument with its punk-haired lion, through the Napoleonic gardens and past the Biennale pavilions to Sant'Elena, making this the largest park in Venice.

DON'T MISS...

➡ Venezuelan Pavilion
➡ Austrian Pavilion
➡ Monument to the Partisan Woman
➡ Parco delle Rimembranze

PRACTICALITIES

➡ Map p320
➡ www.labiennale.org
➡ 🚊Giardini, Biennale

Biennale Pavilions

A large portion of the gardens is given over to the Biennale exhibition arena, hosting international art (odd years) and architecture (even years) events in 30 modernist pavilions, each allocated to a different nation. During the **Art Biennale's** June–September run, connoisseurs swarm national showcases ranging from Geza Rintel Maroti's 1909 Secessionist-era **Hungarian Pavilion** to Philip Cox's 1988 boxy, yellow **Australian Pavilion**, frequently mistaken for a construction trailer.

The pavilions tell a fascinating story of 20th-century architecture – not least because Venetian modernist master Carlo Scarpa contributed to the Biennale from 1948 to 1972, trying to make the best of Duilio Torres' Fascist 1932 Italian Pavilion (now the **Palazzo delle Esposizioni**). Scarpa is also responsible for the daring 1956 raw-concrete-and-glass **Venezuelan Pavilion** and the winsome, bug-shaped **Biglietteria** (Ticket Office). The closest spiritual neighbour is the white-washed **Austrian Pavilion**, a Secessionist masterpiece designed by Josef Hoffman in 1934. More recently, the post-modern 1996 **Korean Pavilion** has taken over an electrical plant in ingenious ways. Note that the Biennale grounds are only open during Biennale events.

Monument to the Partisan Woman

Located purposefully in the lapping water off the Riva dei Sette Martiri – where seven Venetian partisans were shot and killed in 1944 – lies the 1200kg bronze figure of a woman partisan. Sculpted by Augusto Murer, the figure reclines, exhausted it seems, on an arrangement of Istrian stone platforms designed by Scarpa to catch the eye as she appears and disappears beneath the rising and falling tide.

La Serra

In 1894 Napoleon's gardens were furnished with a fashionable iron-framed, greenhouse (p154), originally intended to house the palms used in Biennale events. It rapidly expanded into a community hub and a centre for propagation: many plants grown here went to adorn the municipal flowerbeds of the Lido and the ballrooms of aristocratic *palazzi*. Restored in 2010, it now hosts events and workshops from paper making to yoga.

Parco delle Rimembranze

At the eastern limit of the gardens, on the island of Sant'Elena, is this memorial park. Planted with umbrella pines, each originally commemorating a fallen soldier of WWI, it's a tranquil spot with postcard views of the Bacino di San Marco. Families gather here to sit on the benches, roller skate around the rink and play on the slides and swings. Apart from providing a shady respite in a relentlessly urban environment, it offers a real slice of Venetian life.

⊙ SIGHTS

ARSENALE   HISTORIC QUARTER
See p139.

ZANIPOLO   BASILICA
See p141.

GIARDINI PUBBLICI   GARDEN
See p142.

CHIESA DI SAN ZACCARIA   CHURCH
(Map p320; ☑041 522 12 57; Campo San Zaccaria 4693; ◷10am-noon & 4-6pm Mon-Sat, 4-6pm Sun; ⧉San Zaccaria) **FREE** When 15th-century Venetian girls showed more interest in sailors than saints, they were sent to the convent adjoining San Zaccaria. The wealth showered on the church by their grateful parents is evident. Masterpieces by Bellini, Titian, Tintoretto and Van Dyck crowd the walls. Bellini's altarpiece is such a treasure that Napoleon whisked it away to Paris for 20 years when he plundered the city in 1797.

Founded in the 9th century, the church offers a brief history of Venetian architecture, from its watery Romanesque crypt to its early-Renaissance facade. The latter, begun by Antonio Gambello in the Gothic style, was finished with a flourish by Mauro Codussi, who crowned it with a crescendo of rounded embellishments in white Istrian stone. The church also claims to possess the remains of St Zacharias, father of John the Baptist, as well as the oldest tombs of the doges in Venice.

To your right as you enter, the **Cappella di San Atanasio** (admission €1) holds Tintoretto's *Birth of St John the Baptist*, while Tiepolo depicts the Holy Family fleeing to Egypt in a typically Venetian boat. Both hang above magnificently crafted choir stalls. Behind this chapel you'll find the Gothic **Cappella di San Tarasio** (also called Cappella d'Oro or the Golden Chapel), with impressive Renaissance-style frescoes by Andrea del Castagno and Francesco da Faenza from the 1440s.

The star of the show, though, is undoubtedly Giovanni Bellini's *Virgin Enthroned with Jesus, an Angel Musician and Saints* (1505), which glows like it's plugged into an outlet. Bellini was in his 70s when he painted it and had already been confronted by the first achievements of Giorgione (1477–1510), with his softer *sfumato* ('smokey') technique, which blurred hard lines, enhancing the emotional quality of the light, colour and perspective. Bellini's assimilation of the technique is clear. Not only are his colours typically vivid, but as shafts of sunlight strike, the saintly arrangement glows with a diffuse sense of devout spirituality.

RIVA DEGLI SCHIAVONI   PROMENADE
(Map p320; ⧉San Zaccaria) Stretching west from San Marco, this paved boardwalk is one of the world's great promenades. *Schiavoni* (literally, 'Slavs') refers to the fishermen from Dalmatia who arrived in Venice in medieval times and found this a handy spot for casting their nets. For centuries, vessels would dock and disembark here, the waterfront a Babel of languages, as traders, dignitaries and sailors arrived from ports around the Mediterranean and beyond.

Paolo Veronese's *Feast in the House of Levi*, in the Gallerie dell'Accademia (p84), gives you some idea of how the crowd might have looked and dressed, with Turkish, German, North African and Greek merchants wheeling and dealing along the banks. The great poet Petrarch was among those who found lodgings and inspiration at No 4175, east of Rio della Pietà. Now many of the grand old mansions serve as pricey hotels, so you too can bunk here like the merchants of yesteryear.

LA PIETÀ   CHURCH
(Map p320; ☑041 522 21 71; www.pietavenezia.it; Riva degli Schiavoni; admission €3, guided tour €5; ◷10.15am-noon & 3-5pm Tue-Fri, 10.15am-1pm & 2-5pm Sat & Sun; ⧉Pietà) Originally called Chiesa di Santa Maria della Visitazione but fondly nicknamed La Pietà, this harmonious church designed by Giorgio Massari is known for its association with the composer Vivaldi, who was concertmaster here in the early 18th century. Though the current church was built after Vivaldi's death, its acoustic-friendly oval shape honours his memory, and it is still regularly used as a concert hall.

Be sure to look up: on the ceiling, Giambattista Tiepolo's gravity-defying *Coronation of the Virgin* seems to open up the church to the vast heavens themselves.

CHIESA DI SAN GIOVANNI IN BRAGORA   CHURCH
(Map p320; ☑041 296 06 30; Campo Bandiera e Mori 3790; ◷9-11am & 3.30-5.30pm Mon-Sat, 9.30-noon Sun; ⧉Arsenale) **FREE** This serene,

TOP SIGHT **SCUOLA DI SAN GIORGIO DEGLI SCHIAVONI**

In the 15th century, Venice annexed Dalmatia – an area roughly corresponding to the former Yugoslavia – and large numbers of Dalmatians, known as Schiavoni, emigrated to Venice. In a testament to Venetian pluralism, they were granted their own *scuola* (religious confraternity) in 1451. Around 1500, they began building their headquarters, making the brilliant decision to hire Vittore Carpaccio (also of Dalmatian descent) to complete an extraordinary cycle of paintings of Dalmatia's patron saints George, Tryphone and Jerome.

Though Carpaccio never left Venice, his scenes with Dalmatian backdrops are minutely detailed. But the real brilliance of Carpaccio's imagined worlds are their engaging narrative power: St George charges a lizard-like dragon across a Libyan desert scattered with half-eaten corpses; St Jerome leads his tame-looking lion into a monastery, scattering friars like a flock of lagoon birds; and St Augustine, watched by his dog, is distracted from correspondence by a heavenly voice informing him of Jerome's death.

DON'T MISS...

➡ Carpaccio's *St George and the Dragon*

➡ Carpaccio's *St Jerome and the Lion*

PRACTICALITIES

➡ Map p320

➡ ☑041 522 88 28

➡ Calle dei Furlani 3259a

➡ adult/reduced €5/3

➡ ⊙2.45-6pm Mon, 9.15am-1pm & 2.45-6pm Tue-Sat, 9.15am-1pm Sun

➡ 🚶

➡ 🚤Pietà

15th-century brick church harmonises Gothic and Renaissance styles with remarkable ease, setting the tone for a young Antonio Vivaldi, who was baptised here. Look for Bartolomeo Vivarini's 1478 *Enthroned Madonna with St Andrew and John the Baptist*, which shows the Madonna bouncing a delighted baby Jesus on her knee.

Bartolomeo's nephew Alvise depicts Jesus in later years in his splendidly restored 1494 *Saviour Blessing*, in which Christ has a cloudlike beard and eyes that seem to follow you around the room.

CHIESA DI SAN GIORGIO DEI GRECI   CHURCH
(Map p320; ☑041 522 65 81; Campiello dei Greci 3412; ⊙9am-12.30pm & 2.30-4.30pm Wed-Sat & Mon, 9am-1pm Sun; 🚤Pietà) **FREE** Greek Orthodox refugees who fled to Venice from Turkey with the rise of the Ottoman Empire built a church here in 1536, with the aid of a special dispensation from Venice to collect taxes on incoming Greek ships. Nicknamed 'St George of the Greeks', the little church has an impressive iconostasis, and clouds of fine incense linger over services. The separate, slender **bell tower** was completed in 1603, though it began to lean right from

the start; these days, it seems poised to dive into the canal on which the church sits.

Permission for the church was granted in the late 15th century in acknowledgement of the growing importance of the Greek community in the city, which at its peak numbered around 4000. Greek scholars contributed greatly to Venice's dominance in the printing trade, and thereby to its eminence as a seat of Renaissance learning.

While the exterior is classically Venetian, the interior is Orthodox in style: the aisle-less nave is surrounded by dark, wooden stalls and there's a *matroneo* (women's gallery). All eyes, however, are drawn to the golden iconostasis with its 46 icons, the majority of which are the work of 16th-century Cretan artist Michael Danaskinàs. Other fabulous works by the Venetian school of icon painters can be found in the Museo delle Icone (p144).

MUSEO DELLE ICONE   MUSEUM
(Museum of Icons; Map p320; ☑041 522 65 81; www.istitutoellenico.org; Campiello dei Greci 3412; adult/student €4/2; ⊙10am-5pm; 🚤Pietà) Glowing colours and all-seeing eyes fill this treasure box of some 80 Greek icons

made in 14th- to 17th-century Italy. Keep your own eye out for the expressive *San Giovanni Climaco,* which shows the saintly author of a Greek spiritual guide distracted from his work by visions of souls diving into hell.

The museum goes by a confusing variety of names: it's also known as the 'Museo dei Dipinti Sacri Bizantini' (Museum of Holy Byzantine Paintings), and technically it's housed in the Istituto Ellenico (Hellenic Institute).

MUSEO DIOCESANO DI VENEZIA   MUSEUM
(Map p320; ☑041 522 91 66; www.veneziaubc. org; Chiostro di Sant'Apollonia 4312; adult/ reduced €4/2.50, cloister only €1; ☺10am-5pm Thu-Tue; ☺San Zaccaria) Housed in a former Benedictine monastery dedicated to Sant'Apollonia, this museum has a fairly predictable collection of religious art and the occasional standout temporary show – but the exquisite Romanesque cloister is the sole example of the genre in Venice. The adjoining building was a church until 1906, and now houses exhibition spaces.

PALAZZO GRIMANI   MUSEUM
(Map p320; ☑041 520 03 45; www.palazzo grimani.org; Ramo Grimani 4858; adult/reduced €7/6; ☺8.15am-2pm Mon, 8.15am-7.15pm Tue-Sun; ☺Ospedale, Rialto) The Grimani family built their Renaissance *palazzo* to house an extraordinary Graeco-Roman collection, which was destined to become the basis of the archaeological museum now housed in the Museo Correr (p73). Unusually for Venice, the palace has a Roman-style courtyard, which shed a flattering light on the archaeological curiosities. These days, the empty halls host temporary exhibitions, though their bedazzling frescoed interiors are reason enough to visit.

There is debate about who designed the building. However, it's certain that Giovanni Grimani (1501–93) himself played a large role in a design that consciously recalls the glories of ancient Rome. Grimani also hired a dream team of fresco painters specialising in fanciful grotesques and Pompeii-style mythological scenes. Francesco Salviati applied the glowing, Raphael-style colours he'd used in Rome's Palazzo Farnese, while Roman painter Giovanni da Udine, considered among the brightest pupils of Raphael and Giorgione, devoted three rooms to the stories of Ovid.

The Sala ai Fogliami (Foliage Room) is the most memorable, though. Painted by Mantovano, ceiling and walls are awash with remarkably convincing plant and bird life. They even include New World species that had only recently been discovered by Europeans, including two that would come to be staples of Venetian life: tobacco and corn.

PALAZZO QUERINI STAMPALIA   MUSEUM
(Map p320; ☑041 271 14 11; www.querinistampa lia.it; Campiello Querini Stampalia 5252; ☺Rialto, San Zaccaria) In 1869 Conte Giovanni Querini Stampalia made a gift of his ancestral *palazzo* to the city on the forward-thinking condition that its 700-year-old library operate late-night openings. Downstairs, savvy drinkers take their *aperitivi* with a twist of high modernism in the Carlo Scarpa-designed **garden**, while the *palazzo*'s temporary contemporary shows add an element of the unexpected to the silk-draped salons upstairs.

Enter through the Botta-designed QShop to get a free pass to the cafe and its garden. You can also buy tickets for the **Museo della Fondazione Querini Stampalia** (Map p320; adult/reduced €10/8; ☺10am-6pm Tue-Thu & Sun, to 10pm Fri & Sat; ☺Rialto, San Zaccaria) here. Located in the duke's apartments, the museum reflects the 18th-century tastes and interests of the count: beneath the stuccoed ceilings you'll find rich furnishings and tapestries, Meissen and Sèvres porcelain, marble busts and some 400 paintings. Of these, many are dynastic portraits and conversation pieces, such as Alessandro and Pietro Longhi's genre scenes of masked balls, gambling dens and 18th-century *bon vivants*.

The clear standout in the collection is Giovanni Bellini's arresting *Presentation of Jesus at the Temple*, where the hapless child looks like a toddler mummy, standing up in tightly wrapped swaddling clothes. Other engaging pieces are the 39 winningly naïve *Scenes of Public Life in Venice* by Gabriele Bella (1730–99), which document scenes of the city and its customs during the period. Although rather crude in their realisation, the subject matter – a football game in Sant'Alvise, the frozen lagoon in 1708, the courtesans' race on the Rio de la Sensa – is fascinating.

In summer the *palazzo* hosts chamber-music concerts on Friday and Saturday. Tickets cost €3.

SESTIERE DI CASTELLO SIGHTS

1. Vogalonga (p174)
This popular regatta each May sees enthusiasts sailing wooden boats from Venice to Murano and Burano and back.

2. Grand Canal (p68)
The 3.5km route of *vaporetto* No 1 is public transport at its most glamorous.

3. Water Taxi (p279)
Private water taxis shuttle visitors around Venice.

4. Vaporetto (p281)
These passenger ferries are the city's main form of public transport.

CHIESA DI SANTA MARIA FORMOSA   CHURCH

(Map p320; www.santamariaformosa.it; Campo Santa Maria Formosa 5267; admission €3 or with Chorus Pass; ⊙10am-5pm Mon-Sat, 1-5pm Sun; ⊛Rialto, San Zaccaria) Originally built from wood and thatched with straw, Santa Maria Formosa was the first church on the Rialto to be dedicated to the Virgin Mary, in 842. According to legend, its curious name, 'Shapely St Mary', was inspired by a vision of San Magno, Bishop of Oderzo, although another, more likely, version of events claims the name was confused with the address of a comely courtesan, who lived on the square in the 16th century.

Certainly, Veronica Franco (1546–91), one of Venice's most famous courtesans and an accomplished poet, frequented literary salons at Ca'Vernier opposite the church, and the stage-set *campo* was a lively social hub, often used for open-air theatre.

Destroyed by fire in 1106, the church was refashioned by Mauro Codussi in 1492 with new baroque curves and serene symmetries that make good on its shapely name. So does Palma il Vecchio's polyptych of the forceful-looking St Barbara swathed in a billowing red cape atop the Third Altar dedicated to the Scuola di Bombardieri (School of Shipbuilders), of whom she is patron saint. Vasari thought it one of his best works. Similarly eye-catching is Bartolomeo Vivarini's triptych of the *Madonna della Misericordia* in the first chapel to the right of the nave.

CHIESA DI SAN LIO   CHURCH

(Map p320; Campo San Lio; donations appreciated; ⊙9-11.30am & 3-4pm Mon-Fri; ⊛Rialto) FREE Giandomenico Tiepolo sure did know how to light up a room. Duck into the atmospheric gloom of San Lio's baroque interior and, as your eyes adjust, look up at Tiepolo's magnificent ceiling fresco, *The Glory of the Cross and St Leon IX*. On your left by the main door is Titian's *Apostle James the Great*, but this church is better known for yet another Venetian artist: the great *vedutista* (landscapist) Canaletto, who was baptised and buried in this, his parish church.

STATUE OF BARTOLOMEO COLLEONI   MONUMENT

(Map p320; Campo SS Giovanni e Paolo; ⊛Ospedale) Bartolomeo Colleoni's galloping bronze equestrian statue is one of only two such public monuments in Venice – and it's an extraordinary example of early-Renaissance sculpture. It commemorates one of Venice's most loyal mercenary commanders. From 1448, Colleoni commanded armies for the Republic, though in true mercenary form he switched sides a couple of times when he felt he'd been stiffed on pay or promotions.

On his death in 1474, he bequeathed 216,000 gold and silver ducats to Venice, on one condition: that the city erect a commemorative statue to him in Piazza San Marco. Since not even a doge had ever won such pride of place in Venice, the Senate found a rather dubious workaround, placing the monument in front of the Scuola Grande di San Marco instead. At least the Republic didn't scrimp on the statue: sculpted with imposing grandeur by Florentine master Andrea del Verrocchio (1435–88), it is embellished with Colleoni's emblematic *coglioni* (cullions or testicles) – a typically crude Renaissance pun. You can spot them on the base, looking like emphatic quotation marks.

SCUOLA GRANDE DI SAN MARCO   NOTABLE BUILDING

(Map p320; Campo Zanipolo; ⊛Ospedale) Instead of a simple Saturday father-son handyman project, sculptor Pietro Lombardo and his sons had something more ambitious in mind: a high-Renaissance polychrome marble facade for the most important confraternity in Venice; Mauro Codussi was brought in to put the finishing touches on this gem. Magnificent lions of St Mark prowl above the portals, while sculpted *trompe l'œil* perspectives beguile the eye.

The *scuola* now serves as the main entrance to the Ospedale Civile, the city's public hospital. You are welcome to peek inside at the ancient hall with its beamed ceiling held up by two ranks of five columns. However, sightseeing among the sick is considered poor form.

OSPEDALETTO   CHURCH

(Map p320; ☑041 271 90 12; www.scalabovolo. org; Barbaria delle Tole 6691; guided visits for groups €60; ⊙by reservation only; ⊛Ospedale) This Ruskin-baiting baroque affair, which the celebrated art critic thought 'the most monstrous example of the Grotesque Renaissance...in Venice' was, like Vivaldi's Pietà (p155), famous for its female musicians. The accomplished girls came from the adjoining orphanage and hospice, designed by Antonio Sardi, and played amid the trumpeting angels of Baldassare Longhena's 1660s chapel, complete with music room.

In the recently restored **Sala da Musica**, charming *trompe l'oeil* frescoes by Jacopo Guarana and Antonio Mengozzi Colonna adorn the ceiling and walls showing the orphaned girls performing in celebrated concerts. In one, a girl bends down to feed her pet greyhound what appears to be a doughnut.

The smallest of Venice's four historic hospices (hence the nickname, 'Small Hospital'), the complex is now owned by IRE, a public institution that still runs homes for the elderly. At the time of writing, restoration on the church continues and it remains open by appointment only. Reserve at least a week in advance.

CHIESA DI SAN FRANCESCO DELLA VIGNA
CHURCH

(Map p320; ☑041 520 61 02; www.sanfrancescodellavigna.it; Campo San Francesco della Vigna 2786; ⊙9.30am-12.30pm & 3-6pm Mon-Sat, 3-6pm Sun; ⛴Celestia, Ospedale) **FREE** Designed and built by Jacopo Sansovino with a facade by Palladio, this enchanting Franciscan church is one of Venice's most underappreciated attractions. The Madonna positively glows in Bellini's 1507 *Madonna and Saints* in the **Cappella Santa**, just off the flower-carpeted **cloister**, while swimming angels and strutting birds steal the scene in the delightful *Virgin Enthroned,* by Antonio da Negroponte (c 1460–70). Bring €0.20 to illuminate them.

Palladio and the Madonna are tough acts to follow, but father-son sculptors Pietro and Tullio Lombardo make their own mark with their 15th-century marble reliefs that recount the lives of Christ and an assortment of saints. Housed in the **Cappella Giustiniani**, just left of the altar, they are storytelling triumphs. Breezes seem to ripple through carved-marble trees, and lifelike lions seem prepared to pounce right off the wall. And keep your eye on the expressive reactions of minor figures in these biblical narratives. They provide a running commentary on the action, right down to the startled mule.

Out the back, the bell tower looks like the long-lost twin of the Campanile di San Marco and, facing north, a couple of steps leading to a portico of classical columns make the *campo* look like a proper ancient-Roman *agora* (market place). This makes a sociable setting for Venice's best annual block party, the **Festa di Francesco della Vigna**, with wine and rustic fare served up in the stately shadow of Palladio; it's usually held the third week in June.

CHIESA DI SAN MARTINO
CHURCH

(Map p320; ☑041 523 04 87; Campo San Martino 2298; ⊙8.45-11.45am & 4.30-7.30pm Mon-Sat, 8am-noon Sun; ⛴Arsenale) **FREE** The neighbourhood church of San Martino is named after St Martin of Tours (AD 316–97), a Hungarian priest and the first Christian saint to die a natural death rather than suffer some irksome martyrdom. Inside, Sansovino's Greek cross interior is lined with eight chapels and topped by a *trompe l'oeil* ceiling by Domenico Bruni. Palma di Giovane's canvases of Jesus being flogged and then marched towards Calvary are tucked out of sight in the choir stalls.

The church's other modest treasures include Tullio Lombardo's marble altar effortlessly held aloft by two fervently praying angels and, over the side door, the tomb of Doge Francesco Erizzo, which cleverly mirrors the facade of his *palazzo* seen through the door.

To the right of the church is the former **Scuola di San Martino**, where secondhand sales are sometimes held. It was built by the Guild of Ship Caulkers in the 16th century and sports a relief above the door of St Martin offering to share his cloak with a beggar. On the saint's feast day, 11 November, when children run through the streets banging

THE MOUTH OF THE LION

Next to the door of the Chiesa di San Martino you'll notice the face of a grimacing lion with his mouth agape. There are a number of these *bocca di leoni* around Venice, dating from the 14th century, when Venetians were encouraged to post anonymous denunciations of their neighbours 'in the mouth of the lion'. These slanders reported any number of unholy acts from cursing and tax avoidance (forgiveable) to Freemasonry (punishable by death) and were investigated by Venice's dreaded security service, led by the Council of Ten.

SESTIERE DI CASTELLO SIGHTS

VENICE'S SECRET WEAPON: ARSENALOTTI

In an early version of the assembly line, ships built in the Arsenale progressed through sequenced design phases, each staffed by *arsenalotti* (Arsenale workers) specialised in a particular aspect of construction, ranging from hull assembly and pitch application through to sail rigging. Women specialised in sails; children started apprenticeships at age 10, and did their part twisting hemp into rope.

But this wasn't a low-paid, low-status job. The *arsenalotti* were well remunerated, with cradle-to-grave fringe benefits. This helped keep them remarkably faithful to the Republic, and throughout Venetian history, *arsenalotti* repeatedly proved both their loyalty and their brawn during periods of war and rebellion. Using their proven shipbuilding techniques, they also constructed the vast *carena di nave* (ship's keel) ceilings you see in Venetian churches and in the Palazzo Ducale's Sala del Maggior Consiglio.

Job requirements for *arsenalotti* included manual dexterity, strength and silence. Even in raucous Castello *bacari* (old-style bars), *arsenalotti* remained carefully vague about the specifics of their workday, in an 'I could tell you, but then I'd have to kill you' kind of way. Shipbuilding processes were top secret, and industrial espionage was considered an act of high treason, punishable by exile or death. For centuries the crenellated walls of the Arsenale hid the feverish activity inside from view. Even outside the walls, the *arsenalotti* tended to stick to their own kind. They intermarried, and even had their own market gardens to reduce contact with the rest of the city.

If other maritime powers had learned to make warships as fast and as fleet as Venice's, the tiny lagoon republic might have lost its outsized advantage and been obliterated by its foes. In 1379, when Venetian commander Carlo Zeno's fleet was otherwise engaged, maritime rival Genoa surrounded Venice and tried to starve it into submission. But Genoa hadn't counted on the *arsenalotti,* who worked furiously to produce a fleet able to sustain a counterattack until Zeno arrived on the horizon. In 1570, when requested to produce as many ships as possible for an emergency fleet, the *arsenalotti* put out an astounding 100 galleys in just two months – despite a fire that had decimated the Arsenale the previous year.

However, things eventually went downhill. A bout of plague wiped out a third of the city's population, and Venice's maritime rivals Austria and the Ottoman Empire discovered their own secret weapon: free-trade agreements that excluded Venice. By 1797 naval production had all but ceased, and La Serenissima surrendered to Napoleon without a fight.

cooking pots and hoping for sweets, you'll see the same image reproduced in the shape of hundreds of sugar-coated cookies.

MUSEO STORICO NAVALE MUSEUM

(Map p320; ☎041 244 13 99; Riva San Biagio 2148; adult/student €1.55/free; ◷8.45am-1.30pm Mon-Fri, to 1pm Sat; 🚼; ⛴Arsenale) Maritime madness spans 42 rooms at this museum of Venice's seafaring history, featuring scale models of Venetian-built vessels as well as Peggy Guggenheim's not-so-minimalist gondola. On the ground floor, 'the barn', you'll find sprawling galleries of fearsome weaponry and 17th-century dioramas of forts and ports. Upstairs you can gawk at a sumptuous model of the *bucintoro*, the doge's gilded ceremonial barge, destroyed by Napoleonic troops in 1798.

Although the minutiae of some of the exhibits will mostly be of interest to enthusiasts and specialists, the display illustrates the incredible span of Venetian power across the Adriatic and Mediterranean over the centuries. In addition, the 2nd floor covers Italian naval history and memorabilia, from unification to the present day, and on the 3rd floor is a room devoted to gondolas, including Peggy Guggenheim's pimped-up ride.

The ticket also gets you entrance to the **Padiglione delle Navi** (Ships Pavilion; Map p320; Fondamenta della Madonna; ⛴Arsenale), though at the time of writing it was only open for special exhibitions. Of the many boats on display here, the most eye-catching is the Scalé Reale, an early-19th-century ceremonial vessel used to ferry King Vittorio Emanuele to Piazza San Marco in 1866 when Venice joined the nascent Kingdom of Italy. The ship last set sail in 1959, when it brought the body of the Venetian Pope Pius X to rest at the Basilica di San Marco

CATTEDRALE DI SAN PIETRO DI CASTELLO
CHURCH

(Map p320; ☑041 275 04 62; Campo San Pietro 2787; admission €3, or with Chorus Pass; ☺10am-5pm Mon-Sat; ⛴San Pietro) This sleepy church on the far-flung island of San Pietro served as Venice's cathedral from 1451 to 1807. An almost-but-not-quite Palladio design with a white **bell tower** of Istrian stone by Codussi, its expansive 54m **dome** rivals Michelangelo's at the Vatican in width (though not height). The most intriguing piece inside the church is **St Peter's Throne**, which according to legend was used by the Apostle Peter in Antioch and once hid the Holy Grail.

While the story has all the makings of an *Indiana Jones* sequel, sadly there's very little truth to it: the intricately carved stone back is in fact made from a scavenged Muslim tombstone that postdates the Apostle's death by many centuries. Still, it seems a fitting tale for such a historic location, given that the island of San Pietro (originally known as Olivolo) was among the first to be inhabited in Venice, and the original church here was the seat of a bishopric as early as 775.

✖ EATING

The most sprawling *sestiere* in Venice, Castello is also largely residential, which means its upmarket restaurants, neighbourhood *trattorie* and raucous *cicheti* **bars offer extremely varied dining choices. Eateries cluster around the stage-set *campi* of Santa Maria Formosa, San Zaccaria and SS Giovanni e Paolo, as well as down the narrow alleys around the Arsenale and along Napoleon's grand boulevard, Via Garibaldi.**

★PASTICCERIA DA BONIFACIO
PASTRIES & CAKES €

(Map p320; ☑041 522 75 07; Calle degli Albanesi 4237; pastries €1.50-4; ☺7am-8pm Fri-Wed; ⛴San Zaccaria) Pastry awards line the wall in this tiny bakery where gondoliers and Venetian housewives flock to devour the buttery, just-baked sweetness of almond croissants and take-home boxes of Venetian specialities such as *zaletti* (cornmeal biscuits with sultanas). As afternoon wanes, the bakery turns into a makeshift bar as locals pop in for the signature *spritz* and *mammalucchi* (deep-fried batter balls with candied fruit).

ZENZERO
CAFE €

(Map p320; ☑041 241 28 28; http://barzenzero.it; Campo Santa Marina 5902; sandwiches €2-4; ☺7am-8pm Mon-Fri, to 7.15pm Sat; ⛴Rialto) One of the best quick eats in Venice, Zenzero pairs the eye-opening powers of espresso with great little sandwiches and freshly baked pastries that tend to disappear in a flash. Return for top-shelf *aperitivi* in the *campo*. It's closed for two weeks at Christmas and two weeks in August.

TRATTORIA ALLA RAMPA
VENETIAN €

(Map p320; ☑041 528 53 65; Via Garibaldi 1135; meals €12-22; ☺noon-2pm Mon-Fri; ⛴Giardini) Hidden behind a little working-class bar is

---

THE VENETIAN 'BURBS

At the easternmost reaches of Venice, Sant'Elena is the city's most far-flung island. Most of it, with the exception of the 12th-century church and monastery of the eponymous saint, was built upon reclaimed swampland dredged up in the process of creating shipping lanes in the early 20th century.

The island took on its current aspect during the 1920s, when it was developed as the city's newest residential area. Deliberately eschewing the Modernist trends of its time, the middle-class apartments are faithful copies of the city's aristocratic palaces. However, they lack the quirks and elegant decay that define the rest of Venice. In fact, the whole neighbourhood feels a little like a Disney version of the city of which, ironically, it is an integral part.

Today Sant'Elena has become a favourite of joggers for its shady byways and distinct lack of crowds. But it is also worth a stroll just for its anachronistic charms – and as a lesson, by way of contrasts, in what makes Venice inimitable.

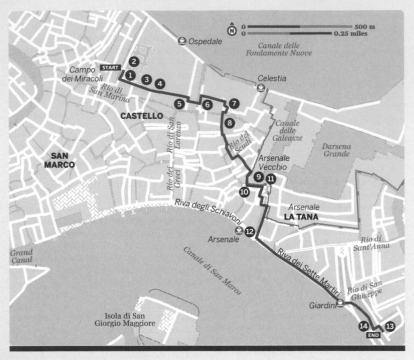

🏃 Neighbourhood Walk
Castello's Byways

START CAMPO ZANIPOLO (CAMPO SS
GIOVANNI E PAOLO)
END PARADISO
LENGTH 6.5KM; THREE HOURS

Start in Campo Zanipolo, where you can't miss the **①** **Bartolomeo Colleoni statue** (p148). A 15th-century mercenary commander, Colleoni left the city a fortune on condition that Venice erect a statue in his honour in Piazza San Marco. Venice took the money but bent the rules, erecting the statue in front of the **②** **Scuola Grande di San Marco** (p148). Next door rise the imposing Gothic heights of the treasure-packed **③** **Zanipolo** (p141).

A block east, pass the **④** **Ospedaletto** (p148), an orphanage chapel designed by Palladio and Longhena. Continue to stroll east down Barbaria de le Tole, past bric-a-brac haven **⑤** **Ballarin** (p157) and aross the canal in front of the **⑥** **Liceo Scientifico**, with another fine Longhena facade.

Dog-leg left for Palladio's massive, classical **⑦** **Chiesa di San Francesco della Vigna** (p149), home to a fine Bellini and Antonio Negroponte's gorgeous *Virgin and Child Enthroned.*

Turn south and back to the future – just over the Rio di San Francesco lies the **⑧** **Laboratorio Occupato Morion** (p155), an avant-garde cultural centre. Further south, past Campo delle Gatte, cross a canal and enter a tight nest of alleys, once housing works of the **⑨** **Arsenale** (p139), whose walls rear up ahead. Turn right at Campo de le Gorne and follow the walls round to **⑩** **Chiesa di San Martino** (p149). To the right of its doorway is the *bocca di leoni* (mouth of the lion), in which Venetians could slip denunciations of their neighbours.

Keep following the Arsenale's walls until you reach the **⑪** **Porta Magna** (Main Gate), considered the city's earliest example of Renaissance architecture. From here, turn south onto the **⑫** **Riva degli Schiavoni** (p143) and gawk at the views across the Bacino before finishing your walk with a herbal tisane at **⑬** **La Serra** (p154) or a *spritz* and lagoonside seat at **⑭** **Paradiso** (p155).

a low-slung dining room serving up some of Venice's heartiest lunch specials. A largely male, Venetian crowd tucks in hungrily to generous portions of roasted meat and fish, accompanied by seasonal vegetables and plentiful hunks of bread to sop up the sauces – all for €13.

LE SPIGHE
VEGETARIAN €

(Map p320; ☑041 523 81 73; Via Garibaldi 1341; meals €10-15; ☺9.30am-2pm & 5.30-7.30pm Mon-Sat; ☑; ☑Giardini) All vegetarian, all organic and vegan-friendly, this little spot offers quick but delicious eats based on seasonal produce, from crunchy fennel salads to delicious potato-and-squash pies. And the vegan chocolate cake tastes divine, whatever its other virtues might be.

CIP CIAP
PIZZERIA €

(Map p320; ☑041 523 6621; Calle del Mondo Novo 5799a; pizza per kilo €12; ☺9.30am-9pm Wed-Mon; ☑; ☑Rialto) The cooks at this to-go pizza joint (where slices and pies are sold by weight) take their job seriously enough to dress in traditional chef's whites, and their thick-crust pizzas are a cut above the competition, thanks to fresh, high-quality ingredients. If you can snag one of the half-dozen stools, you'll even get a canal view thrown in with your meal.

★OSTERIA
ALLA STAFFA
MODERN VENETIAN €€

(Map p320; ☑041 523 91 60; Calle de l'Ospedaleto 6397a; meals €20-35; ☺11.30am-3pm & 6-11pm; ☑Ospedale) With fish fresh from the Rialto every morning and a preference for organic veg and cheese, Alberto's takes on Venetian classics have flavourful foundations. But this is home cooking with a twist: the seafood selection looks like a modernist masterpiece with its creamy, coiffed *baccalà* bedded on a rich, red radicchio leaf and baby octopus set like lagoon flowers against a splash of apricot salmon.

If you can't find a seat, grab *cicheti* at the bar. You won't be disappointed.

TAVERNA SAN LIO
MODERN VENETIAN €€

(Map p320; ☑041 277 06 69; www.tavernasanlio.com; Salizada San Lio 5547; meals €25-40; ☺noon-11pm Tue-Sat; ☑; ☑Rialto) Modern without losing Venice's essential quirkiness, the seafood dishes here are delicately handled: think scallops infused with thyme or a tuna steak in a clam and lobster sauce. The veal with ricotta is also tempting. Low

tables encourage diners to lean towards one another conspiratorially, amoeba-shaped lamps set the mood for free-form conversation, and huge windows let you in on the catwalk action outdoors.

ALLA RIVETTA
VENETIAN €€

(Map p320; ☑041 528 73 02; Salizada San Provolo 4625; meals €20-25; ☺noon-2.30pm & 7-10.30pm Tue-Sun; ☑San Zaccaria) Tucked behind the Ponte San Provolo, this trattoria hums with the chatter of contented diners even in the dead of winter. Manned by a clutch of senior *camerieri* in jovial red gilets, who'll dispense free nibbles and a glass of strawberry wine as you wait for your table. Then they'll cordially serve you a feast of traditional lagoon platters: raw seafood antipasti, pasta with clams and *fritto misto* (mixed fried seafood).

OSTARIA DA SIMSON
VENETIAN €€

(Map p320; ☑041 528 99 29; www.ostariadasimson.it; Fondamenta dei Felzi 6316; meals €25; ☺11am-midnight; ☑Ospedale) Taking in dreamy canal views in this tiny, wood-clad interior just like a ship's cabin, you could be forgiven for thinking you'd been cast adrift on the lagoon with gregarious *oste* Andrea as your captain. You're in good hands. He'll supply something memorable to drink while Mirco sends forth plates of parsley-dusted razor clams and steaming Gò risotto.

Landlubbers can look forward to a variety of salami and proscuitto from the Veneto, Friuli and Parma, alongside duck, goose and, occasionally, horse.

TRATTORIA DA REMIGIO
VENETIAN €€

(Map p320; ☑041 523 00 89; Salizada dei Greci 3416; meals €30-40; ☺12.30-2.30pm & 7.30-10.30pm Wed-Sun, 12.30-2.30pm Mon; ☑; ☑San Zaccaria) It's not often you find a restaurant that can post a sign in the window saying *completo* (full), but this place can. The secret: perfectly prepared Adriatic classics such as *gnocchi alla pescatora* (homemade gnocchi in a tomato-based seafood sauce) or a feast of delicately flavoured *rombo* (turbot) simmered in white wine. Service can be brusque when the restaurant is busy.

★TRATTORIA
CORTE SCONTA
MODERN VENETIAN €€€

(Map p320; ☑041 522 70 24; Calle del Pestrin 3886; meals €50-65; ☺12.30-2.30pm & 7-9.30pm Tue-Sat, closed Jan & Aug; ☑; ☑Arsenale) Well-informed visitors and celebrating locals

SESTIERE DI CASTELLO EATING

seek out this vine-covered *corte sconta* (hidden courtyard) for its trademark seafood antipasti and imaginative house-made pasta. Inventive flavour pairings transform the classics: clams zing with the hot, citrus-like taste of ginger; prawn and courgette linguine is recast with an earthy dash of saffron; and the roast eel loops like the Brenta River in a drizzle of balsamic reduction.

The evolving wine list now features a notable selection of organic and biodynamic wines.

AL COVO
VENETIAN €€€

(Map p320; ☎041 522 38 12; www.ristorantealcovo. com; Campiello della Pescaria 3968; meals €55-80; ⊘12.45-2pm & 7.30-10pm Fri-Tue; ❀; ⚑Arsenale) For years Diane Rankin and Cesare Benelli have dedicated themselves to the preservation of heritage products and lagoon recipes, which has placed them firmly on the gourmet map. Only the freshest seasonal fish gets the Covo treatment, accompanied by artichokes, aubergines, *cipollini* onions and mushrooms from the lagoon larders of Sant'Erasmo, Vignole, Treporti and Cavallino. Meat, too, is carefully sourced and much of it is Slow Food accredited, too.

Prices are offset by reasonably priced, limited-production wine.

OSTERIA DI SANTA MARINA
MODERN VENETIAN €€€

(Map p320; ☎041 528 52 39; www.osteriadisantamarina.com; Campo Santa Marina 5911; meals €55-80; ⊘12.30-2.30pm & 7.30-9.30pm Tue-Sat; ❀; ⚑Rialto) Don't be fooled by the casual piazza seating; this restaurant is saving up all the drama for your plate. Each course of the €75 tasting menu brings two bites of reinvented local fare – a prawn in a nest of shaved red pepper, artichoke and soft-shelled crab with squash *saòr* marinade – while homemade pastas marry surprising flavours such as the shrimp and chestnut ravioli.

Bookings are essential and in busy periods you're required to reconfirm – otherwise you'll likely face the cold shoulder of the wait staff.

🍷 DRINKING & NIGHTLIFE

Around sunset, the inhabitants of Castello converge on the waterfront and the Giardini for the *passeggiata* (evening stroll), then disperse into the *campi* for *aperitivi*. Cafes in Campo Santa Maria di Formosa, Campo Zanipolo and along Via Garibaldi become prime drinking spots by night – though for cocktails with views of glowing Palladio monuments across the lagoon, you should splash out at hotel bars along the Riva degli Schiavoni.

BACARO RISORTO
BAR

(Map p320; Campo San Provolo 4700; cicheti €1.50-4; ⊘9am-9pm Mon-Sat; ⚑San Zaccaria) Just a footbridge from San Marco, this shoebox of a corner bar overflowing with happy drinkers offers quality wines and abundant *cicheti,* including *crostini* heaped with *sarde in saòr,* soft cheeses and melon tightly swaddled in prosciutto. Note that opening times are 'flexible.'

LA SERRA
CAFE

(Serra dei Giardini; Map p320; ☎041 296 03 60; www.serradeigiardini.org; Viale Giuseppe Garibaldi 1254; snacks €4-15; ⊘11am-8pm Tue-Fri, 10am-9pm Sat & Sun; 🛜🚼; ⚑Giardini) Order a herbal tisane or the signature pear bellini and sit back amid the hothouse flowers in Napoleon's fabulous greenhouse. Cathedral-like windows look out onto the tranquil greenery of the public gardens, while upstairs workshops in painting and gardening are hosted on the suspended mezzanine. Light snacks and homemade cakes are also available alongside unique micro-brews and Lurisia sodas flavoured with Slow Food Presidia products.

BAR TERAZZA DANIELI
HOTEL BAR

(Map p320; ☎041 522 64 80; www.starwoodhotels.com; Riva degli Schiavoni 4196; cocktails €18-22; ⊘3-6.30pm Apr-Oct; ⚑San Zaccaria) Gondolas glide in to dock along the quay, while across the lagoon the white-marble edifice of Palladio's San Giorgio Maggiore turns from gold to pink in the waters of the canal: the late-afternoon scene from the Hotel Danieli's top-floor balcony bar definitely calls for a toast. Linger over a *spritz* (€10) or cocktail – preferably the sunset-tinted signature Danieli cocktail of gin, apricot and orange juices, and a splash of grenadine.

AL PORTEGO
BAR

(Map p320; ☎041 522 90 38; Calle de la Malvasia 6015; cicheti €1.50-3; ⊘noon-3pm & 6-10pm; ⚑Rialto) Beneath the portico that gives this *bacaro* its name is a walk-in closet that somehow manages to distribute wine and *cicheti* to the overflowing crowd of young Venetians in approximate order of arrival. Wine is cheap (€2 to €3) and plentiful, and the bar groans with classic nibbles. If that's not enough, make a dash for one of the five tables round the back where enormous plates of *fritto misto* and pasta with scampi are served.

QCOFFEE BAR   CAFE
(Map p320; ☑041 099 13 07; Fondazione Querini Stampalia, Campo Santa Maria Formosa 5252; ⊙10am-10.30pm Tue-Sat, to 7pm Sun; 🛜; 🚊San Zaccaria) One drink grants you access to the works of two modernist master architects through the Querini Stampalia bookshop. Rainy days are right for hot chocolate in Mario Botta's neoclassical cafe, with white walls framed with black polished-concrete floors. Outside, Carlo Scarpa's clever, Levant-inspired concrete irrigation channels bring Venice's canals indoors, adding industrial cool to your *spritz* in the sunny garden.

EL RÈFOLO   BAR
(Map p320; Via Garibaldi 1580; sandwiches & salads €1.5-5; ⊙5.30pm-12.30am Tue-Sun, 10.30-12.30am Tue-Sun during Biennale; 🚊Giardini) Although the bars along Via Garibaldi may look interchangeable, the queue for el Rèfolo's pavement tables says otherwise. Part of the draw is the ever-friendly Massimiliano dispensing Italian micro-brews and glasses of wine; then there are the plump sandwiches stuffed with wild boar mortadella, Sauris speck and pungent cheeses such as *puzzone di Moena*; and, finally, there's the live summer music (May to October).

PARADISO   CAFE
(Map p320; ☑041 241 39 72; Giardini della Biennale 1260; ⊙9am-7pm, later during Biennale; 🚊Biennale) This cheery yellow mini-*palazzo* is fuelled by a steady stream of coffee and cocktails that cost less than you'd expect given the designer chairs, waterfront terrace and lack of competition – this is the only cafe within reach of anyone in stilettos at the Biennale.

ACIUGHETA ENOTECA   WINE BAR
(Map p320; ☑041 522 42 92; www.aciugheta-ho telrio.it; Campo SS Filippo e Giacomo 4357; cicheti €3-15; ⊙11am-midnight; 🚊San Zaccaria) Never mind the lacklustre pizza menu: follow the locals' lead and stick to the sleek modern

bar, which is moored in the centre of the marble space like the prow of a ship. Come early or late for a range of mini-pizzas, meatballs, *arancini* (stuffed rice balls) and an array of *crostini*.

ENTERTAINMENT

CONCERTS AT LA PIETÀ   LIVE MUSIC
(Map p320; ☑041 522 21 71; www.pietavenezia. org; Riva degli Schiavoni; adult/reduced €25/20; ⊙concerts 8.30pm; 🚊Pietà) With fine acoustics, soaring Tiepolo ceilings and a long association with Vivaldi, this church makes an ideal venue for live baroque music.

LABORATORIO OCCUPATO
MORION   CULTURAL CENTRE
(Map p320; ☑041 520 84 37; Calle di Morion 2951; 🚊Celestia) When not busy staging environmental protests or avant-garde performance art, this counterculture social centre throws one hell of a dance party, with performances by bands from around the Veneto. Events are announced via wheat-paste posters thrown up around town and on its Facebook page (facebook.com/laboratorio occupatomorion).

🛍 SHOPPING

Castello is more of a residential area than a tourist zone, so the artisans you'll find in these quiet alleyways are less beholden to the mainstream tourist trade.

⭐SIGFRIDO CIPOLATO   JEWELLERY
(Map p320; ☑041 522 84 37; sigfridocipolato.com; C Casseleria 5336; ⊙11am-8pm Tue-Sun; 🚊San Zaccaria) Booty worthy of pirates is displayed in a fishbowl-size window display:

LOCAL KNOWLEDGE

ART BIENNALE: A LOCAL'S GUIDE

For the last decade, designer and art director **Pamela Berry** (www.pamelaberry.com) has made Venice her home – and helped create tailor-made itineraries for the city and its surrounding countryside. An Art Biennale veteran, she's learned to navigate the crowds and wring the most from the sprawling phenomenon.

If you only have a weekend The first day, I would visit the pavilions in the Giardini Pubblici (p142) and then head over to the Arsenale (p139). The second day, I'd choose from the list of other exhibitions and just start wandering throughout the city.

Beating the crowds The first week of Art Biennale is the busiest, though in some ways the most interesting – the crowd is educated, sophisticated and international. After June it really quiets down, and you can easily visit without elbowing others. However, the rest of the city grows hot and crowded. September and October are wonderful, after the summer crowds and heat subside.

For the glamour of it all The opening of the Biennale is very glamorous – the city fills with cocktails, events and parties until late. Yachts and celebrities are eager to out-do, out-party and out-glam one another. For the best people-watching, head to Harry's Bar (p77) or **B-Bar** (Map p308; ☑041 240 68 19; Campo di San Moisè 1455; ⊙6.30pm-1am Wed-Sun; 🛲Vallaresso) at the Bauer's L'Hotel.

Refuelling Favourite places within a stone's throw of the Giardini include Corte Sconta (p153) and al Covo (p154). For fresh, organic and vegetarian takeaway, head to Le Spighe (p153). And for inexpensive *casalinga* (homemade) meals, try Trattoria alla Rampa (p151). If you have your heart set on a particular place, be sure to reserve well ahead during the weeks of Biennale.

Treasure hunting There are collateral exhibitions and temporary pavilions scattered throughout the city during the Biennale (printed material with indications and maps is available at the entrances). Some are interesting, some not, but even if you don't end up liking the art, the locations are often worth visiting. It's like going on a treasure hunt to find some of them. There are exhibitions in palaces and churches, galleries and monasteries, abandoned buildings and far-flung islands.

Favourite far-flung venue The Scuola della Misericordia in Cannaregio is worth the hike. It was built in the mid-1500s, and its high ceilings and massive columns are attributed to the architect Jacopo Sansovino. Many Venetians still remember it as a basketball court and gym in the '70s. It's especially worth seeking out since it's only open to the public during Biennale.

SESTIERE DI CASTELLO SHOPPING

a constellation of diamonds in star settings on a ring, a tiny enamelled green snake sinking its fangs into a pearl, and diamond drop earrings that end in enamelled gold skulls. Though they look like heirlooms, these small wonders were worked on the premises by master jeweller Sigfrido.

QSHOP   MUSEUM SHOP
(Map p320; ☑041 523 44 11; Campiello Querini Stampalia 5252; ⊙10am-6pm Tue-Sun; 🛲Rialto, San Zaccaria) Aside from its sumptuous range of art and design books, the shop of the Querini Stampalia Foundation offers a highly curated selection of glass, jewelry, household items, silverware and textiles. Pieces from design greats such as Carlo Scarpa, Carlo Moretti and San Lorenzo

sit beside the work of emerging talents such as Benjamin Hubert's pleated, Plicate watches and Mad am I? Madam's range of jewelry in rodium, stainless steel and methacrylate.

KALIMALA CUOIERIA   ARTISANAL, LEATHER
(Map p320; ☑041 528 35 96; www.kalimala.it; Salizada San Lio 5387; ⊙9.30am-7.30pm Mon-Sat; 🛲Rialto) Sleek, supple belts with brushed-steel buckles, modern satchels, man-bags and knee-high red boots: Kalimala makes beautiful leather goods in practical, modern styles. Shoes, sandals and gloves are crafted from vegetable-cured cow hide and dyed in a mix of earthy tones and vibrant lapis blues. Given the natural tanning and top-flight leather, the prices are remarkably

reasonable, with handmade shoes starting at €100.

ATELIER ALESSANDRO
MERLIN
ARTISANAL, CERAMICS

(Map p320; ☎041 522 58 95; Calle del Pestrin 3876; ⊘3-7pm Fri & Sun, 10am-noon & 3-7pm Mon-Thu & Sat; ⓢArsenale) Enjoy your breakfast in the nude, on a horse or atop a jellyfish – Alessandro Merlin paints them all on striking black and white cappuccino cups and saucers. His expressive characters are modern, but the *sgraffito* technique he uses on some of his work dates back to Roman times: designs are scratched white lines against a black background.

AL CAMPANIL
JEWELLERY, GLASS

(Map p320; ☎041 523 57 34; Calle Lunga Santa Maria Formosa 5184; ⊘9.30am-12.30pm & 3.30-7.30pm Mon-Sat; ⓢOspedale, San Zaccaria) Utilising traditional Murano techniques and materials, including oxides and resins, Sabina Melinato conjures up contemporary glass and costume jewellery. Her deco-inspired glass pendants are so highly polished they look like lacquerwork – just what you'd expect from a teacher at Murano's International School of Glass.

BARBIERI ARABESQUE
ACCESSORIES

(Map p320; ☎041 522 81 77; Ponte dei Greci 3403; ⊘10am-12.30pm & 3.30-7.30pm Mon-Sat; ⓢPietà) Although the luxe cashmere pashminas, merino scarves, silk ties and leather goods all hail from Lombardy, the colours and styles in Adelia's shop are pure Venice. Check out the suede belts in teal and fuchsia, which mirror the colour of the canals and the outrageous Venetian sunsets. Barbieri supplies brands such as Moschino, Pollini and Iceberg, but you can buy non-branded products here at nearly half the price.

BALLARIN
ANTIQUES

(Map p320; ☎347 779 24 92; Calle del Cafetier 6482; ⊘10am-1pm & 4.30-7.30pm Mon-Sat; ⓢOspedale) If you're looking for something distinctively Venetian join the bargain-hunters in Valter Ballarin's Aladdin's cave. An old-fashioned dealer and artisan restorer, Valter has a knack for tracking down period furnishings, hand-painted glassware, prints, books, toys and lamps. The best souvenir, though, is a handful of colourful, hand-blown glass flowers from dismembered Murano chandeliers.

GIOVANNA ZANELLA
SHOES

(Map p320; ☎041 523 55 00; www.giovannazanella.com; Calle Carminati 5641; ⊘9.30am-1pm & 3-7pm Mon-Sat; ⓢRialto) Woven, sculpted and crested like lagoon birds, Zanella's shoes practically demand that red carpets unfurl before you. The Venetian designer makes shoes custom, so the answer is always: yes, you can get those peep-toe numbers in yellow and grey, size 12, extra narrow. Closed last two weeks of August.

BANCO LOTTO 10
FASHION, ACCESSORIES

(Map p320; ☎041 522 14 39; Salizada da Sant'Antonin 3478a; ⊘3.30-7.30pm Mon, 10am-1pm & 4-7pm Tue-Sat; ⓢPietà) Prison orange is out and plum silk velvet is in at this non-profit boutique, whose hand-sewn fashions are the fruit of a retraining program at the women's prison on Giudecca. Designed and made by inmates, the smartly tailored jackets (€80 to €140) and handbags often incorporate opulent silks, velvets and tapestry donated by Fortuny and Bevilacqua. Even La Fenice has dressed its divas in Banco Lotto ensembles.

Volunteers run the boutique and purchases fund the women prisoners' continuing career training and reintegration into society after their release.

PAOLO BRANDOLISIO
ARTISANAL

(Map p320; ☎041 522 41 55; www.paolobrandolisio.altervista.org; Sotoportego Corte Rota 4725; ⊘vary; ⓢSan Zaccaria) Beneath all the marble, gilding and lacquering, Venice is a city of wood long supported by its carpenters, caulkers, oarmakers and gilders. Master woodcarver Paolo Brandolisio continues the traditions, crafting the sinuous rowlock *(forcola)* that supports the gondolier's oar. Made of walnut or cherry wood, each one is crafted specifically for boat and gondolier. Miniature replicas, which make great gifts, are for sale in the workroom.

Giudecca, Lido & the Southern Islands

GIUDECCA | LIDO DI VENEZIA | PELLESTRINA | ISOLA DI SAN LAZZARO DEGLI ARMENI | ISOLA DI SAN SERVOLO

Neighbourhood Top Five

1 Immersing yourself in the bright serenity of Palladio's **Chiesa di San Giorgio Maggiore** (p160) and admiring the classical proportions of Longhena's elegant library, now part of the **Fondazione Giorgio Cini** (p162).

2 Ascending San Giorgio Maggiore's soaring **cam-** panile (p160) to gain purchase on the labyrinth that is Venice.

3 Renting a bike on the **Lido** (p168) and pedalling your way along the seafront promenade to the **Alberoni pine forest** (p163) at the southern tip.

4 Rubbing elbows with locals at Giudecca's **farm-** ers market (p161) and **El Pecador** (p166), the Lido's double-decker food bus.

5 Feasting on prize Malamocco artichokes at **Le Garzette** (p166) and the freshest lagoon-sourced molluscs at **da Celeste** (p166).

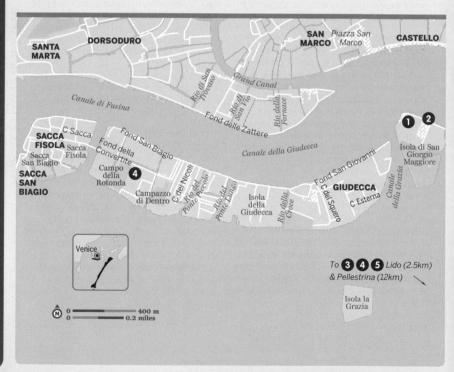

For more detail of this area see Map p323 and p324 ➡

Explore Giudecca, Lido & the Southern Islands

Other cities have suburban sprawl; Venice has primordial monasteries floating in teal-blue waters. To the south, the seaward side of the lagoon is sheltered from the Adriatic by the Lido, for centuries the beach and bastion of the city. In the 19th century, it found a new lease of life as a bathing resort and a place of welcome natural beauty after the urban rigours of the Rialto.

Smaller islands dot the foreground of remarkable views back across the lagoon to San Marco: Sacca Sessola, San Lazzaro degli Armeni, San Servolo and San Giorgio Maggiore. In the past they served the Republic well as quarantine islands, convents for wayward nuns, hospitals and mental asylums.

In the shadow of San Giorgio Maggiore lies La Giudecca, Venice's unofficial seventh *sestiere*. It was once an aristocratic retreat and later the city's industrial centre, the redeveloped Molino Stucky flour mill standing in counterpoint to Palladio's Chiesa di San Giorgio. You can easily visit both islands in half a day – weekends are best, when you can also visit the Fondazione Giorgio Cini.

Note that many island restaurants close from November to March, especially on the Lido.

Local Life

➡ **Cicheti hot spots** Join artists and rough-and-ready locals for generous *cicheti* at Al Pontil Dea Giudecca (p165), Jeroboam (p167), Al Ponte di Borgo (p166) and al Mercà (p165).

➡ **Cocktails with a view** Even Venetians head to Skyline Rooftop Bar (p167) for the views, while Lido alternatives take a break in double-decker bus El Pecador (p166).

➡ **Off-the-beaten-track beaches** Pack a picnic and head for the dunefields of Alberoni (p163), and enjoy the winter sun with Lido families at the Blue Moon (p168).

Getting There & Away

➡ **Vaporetto Giudecca** *Vaporetto* lines 2, 41, 42 and N (night) make Giudecca an easy hop from San Marco or Dorsoduro.

➡ **Vaporetto San Giorgio Maggiore** Line 2 leaves from San Zaccaria.

➡ **Vaporetto Lido** Lines 1, 2, 51, 52, 61 and 62 connect the Lido with all major stops in Venice.

➡ **Vaporetto San Servolo & San Lazzaro** Line 20 from San Zaccaria serves both these islands.

Lonely Planet's Top Tip

Instead of braving the lines at San Marco's campanile, seek out San Giorgio Maggiore's campanile, which offers comparable views for a fraction of the wait time.

✗ Best Places to Eat

➡ I Figli delle Stelle (p165)
➡ La Favorita (p166)
➡ Le Garzette (p166)
➡ El Pecador (p166)

For reviews, see p165➡

▢ Best Places to Drink

➡ Skyline Rooftop Bar (p167)
➡ Harry's Dolci (p165)
➡ Jeroboam (p167)
➡ Lion's Bar (p167)

For reviews, see p167➡

🔒 Best Places to Shop

➡ Giudecca 795 (p162)
➡ Fortuny Tessuti Artistici (p161)
➡ Monastero di San Lazzaro degli Armeni (p164)

For reviews, see p162➡

TOP SIGHT
CHIESA DI SAN GIORGIO MAGGIORE

Most visitors only see San Giorgio across the water. It's quite a view – Palladio chose the white Istrian stone to stand out against the blue lagoon waters, and set it at an angle to create visual drama while also ensuring that it catches the sun all afternoon.

Palladio's Facade

Palladio's radical 15th-century facade gracefully solved the problem bedevilling Renaissance church design: how to graft a triangular, classical pediment onto a Christian church, with its high, central nave and lower side aisles. Palladio's solution: use one pediment to crown the nave, and a lower, half-pediment to span both side aisles. The two interlock with rhythmic harmony, while prominent three-quarter columns, deeply incised capitals and sculptural niches create depth with clever shadow-play.

Church Interior & Tintorettos

Likewise, the interior is an uncanny combination of brightness and serenity. Sunlight enters through high thermal windows and is then diffused by acres of white stucco. Floors inlaid with black, white and red stone draw the eye toward the altar. With its rigorous application of classical motifs, it's reminiscent of a Roman theatre.

Two outstanding late works by Tintoretto flank the church's altar. On one side hangs his *Fall of Manna*; on the other side, *Last Supper* depicts Christ and his apostles in a scene that looks suspiciously like a 16th-century Venetian tavern. Nearby, in the Cappella dei Morti, hangs Tintoretto's last work, the moving *Deposition of Christ*.

DON'T MISS...

➡ Tintoretto's *Fall of Manna* and *Last Supper*

➡ Views from the 60m-high bell tower

PRACTICALITIES

➡ Map p323

➡ ☏041 522 78 27

➡ Isola di San Giorgio Maggiore

➡ bell tower adult/reduced €3/2

➡ ⊙9am-12.30pm & 2.30-6.30pm Mon-Sat May-Sep, to 5pm Oct-Apr

➡ ⛴San Giorgio Maggiore

⊙ SIGHTS

⊙ Giudecca

Giudecca's disputed history begins with its name. The name comes not from onetime Jewish inhabitants (the Italian word for Jews is *ebrei*), but from the Venetian *zudega*, meaning 'the judged' – referring to rebel aristocratic families banished here during the 9th century.

Giudecca's most illustrious exile, however, was not Venetian but Florentine. Michelangelo fled here from Florence in 1529, though by the time he arrived the aristocratic Dandolos, Mocenigos and Vendramins had transformed the island from a prison into a neighbourhood of garden villas. When the nobles headed inland in the 18th century to build villas along the Riviera Brenta (p183), the gardens gave way to factories, tenements and military barracks.

In recent years, these large abandoned spaces attracted a new set of exiles – artists who could no longer afford rents in central Venice. Today, SS Cosma e Damiano, first a church and then a factory, has live-work loft spaces, while a munitions depot is now the cutting-edge Teatro Junghans (p167).

CHIESA DELLE ZITELLE CHURCH
(Map p323; ☑041 260 19 74; Fondamenta delle Zitelle; ⬛Zitelle) Designed by Palladio in the late 16th century, the Chiesa di Santa Maria della Presentazione, known as the Zitelle, was a church and hospice for orphans and poor young women (*zitelle* is old local slang for 'old maids'). The doors are rarely open, but you can get a spa treatment in the adjoining convent and sleep in the orphanage. The Palladio Hotel & Spa (p223) has creatively tweaked the original structure without altering Palladio's blueprint or the original cloister garden.

CASA DEI TRE OCI CULTURAL CENTRE
(Map p323; ☑041 220 12 11; www.fondazionedi venezia.org; Fondamente de la Croce 43; ⊙10am-6pm during exhibitions only; ⬛Zitelle) **FREE** Acquired by the Fondazione di Venezia in 2000, the Casa dei Tre Oci was once the home of early-20th-century artist and photographer Mario de Maria, who conceived of its distinctive, neo-Gothic brick facade with its three arched windows (its namesake 'eyes') in 1910. Now it hosts his archive

and international exhibitions of contemporary art and photography.

The views of San Marco and the Punta della Dogana alone are worth the visit.

CHIESA DEL SANTISSIMO REDENTORE CHURCH
(Church of the Redeemer; Map p323; Campo del SS Redentore 194; adult/reduced/child €3/1.50/ free or with Chorus Pass; ⊙10am-5pm Mon-Sat; ⬛Redentore) Built to celebrate the city's deliverance from the Black Death, Palladio's Il Redentore was completed under Antonio da Ponte (of Rialto bridge fame) in 1592. Inside there are works by Tintoretto, Veronese and Vivarini, but the most striking is Paolo Piazza's 1619 *Gratitude of Venice for Liberation from the Plague.*

Survival is never taken for granted in this tidal town, and to give thanks during the **Festa del Redentore** (Feast of the Redeemer; www.turismovenezia.it) Venetians have been making the pilgrimage across the canal on a shaky pontoon bridge from the Zattere since 1578.

CHIESA DI SANT'EUFEMIA CHURCH
(Map p323; ☑041 532 29 20; Fondamenta Sant'Eufemia 680; ⊙by appointment for groups of 20 or more; ⬛Palanca) Four women saints were crowded under the roof of the original AD 890 church here, but Sts Dorothy, Tecla and Erasma weren't as big a draw as Byzantine Christian martyr Euphemia. She was thrown to hungry lions, but after biting off her hand, the lions refused to eat her holy virgin flesh. The simple Veneto-Byzantine structure you see today dates from the 14th century.

FORTUNY TESSUTI ARTISTICI FACTORY OUTLET
(Map p323; ☑041 522 40 78; www.fortuny.com; Fondamenta San Biagio 805; ⊙10am-1pm &

LOCAL KNOWLEDGE

ORGANIC PRISON MARKET

Every Thursday morning, locals jostle for the best of the organic produce available at this unusual twist on a farmer's **market** (Map p323; Fondamenta delle Convertite, Giudecca; ⊙9am-10am Thu; ⬛Palanca). In this case, the farmers happen also to be prisoners of the adjacent women's correctional facility. Proceeds help pay for job retraining and postrelease reintegration.

2-6pm Mon-Sat; ⬛Palanca) Marcel Proust waxed rhapsodic over Fortuny's silken cottons printed with boho-chic art nouveau patterns. Find out why at Fortuny's version of a factory outlet. Visitors can browse 260 textile designs in the showroom, but fabrication methods have been jealously guarded in the garden studio for a century. To see more of Fortuny's original designs and his home studio, head over to Museo Fortuny (p67).

GIUDECCA 795   ART GALLERY
(Map p323; ☑340 879 83 27; www. giudecca795.com; Fondamenta San Biagio 795; ⏰11am-7pm Tue-Sun Apr-Oct, 4.30-7pm Tue-Sun Nov-Mar; ⬛Palanca) Founded to promote local artists of all kinds, this quirky and welcoming gallery displays (and sells) a wide range of works by both established and young artists, most of whom have a strong connection with Venice itself.

⦿ Lido di Venezia

There's no doubt that the Lido is no longer the unspoilt natural haven that Lord Byron used to gallop across in the 19th century, nor the glamorous summer bolt-hole of Hollywood starlets and European aristocracy, but neither is it the vulgar, unremarkable tourist resort that many detractors would have us believe. In fact, with its groomed shellac beaches, bronzed lifeguards and old ladies sipping *prosecco* beneath candy-striped awnings, the Lido is a rather diverting seaside escape.

ANTICO CIMITERO ISRAELITICO   CEMETERY
(Map p324; ☑041 71 53 59; www.museoebraico. it; Riviera San Nicolò; group tours adult/student €10/8, individual tours €80; ⏰by reservation Apr-Oct; ⬛Lido, San Nicoló) This quiet, overgrown garden was Venice's main Jewish cemetery from 1386 until the 18th century. It fell into disuse after the establishment of a new cemetery on Via Cipro. The tombstones were rediscovered by construction workers in the 1920s and it was decided to set them in some sort of order. They range in design from Venetian Gothic to distinctly Ottoman, and many of them bear decorations dramatically at variance with Jewish Orthodoxy.

⦿ TOP SIGHT
FONDAZIONE GIORGIO CINI

In 1951, industrialist and art patron Vittorio Cini – a survivor of Dachau – acquired the monastery of San Giorgio and lovingly restored it in memory of his son, Giorgio Cini. The rehabilitated complex, now home to Cini's cultural foundation, is an architectural treasure incorporating a **refectory** and **cloister** by Palladio, and Baldassare Longhena's **monumental staircase** and 17th-century **library**. Palladio's impressive refectory, refurbished in 2011–12, now features a glorious video projection of Paolo Veronese's *Nozze di Cana* (Wedding at Cana), which once hung on the end wall until Napoleon transplanted it to the Louvre in 1797.

The foundation continues the tradition of scholarship that the Benedictines became renowned for during the Renaissance, when Cosimo de' Medici was exiled here from Florence and funded the creation of a library. Two are still open to the public.

Weekend tours allow you to stroll through the **Borges Labyrinth** and contemplate the tranquil **Chiostro dei Cipressi**, the oldest extant part of the complex, completed in 1526 by Andrea Buora. Check the website for other exhibitions as well as performances in the open-air **Teatro Verde**.

DON'T MISS...
➡ Chiostro dei Cipressi

PRACTICALITIES
➡ Map p323
➡ ☑041 220 12 15
➡ www.cini.it
➡ Isola di San Giorgio Maggiore
➡ adult/reduced €10/8
➡ ⏰guided tours in English & French 11am, 1pm, 3pm & 5pm Sat & Sun; in Italian 10am, noon, 2pm & 4pm Sat & Sun
➡ ⬛San Giorgio Maggiore

LIDO BEACHES

All Lido beaches are to be found on the seaward side of the island, easily accessed from the *vaporetto* along the Gran Viale. In May 2012 they were awarded Blue Flag eco-accreditation (www.blueflag.org), and their shallow gradient makes them ideal for young children and even toddlers.

There are only three 'free' beaches open to the public: the *spiaggia comunale* accessed through the Blue Moon (p168) complex, the San Nicolò beach to the north and the Alberoni beach at the southern end of the island. The latter is the most scenic.

The rest of the shoreline is occupied by *stabilimenti*: privately managed sections of beach lined with wooden *capannas* (cabins), a relic of the Lido's 1850s bathing scene. Many of them are rented by the same families year in, year out, or are reserved for guests of the grand hotels. The *stabilimenti* also offer showers, sun loungers (€6 to €9), umbrellas (€11 to €16) and small lockers (€18.50 to €28). Rates drop a few euros after 2pm.

Nor are the lions those of St Mark or Judah; they are the lions of Castile and León, brought to Venice on the armorials of Sephardic Jews expelled from Spain by the Grand Inquisitor in 1492. Tours must be pre-booked with the Museo Ebraico (p125) in Cannaregio.

MALAMOCCO TOWN

(⚓Lido) Pass over Ponte di Borgo to explore the canals and *calli* (lanes) of a less overwhelming lagoon town, with just a few churches and a Gothic *palazzo* (mansion). A miniature version of Venice right down to the lions of St Mark on medieval facades, Malamocco was actually the lagoon capital from 742 to 811.

PINETA DEGLI ALBERONI PINE FOREST, BEACH

(🚴; ⚓Lido) Right at the southern tip of the island the Alberoni pine forest slopes down to the Lido's wildest, most scenic beach. These enchanting dunefields are the stuff of Shelley's poems and Byron's early-morning rides.

Kentish plovers, rare bee-eaters and a plethora of marine birds fish in shallow sea pools. Out of season, the forest and beach are virtually deserted, while in summer tanned volleyball players leap about the dunes. The majority of the beach is open to the public, but if you feel the need for a restaurant and sun-loungers, head for the **Bagni Alberoni** (📞041 73 10 29; www.bagnialberoni.com; Strada Nuova dei Bagni 26; umbrella/sun-lounger/deck chair €8/7/5; ⊙8am-midnight Jun-Sep; 🚴; ⚓Lido). To reach Alberoni, take bus A from the *vaporetto* stop.

⊙ Pellestrina

Stretching south of the Lido and repeating its long, sinuous shape, Pellestrina reminds you what the lagoon might have been like if Venice had never been dreamed of. The 11km-island is home to three tight-knit fishing communities – San Pietro in Volta, Porto Secco and Pellestrina – strung out along the water's edge in jaunty pastel colours. There are no hotels here, or sun loungers, just elderly women sitting on their porches and fishermen mending their nets.

The island is also blissfully flat, making it ideal biking country. Your best bet is to rent a bike near the Lido *vaporetto* stop and hop across on the ferry. On the lagoon side, look out for the shantylike fishermen's shacks built over beds of mussels. Towards the southern end of the island, you'll find a bird-watching sanctuary in the region of Ca' Roman.

Bus 11 travels from the Lido *vaporetto* stop to Pellestrina aboard the ferry.

MURAZZI LANDMARK

(⚓Pellestrina) Much of Pellestrina's seafront is lined by a remarkable feat of 18th-century engineering known as the Murazzi. Although it's not immediately impressive to modern eyes, these massive sea walls represent Herculean handiwork from a preindustrial age. Designed to keep high seas from crashing into the lagoon, they remain an effective breakwater even today. On calm days, long stretches of grey-sand beaches separate the Murazzi from the sea.

LIDO STYLE

Between 1850 and WWI the Lido became the world's most exclusive seaside resort and is still defined by the Stile Liberty (art nouveau) of the period. Walking itineraries around the most extravagant villas are available to download at www2.comune.venezia.it/lidoliberty.

Sensing an opportunity, canny business tycoon Nicolò Spada (founder of the Italian hotel group CIGA) started buying up Lido land, opening the island's two grandest hotels, the **Grand Hotel Excelsior** and the **Grand Hotel des Bains**, in 1908 and 1909 respectively. Giovanni Sardi's Excelsior, which sits directly on the beach, is a Veneto-Moorish fantasy palace with interiors decorated by Mariano Fortuny, while the more conservative Hotel des Bains, designed by Francesco Marsich, is an art nouveau monolith, recalling the great luxury spas of Baden Baden. The latter was immortalised in Thomas Mann's best-selling novella *Death in Venice*, adapted for the screen by Luchino Visconti in 1971 and filmed in the hotel.

These days the Hotel des Bains is once again the jewel in the crown of Lido redevelopment. EST Capital, in partnership with the Comune di Venezia, is working to restore some of the island's faded glamour with a €330-million redevelopment of the hotel, Malamocco, the Ospedale del Mare and a new 1000-berth marina. The vast 200-room villa, where luminaries such as Marlene Dietrich, Serge Diaghilev, Coco Chanel and Elizabeth Taylor whiled away their summers, is set to become an uberluxe 15-suite hotel and a collection of private residences.

◎ Isola di San Lazzaro degli Armeni

Once the site of a Benedictine hospice for pilgrims and then a leper colony, this island was given to Armenian monks fleeing Ottoman persecution in 1717. The entire island is still a working monastery, so access is by tour only. Take the 3.10pm *vaporetto* 20 from San Zaccaria.

MONASTERO DI SAN LAZZARO DEGLI ARMENI   MONASTERY

(Map p324; ☑041 526 01 04; Isola di San Lazzaro degli Armeni; adult/student & child €6/4.50; ☺tours 3.25-5pm Sun; 🛱; 🚢San Lazzaro degli Armeni) Tours start in the glittering **church** and are conducted by multilingual monks, who amply demonstrate the order's reputation for scholarship. After passing through the 18th-century **refectory**, you'll head upstairs to the **library**. In 1789 the monks set up a polyglot printing press here and translated many scientific and literary works into Armenian. Those works are still housed in the 150,000-strong collection alongside curios from Ancient Egypt, Sumeria and India.

An Egyptian mummy and a 15th-century Indian throne are the rather quirky main features of the room dedicated to the memory of Lord Byron, who spent six months here in 1816 helping the monks to prepare an English-Armenian dictionary. True to his eccentric nature, he could often be seen swimming from the island to the Grand Canal.

Before leaving be sure to browse the shop, which is a great source of unusual gifts. Try the Vartanush jam made from rose petals from the monastery's exotic gardens. Byron was particularly fond of it.

◎ Isola di San Servolo

Step off *vaporetto* 20 from San Zaccaria amid the students of Venice International University and you'll be struck by the island's balmy beauty. But despite the exotic palms, San Servolo has long sent a chill down Venetian spines, serving as it did as the city's main insane asylum from the 18th century until 1978.

Home to Benedictine monks since the 7th century, the island's medicinal flora saw it granted an apothecaries' license in 1719 so the monks could better supply the Republic's on-site military hospital. Not long afterwards, in October 1725, San Servolo's first 'insane' patient, Lorenzo Stefani, arrived, starting a trend among aristocratic families to have their afflicted relatives committed. At its peak the asylum held hundreds of inmates, a large portion of them former ship's hands and Italian and Austrian servicemen, many of whom were simply suffering trauma or were afflicted by conditions caused by poverty and poor nutrition. A dedicated museum now documents their stories and some of the nightmarish 'treatments' practised on them.

MUSEO DELLA FOLLIA MUSEUM

(Museum of Madness; Map p324; ☑041 524 011 914; www.coopculture.it; Isola di San Servolo; adult/reduced €3/2; ☉phone bookings 9.30am-5.30pm Mon-Thu, to 3pm Fri; ☻San Servolo) As well as a poignant photographic collection displaying portraits of patients before and after treatment, San Servolo's Museo della Follia contains the full paraphernalia of psychiatric treatment of the day, including chains, handcuffs, cages for ice showers, early electro-therapy machines and a rare plethysmograph (the precursor of the lie detector).

The tour also takes in the reconstructed anatomy theatre beside the church and the ancient pharmacy. For centuries many of Venice's medicines were concocted here – including various 'cures' for syphilis, a common cause of mental-health problems, even after the discovery of penicillin. Since most penicillin in Italy was set aside for the military well into the 20th century, it remained a sought-after street drug.

✗ EATING

✗ Giudecca

AL PONTIL DEA GIUDECCA VENETIAN €

(Map p323; ☑041 528 69 85; Calle Redentore 197a; meals €15; ☉8am-8pm Mon-Sat; ☻Redentore) Asking for a menu here is like asking for one at your grandma's house. You'll have one of the three daily specials and like it – really – and by the time lunch is over you'll feel as though you should offer to help tidy up. For €12 you can expect a generous plate of pasta, a savoury meat or fish dish, a *contorno* (veggie side dish), and a view of Venice – if you get the one window seat. Note that the bar is open for *cicheti* all day, but meals are only available at lunchtime Monday to Friday.

★I FIGLI DELLE STELLE ITALIAN €€

(Map p323; ☑041 523 00 04; www.ifiglidelles telle.it; Zitelle 70; meals €30-40; ☉12.30-2.30pm & 7-10pm Tue-Sun, closed mid-Nov–mid-Mar; ☻Zitelle) Beware of declarations of love at one of Venice's most romantic restaurants: are you sure that's not Pugliese chef Luigi's velvety pasta and soup talking? A creamy fava-bean mash with biting chicory and fresh tomatoes coats the tongue in a naughty way, and the mixed grill for two with langoustine, sole and fresh sardines is quite a catch.

MISTRÀ VENETIAN €€

(Map p323; ☑041 522 07 43; Calle Michelangelo 53c; meals €20-35; ☉noon-3pm & 7-11pm Tue-Sun; ☻Zitelle) Head here for authentically Venetian seafood, including generous plates of briny clam pasta and genuine Genovese pesto. The chef, who hails from Liguria, also recommends *zuppa di pesce* (soup thick with seafood) and ravioli stuffed with shrimp. Boat-yard workers fill the place with raucous chatter at lunchtime, while evenings are a more sedate affair.

LA PALANCA VENETIAN €€

(Map p323; ☑041 528 77 19; Fondamenta al Ponte Piccolo 448; meals €20-30; ☉8am-8.30pm Mon-Sat; ☻Palanca) Lunchtime competition for canalside tables is stiff, but the views of the Zattere make *tagliolini ai calamaretti* (narrow ribbon pasta with tiny calamari) and tuna steak with balsamic vinegar taste even better. At €7 to €9 for plates of pasta, you'll be forking out half what diners pay along the waterfront in San Marco. Dinner is not served, but you can get *cicheti* at the bar right up to closing time.

HARRY'S DOLCI MODERN VENETIAN €€€

(Map p323; ☑041 522 48 44; www.cipriani.com; Fondamenta San Biagio 773; meals €80-120; ☉11am-11pm Wed-Mon, lunch Apr-Oct; ☻Palanca) The sun-washed Tiffany-blue canopy along the waterfront marks out this home away from home for the designer-sunglasses set. The service is low-key and the decor retro (think bistro chairs and subway tile), though the prices have more than kept up with inflation. Still, for the €15 price of *dolci* (sweets), you could linger through the better part of an afternoon.

✗ Lido di Venezia

AL MERCÀ CICHETI BAR, SEAFOOD €

(Map p324; ☑041 526 45 49; Via Enrico Dandolo 17a; cicheti €2.50-3.50, meals €15-25; ☉12.30am-3pm & 6-10pm Tue-Sun; ☻Lido) Located in the

LOCAL KNOWLEDGE

EL PECADOR

No, you're not suffering from heat stroke; that really is a red double-decker bus parked against the kerb, and what's more it's dishing out the Lido's finest sandwiches and *spritz*, so climb aboard and take a seat on the canopied top deck.

El Pecador (Lungomare Gabriele d'Annunzio; sandwiches €2.50-5; ⊘11am-3am May-Sep; 🚊Lido) means 'The Sinner' – a tongue-in-cheek allusion to its ongoing struggle with the Lido comune over local permits. But despite the party-pooper behaviour, the bus marks out its territory on the Lungomare d'Annunzio each summer and attracts an alternative crowd to its very own block party.

old Lido fish market, al Mercà is popular with students who come for the abundant *cicheti*, outdoor seating and well-priced wine by the glass. Take a pew at one of the marble counters and order up a seafood storm of *folpetti* (mini octopus), fried *schìe* (shrimps) and creamy salt cod.

AL PONTE DI BORGO   VENETIAN €

(☑041 77 00 90; Rio Terà Mercerie 27, Malamocco; meals €20-25; ⊘12.30-2.30pm & 7-10pm Tue-Sun Apr-Oct; 🚊Lido) This local trattoria in Malamocco draws in the punters with its abundant *cicheti*. Local favourites such as *nervetti* (nerves with onion) and baby squid are washed down with slugs of *prosecco*, while out back, beneath the ramshackle pergola, bowls brim with pasta *alla malamocchina* (with mussels, tomatoes, oregano and smoked cheese).

MAGICHE VOGLIE   GELATERIA €

(Map p324; ☑041 526 13 85; Gran Viale 47g; cones €2.50-4.50; 🚊Lido) The best ice cream in the Lido is made every morning on the premises at this family-owned place right between the *vaporetto* stop and the beach. Mull over the soft peaks of new-world flavours such as acai and caja, or plump for the classic purplish-black cherry or Sicilian pistachio.

★LE GARZETTE   FARMSTAY €€

(☑041 712 16 53; www.legarzette.it; Lungomare Alberoni 32, Lido; meals €35-45; ⊘12.30-2.30pm & 7-10.30pm mid-Jan–mid-Dec; ❋🐾; 🚊Lido) 🌿

Nestled amid gardens overflowing with red radicchio, astringent fennel, handsome pumpkins and dark-green courgettes is the rust-red *agriturismo* of Renza and Salvatore. Choose between a meat or a fish menu and wait for the parade of organic dishes: crepes filled with juicy asparagus, lightly fried Malamocco artichokes and mouthwatering pear tart made with farm eggs.

If you aren't staying the night, reservations are essential for the restaurant.

BUDDHA   INDIAN €€

(Map p324; ☑041 77 06 18; Gran Viale 28b; meals €15-30; ⊘10am-midnight Tue-Sun, to 2am Jun-Aug; 🐾; 🚊Lido) A short walk from the beach, this simple but stylishly mod eatery offers up an intriguing fusion of Italian and Indian cuisines, from curry-inflected *cicheti* (available all day) to mains combining Veneto produce and fish infused with Indian spices and condiments. There's also a good vegetarian selection.

★LA FAVORITA   SEAFOOD €€€

(Map p324; ☑041 526 16 26; Via Francesco Duodo 33; meals €35-50; ⊘12.30-2.30pm & 7.30-10.30pm Wed-Sun, 7.30-10.30pm Tue, closed Jan–mid-Feb; 🚊Lido) For long, lazy lunches, bottles of fine wine and impeccable service, look no further than La Favorita. The menu is as elegant as the surroundings: giant *rhombo* (turbot) simmered with capers and olives, spider-crab *gnochetti* (mini-gnocchi) and classic fish risotto. Book ahead for the wisteria-filled garden and well ahead during the film festival, when songbirds are practically out-sung by the ringtones of movie moguls.

🍴 Pellestrina

RISTORANTE DA CELESTE   SEAFOOD €€€

(☑041 96 73 55; Sestier Vianelli 625; meals €60-80; ⊘12.30-3pm & 7-10.30pm Thu-Tue; 🚊Pellestrina) At the furthest end of the island, da Celeste has been serving up lagoon-fresh fish on its pontoon terrace for generations. Go at sunset, when the rose-tinted sky kisses the glassy lagoon, and let Rossano guide you through the best daily offerings from polenta with tiny shrimp to a whole host of cockles, clams, scallops, spider crab and – the house special – fish pie. Reservations are advised.

DRINKING & NIGHTLIFE

SKYLINE ROOFTOP BAR BAR
(Map p323; ☑041 272 33 11; www.molinos
tuckyhilton.com; Fondamenta San Biagio 810,
Giudecca; ⊙noon-3.30pm & 6pm-1am, closed
Mon Nov-Feb; ⛴Palanca) From white-sneaker
cruise passengers to the €1000-sunglasses
set, the rooftop bar at the Hilton Molino
Stucky wows everyone with its vast pano-
rama over Venice and the lagoon, with
drink prices to match. From May to September, the bar offers a lunch buffet from
noon to 3pm.

LION'S BAR BAR
(Map p324; ☑041 887 66 42; www.cafecentrale
venezia.com; Lungomare Marconi 31, Lido; sandwiches €2-7, salads €8-12; ⊙8am-3am Aug & Sep;
⛴Lido) With its sexy baroque curves, stately
porticos and exuberant sunburst demilune
above the front door, the Lion's Bar is the
Lido's most prestigious drinking den, although sadly it's only open during the Film
Festival (p24). Designed by Giovanni Sicher
in the 1920s, it's a classic art nouveau extravagance with a sweeping staircase, mul-
lioned windows and a large terrace ideal for
late-night DJ sets.

Inside, festival glitterati and journalists
neck an endless supply of coffee and lunch
on spartan salads beneath an enormous
glitter ball.

B.EACH BEACH BAR, CLUB
(Map p324; Lungomare D'Annunzio 20, Lido;
⊙9am-9pm Mon-Tue, Thu & Sun, to 2am Wed &
Fri-Sat May–mid-Sep; ⛴Lido) After a taxing
day on a Lido lounge chair, there's nothing
better than unwinding on a four-poster
beach bed. At this bold venue, days flow
into nights with a parade of diversions:
free library books, designated beach sport,
massage, live-music sets, open-air cinema and weekend DJ sets that will keep
you dancing until you face-plant on the
sand.

JEROBOAM BAR, CAFE
(Map p324; Piazzetta Lepanto 1l; sandwiches &
salads €2.50-5; ⊙7.30-2am Wed-Mon; ⛴Lido)
With its gleaming wooden bar lined with
multicoloured booze bottles, this bustling
place in Piazzetta Lepanto is a year-round
favourite. Come for coffee in the morning, generous sandwiches and salads at
lunchtime and the best Manhattan and
aperitivo bar on the Lido in the early
evening.

☆ ENTERTAINMENT

TEATRO JUNGHANS THEATRE
(Map p323; ☑041 241 19 74; www.teatrojunghans.
it; Piazza Junghans 494, Giudecca; prices vary;
⛴; ⛴Redentore) This experimental theatre, nicknamed Teatro Formaggino (Little
Cheese), seats 150 around its three-sided
stage. But you're not expected to just sit
there: Teatro Junghans offers workshops
on costume design, mask-acting, and *commedia dell'arte* (improvisational comedy).
If you'd rather leave that sort of thing to
professionals, check the online calendar for
performances.

THE PALACE OF CINEMA

Eugenio Miozzi's rigid, Rationalist **Palazzo della Mostra del Cinema** seems as
ill-suited to the playboy Lido as a woolly bathing suit. But its severe Fascist lines were
well in keeping with the ambitious modernism of the era, when business tycoon and
Fascist minister Count Giuseppe di Volpi conceived of the film festival as a means of
fostering the Lido's upmarket tourism industry.

Bolted onto the already successful Biennale, it was an inspired idea in keeping with
Volpi's other modernising projects – the Schneider Trophy air race, the Casino and
an international motor-boat race – all of which lured a new breed of monied American, English and French holidaymakers to the city. Inaugurated in August 1932 on
the terrace of the Excelsior, the festival was the first of its kind (Cannes was a relative
latecomer in 1946) and capitalised on the boom in the film-making industry. So great
was its success, in fact, that Miozzi's *palazzo* was commissioned within three years
and remains the main festival venue – at least until the much-delayed new cinema is
completed.

SPORTS & ACTIVITIES

Lido di Venezia

BLUE MOON BEACH COMPLEX
(Map p324; Piazzale Bucintoro 1; ☻10am-6.30pm May-Sep; ⛟; ⛴Lido) FREE Named after a glamorous nightclub that once stood on the beach, the Blue Moon serves the *spiaggia comunale* (public beach) at the northern end of the Lido. Designed by Giancarlo de Carlo, professor emeritus at the Venice School of Architecture, in 1999, it marked the start of the Lido's most recent wave of redevelopment.

The bizarre, sci-fi structure – which consists of a semicircular, domed rotunda, containing a bar and restaurant, and a 30m-high aluminium flag tower and extended viewing platform – begs to be explored. Ramps and staircases lead to different levels and a raised dance floor, while the semicircular shape of the main building creates a piazza-like effect on the beach. In summer it's a hive of democratic events and activities, which is precisely what Giancarlo envisaged.

LIDO ON BIKE CYCLING
(Map p324; ☎041 526 80 19; www.lidoonbike.it; Gran Viale 21b; bikes per 90min/day €5/9; ☻9am-7pm mid-Mar–Oct; ⛴Lido) To tour at your own pace, rent a set of wheels from this friendly bike place near the Lido *vaporetto* stop, with reasonable prices that include a free map with recommended routes. It's a great way to island-hop to Pellestrina. You must have official identification showing you're at least 18 to rent.

CIRCOLO DEL GOLF VENEZIA GOLF
(☎041 73 13 33; www.circologolfvenezia.com; Via Strada Vecchia 1, Alberoni; green fees weekdays/weekends €97/109; ☻8.30am-6.30pm Tue-Sun; ⛟; ⛴Lido) Preserving some of the Lido's natural beauty, the golf club sits on a 100-hectare site protected by the World Wildlife Fund. The original nine-hole course (there are now 18) was designed by Cruikshank of Glasgow in 1928 and incorporates the walls of the old Alberoni fort as key elements in a number of holes.

Even if you don't play golf it's a lovely place for a stroll. Photos of club regulars such as the Duke of Windsor still hang in the bar; the club's most notorious guest was Adolf Hitler, who visited in 1934.

Murano, Burano & the Northern Islands

TORCELLO | BURANO & MAZZORBO | MURANO | ISOLA DI SAN MICHELE | SANT' ERASMO | LE VIGNOLE | ISOLA DELLA CERTOSA

Neighbourhood Top Five

❶ Engaging with vivid biblical tales at **Basilica di Santa Maria Assunta** (p171), where devilish imps steal all the attention away from a glittering, golden heaven.

❷ Witnessing artistry in action at the glass-blowing showrooms in **Murano** (p180) and rewarding their originality by making purchases.

❸ Basking in sun and culinary glory on the vineyard patio at **Venissa** (p179) or beneath the rose pergola at **Locanda Cipriani** (p179).

❹ Watching colourful houses wiggle with delight at their reflections in the canals of **Burano** (p172).

❺ Exploring religious retreats, off-the-beaten track beaches and ruined **Forte Sant'Andrea** by sailboat, barge (p172) or *batèla* (p174).

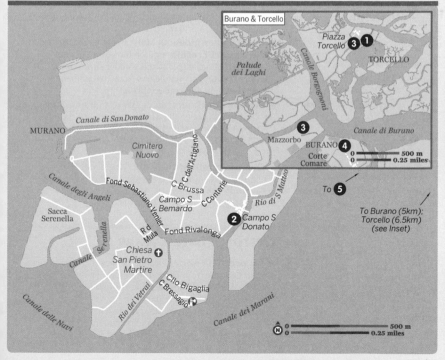

For more detail of this area see Map p325 and p326 ➡

Lonely Planet's Top Tip

Plan your trip carefully around your priorities – or it can be tricky to squeeze in Murano glass, Burano photography, Mazzorbo lunches and Torcello nature and history between the *vaporetto* hours (9am-5.30pm). Hit the outer islands first, and work your way back to Murano – it's faster and easier to reach from Venice if you need to return for more glass.

Best Places to Eat

→ Venissa (p179)

→ Locanda Cipriani (p179)

→ Acquastanca (p178)

→ Trattoria al Gatto Nero (p178)

For reviews, see p178➡

🍷 Best Places to Drink

→ Terrazzamare (p181)

→ Venissa (p179)

→ Caffè-Bar Palmisano (p178)

→ Terre di Venezia (p178)

For reviews, see p181➡

◉ Best Lagoon Photo-Ops

→ Brightly painted houses reflected in Burano canals.

→ Poses in Attila the Hun's throne in Torcello.

→ Flowers on poets' graves at Isola di San Michele. (p174)

→ Cormorants holding their wings out to dry on Mazzorbo.

→ Rock-star shots at ruined Forte Sant'Andrea on Le Vignole.

For reviews, see p172➡

Explore Murano, Burano & the Northern Islands

A multitude of small islands dot the northern lagoon, shards of greenery splintering off the mainland. The earliest Venetian refugees were able to island-hop to safety on Torcello in the 5th century when Mongol hordes threatened to overwhelm the Roman stronghold of Altinum. There they raised the first church of the lagoon, Santa Maria Assunta, decorating it with glittering mosaics telling cautionary tales in over a million handcut glass *tesserae*. As vivid as these mosaics, the glass workshops of Murano continue to conjure writhing chandeliers, swirling goblets and gem-bright jewellery from their red-hot furnaces, tempting a more modern type of pilgrim. Between these two islands you'll pass the haunting cemetery of San Michele, lagoon gardens on Sant'Erasmo and colourful fishers' houses on Burano – and with fresh seafood, island-grown vegetables and even local vineyards, you'll want to linger longer on the lagoon.

Local Life

→ **Picnics** Lunch is a highlight of sunny northern lagoon days, even without reservations at Venissa (p179). Pack a picnic to enjoy on Mazzorbo, in the meadow behind Basilica di Santa Maria Assunta (p171) on Torcello, or among the picturesque ruins of Forte Sant'Andrea on Le Vignole.

→ **Local lagoon hideouts** Make a beeline for the beach scene on **Sant'Erasmo**, sign up for sailing lessons at Vento di Venezia (p178) and wander through the long grasses on Le Vignole to a homemade lunch at Agriturismo da Zangrando (p175).

→ **Islands after hours** Stores and restaurants close up shop quickly once day-trippers clear out around 5.30pm, but stick around to enjoy happy hour with the crowd at Caffè-Bar Palmisano (p178), Gelateria al Ponte (p178) or Acquastanca (p178).

→ **Overnight retreats** Quit worrying about ferry schedules and enjoy a relaxed stay at affordable rates at Locanda Cipriani (p224), Murano Palace (p224) or Venissa (p224).

Getting There & Away

→ **Vaporetto** To reach Murano, the most regular services are the DM line from Ferrovia and lines 41 and 42 from Fondamente Nuove. To reach Burano and Mazzorbo, take the LN line from Fondamente Nuove or from the Murano-Faro stop. From Burano, the T line is a short hop to Torcello. Line 13 heads from Fondamente Nuove to Murano and onward to Le Vignole and Sant'Erasmo.

TOP SIGHT
BASILICA DI SANTA MARIA ASSUNTA

Life choices are presented in no uncertain terms in Santa Maria Assunta's vivid cautionary tale: look ahead to a golden afterlife amid saints and a beatific Madonna, or turn your back on her to face the wrath of a devil gloating over lost souls. In existence for more than a millennium, the cathedral is the lagoon's oldest Byzantine-Romanesque monument.

Madonna & Last Judgment Mosaics
The restrained brick exterior (c 824) betrays no hint of the colourful scene that unfolds as you enter. The Madonna rises in the east like the sun above a field of corn poppies in the 12th-century apse mosaic, while the back wall vividly depicts the dire consequences of dodging biblical commandments. This extraordinary Last Judgment mosaic shows the Adriatic as a sea nymph ushering souls lost at sea towards St Peter while a sneaky devil tips the scales of justice, and the Antichrist's minions drag sinners into hell.

Chapel Mosaics & Other Key Works
The right-hand chapel is capped with another 12th-century mosaic showing Sts Augustine, Ambrose, Martin and Gregory amid splendid, symbolic plants: lilies (representing purity), grapes and wheat (representing the wine and host of the holy sacrament), and corn-poppy buds (evoking Torcello's island setting).

Polychrome marble floors are another medieval masterpiece, with swirling designs and interlocking wheels symbolising eternal life. Saints line up atop the gilded iconostasis, their gravity foiled by a Byzantine screen teeming with peacocks, rabbits and other fanciful beasts.

DON'T MISS...
➡ Last Judgement mosaic
➡ Madonna apse mosaic
➡ Chapel saints mosaic
➡ Polychrome marble floors
➡ Iconostasis

PRACTICALITIES
➡ Map p326
➡ Piazza Torcello
➡ adult/reduced €5/4, incl museum €8/6
➡ ⏱10.30am-6pm Mar-Oct, 10am-5pm Nov-Feb
➡ 🚤Torcello

◉ SIGHTS

◉ Torcello

On the pastoral island of Torcello, sheep outnumber the 14 or so human residents. This bucolic backwater was once a Byzantine metropolis of 20,000, but rivalry with Venice and a succession of malaria epidemics systematically reduced its population. Of its original nine churches and two abbeys, all that remain are the Basilica di Santa Maria Assunta (p171) and the 11th-century **Chiesa di Santa Fosca** (Map p326; ☺10am-4.30pm daily; ⛴Torcello). On leisurely walks around the island you'll spot a few relics, including a worn stone throne Attila the Hun is said to have occupied when he passed through the area in the 5th century.

From Burano, the T *vaporetto* runs every half-hour until evening. Follow the path along the canal, Fondamenta Borgognoni, which leads you from the ferry stop to the cathedral.

MUSEO DI TORCELLO MUSEUM
(Map p326; ☑041 73 08 75; Piazza Torcello; adult/reduced €3/1.50, incl cathedral €8/5; ☺10.30am-5pm Tue-Sun Apr-Oct, to 5pm Nov-Mar; ⛴Torcello) Across the square from the cathedral in the 13th-century **Palazzo del Consiglio** is this museum dedicated to Torcello's bygone splendours. Downstairs are early Byzantine mosaics; while upstairs you'll find Roman items unearthed at the now-vanished Altinum. The show-stopper is a lively 1st-century Greek marble bust of a baby, lips parted as though to utter his first word.

◉ Burano & Mazzorbo

Once Venice's lofty Gothic architecture leaves you feeling slightly loopy, Burano brings you back to your senses with a reviving shock of colour. The 50-minute Laguna Nord (LN) ferry ride from the Fondamente Nuove is packed with photographers bounding into Burano's backstreets, snapping away at pea-green stockings hung to dry between hot-pink, royal-blue and caution-orange houses.

◉ TOP SIGHT
A NORTHERN LAGOON BOAT TRIP

Whereas other cities sunk their history in foundations, Venice cast out across the lagoon's patchwork of shifting mudflats, so seeing and understanding something of the lagoon is integral to understanding Venice. Unesco recognised this by specifically including the 550-sq-km (212-sq-mile) lagoon – the largest coastal wetland in Europe – in its designation of Venice as a World Heritage Site in 1987.

Rich in unique floral and fauna, the tidal *barene* (shoals) and salt marshes are part of the city's psyche. Between September and January over 130,000 migrating birds nest, dive and dabble in the shallows; while year-round fishermen tend their nets and traps, and city-council workers dredge canals and reinforce shifting islands of cord-grass and saltwort so essential to the lagoon's ecology.

Take a boat tour with **Terra e Acqua** (☑347 420 50 04; www.veneziainbarca.it; day-long trips incl lunch for 9-12 people €380-460) and dock for wine tasting at the Sant'Erasmo *cantina*, tour the quarantine island of Lazzaretto Nuovo and explore Sant'Andrea, the finest fort in the lagoon. Then return to Venice as a rosy-tinted sunset frames the city's campaniles.

DON'T MISS

➡ Tour of San Francesco del Deserto (p173)
➡ Fisherman's lunch on board
➡ Lazzaretto Nuovo
➡ Forte Sant'Andrea

WORTH A DETOUR

ISOLA DI SAN FRANCESCO DEL DESERTO

Given that the Venetian lagoon is situated on one of the most important migration routes in Europe, it only seems right that Francis of Assisi, the saint so famous for talking to birds, should have sought shelter here after his journey to Palestine in 1220. He built a chapel and a cell and after his death, Jacopo Michiel, the owner of the island, decided to give it to the Franciscans in perpetuity. In 1420 the friars were forced to desert the island (hence the name) due to rampant malaria, but in 1856 Monsignor Portogruaro brought them back and here they have remained as caretakers ever since.

Today, visits are only possible by prior arrangement with the **monastery** (☑041 528 68 63; www.sanfrancescodeldeserto.it; Isola di San Francesco del Deserto; admission free, donations appreciated; ☺9-11am & 3-5pm Tue-Sun), and are led by a Franciscan brother. As this is a place of prayer visitors are kindly asked to speak in hushed tones as they are led around the two cloisters and into the serene chapel where St Francis himself is said to have prayed. Best of all are the peaceful, cypress-scented gardens with their dreamlike views of Burano.

To get here you'll need to hire a private boat or water taxi, or arrange a visit as part of a day trip boating on the lagoon. From Burano expect to pay about €80 to €100 return for up to four passengers in a taxi, including 40- to 60-minute wait time.

Burano is also famed for its lemon-scented, S-shaped *buranelli* biscuits and its handmade lace, which once graced the décolleté and ruffs of European aristocracy. Unfortunately the ornate styles and expensive tableware fell out of vogue in lean post-WWII times and the industry has since suffered a terminal decline. Some women still maintain the traditions, but few production houses remain – most of the lace for sale in local shops is of the imported, machine-made variety.

If you fancy a stroll, hop across the 60m bridge to Burano's even quieter sister island, Mazzorbo. Little more than a broad grassy knoll, Mazzorbo is a great place for a picnic or a long, lazy lunch. The LN *vaporetto* also stops at Mazzorbo.

MUSEO DEL MERLETTO　　　　MUSEUM
(Lace Museum; Map p326; ☑041 4273 0892; www.visitmuve.it; adult/reduced €5/3.50; ☺10am-6pm Tue-Sun Apr-Oct, to 4.30pm Nov-Mar; ☱Burano) Burano's newly renovated Lace Museum tells the story of a craft that cut across social boundaries, endured for centuries and evoked the epitome of civilisation reached during the Republic's heyday. From the triple-petalled corollas on the fringes of the Madonna's mantle in Torcello's 12th-century mosaics to Queen Margherita's spider web–fine 20th-century mittens, lace-making was both the creative expression of female sensitivity and a highly lucrative craft.

The exhibit starts downstairs with a video explaining the early origins of lace-making and its geographical spread from Northern France to Bohemia, Malta and Turkey, while upstairs four rooms cover the major developments from the 16th to the 20th century. Pattern books, journals, paintings, furniture and costumery place the evolving art in context, starting with ecclesiastical garments and delicate *trinette* (accessories), and branching out into naughty, fringed underwear and sumptuously embroidered bodices shot through with silver thread. In the final room, bringing it all to life, a group of local lacemakers sit tatting and gossiping beneath pictures of the Lace School (where many of them learnt their craft), which was located here from 1872 to 1970. Don't be shy to ask questions about their work – your interest is welcome and provides a break from the mind-blowing concentration required for Burano-point stitching.

CHIESA DI SAN MARTINO　　　　CHURCH
(Map p326; ☑041 73 00 96; Piazza Galuppi; ☺8am-noon & 3-7pm Mon-Sat; ☱Burano) **FREE** This 16th-century church is worth a peek for Giambattista Tiepolo's 1725 *Crocifissione,* showing Mary gone grey with grief, and Giovanni di Niccolo Mansueti's fanciful *Flight from Egypt* (c 1492), which looks suspiciously like Torcello. The Russian icon near the altar is the Madonna di Kazan, a

REGATTA REVELRY

The biggest event in the northern lagoon calendar is the 32km **Vogalonga long row** (www.vogalonga.it) from Venice to Murano and Burano and back each May. It's a fabulously festive day when hundreds of enthusiasts take to the waters in their wooden *batèla* and motorised boats are banned from the lagoon for the day.

Plan in advance and find a grassy picnic spot on Mazzorbo. If you'd like to have a go yourself get in touch with Jane Caporal of **Row Venice** (☑345 241 52 66; www.rowvenice.com; 2hr lessons 1-2 people €80, 4 people €120), who'll soon show you how to wield an oar standing up like a *gondolieri*.

masterpiece of enamelwork with astonishingly bright, lifelike eyes.

◉ Murano

Venetians have been working in crystal and glass since the 10th century, but due to the fire hazards of glass-blowing, the industry was moved to the island of Murano in the 13th century. Woe betide the glass-blower with wanderlust: trade secrets were so jealously guarded that any glass worker who left the city was guilty of treason and subject to assassination. Today, glass artisans ply their trade at workshops along Murano's **Fondamenta dei Vetrai** marked by '*Fornace*' (Furnace) signs, secure in the knowledge that their wares set a standard that can't be replicated elsewhere.

To Murano, the most regular *vaporetto* services are the 41 and 42.

MUSEO DEL VETRO   MUSEUM

(Glass Museum; Map p325; ☑041 73 95 86; www.museovetro.visitmuve.it; Fondamenta Giustinian 8; adult/reduced €8/5.50; ☉10am-6pm Apr-Oct, to 5pm Nov-Mar; ⬛Museo) Since 1861, Murano's glass-making prowess has earned pride of place in Palazzo Giustinian (the seat of the Torcello bishopric from 1659 until its dissolution). Downstairs there are priceless 1500-year-old examples of iridescent Roman glass, but upstairs, Murano shows off in the frescoed **Salone Maggiore** (Grand Salon), with displays ranging from gold-flecked 17th-century winged aventurine goblets to a botanically convincing 1930s glass cactus.

An adjoining salon geeks out with the technical details of glass-making processes innovated on Murano, helpfully illustrated with examples of Murano specialities ranging from mosaic miniatures to *murrine* (flower-patterned beads), including blue-and-white Venetian trade beads.

BASILICA DEI SS MARIA E DONATO   CHURCH

(Map p325; Campo San Donato; ☉9am-noon & 3.30-7pm Mon-Sat, 3.30-7pm Sun; ⬛Museo) **FREE** Fire-breathing is the unifying theme of Murano's medieval church, with its 12th-century gilded glass Madonna apse mosaic made in Murano's *fornaci* and the legendary bones of a dragon hanging behind the altar. According to legend, these are the bones of a beast slayed by San Donato, whose mortal remains rest here. The other masterpiece here is underfoot: a Byzantine-style 12th-century mosaic pavement.

◉ Isola di San Michele

Shuttling between Murano from the Fondamente Nuove, *vaporetti* 41 and 42 stop at Venice's **city cemetery**.

CIMITERO   HISTORIC SITE

(☉7.30am-6pm daily Apr-Sep, to 4pm Oct-Mar; ⬛Cimitero) **FREE** Until Napoleon established a city cemetery on Isola di San Michele, Venetians had been buried in parish plots across town – not the most salubrious solution, as Napoleon's inspectors realised. Today, goths, incorrigible romantics and music-lovers pause here to pay respects to Ezra Pound, Joseph Brodsky, Sergei Diaghilev and Igor Stravinsky. Architecture buffs stop by to see the Renaissance **Chiesa di San Michele in Isola**, begun by Codussi in

❶ CIVIC MUSEUM PASS

If you're interested in artisanal work and plan on visiting both Murano's Glass Museum and the Lace Museum on Burano, then consider investing in a Civic Museum Pass (adult/reduced €20/14). The pass will also give you access to nine other museums, including the home of fabric icon Fortuny (p67).

LAGOON SUMMER CAMPS

Every summer since 1988 amateur archaeologists, university graduates and school-children have made the journey out to the island of Lazzaretto Nuovo to work on one of the most fascinating historic sites in the lagoon, the **Tezon Grande**.

The quarantine depot for the Republic between 1468 and the 1700s, the Tezon measures 100m in length and is the second-largest public building in the lagoon after the Corderie at the Arsenale. Around its perimeter it was surrounded by hundreds of one-room cottages, where travelling merchants waited out their 40-day exile trying to avoid the plague while city officials fumigated their cargoes with burning juniper and rosemary branches. Archaeological groups have so far catalogued hundreds of artefacts and uncovered extensive graffiti itemising ships' cargoes and describing harrowing voyages from Cyprus and Constantinople.

To enjoy an active role in the Lazzaretto's rehabilitation, check out the **Ekos Club** (⏺041 244 40 11; www.lazzarettonuovo.com; Isola di Lazzaretto Nuovo; ⏱9.45am-4.30pm Sat & Sun Apr-Oct; ⌖; ⛴Lazzaretto Nuovo) summer program. Between April and October it's also possible to visit the island on Saturday and Sunday. Take *vaporetto* 13 from the Fondamente Nuove and request the stop.

1469, and the ongoing **cemetery extension** by David Chipperfield Architects (scheduled for completion in 2016), including the recently completed **Courtyard of the Four Evangelists** – a sunken bunker, with a concrete colonnade and basalt-clad walls engraved with the Gospels.

⊙ Sant' Erasmo

Sant' Erasmo is known as the *orto di Venezia* (Venice's garden), and if you're visiting in mid-May, don't miss the island's **Sagra di Violetti** (Festival of Sant'Erasmo purple artichokes; www.carciofosanterasmo.it), when the island celebrates its purple-hued artichokes. At 4.5km (2.8 miles) long, Sant'Erasmo is as long as Venice, although it's just 1km (0.6 miles) wide at its widest point. Seven hundred and fifty farmers still plough its fields, supplying not only artichokes but also asparagus, squash, tomatoes and cardoons to the Rialto market and Venice's restaurants.

Once a rural retreat for aristocrats, the island now provides a largely tourist-free refuge for Venetian families who moor their boats along its mudbanks and picnic on the sandy beaches. Essential shots of coffee and pizza lunches are provided by the seasonal bar behind the beach, while bikes can be rented at the island's only accommodation, Il Lato Azzurro (p224), a favourite summertime retreat for artists.

Vaporetto 13 docks at Chiesa, from where it's a half-hour walk to the southern Capannone stop, and another 15 minutes east to the beach near the partly ruined **Torre Massimiliana**, a 19th-century Austrian fort sometimes used for art exhibitions. In summer only, line 18 departs from the Lido and stops right by the action at Torre Massimiliana.

⊙ Le Vignole

Welcome to the Venetian countryside! Together the two islands of Vignole Vecchie and Vignole Nuove long produced the doge's wine, and their 50 inhabitants still live mainly from agriculture. Like that of nearby Sant'Erasmo, the landscape is covered in fields, groves and vineyards and people are few and far between. *Vaporetto* 13 runs to Le Vignole from Fondamente Nuove via Murano (Faro stop).

A couple of *osterie* – **Trattoria alla Vignole** (⏺041 528 97 07; www.trattoriaallevignole. com; Isola Vignole 12; meals €30-40; ⏱10am-10pm Tue-Sun Apr-Sep) and **Agriturismo da Zangrando** (⏺041 528 40 20; Via delle Vignole 11; meals €25-35; ⏱12.30-2.30pm Thu-Mon Apr-Sep) – on the southwestern shore open in summer to accommodate weekending Venetians and intrepid lagoon explorers. At the southeastern tip a promontory ends in the Isola di Sant'Andrea, the location of the best-preserved fort on the lagoon: 16th-century **Forte Sant'Andrea**. Visits to the fort – more commonly known as the Castello da Mar (Sea Castle) – are only possible on lagoon boat trips.

Venetian Artistry

Glass

Venetians have been working in crystal and glass since the 10th century, though fire hazards prompted the move of the city's furnaces to Murano in the 13th century. Trade secrets were so closely guarded that any glass-worker who left the city was considered guilty of treason. By the 15th century Murano glass-makers were setting standards that couldn't be equalled anywhere in the world. They monopolised the manufacture of mirrors for centuries, and in the 17th century their skill at producing jewel-bright crystal led to a ban on the production of false gems out of glass. For a short course in Murano's masterly skill, head to the **Museo del Vetro** (p174).

Today, along Murano's Fondamenta dei Vetrai, centuries of tradition are upheld in Cesare Toffolo's winged goblets and Davide Penso's lampworked glass beads, while striking modern glass designs by Nason Moretti at ElleElle, Marina e Susanna Sent and Venini keep the tradition moving forward.

Paper

Embossing and marbling began in the 14th century as part of Venice's burgeoning publishing industry, but these bookbinding techniques and *ebru* (Turkish marbled paper) endpapers have taken on lives of their own. Artisan Rosanna Corrò of Cárte uses bookbinding techniques to create marbled, book-bound handbags and even furniture, while Cartavenezia turns hand-pulped paper into embossed friezes and free-form lamps. Gianni Basso uses 18th-century book symbols to make letter-pressed business cards with old-world flair, and you can watch a Heidelberg press in

1. Glass-shop window display **2.** Lace-making **3.** Paper in a bookbinder's shop

action at Veneziastampa, churning out menus and ex-libris (bookplates).

Textiles

Anything that stands still long enough in this city is liable to end up swagged, tasselled and upholstered. Venetian lace was a fashion must for centuries as Burano's **Lace Museum** (p173) attests, and Bevilacqua still weaves luxe tapestries (and donates scraps to nonprofit Banco Lotto 10 to turn into La Fenice costumes and handbags).

But the modern master of Venetian bohemian textiles is Fortuny, whose showroom on Giudecca features hand-stamped wall coverings created in strict accordance with top-secret techniques. But though the methods are secret, Fortuny's inspiration isn't: it covers the walls of his home studio, from Persian armour to portraits of socialites who tossed aside their corsets for Fortuny's Delphi gowns – now available for modern boho goddesses at Venetia Studium.

TOP FIVE NON-TOURISTY SOUVENIRS

➡ Customised business cards at **Gianni Basso** (p135).

➡ Lilac smoking jacket with handprinted scarlet skulls from **Fiorella Gallery** (p78).

➡ Blown-glass soap-bubble necklaces from **Marina e Susanna Sent** (p96).

➡ An overnight bag in swirling **Bevilacqua** (p79) tapestry.

➡ Orange marbled-paper cocktail rings from **Cárte** (p117).

⊙ Isola della Certosa

Once home to Carthusian monks (hence the island's name), La Certosa was the site of a grand monastery, its church graced with ducal tombs and rich artworks. All of that was lost, however, when the island was taken over by the military in the 19th century. Even its cloister was purchased by Prince Charles of Prussia and rebuilt in his summer castle in Berlin in 1850.

Today, thanks to EU funding and a huge local effort, La Certosa has been revived as a marina complex under the Vento di Venezia umbrella headed by former Italian sailing champion Alberto Sonino. Years of work have also been invested in the historic parkland with its groves of poplar and ash. In 2012 this work received a damaging setback when a tornado ripped across the island, felling trees and smashing boats. Although most of the park has now reopened, areas will remain closed for many months to ensure safety and complete ongoing restoration.

Between 6am and 8pm, *vaporetti* 41 and 42 connect San Pietro and Sant'Elena with Certosa, but you must request the stop. At night the hotel provides a shuttle from Sant'Elena, Lido and San Pietro di Castello.

VENTO DI VENEZIA   MARINA
(✆041 520 85 88; www.ventodivenezia.it; Isola della Certosa; 🚹; 🚤Certosa) ⛵ The initiative behind Certosa's yacht marina now embraces a fully fledged sustainable-tourism project, with a sailing school, a yoga centre, public nature trails and a restored 15th-century charterhouse for educational programs. To accompany it an 18-room hotel offers a range of sailing, kayaking and cycling packages and an alfresco restaurant-bar. It's a great place to escape the crowds on a hot summer day, and share a drink with the sailing fraternity on the patio of the **Terre di Venezia** (✆041 277 86 32; www.ventodivenezia.it; Isola della Certosa; ⊙8am-10pm; 🛜) bar.

✖ EATING

✖ Murano

GELATERIA AL PONTE   GELATO, SANDWICHES €
(Map p325; ✆041 73 62 78; Riva Longa 1c; snacks €2-5; ⊙9am-5pm Mon-Sat; 🚹; 🚤Museo) Toast-

ed prosciutto-and-cheese *panini* and gelato give shoppers a second wind, without cutting into Murano glass-buying budgets – sandwiches run at €3 to €5 and ice creams are €2.

★ACQUASTANCA   OSTERIA €€
(Map p325; ✆041 319 51 25; www.acquastanca.it; Fondamenta Manin 48; meals €30-40; ⊙9am-8pm Tue-Sun, to 10pm Fri; 🚤Faro) Caterina and Giovanna's old bakery has been transformed into a warm, modern space with nary a garish Murano trinket in sight. Sit down amid a symphony of marble, concrete and brushed steel and order plump prawns in a web of filo pastry or exquisitely sweet tuna tartare and homemade gnocchi with scallops.

There's also a generous bar, where you can grab a coffee and homemade cake in the morning or glasses of wine and platters of cheese come early evening.

BUSA ALLA TORRE   SEAFOOD €€
(Map p325; ✆041 73 96 62; Campo Santo Stefano 3; meals €35-50; ⊙11.45am-3.30pm; 🚤Faro) Glassy-eyed shoppers are drawn to Murano's classic eatery for its sunny disposition and €13 set menu. Arrive early for piazza seating with tempting views of glass showrooms, and settle in for seasonal lagoon treats like fried *moeche* (lagoon crab) cooked with pine nuts and sultanas and ribbons of tagliatelle with sweet winter *canòce* (mantis shrimps).

✖ Burano & Mazzorbo

CAFFÈ-BAR PALMISANO   CAFE €
(Map p326; Via San Martino 351, Burano; snacks €2-5; ⊙7am-8pm; 🚤Burano) Refuel with espresso and a sandwich at this cafe on the sunny side of the street, and return later to celebrate photo-safari triumphs over *spritz* or DOC wine with regular crowds of fishermen and university students.

TRATTORIA AL GATTO NERO   SEAFOOD €€
(Map p326; ✆041 73 01 20; www.gattonero.com; Fondamenta della Giudecca 88, Burano; meals €30-40; ⊙noon-3.30pm & 7.30-10pm Tue-Sun; 🚤Burano) Once you've tried the homemade *tagliolini* with spider crab, whole grilled fish, and perfect house-baked Burano biscuits, the ferry ride to Burano seems a minor inconvenience – a swim back here from Venice would be worth it for that decadent

VENISSA

During the Renaissance, most of the wine served at Venice's high tables came from vineyards on the lagoon islands. It was fermented from hardy, ancient varieties like Dorona and was golden hued in colour and bone dry to taste. But as the empire expanded, the Venetians abandoned their unyielding island vineyards for more productive possessions around Soave and Valpolicella. That is, until Gianluca Bisol, a *prosecco* producer from Valdobbiadene, heard of an ancient vineyard for sale on Mazzorbo in 1999. Since then, Bisol has worked magic rehabilitating orchards and vegetable patches, and restocking the brick-lined *peschiera* with eels, mullet and crabs. Then he renovated the farm building into a low-key, six-room guesthouse, and in 2006 **Venissa Ristorante Ostello** (Map p326; ☑041 527 22 81; www.venissa.it; Fondamenta Santa Caterina 3; ☺noon-3pm & 7-9.30pm Tue-Sun; 🚢Mazzorbo) 🍴 was opened to the public. But his greatest act of reclamation was undoubtedly the reintroduction of the 600-year-old Dorona grape at the heart of the new vineyard, so now you, too, can sup the nectar of Renaissance princes alongside lagoon langoustine and salicornia seaweed.

langoustine risotto alone. Call ahead and plead for canalside seating.

TRATTORIA DA ROMANO
SEAFOOD €€
(Map p326; ☑041 73 00 30; www.daromano.it; Via San Martino 221, Burano; meals €35-45; ☺noon-3pm & 7-9pm Apr-Oct, noon-3pm Nov-Dec & Feb; 🚢Burano) Da Romano have been perfecting its Gò risotto for over a century, and it's got so good at it that the restaurant is now crammed with paintings donated in gratitude by visiting artists. The risotto is made from the humble Gò fish, which is unique to the lagoon. Full of needle-like bones, they're boiled down to a broth that is then used to give the risotto its subtle, aromatic flavour.

TRATTORIA AL RASPO DE UA
VENETIAN €€
(Map p326; ☑041 73 00 95; www.alraspodeua.it; Via Galuppi 560, Burano; meals €20-30; ☺noon-3pm; 🚢Burano) Lunches alongside the piazza let you take in the lace-shopping frenzy from a safe distance while enjoying a plate of delicate prawn pasta. Linger over *vin santo* and *essi buranelli* – postprandial spirits served with the classic S-shaped Burano biscuit.

ALLA MADDALENA
SEAFOOD €€
(Map p326; ☑041 73 01 51; www.trattoriamaddalena.com; Fondamenta di Santa Caterina 7c, Mazzorbo; meals €30; ☺8am-8pm Fri-Wed; 🚢Mazzorbo) 🍴 Just a footbridge away from Burano's frantic, photo-snapping crowds are lazy seafood lunches on the island of Mazzorbo. Relax by the canal or in the garden out the back with fresh fish dishes and,

during autumn hunting season, the signature pasta with wild duck ragú.

🍴 Torcello

LOCANDA CIPRIANI
ITALIAN €€€
(Map p326; ☑041 73 01 50; www.locandacipriani.com; Piazza Santa Fosca 29; meals €40-55; ☺by reservation, closed Tue & Jan; 🚢Torcello) A rustic retreat run by the Cipriani family since 1934, the Locanda is Harry's Bar gone wild. Go with seasonal specialities like *bigoli* (fat wholewheat spaghetti) with rabbit, lamb with wild herbs, or plan a lazy afternoon around the €45 Torcello menu fit for a famished Hemingway. Lunches and dinners are served by the fireplace or in the garden under the rose pergola.

🛍 SHOPPING

Watch red-hot home decor emerge from the fiery *fornaci* of Murano, hidden behind the showrooms along Fondamenta Vetrai and Ramo di Mula. Showroom staff let you handle pieces if you ask first, but wield parcels and handbags with care – what you break, you buy. On sunny Burano days, you might glimpse local ladies tatting lace on brightly painted front stoops. The island's main drag, Via Galuppi, is lined with lace shops. Look for *'fatto a Burano'* (made in Burano) and 'Vero Artistico Murano' guarantees, since much of the less expensive stock is imported.

🏠 Murano

⭐ELLEELLE ARTISANAL, GLASS

(Map p325; 🕿041 527 48 66; www.elleellemurano. com; Fondamenta Manin 52; ☺10am-6pm Mon-Sat; 🚤Colonna) Burlesque dancers inspire curvy, red-hot wineglasses, crystal icebergs become champagne flutes and lagoon waters seem to swirl inside free-form, two-tone green and blue vases. Nason Moretti have been making modernist magic happen in glass since the 1950s, and the third-generation glass designers are in rare form in this showroom. Prices start at €30 for signed, hand-blown drinking glasses.

⭐DAVIDE PENSO ARTISANAL, GLASS

(Map p325; 🕿041 527 56 59; www.davidepenso. com; Fondamenta Rivalonga 48; ☺10am-5.30pm Mon-Sat; 🚤Museo) Davide Penso has taken the art of bead making to dizzying heights with exhibits at the Museo Correr, Boston's Fine Arts Museum and the San Marco Museum of Japan. Made using the lamp-working process, each bead is individually painted in strikingly modern styles. The collar of gold lozenges looks satisfyingly like the real thing.

VENINI ARTISANAL, GLASS

(Map p325; 🕿041 273 72 04; www.venini.it; Fondamenta Vetrai 47; ☺9.30am-6pm Mon-Sat; 🚤Colonna) Even if you don't have the cash to buy a Venini, pop into its gallery to see how it's done by the experts. Of the big houses – Seguso, Salviati, Barovier & Toso and C.A.M – Venini remains the most relevant, having embraced modernist trends since the 1930s.

Its enviable range is bolstered by collaborations with design greats such as Carlo Scarpa, Gae Aulenti, Emmanuel Babled and, most recently, Fabio Novembre, whose 'Happy Pills' hit the shelves in 2012.

MARINA E SUSANNA
SENT STUDIO ARTISANAL, GLASS

(Map p325; 🕿041 527 46 65; www.marinaesu sannaset.com; Fondamenta Serenella 20; ☺Sep-Jul; 🚤Colonna) At last the Sent sisters have opened their workshop in Murano, causing countless holiday hours lost in indecision. The two-storey space is as sleek as their jewellery: exposed-concrete walls, a double-height ceiling and white light streaming through the windows and setting signature pieces ablaze. The collection is displayed in colour groups and neatly stashed in draw-

ers – don't be too shy to ask for assistance; there's a lot to see.

Two other shops, with a more highly curated selection, can be found in Dorsoduro (p96) and San Marco.

LUIGI CAMOZZO ARTISANAL, GLASS

(Map p325; 🕿041 37 68 75; www.luigicamozzo. com; Fondamenta Venier 3; 🚤Museo) If you're lucky you'll find master glass engraver Luigi Camozzo sat at one of his diamond-point wheels etching painstakingly detailed scenes into all manner of glass objects. Some are embedded with richly coloured enamels and gold, while other cold-worked *battuto* (literally 'beaten') vases in browns, reds and gold look like basketry or wood sculpture.

Apprentice Amy West, who hails from Kansas, also exhibits her work in the gallery, including super mod rings that sit like shiny, dark beetles on long slender fingers.

CAMPAGNOL & SALVADORE ARTISANAL, GLASS

(Map p325; 🕿041 73 67 72; Fondamenta Vetrai 128a; ☺10.30am-6pm Mon-Sat; 🚤Colonna) The Japanese-Murano couple behind Campagnol & Salvadore specialise in light-hearted creations: their aqua and sunshine-yellow bead necklaces look like strands of tiny beach balls. Psychedelic colour schemes make these baubles runway-ready, and aspiring designers are encouraged to create their own looks from individual blown-glass beads (€3 to €15 per bead).

TOFFOLO GALLERY ARTISANAL, GLASS

(Map p325; 🕿041 73 64 60; www.toffolo.com; Fondamenta Vetrai 37; ☺10am-6pm Mon-Sat; 🚤Colonna) Classic gold-leafed winged goblets and mind-boggling miniatures are the trademarks of this Murano glass-blower, but you'll also find some dramatic departures: chiselled cobalt-blue vases, glossy black candlesticks that look like Dubai minarets, and highly hypnotic pendants.

LINEA ARTE VETRO ARTISANAL, GLASS

(Map p325; 🕿041 73 97 48; Fondamenta Rivalonga 53; ☺10.30am-5.30pm Mon-Tue & Thu-Sat; 🚤Museo) Mounds of flaming orange beads and shelves of octopus-tentacle glass rings keep DIY designers and bargain shoppers enthralled at this collective of emerging Murano glass artists. Prices like these are how Murano glass collections begin: beads start at €30 and rings at €7.

LIDO DI JESOLO

This strand of sand a couple of kilometres away from Jesolo is far and away Venetians' preferred beach, with fine, clean sand, warm, calm waters and beach nightclubs. The most memorable entertainment options are often spontaneous – so in July and August keep an eye out for flyers offering free admission to clubs (a €5 to €20 value) and announcements of free beach concerts often featuring international acts.

With open cabanas on a raised platform, dance scenes on the sand and occasional DJ duels, **Terrazzamare** (☑0421 37 00 12; www.terrazzamare.com; Vicolo Faro 1; admission €15; ☺6pm-4am Tue-Sat Apr-Jun, nightly Jul-Sep) earns its 'theatre-bar' fame and is populated by bronzed regulars in enormous sunglasses. Inland from Jesolo, an army of DJs spins mostly house music at one of the hippest summer dance locales, **Il Muretto** (☑393 410 11 20; www.ilmuretto.net; Via Roma Destra 120d; admission from €20; ☺11pm-5am Wed & Fri-Sun Mar-Sep), although you'll need a car or taxi to get here. While clubbers at Muretto watch dawn arrive through the retractable roof, hook-ups head down the road to **Marina Club** (☑0421 37 06 45; www.marinaclubjesolo.com; Via Roma Destra 120b, Lido di Jesolo; admission free; ☺8pm-4am Apr-Sep) FREE, where breezy gazebos, candles and weekend DJs set the mood for private convos.

Getting to Jesolo takes about an hour by car, and can be reached by public transport: take ATVO bus 10a (€3.80, 70 minutes) from Piazzale Roma. The problem is getting back – the last bus usually leaves at 11.20pm in summer, and taxis cost upwards of €80. If you can make it to Punta Sabbioni at the tip of the peninsula, you might be able to catch the LN late-night *vaporetto* back to Venice. For more information, try the **Palazzo del Turismo** (☑041 37 06 01; www.jesolo.it) in Jesolo.

⛪ Burano

EMILIA   ARTISANAL, LACE

(Map p326; ☑041 73 52 99; www.emiliaburano.it; Piazza Galuppi 205; ⛴Burano) Doyenne Emilia di Ammendola is a third-generation lacemaker and has passed on her skills to her son and daughter. You'll often find her son, Lorenzo, at the drawing board designing elaborate floral schemes, which are then brought to life by a team of local women. Prices for off-the-shelf tablewear start at €60 and rise rapidly into the hundreds for tablecloths.

Cut Egyptian cottons, embroidered Irish linens and towels are also available. Upstairs Emilia's personal collection showcases priceless antique pieces, including an 18th-century wedding dress, which took seven women three years to complete.

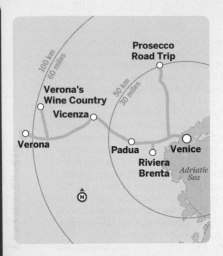

Day Trips from Venice

Riviera Brenta p183
See where Venetian elites gambled away their summers in Palladian-style villas.

Padua p185
This vibrant university town is also a treasure trove of fresco cycles from its medieval golden age.

Vicenza p192
Palladio's adopted home is defined by the architect's classical restraint, while the countryside is dotted with his elegant villas.

Prosecco Road Trip p198
Share a glass of *prosecco* with hardworking locals in one of the Veneto's most under-appreciated areas.

Verona p201
Romeo and Juliet might have been fictional, but Verona's real history is evidenced by its Roman arena, Romanesque churches and Renaissance gardens.

Verona's Wine Country p208
Valpolicella yields up some of Italy's biggest, boldest reds. Soave is synonymous with crisp whites.

Riviera Brenta

Explore

For centuries, summer officially started on 13 June as a flotilla of fashionable Venetians headed for their summer residences along the banks of the Brenta. There were once over 3000 villas in the Venetian hinterland, built between the 15th and the 18th century; now fewer than 80 survive and of those four are open as museums, including Palladio's exquisite La Malcontenta and the grand Villa Pisani. They can be seen in a day, especially on a river cruise aboard the traditional *burchiello*. If on your own, note that sites are scattered, so cars are a better option than trains – this very flat country also begs for biking. If you decide to linger, seek shelter in a villa-turned-B&B – or spend the night in nearby Padua, where the cruise ends.

The Best...

➡ **Sight** Villa Foscari (p183)
➡ **Place to Eat** Da Conte (p185)
➡ **Place to Drink** Da Conte (p185)

Top Tip

The Riviera Brenta is best seen from the decks of flat-bottomed riverboats – the same way Venetians did, at least until Napoleon's troops shut down the centuries-long party in 1797.

Getting There & Away

➡ **Boat** Organised boat tours leave from both Venice and Padua (p184).

➡ **Train** Regional trains between Venice and Padua stop at Dolo (€2.85, 30 minutes, one to two per hour) en route to Padua.

➡ **Bus** ACTV's Venezia–Padova Extraurbane bus 53 leaves from Venice's Piazzale Roma about every half-hour, stopping at key Brenta villages en route to Padua.

➡ **Car** Take SS11 from Mestre-Venezia towards Padova (Padua), and take the Autostrada A4 towards Dolo/Padova.

Need to Know

➡ **Area Code** 041
➡ **Location** 15km to 30km west of Venice

---

❶ THE BRENTA BY BIKE

Speed past tour boats along 150km of cycling routes along the Brenta Riviera. Veloce (p283) offers a handy pick-up and drop-off service at railway stations and hotels in many Veneto towns, including Padua, Venice and Mira. City and mountain bikes are available, along with GPS units pre-loaded with multi-lingual Brenta itineraries (€10).

➡ **Tourist Office** (☑041 560 06 90; Via Nazionale 420, Villa Widmann Foscari, Mira Porte; ☺10.30am-1pm, 1.30-4.30pm)

◉ SIGHTS

The Brenta River had long acted as a commercial waterway between inland farms and Venice, transporting meat, fruit, vegetables, flour and even fresh water to the city, and exporting its spices, cloth, soap, glass and fish inland. But the river's regular and ferocious torrents, coupled with a pre-1345 decree forbidding Venetians to own mainland property, meant the area remained largely undeveloped until the 15th century.

That all changed in 1407, when Padua came under Venetian control and the Brenta's flow was finally tamed by hydraulic intervention. Almost immediately life on the river began to change as aristocratic families set up fabulous country estates, enhancing their incomes with farming and indulging in wild parties. Famous artists and architects were brought in to design and decorate their homes, and soon the river was traffic-logged with nobles who spent the days cruising between villas, engaging in what became known as *villeggiatura*.

VILLA FOSCARI   HISTORIC BUILDING
(☑041 520 39 66; www.lamalcontenta.com; Via dei Turisti 9, Malcontenta; adult/student €10/8; ☺9am-noon Tue & Sat, closed Nov-Apr) The most romantic Brenta villa, the Palladio-designed 1555–60 Villa Foscari got its nickname 'La Malcontenta' from a grande dame of the Foscari clan who was reputedly exiled here for cheating on her husband – though these bright, highly sociable salons hardly constitute a punishment. The villa was abandoned for years, but Giovanni Zelotti's

frescoes have been restored to daydream-inducing splendour from *Fame* in the study to the Bacchanalian bedroom.

Palladio's glorious facade faces the river, with soaring Ionic columns capped by a classical tympanum that draw the eye and spirits upward.

VILLA WIDMANN REZZONICO FOSCARI HISTORIC BUILDING

(☑041 560 06 90; Via Nazionale 420, Mira; adult/student €5/4; ⊗10am-5pm Tue-Sun May-Sep, 10am-5pm Sat & Sun Nov-Feb) To appreciate both gardening and Venetian-style social engineering, stop just west of Oriago at Villa Widmann Rezzonico Foscari. Originally owned by Persian-Venetian nobility, the 18th-century villa captures the Brenta's last days of rococo decadence, with Murano sea-monster chandeliers and a frescoed grand ballroom with upper viewing gallery.

Head to the gallery to reach the upstairs ladies' gambling parlour where, according to local lore, villas were once gambled away in high-stakes games. Ignore the incongruously modernised bathrooms and puzzling modern crafts displays in the bedrooms and head instead into the garden, where an albino peacock loudly bemoans bygone glories.

VILLA BARCHESSA VALMARANA HISTORIC BUILDING

(☑041 426 63 87; www.villavalmarana.net; Via Valmarana 11, Mira; admission €6; ⊗10am-6pm Tue-Sun Mar-Oct, by appointment rest of year) Across the Brenta from Villa Widmann is the Villa Barchessa Valmarana. What you see is just one of the wings of the original 17th-century villa, as the main structure was torn down in the 19th century to avoid paying luxury taxes. Originally built as the boathouse, this wing was soon upgraded to a guesthouse when the Valmaranas found that they couldn't accommodate all their summer visitors.

Now the double-height dining room with its glorious frescoes by Michelangelo Schiavoni (1712–72) serves mainly as a conference centre – something of a comedown from the days when Prospero Valmarana hosted the Bey of Tripoli.

VILLA PISANI NAZIONALE HISTORIC BUILDING

(☑049 50 20 74; www.villapisani.beniculturali.it; Via Doge Pisani 7, Stra; adult/reduced €7.50/3.75, park only €4.50/2.25; ⊗9am-5pm Tue-Sun Nov-Mar, to 7pm Apr-Sep) To keep hard-partying Venetian nobles in line, Doge Alvise Pisani provided a Versailles-like reminder of who was in charge. The 1774 Villa Pisani Nazionale is surrounded by huge gardens, a labyrinthine hedge-maze and pools to reflect the doge's glory. Occasionally there are also some outstanding temporary exhibitions in upstairs salons, from Old Masters to contemporary artists.

And if the walls of these 114 rooms could talk, they'd name-drop shamelessly. Here you'll find the gaming rooms where Venice's powerful Pisani family racked up debts

RIVER CRUISES

When Venetians set out from Piazza San Marco for the the Brenta, many of them would step aboard the commodious barge *Il Burchiello*, which was drawn along the tow-path by a team of horses. Goethe arrived on the lagoon in this fashion in 1786, and today a small fleet of modern *burchielli* ply the river between Venice and Padua.

There's no doubt that seeing the Brenta from the perspective of a boat (rather than through the snarl of Venetian and Padovan suburbs) is the best way to experience the river and its villas, most of which where designed to show their best face to the water. As you pass through the five locks and nine swing bridges, you'll appreciate the 15th-century hydraulic locks system, which diverted the main floodwaters of the river to Chioggia, putting a stop to the accumulation of silt in the lagoon.

Il Burchiello (☑049 876 02 33; www.ilburchiello.it; adult/reduced half-day cruise €55/45, full day from €94/55) is a modern luxury barge offering full-day cruises that stop at Malcontenta, Widmann and Pisani villas; half-day tours cover two villas. Full-day cruises leave from Venice's Stazione Maritima (Tuesday, Thursday and Saturday) or Padua (Wednesday, Friday and Sunday), with bus transfers to train stations.

I Batelli del Brenta (☑049 876 02 33; www.battellidelbrenta.it; adult/reduced half-day tours from €50/40, full day from €89/50; ⊗by reservation Tue-Sun Mar-Nov) offers a range of half- and full-day excursions, with departures from both Venice and Padua.

DAY TRIPS FROM VENICE PADUA (PADOVA)

SLEEPING IN RIVIERA BRENTA

Villa Tron Mioni (☑041 41 01 77; www.
villatron.it; Via Ca' Tron 23, Dolo; d €92-
130, ste €120-170; ❀❀) Surrounded
by gardens, this 19th-century villa
provides aristocratic flourishes at
middle-class prices. Rooms in the
main villa are done up in simple good
taste, and a few new apartments are
handsomely decorated in rustic-chic
style. However, the ramblingly romantic gardens are the real draw. Works
best if you have your own car.

that forced them to sell the family mansion
to Napoleon; the grand bathroom with a
tiny wooden throne used by Napoleon during his 1807 reign as king of Italy; a sagging
bed where Vittorio Emanuele II apparently
tossed and turned as the head of newly independent Italy; and, in historical irony, the
grand reception hall where Mussolini and
Hitler met for the first time in 1934 under
Tiepolo's ceiling depicting the Geniuses of
Peace.

VILLA FOSCARINI ROSSI   HISTORIC BUILDING
(☑049 980 10 91; www.villafoscarini.it; Via
Doge Pisani 1/2, Stra; adult/reduced €5/2.50;
⊗9am-1pm & 2-6pm Mon-Fri, 2.30-6pm Sat &
Sun Apr-Oct, 9am-1pm Mon-Fri Nov-Mar) Well-
heeled Venetians wouldn't have dreamt
of decamping to the Brenta without their
favourite cobblers, sparking a tradition
of high-end shoemaking. Today, 950 companies produce 22 million pairs of shoes
annually. The lasting contribution of
Brenta cobblers is commemorated with a
Shoemakers' Museum at Villa Foscarini,
a multiroom dream that includes 18th-
century slippers, kicks created for Marlene
Dietrich, and heels handcrafted for Yves
Saint Laurent.

✗ EATING

OSTERIA DA CONTE   MODERN VENETIAN €€
(☑049 47 95 71; www.osteriadaconte.it; Via
Caltana 133, Mira; meals €35-45; ⊗10am-4pm
& 6-10pm Tue-Sat) This unlikely bastion of
sophistication is lodged practically underneath an overpass. Da Conte has one of the
best wine lists in the region and uses much

Slow Food–accredited produce in its dishes.
Expect creative takes on classic lagoon cuisine, from roasted quail to ginger-infused
langoustines.

Padua
(Padova)

Explore

Though under an hour from Venice, Padua
(population 214,900) seems a world away
with its medieval marketplaces, Fascista-
era facades and hip student population. As
a medieval city-state and home to Italy's
second-oldest university, Padua challenged
both Venice and Verona for regional he-
gemony. A series of extraordinary fresco
cycles recalls this golden age – including
Giotto's remarkable Capella degli Scrovegni, Menabuoi's heavenly gathering in the
Bapistry and Titian's *St Anthony* in the
Scoletta del Santo. With convenient train
connections and a dense historic centre,
Padua is an easy day trip from Venice, although its many and varied sites could
fill a number of days. Be sure to stay overnight and watch the *piazze* come alive as
the highly social Padovans gather for their
evening *aperitivo*.

The Best...

➔ **Sight** Capella degli Scrovegni (p187)
➔ **Place to Eat** L'Anfora (p190)
➔ **Place to Drink** Enoteca Il Tira
Bouchon (p191)

ⓘ MAKING THE MOST OF
YOUR EURO

A **PadovaCard** (www.padovacard.it; per
48/72hr €16/21) gives one adult plus
one child under 14 free use of city public transport and access to almost all
of Padua's major attractions, including the Cappella degli Scrovegni (plus
€1 booking fee; reservation essential).
They are available at Padua tourist
offices and monuments covered by
the pass.

Padua

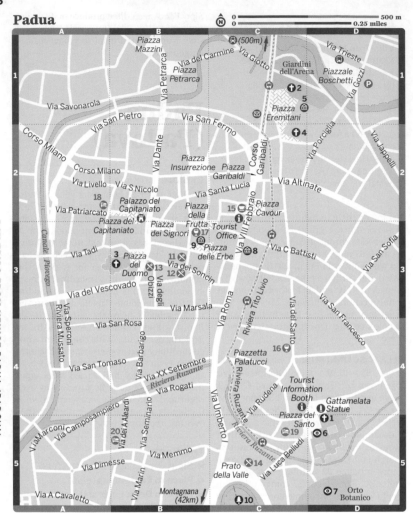

Top Tip

Reservations are required to see Giotto's extraordinary Capella degli Scrovegni – sometimes as much as a few weeks ahead for summer weekends and during holidays.

Getting There & Away

➜ **Car** The A4 (Turin–Milan–Venice–Trieste) passes to the north of town, while the A13 to Bologna starts south of town.

➜ **Bus** SITA buses (☏049 820 68 34; www.fsbusitalia.it) from Venice's Piazzale Roma (€4.10, 45 to 60 minutes, hourly) arrive at Piazzale Boschetti, 500m south of the train station. Check online for buses to Colli Euganei towns.

➜ **Train** Trains are the easiest way to reach Padua from Venice (€4 to €19.50, 25 to 50 minutes, three or four per hour).

Need to Know

➜ **Area Code** 049

➜ **Location** 37km west of Venice

➜ **Tourist Office** (www.turismopadova.it) Train Station (☏049 875 20 77; Train Station; ⊙9.15am-7pm Mon-Sat, 9am-noon Sun); Galleria

Padua

◎ Sights

⊗ Eating

⊜ Drinking & Nightlife

⊜ Sleeping

Pedrocchi (☑049 876 79 27; Galleria Pedrocchi; ◎9am-1.30pm & 3-7pm Mon-Sat)

◉ SIGHTS

CAPPELLA DEGLI SCROVEGNI   CHURCH
(☑049 201 00 20; www.cappelladegliscrovegni.it; Piazza Eremitani 8; adult/reduced €13/8; ◎9am-7pm Mon, to 10pm Tue-Sun Mar-Oct, 9am-7pm Nov-Dec, by reservation only) Dante, da Vinci and Vasari all honour Giotto as the artist who ended the Dark Ages with his 1303–05 frescoes. Giotto's moving, modern approach changed how people saw themselves: not as lowly vassals but as vessels for the divine, however flawed. This was especially well suited to the chapel Enrico Scrovegni commissioned in memory of his father, who as a moneylender was denied a Christian burial.

Previously medieval churchgoers had been accustomed to blank stares from saints perched on high, golden Gothic thrones, but Giotto introduced biblical figures as characters in recognisable settings. Onlookers gossip as middle-aged Anne tenderly kisses Joachim; exhausted new dad Joseph falls asleep standing up in the manger; and Jesus stares down Judas as the traitor puckers up for the fateful kiss. A 10-minute introductory video provides some helpful insights before you enter the church itself.

Visits are by reservation only and booking is required online or by phone. Pick up tickets at the Musei Civici agli Eremitani, where you access the chapel. Book well ahead for weekends and any time from April to October. Chapel visits last 15 minutes, plus another 15 minutes for the video, though the 'double turn' night-session ticket (adult/reduced/child under seven years €12/6/1) allows a 30-minute stay in the church.

MUSEI CIVICI AGLI EREMITANI   MUSEUM
(☑049 8204 5450; Piazza Eremitani 8; adult/reduced €10/8; ◎9am-7pm Tue-Sun) The ground floor of this monastery houses artefacts dating from Padua's Roman and pre-Roman past. Upstairs, a rambling but interesting collection boasts a few notable 14th- to 18th-century works by Bellini, Giorgione, Tintoretto and Veronese. The showstopper is a crucifix by Giotto, showing a heartbroken Mary wringing her hands as Jesus' blood drips into the eye sockets of a human skull.

CHIESA DEGLI EREMITANI   CHURCH
(☑049 875 64 10; Piazza Eremitani; ◎8.15am-12.15pm & 4-6pm Mon-Sat, 9.30am-12.15pm & 4-6pm Sun) When a 1944 bombing raid demolished the extraordinary 1448–57 frescoes by Andrea Mantegna in the Capella Overtari in the Chiesa degli Eremitani, the loss to art history was incalculable. After half a century of painstaking reconstruction, the shattered, humidity-damaged stories of Sts James and Christopher have been puzzled together, revealing action-packed compositions and extreme perspectives that make Mantegna's saints look like superheroes.

PALAZZO DEL BÒ   HISTORIC BUILDING
(☑049 827 30 47; Via VIII Febbraio; adult/reduced €5/3.50; ◎tours 9.15am, 10.15am & 11.15am Tue, Thu & Sat, 3.15pm, 4.15pm & 5.15pm Mon, Wed & Fri) This Renaissance *palazzo* is the seat of Padua's history-making **university**. Founded by renegade scholars from Bologna seeking greater intellectual freedom, the university has employed some of Italy's

greatest and most controversial thinkers, including Copernicus, Galileo, Casanova and the world's first woman doctor of philosophy, Eleonora Lucrezia Cornaro Piscopia (her statue graces the stairs). Guided tours cover **Galileo's lecture hall** and the world's first **anatomy theatre**.

Built for autopsy in 1594, this six-tiered wooden hall is an ingenious spiral: students circulated continuously so everyone got a close-up look at the dissection, while high handrails prevented those in the heights, giddy from the overwhelming smell, from fainting into the pit. Afterwards don't forget to pay your respects to the skulls of noble professors in the **graduation hall**. They donated themselves for dissection, given the difficulty involved in acquiring fresh corpses.

Note that there are generally only two tours per day from November to March.

PALAZZO DELLA RAGIONE   HISTORIC BUILDING
(☑049 820 50 06; Piazza delle Erbe; adult/reduced €4/2; ☺9am-7pm Tue-Sun, to 6pm Nov-Jan) Ancient Padua can be glimpsed in elegant twin squares separated by the triple-decker Gothic Palazzo della Ragione, the city's tribunal dating from 1218. Inside, frescoes by Giotto acolytes Giusto de' Menabuoi and Nicolò Mireto depict the astrological theories of Padovan professor Pietro d'Abano, with images representing the months, seasons, saints, animals and noteworthy Paduans (not necessarily in that order).

D'Abano's work, which drew on Arab sources, brought him into conflict with the Church, and he was convicted posthumously of heresy. Unfortunately, the frescoes had to be restored after a fire in 1420 and storm damage in 1756, but the reproductions are of high quality.

CATHEDRAL   CHURCH
(☑049 66 28 14; Piazza del Duomo; ☺7.30am-noon & 4-7.30pm Mon-Sat, 8am-1pm & 3-8pm Sun & holidays) FREE Built from a much-altered design of Michelangelo's, the whitewashed symmetry of Padua's cathedral is a far cry from its rival in Piazza San Marco. The adjoining 13th-century **Baptistry** (☑049 65 69 14; adult/child €2.80/1; ☺10am-6pm), however, is a Romanesque gem frescoed with luminous biblical scenes by Giusto de' Menabuoi. Hundreds of male and female saints congregate in the cupola, posed as though for a school graduation photo, ex-

changing glances and stealing looks at the Madonna.

At the centre of the dome Christ Pantocrator holds open a book inscribed with the words *Ego sum alpha et omega* (I am the beginning and the end), and the rear apse wall illustrates his meaning with frescoes that illuminate biblical stories of creation, redemption and the apocalypse.

BASILICA DI SANT'ANTONIO   CHURCH
(Il Santo; www.basilicadelsanto.org; Piazza del Santo; ☺6.20am-7.45pm Apr-Oct, to 7pm Nov-Mar) FREE Il Santo is the soul of Padua, a key pilgrimage site and the burial place of patron saint St Anthony of Padua (1193–1231). Begun in 1232, its polyglot style incorporates rising eastern domes atop a Gothic brick structure crammed with Renaissance treasures. Behind the high altar nine radiating chapels punctuate a broad ambulatory homing in on the **Cappella del Tesoro** (Treasury Chapel), where the relics of St Anthony reside.

Renowned for his oratorical skills, Anthony was a notable public mediator in times of civil strife. Legend has it that when his tomb was opened in 1263 his body had disintegrated, with the exception of his chin and grey-green tongue, which are now on display in enormous golden reliquaries.

You'll also notice dozens of people clustering along the right transept waiting their turn to enter the **Cappella del Santo**, where Anthony's tomb is covered with requests and thanks for the saint's intercession in curing illness and recovering lost objects. The chapel itself is a light-filled Renaissance confection lined with nine panels vividly depicting the story of Anthony's life in extraordinary relief sculptures attributed to the Padua-born Lombardo brothers and completed around 1510.

Other notable works include the lifelike 1360s crucifix by Veronese master Altichiero da Zevio in the frescoed **Cappella di San Giacomo**; the wonderful 1528 sacristy fresco of St Anthony preaching to spellbound fish by a follower of Girolamo Tessari; and 1444–50 high altar reliefs by Florentine Renaissance master Donatello (ask guards for access). Through the east door of the basilica you reach the attached monastery with its five cloisters. The oldest (13th century) is the **Chiostro della Magnolia**, so called because of the magnificent tree in its centre. Nearby, the **Museo Antoniano** (☑049 860 32 36; Piazza del Santo;

adult/reduced €2.50/1.50; ⊙9am-1pm & 2-6pm Apr-Sep, 9am-1pm Mon-Fri, 9am-1pm & 2-6pm Sat & Sun Oct-Mar) holds a kitschy collection of art and religious objects donated by grateful pilgrims.

Outside, in the **Piazza del Santo**, is Donatello's 1453 equestrian statue of the 15th-century Venetian mercenary leader known as **Gattamelata** (Honeyed Cat). It's considered the first great Italian Renaissance bronze.

ORATORIO DI SAN GIORGIO ORATORY

(☎049 822 56 52; Piazza del Santo; excl/incl Scoletta del Santo €3/5; ⊙9am-12.30pm & 2.30-7pm Apr-Oct, to 5pm Nov-Mar) Anywhere else the fresco cycle of the **Oratorio di San Giorgio** and the paintings in the **Scoletta del Santo** would be considered highlights, but in Padua they must contend with Giotto's Scrovegni brilliance. This means you'll have Altichiero da Zevio's and Jacopo Avanzi's jewel-like, 14th-century frescoes of St George, St Lucy and St Catherine all to yourself, while upstairs in the *scoletta* (confraternity house) Titian paintings are seldom viewed in such tranquility.

Completed in 1377, the Oratory was the burial chapel of the Marquis Raimondino Lupi and is similar in structure to the Scrovegni chapel. A single nave with high, smooth walls is capped by a generous barrel vault sprinkled with golden stars. To the left, scenes from the life of St George include not only feats of dragon-slaying but miraculous survival stories and superhero prayer power that lays low a temple of idols. Likewise, to the right, St Lucy remains steadfast as a team of burly oxen attempt to drag her to a house of ill repute, and St Catherine frees herself from the torture wheel.

Upstairs, the 1427 *scoletta* was built soon after St Anthony's canonisation, although the cycle of 15 paintings lining its walls was only added in 1510–11. Large uplighters cast glowing pools of light on paintings by Titian and his brother Francesco Vecellio. Most engaging are Titian's *Miracle of a Jealous Husband* and his portrait of St Anthony calmly reattaching his own foot as an onlooker gasps. There is also a riveting parable by his brother, in which a doctor discovers a miser's heart is missing, just as a neighbour pulls the bloody organ from a treasure chest.

ORTO BOTANICO GARDEN

(☎049 827 21 19; www.ortobotanico.unipd.it; Via dell'Orto Botanico 15 ; adult/reduced €4/3; ⊙9am-1pm & 3-7pm Apr-Oct, 9am-1pm Mon-Sat Nov-Mar) South of Piazza del Santo, a Unesco World Heritage Site is growing. Padua's Orto Botanico was planted in 1545 by Padua University's medical faculty to study the medicinal properties of rare plants, and served as a clandestine Resistance meeting headquarters in WWII. The oldest tree in here is nicknamed 'Goethe's palm'; it was planted in 1585 and mentioned by the great German writer in his *Voyage in Italy*.

PRATO DELLA VALLE PARK

At the southern edge of the historical centre is Italy's largest public piazza, the Prato della Valle. At the centre of the enormous elliptical space is the grassy Memmia island, encircled by a canal and bordered by two concentric circles of statuary. There are 78 statues in all, commemorating the great and good of Paduan history, plus 10 empty

TO MARKET

One of the most enjoyable activities in Padua is browsing the markets in **Piazza delle Erbe** and **Piazza della Frutta**, which operate very much as they've done since the Middle Ages. The rules of the market are surprisingly democratic: stallholders must rotate location, so everyone gets a chance at the main thoroughfares, and all produce must be clearly labelled with provenance, category of freshness and price.

Stalls in Piazza delle Erbe are dedicated to fresh fruit and vegetables and are tiered in terms of quality. Those with less choice products are on the outer perimeter, with better stalls nearer the Palazzo delle Ragione. Beneath the arcades, known locally as **Sotto il Salone** (www.sottoilsalone.it), specialist butchers, cheese makers, fishmongers, *salumerie* and fresh pasta producers sell their wares, while on the other side of the *palazzo*, in Piazza della Frutta, stalls with non-local produce, spices, nuts, dried fruits, herbs and grains cluster.

The markets are open all day, every day except Sunday, although the best time to go is before midday.

pedestals. Ten Venetian dogi once occupied them, but Napoleon had them removed after he took Venice in 1797.

Originally the location of a public market, the square now serves more recreational purposes and it's a favourite spot for locals to soak up the summer sun. It is also the location for Padua's Capodanno (New Year's Day) and Ferragosto celebrations, when the piazza thumps with live music beneath extravagant fireworks.

 **EATING**

★**GODENDA**   MODERN ITALIAN €€
(⌨049 877 41 92; www.godenda.it; Via Squarcione 4/6; meals €25-40; ⊙10am-3pm & 6pm-2am Mon-Sat) Though hidden under an ancient portico, this local foodies' favourite is airy and modern with red-leather loungers, a long, sleek bar and a sultry jazz soundtrack.

The seasonal menu offers creative takes on old Venetian classics such as venison and lentils with sauteed apples, and there's an excellent selection of wines by the glass.

L'ANFORA   OSTERIA €€
(⌨049 65 66 29; Via dei Soncin 13; meals €25-30; ⊙9am-11pm Mon-Sat) Preserving the long tradition of the university tavern, L'Anfora is perpetually filled with a raucous crowd of students and professors pressing home their points fuelled by an ample supply of *spritz* and snacks. On the chalkboard daily dishes feature no-frills *cucina casalinga* (home cooking) of the Veneto, from sardines *in saor* to *orecchiette* pasta with turnip greens and ricotta.

OSTERIA DAL CAPO   OSTERIA €€
(⌨049 66 31 05; www.osteriadalcapo.it; Via degli Obizzi 2; meals €25-35; ⊙12.30-2.30pm & 7.30-10.30pm Mon-Sat) Originally established in

DAY TRIPS FROM VENICE PADUA (PADOVA)

WORTH A DETOUR

COLLI EUGANEI (EUGANEAN HILLS)

Southwest of Padua, the **Euganean Hills** (www.parcocollieuganei.com) feel a world away from the urban sophistication of Venice and the surrounding plains. To explore the walled hilltop towns, misty vineyards and bubbling hot springs, the Padua tourist office offers area maps, hiking and transport information online (www.turismotermeeuganee.it). Trains serve all towns except Arquà Petrarca.

Just south of Padua lie the natural-hot-spring resorts of **Abano Terme** (⌨tourist office 049 866 90 55; Via Pietro d'Abano 18) and **Montegrotto Terme**. They have been active since Roman times, when the Patavini built their villas on Mt Montirone. The towns are uninspired, but the waters do cure aches and pains. Nearby, in **Galzignano Terme**, **Villa Barbarigo** (⌨049 805 92 24; www.valsanzibiogiardino.it; adult/reduced €8.50/5.50; ⊙10am-1pm & 2pm-sunset Mar-Nov) is the location of one of the finest historical gardens in Europe, shot through with streams, fishponds and Bernini fountains.

In the medieval village of **Arquà Petrarca**, look for the elegant little **house** (⌨0429 71 82 94; Via Valleselle 4; adult/reduced €4/2; ⊙9am-12.30pm & 3-7pm Tue-Sun Mar-Oct, 9am-12.30pm & 2.30-5.30pm Tue-Sun Nov-Feb) where great Italian poet Petrarch spent his final years in the 1370s.

At the southern reaches of the Euganei, you'll find **Monselice**, with its remarkable **medieval castle** (⌨0429 729 31; www.castellodimonselice.it; Via del Santuario 11, Monselice; adult/reduced €6/5; ⊙1hr guided tours 9am, 10am, 11am, 3pm & 4pm Tue-Sun Apr-Nov); **Montagnana**, with its magnificent 2km defensive perimeter; and **Este**, with its rich architectural heritage and important **archaeological museum** (⌨0429 20 85; www.atestino.beniculturali.it; Via Guido Negri 9c; adult/reduced €4/free; ⊙8.30am-7.30pm). Este is also home to **Este Ceramiche Porcellane** (⌨0429 22 70; www.esteceramiche.com; Via Zanchi 22a; ⊙9am-noon & 2-5.30pm Mon-Fri), one of the oldest ceramics factories in Europe. It's been making tableware for Dior, Tiffany and Barneys for years, but here you can find some fabulous bargains in its outlet shop.

If you want to overnight, consider staying in one of the two apartments at **Villa Vescovi** (⌨049 993 04 73; www.villadeivescovi.it; Luvigliano; villa tour adult/reduced €7/3.50, apartments €200; ⊙10am-6pm Wed-Fri Apr-Oct, to 5pm Nov-Dec; ☎), one of the best preserved pre-Palladio Renaissance villas in the Veneto.

SLEEPING IN PADUA

The tourist office (p186) publishes accommodation brochures and lists dozens of B&Bs and hotels online. B&B listings outside Padua are listed on an affiliated website: www.bedandbreakfastpadova.it (in Italian).

Albergo Verdi (☑049 836 41 63; www.albergoverdipadova.it; Via Dondi dall'Orologio 7; s €70, d €100; ✴ @ ⓢ) With fresh orchids in the rooms and a bright, modern colour scheme, Albergo Verdi is a breath of fresh air in Padua's conservative hotel scene. Upper rooms benefit from lovely views over Piazza del Capitaniato and the breakfast buffet groans with fresh fruit, pastries, cold meats, eggs and cheese. Staff are happy to get refreshments if you arrive out of hours and will sort out historic-centre permits for rental cars.

Ostello Città di Padova (☑049 875 22 19; www.ostellopadova.it; Via dei Aleardi 30; dm €19-23, d €76; ☻reception 7.15-9.30am & 3.30-11.30pm; ⓢ) This central hostel on a quiet side street has decent dorm rooms with four to six beds. Sheets and wi-fi are free, but there is no open kitchen. Note there is an 11.30pm curfew, except when there are special events, and you must check out by 9.30am. Take bus 3, 8 or 12 or the city's new tram from the train station.

Belludi37 (☑049 66 56 33; www.belludi37.it; Via Luca Belludi 37; s €97, d €120-145; ✴ ⓢ) With its central location, super-efficient staff and mod decor the Belludi is the hotel of choice for many regular travellers to Padua. Although the black-on-brown rooms could do with a little freshening up, the generous-sized beds, free minibar and ample buffet breakfast more than compensate. Staff are always on hand with budget-friendly shopping advice and suggestions for biking itineraries and walking tours.

1936 to cater to the tram traffic in Piazza del Duomo, this tiny place is in Padua's old Jewish ghetto. Rub elbows with locals – literally – at tiny tables piled with traditional dishes such as rabbit, Borgoforte gnocchi with ricotta and *musso in tocio* (stewed donkey). Reservations and a sociable nature advised.

TRATTORIA AL PRATO
TRATTORIA €€

(☑049 66 24 29; Prato della Valle 4/5; meals €20-30; ☻12.15-2.30pm & 7.30-11pm Thu-Tue) Sit in the enclosed conservatory and enjoy the views of the Prato della Valle while you savour rabbit terrine and pumpkin puree or silky tagliatelle with *guanciale* (pig's cheek), followed perhaps by the apple and cinnamon pastry. Illicit lunch dates, well-fed business men and fur-clad female diners are your companions. The two-course, €10 set lunch is an absolute steal.

🍷 DRINKING & NIGHTLIFE

Sundown isn't official until you've had your *spritz* in Piazza delle Erbe or Piazza dei Signori. Also note that Padua is the region's unofficial capital of gay and lesbian life.

CAFFÈ PEDROCCHI
CAFE

(☑049 878 12 31; www.caffepedrocchi.it; Via VIII Febbraio 15; ☻9am-10pm Sun-Wed, to 1am Thu-Sat) Since 1831, this neoclassical landmark has been a favourite of Stendhal and other pillars of Padua's cafe society. Divided into three rooms: red, white and green (the colours of the Italian flag), the Pedrocchi has long been a seat of intrigue and revolution. The green room to the right of the bar was a 'no obligation' lounge where intellectuals could come and talk, while the white room bears a small plaque marking the spot where a bullet struck the wall in the 1848 student rebellion.

The extraordinary 1st floor is decorated in post-Napoleonic styles ranging from ancient Egyptian to Imperial. During the day you can visit the upstairs Museo del Risorgimento e dell'Età Contemporanea, recounting local and national history from the fall of Venice in 1797 until the republican constitution of 1848.

★ENOTECA IL TIRA BOUCHON
BAR

(☑049 875 21 38; www.enotecapadova.it; Sotto il Salone 23/24) With an expert French hand behind the bar, you can be sure of an excellent aperitif at this traditional place beneath the arcades of the Palazzo della

Ragione. Locals crowd in for *spunciotti* (baked bread dough served with olive oil and cheese) and lively glasses of *prosecco* paired with charcuterie from the *salumeria* around the corner.

ENOTECA DA SEVERINO   BAR, WINE SHOP

(☑049 65 06 97; Via del Santo 44; ☺10am-2pm & 5-9.30pm) What better way to sample Veneto wines before purchasing them than in a well-frequented neighbourhood wine shop? Da Severino obliges by hosting a convivial drinking session every evening amid the barrels and crates. You drink what's open at the bar and soak it up with hunks of cheese and salami.

Vicenza

Explore

When Palladio escaped an oppressive employer in his native Padua in the 1520s, few could have guessed that the humble stonecutter would transform not only Vicenza (population 115,900) but also the history of European architecture. Today, Vicenza's historic centre, thick with Palladio's work, has been recognised as a Unesco World Heritage Site. Despite its outsized legacy, this charming town remains quietly unpretentious – a fine place to join locals lingering over rustic lunches. Frequent train connections make it an easy day trip from Venice.

The Best...

➡ **Sight** La Rotonda (p194)
➡ **Place to Eat** Al Bersagliere (p195)
➡ **Place to Drink** Osteria Al Campanile (p198)

Top Tip

Palladio's Teatro Olimpico was built for live performances, and that is still the best way to absorb the complex harmonies of this extraordinary space.

Getting There & Away

➡ **Train** Trains are the easiest way to reach Vicenza from Venice (€5.20 to €15.50, 45 to 90 minutes, three or four per hour).

➡ **Car** Vicenza lies just off the A4 connecting Milan with Venice, while the SR11 connects Vicenza with Verona and Padua. Large car parks are located near Piazza del Castello and the train station.

Need to Know

➡ **Area Code** 0444
➡ **Location** 62km west of Venice
➡ **Tourist Office** (☑0444 32 08 54; www. vicenzae.org; Piazza Matteotti 12; ☺9.30am-6pm Mon-Thu, to 7.30pm Fri-Sun)

◉ SIGHTS

The heart of Vicenza is **Piazza dei Signori**, where Palladio lightens the mood of government buildings with his trademark play of light and shadow. Dazzling white Piovene stone arches frame shady double arcades in the Basilica Palladiana, while across the piazza, white stone and stucco grace the exposed red-brick colonnade of the 1571-designed Loggia del Capitaniato. Palladio's most iconic building, La Rotonda, can be found a short 20-minute walk to the south.

BASILICA PALLADIANA   LANDMARK, ART GALLERY

(☑0444 22 21 14; Piazza dei Signori; temporary exhibtions €9-12; ☺temporary exhibitions only) This immense basilica with its wraparound arcades dominates Piazza dei Signori, its copper dome reminiscent of the hull of an upturned ship. It was modelled on a Roman basilica (hence the name), and in its day it would have housed the law courts and Council of Four Hundred upstairs and a mall of luxury shops downstairs in the tradition of the markets on the Rialto.

Palladio was lucky to secure the commission in 1549 (it took patron Trissano 50 years of lobbying the Council), which involved radically restructuring the original Gothic *palazzo* after the loggia around it collapsed. Palladio's solution: an even more ambitious double order of loggias, supported by Tuscan and Ionic columns topped by soaring statuary.

Inside, the awesome 52m hall is uninterrupted by internal supports and now – after a €20-million refurbishment – serves as a vast exhibition space. If the inaugural show, *Raphael to Picasso*, which featured 85 extraordinary canvases spanning Old Masters such as Bellini, Giorgioni, Rubens and El Greco, to modernist masterpieces by Edvard Munch, Lucien Freud and Andrew Wyeth, is anything to go by, Palladio's basilica could once again put Vicenza on the map.

GALLERIE DI PALAZZO LEONI MONTANARI
MUSEUM

(✆800 57 88 75; www.gallerieditalia.com; Contrà di Santa Corona 25; adult/reduced €5/4; ☺10am-6pm Tue-Sun) From the outside it looks like a bank, but a treasure beyond accountants' imagining awaits inside the Palazzo Leoni Montanari. Ascend past the nymphs along the extravagant stuccoed staircase to grand salons filled with Canaletto's misty lagoon landscapes and Pietro Longhi 18th-century satires such as *Tutors of Venier's House*, in which a sassy child with hand on hip wears out exasperated tutors.

Head upstairs to see Banca Intesa's superb collection of some 400 Russian icons, gorgeously spot lit in darkened galleries in which recordings of soft Gregorian chants set the scene. Such a collection is rare anywhere outside Russia.

CHIESA DI SANTA CORONA
CHURCH

(✆0444 22 28 11; Contrà di Santa Corona; ☺9am-noon & 3-6pm Tue-Sun) **FREE** Built by the Dominicans in 1261 to house a relic from Christ's crown of thorns donated to the Bishop of Vicenza by Louis IX of France, this Romanesque church also houses three light-filled masterpieces: Palladio's 1576 Valmarana Chapel in the crypt; Paolo Veronese's *Adoration of the Magi*, much

praised by Goethe; and Giovanni Bellini's radiant *Baptism of Christ*, where the holy event is witnessed by a trio of Veneto beauties and a curious red bird.

TEATRO OLIMPICO
THEATRE

(✆0444 22 28 00; http://olimpicovicenza.it; Palazzo Matteotti 11; adult/reduced incl Museo Civico €10/8; ☺9am-5pm Tue-Sun) Behind a charming walled garden lies a Renaissance marvel: the Teatro Olimpico, which Palladio began in 1580 with inspiration from Roman amphitheatres. Vincenzo Scamozzi finished the elliptical theatre after Palladio's death, adding a stage set modelled on the ancient Greek city of Thebes, with streets built in steep perspective to give the illusion of a city sprawling towards a distant horizon.

The theatre was inaugurated in 1585 with a performance of *Oedipus Rex* but soon fell into disuse. Eventually the ceiling caved in, and the theatre remained abandoned for centuries until it was finally restored in 1934. Today, Italian performers vie to make an entrance on this gem of a stage; check online for opera, classical and jazz performances.

MUSEO CIVICO
MUSEUM

(Palazzo Chiericati; ✆0444 22 28 11; www.museicivicivicenza.it; Piazza Matteotti 37/39; adult/reduced incl Teatro Olimpico €10/8; ☺9am-5pm Tue-Sun) This civic art museum is housed in one of Palladio's finest buildings, designed in 1550 with a colonnaded ground floor and double-height loggia. The frescoed ground

DAY TRIPS FROM VENICE VICENZA

'BIRDS' OF THE BANCO POPOLARE

Just off Corso Palladio, you'll find the headquarters of the Banca Popolare di Vicenza (the People's Bank of Vicenza), housed rather ironically in Palladio's **Palazzo Thiene** (✆0444 33 99 89; www.palazzothiene.it; Contrà San Gaetano Thiene ; ☺9am-5pm Wed, Thu & Fri Jan-Jun & Sep-Dec) **FREE**, which he fashioned for the aristocratic Thiene family in 1556. The bank purchased the palace in 1872 soon after its founding and has, since then, been filling it with a variety of treasures.

Most interesting of these is the unique collection of *oselle* (silver and gold coins minted by the Doge each year and presented as a Christmas gift to all the noble families of the Great Council of Venice). Originally, the gift was five mallards per family, but given the growing number of nobles and the declining number of mallards, in 1521 the Council decreed that the doge should mint a silver coin instead, hence the name, oselle, which is Venetian for bird.

The bank owns the most complete collection in the world – 275, to be precise – and you can now book to see them, along with the bank's frescoed salons, fine artworks and sculpture.

Vicenza

floor includes the ultimate baroque party room: the *Sala dal Firmamento* (Salon of the Skies), with Domenico Brusasorci's ceiling fresco of Diana, the moon goddess, galloping across the sky to meet a bare-arsed Helios, god of the Sun.

Upstairs galleries present works by Vicenza masters in the context of a handful of major works by Venetian masters such as Veronese, Tiepolo and Tintoretto. Also look out for Hans Memling's minutely detailed Crucifix, action-packed works by Jacopo Bassano, and Giambattista Piazzetta's swirling, high-drama 1729 masterpiece *The Ecstasy of St Francis*.

LA ROTONDA   HISTORIC BUILDING
(☑049 879 13 80; www.villalarotonda.it; Via della Rotonda 45; villa/gardens €10/5; ☺gardens 10am-noon & 3-6pm Tue-Sun mid-Mar–mid-Nov, to 5pm mid-Nov–mid-Mar, villa open Wed & Sat only) No matter how you look at it, this villa is a show-stopper: the namesake dome caps a square base, with identical colonnaded facades on all four sides. This is one of Palladio's most admired creations, inspiring variations across Europe and the USA, including Thomas Jefferson's Monticello (La Rotonda's late owner, Mario di Valmarana, was a retired University of Virginia architecture professor; he died in 2010).

Inside, the circular central hall is covered from the walls to the soaring cupola with *trompe l'oeil* frescoes. Catch bus 8 or 13 (€1.50) from in front of Vicenza's train station, or just walk (about 25 minutes).

VILLA VALMARANA
'AI NANI'   HISTORIC BUILDING
(☑0444 32 18 03; www.villavalmarana.com; Stradella dei Nani 8; adult/reduced €9/6; ☺10am-12.30pm & 3-6pm Tue-Sun Mar-Oct, 10am-12.30pm Tue-Fri, 10am-12.30pm & 2.30-4.30pm Sat & Sun Nov-Jan) From La Rotonda, a path leads about 500m to the elegantly neoclassical Villa Valmarana 'ai Nani', where the

Vicenza

interior shelters 1757 frescoes by Giambattista Tiepolo and his son Giandomenico. Giambattista painted the Palazzina wing with his signature mythological epics, while his son painted the Foresteria with rural, carnival and Chinese themes.

Nicknamed 'ai Nani' (gnomes) for the 17 garden-gnome statues around the perimeter walls, this estate, with its carefully maintained grounds, is a superb spot for the occasional summer concert; check dates online.

EATING

GASTRONOMIA IL CEPPO   DELI €
(☑0444 54 44 14; www.gastronomiailceppo.com; Corso Palladio 196; prepared dishes per 100g €3-5; ⊙8am-1pm & 3.30-7.45pm Mon, Tue & Thu-Sat, 8am-1pm Wed) San Daniele hams dangle over the vast glass counter, which is filled with ready-made items like fresh seafood salads, house-made pastas and speciality cheeses. Never mind that there's no seating available at this temple to local gastronomy; ask counter staff to pair your food selections with a local wine from their shelves for a gourmet picnic.

JULIEN   MODERN ITALIAN €
(☑0444 32 61 68; Contrà Jacopo Cabianca 13; meals €18-25; ⊙8.30-2am) It's cool, it's crowded and with its floor-to-ceiling windows this is where Vicenza's beautiful people gather to see and be seen. Fusion food includes basmati rice with shrimp and courgette, Caesar salads and classic grilled steaks, but you're not really here for the food. Do as the locals do and grab yourself a cocktail or glass of wine and spend the evening exchanging glances and grazing *aperitivi*.

★AL BERSAGLIERE   OSTERIA €€
(☑0444 32 35 07; Contrà Pescaria 11; meals €25-35; ⊙12.30-2pm & 7.30-10pm Tue-Sat, 12.30-2pm Sun) Savour the taste of summer in Maria's *datterino* tomato and mozzarella salad or nurse a glass of Recioto with your stuffed quails or guinea-fowl pasta – Bersagliere's kitchen is first class, although the bill is surprisingly democratic. What's more, the warm, exposed-brick interior with its hanging mezzanine is stylish and intimate. Reservations are recommended.

ANTICO RISTORANTE
AGLI SCHIOPPI   OSTERIA, VICENTINA €€
(☑0444 54 37 01; www.ristoranteaglischioppi.com; Contrà Piazza del Castello 26; meals €30-40; ⊙dinner Mon, lunch & dinner Tue-Sat) Tucked under an arcade just off Piazza del Castello lies one of the city's oldest family restaurants. The owners are devotees of locally sourced products, from wild forest greens to baby river trout, but without any pretensions; it's just what they know best. The menu changes with the season, but they are famous for their *baccalà alla vicentina* (dried cod on a bed of creamy polenta).

ANTICO GUELFO   MODERN ITALIAN €€
(☑0444 54 78 97; www.anticoguelfo.it; Contrà Pedemuro San Biagio 90; meals €30-40; ⊙7-10.30pm Mon-Sat) This culinary hideaway is a hit with slow foodies for its inventive daily market menu, making the most of local specialities in such dishes as Amarone risotto or buckwheat crepes with Bastardo di Grappa cheese. The chef is a specialist in gluten-free cooking, and is usually willing to adapt dishes to any food sensitivity.

Wonderful Palladio

When it comes to coffee-table architecture, no one beats Andrea Palladio. As you flip past photos of his villas, your own problematic living space begins to dissolve, and you find yourself strolling through more harmonious country. Nature is governed by pleasing symmetries. Roman rigour is soothed by rustic charms. He managed to synthesise the classical past without doggedly copying it, creating buildings that were at once inviting, useful and incomparably elegant. From London to St Petersburg, his work – cleverly disseminated by his own 'Quattro Libri', a how-to guide for other architects – shaped the way Europe thought about architecture.

And yet when Palladio turned 30 in 1538, he was little more than a glorified stonecutter in Vicenza. His big break came when nobleman and amateur architect Giangiorgio Trissino recognised his potential and noticed his inclination towards mathematics. He introduced Palladio to the work of Roman architectural theorist Vitruvius, and sent him to Rome (1545–47) to sketch both crumbling antiquities and new works like Michelangelo's dome for St Peter's.

Something mysterious happened on those trips, because when Palladio returned to Vicenza he was forging a new way of thinking about architecture – one that focused on the relationship between ratios to create spatial harmony. So a room in which the shorter wall was one-half (1:2), two-thirds (2:3) or three-quarters (3:4) the length of the longer would inevitably *feel* more satisfying because it was rationally harmonious. Like Pallas Athena, the goddess of wisdom, from whom he took his name,

1. Teatro Olimpico (p193) **2.** Basilica Palladiana (p192) **3.** Villa di Masèr (p200)

Palladio's ideas seemed to spring fully formed from his head.

This search for perfection was never at odds with practicality. In his villas, he squeezed stables beneath elegant drawing rooms. Lacking funds to line San Giorgio Maggiore with marble, he came up with a superior solution: humble stucco walls that fill the church with an ethereal softness. Constraint provided the path to innovation.

A Palladian villa never masters its landscape like, say, Versailles. Palladio makes his mark tactfully, as if he has merely gathered the natural forces of the land and translated them into an ideal, and distinctly human, response. His Rotonda, for example, crowns a rise in the terrain, and looks out on it from four identical facades. Nothing like it had been built before. Yet when you see it *in situ*, it seems to be the inevitable outcome of the site itself.

PALLADIAN HIGHLIGHTS

➡ **Basilica Palladiana** Restored to former glory after a six-year, €20-million refurbishment.

➡ **La Rotonda** Palladio's most inspired design, copied the world over.

➡ **Villa di Masèr** Butter-yellow villa set against a green hillside; Palladio's prettiest composition.

➡ **Villa Foscari** River-facing facade with soaring Ionic columns that draw the eye and spirits upwards.

➡ **Palladio Museum** (Map p194; ☎0444 32 30 14; www.palladiomuseum.org; Contrà Porti 11, Vicenza; adult/reduced €6/4; ☉10am-6pm Tue-Sun) New in 2012 and created by Howard Burns, the world authority on Palladio.

➡ **Teatro Olimpico** Palladio's visionary elliptical theatre.

♀ DRINKING

★OSTERIA AL CAMPANILE   BAR
(☑0444 54 40 36; Piazza della Posta; ⊘9am-2pm & 5-9pm) Owned by the same family for over three generations, Al Campanile is one of Vicenza's historic watering holes, featuring an antique wooden bar and tucked beneath the Roman belltower by the cathedral. As you'd expect from local experts, their cellar is stocked with unusual vintages such as the sparkling Durelio, which is usually overshadowed by its more famous cousin, *prosecco*.

FIASCHETTERIA DA RENZO   BAR
(☑0444 31 13 56; Contrà Frasche del Gambero 36; tartine €1-2; ⊘8am-9pm Mon-Sat) Hidden down a narrow alley off Piazza dei Signori, Fiaschetteria Da Renzo is Vicenza's most popular *aperitivo* spot. In the morning and early evening customers drop by for a *spritz* and one of Fabio's famous tartines – open-faced sandwiches filled with egg, anchovies, shrimps, crab, tuna and, sometimes, truffles or even caviar. They cost a shocking €1.

PASTICCERIA SORARÙ   CAFE
(☑0444 32 09 15; Piazzetta Palladio; ⊘7.30am-12.30pm & 3.30-7.30pm Thu-Tue) Drink in the history at this marble-topped bar, serving bracing espresso and pastries made on the premises. There are also tempting jars of sweets stashed on the elaborately gilded shelves. A few outdoor tables offer views of one of Italy's finest piazzas.

ANTICA CASA DELLA MALVASIA   WINE BAR
(☑0444 54 37 04; Contrà delle Morette 5; ⊘11am-12.30pm Mon-Thu & Sat, 5.30pm-2am Fri) This purveyor of wines has been in business since 1200, when Malvasia wine was imported from Greece by Venetian merchants. Its menu covers 80 wines, including prime Italian Malvasia, plus 100 types of grappa from just up the road in Bassano del Grappa (p200).

Prosecco Road Trip

···

Explore

A road trip north of Venice takes you through one of Italy's most sophisticated, and least visited, stretches of countryside. Some of the Veneto's finest country villas, medieval walled towns and frescoes are to be found here, while a little further north in the foothills of the Dolomites, *prosecco* vines dip and crest across an undulating landscape framed by snowy peaks. To explore it properly you'll need a car of your own; and you'll certainly want one so you can load up with the Veneto's finest fizz and firewater.

···

The Best...

➡ **Sight** Villa di Masèr (p200)
➡ **Place to Eat** Agriturismo Da Ottavio (p201)
➡ **Place to Drink** Azienda Agricola Frozza (p199)

···

Top Tip

Every May the 30 *prosecco*-producing villages in the DOC-denominated area partici-

PROSECCO: A LOCAL'S GUIDE

Since 2007, sommelier **Mario Piccinin** (☎049 60 06 72; www.venicedaytrips.com; Via Saetta 18, Padua; semi-private/private tours per person €165/275) has been designing art, food and wine tours exploring the hidden corners of Venice and the Veneto. We caught up with him over a glass of *prosecco* to get the low-down on the Veneto's favourite *aperitivo*.

The origins of prosecco... *Prosecco* can be traced back to the Romans. It was then known as 'Pucino' and was shipped direct to the court of Empress Livia from Aquileia, where it was produced with grapes from the Carso. During the Venetian Republic the vines were transferred to the Prosecco DOCG (*denominazione d'origine controllata e garantita*; quality-controlled) area, a small triangle of land between the towns of Valdobbiadene, Conegliano and Vittorio Veneto.

The social scene... Here in the Veneto we drink *prosecco* like water – sometimes it's even cheaper than water!

Describe the character of a good prosecco... Straw yellow in colour with sparkling greenish reflections. The naturally formed bubbles are tiny, numerous and long-lasting in your glass. It's fragrant with fresh notes of white fruits and fresh grass. It pleases your mouth with its crispness and aromaticity. Keep in mind that these characteristics are not long-lasting – *prosecco* is meant to be drunk young.

Pairings? *Soppressa* (a fresh local salami), buttery Asiago cheese and roasted chestnuts in season. But it really is a match for many simple dishes such as those served at Agriturismo Da Ottavio (p201).

Best aspect of the tour? I think what people enjoy most is the feeling of having lived like a local for a day – discovering typical places far off the beaten path and being received warmly by the people they meet. Often they're so enthused they want to take a cooking lesson. It's fun to learn hands-on how to prepare some local dishes that pair well with the wines you've just discovered. As for me, I find it very satisfying to show people all that is behind a glass of wine.

pate in the **Primavera di Prosecco** (www. primaveradiprosecco.it). Each village puts on a weekend party with food stalls and *prosecco* tasting all day. *Cin cin.*

Getting There & Away

➡ **Train** Head from Venice to the Mestre station, where there are two to three trains per hour to Conegliano (one hour, €4.15). Castelfranco Veneto is also accessible from Venice (one hour, €4.70).

➡ **Car** Your own wheels are your best option for getting around the region at a reasonable pace and visiting wineries and farmstays. The A27 heads directly north from Mestre to Conegliano.

Need to Know

➡ **Area Code** 0423

➡ **Location** Conegliano 53km north of Venice; Castelfranco Veneto 37km northwest of Venice; Bassano del Grappa 58km northwest of Venice

➡ **Tourist Office** (☎0438 212 30; Via XX Settembre 61, Conegliano; ⊙9am-12.30pm Tue & Wed, 9am-12.30pm & 3-6pm Thu-Sun)

◉ SIGHTS

AZIENDA AGRICOLA FROZZA   WINERY
(☎0423 98 70 69; www.frozza.it; Via Martiri 31, Colbertaldo di Vidor; ℗) Galera vines have grown on this sunny Colbertaldo hillside for hundreds of years thanks to six generations of the Frozza family, who have tended them since 1870. The result: a DOCG *prosecco* with remarkable fragrance and complexity. The 2011 Brut is a particularly good vintage with fruity fragrances and a well-structured, mineral-rich body. Prices range from €4 to €9 per bottle.

AZIENDA AGRICOLA BARICHEL   WINERY
(☎0423 97 57 43; www.barichel.net; Via Zanzago 9, Valdobbiadene; ℗) 🍷 Ultra-marathon runner and vinter Ivan Geronazzo returned

to his grandfather's vineyard in Valdob-biadene after years of working at larger, high-capacity wineries. Here he tends just 7 hectares by hand, producing 60,000 bot-tles of natural, *frizzante*, Extra Dry and Brut *prosecco* with a pale, straw-yellow col-our and apple-and-pear fragrances. Prices range from €4 to €7 per bottle.

VILLA DI MASÈR
HISTORIC BUILDING

(Villa Barbaro; ☑0423 92 30 04; www.villadimaser.it; Via Barbaro 4; adult/reduced €6/5; ☺10.30am-6pm Tue-Sat & 11am-6pm Sun Apr-Jun, Sep & Oct, Tue, Thu, Sat & Sun Mar, Jul & Aug, 11am-5pm Sat & Sun Nov-Feb; ℗) On a vineyard-covered hill-side is Palladio and Paolo Veronese's golden monument to the Venetian *bea vita* (good life). Palladio set the arcaded butter-yellow villa into the verdant hillside, but inside Ve-ronese upstaged the master-architect with wildly imaginative *trompe l'œil* scenery. Vines climb the walls of the *Stanza di Baccho* and in a corner of the grand salon the painter has apparently forgotten his spattered shoes.

In the villa's wine-tasting room, near the parking lot, you can raise a toast to the gifted pair with Masèr estate–grown DOC *prosecco*. Just east of the villa's gates is Pal-ladio's **Tempietto**, a miniature copy of the Pantheon in Rome.

ASOLO
TOWN

Known as the 'town of 100 vistas' for its panoramic hillside location, the medieval walled town of Asolo has long been a fa-vourite of literary types. Robert Browning bought a house here, but the ultimate lo-cal celebrity is Caterina Corner, the 15th-century queen of Cyprus, who was given the town, its castle (now used as a theatre) and the surrounding county in exchange for her abdication. She promptly became queen of the literary set, holding salons that featured writer Pietro Bembo.

ℹ️ LA STRADA DI PROSECCO

Running through a landscape of rolling vineyards, **La Strada di Prosecco** (www.coneglianovaldobbiadene.it) is a driving route that takes you from Con-egliano to Valdobbiadene via some of the region's best wineries. The web-site provides an itinerary, background information on *prosecco*, and details about stops along the way.

In the **Museo Civico** (☑0423 95 23 13; Via Regina Cornaro 74; adult/reduced €4/3; ☺10am-noon & 3-7pm Sat & Sun) you can explore Asolo's Roman past and wander through a small collection of paintings, including a pair of Tintoretto portraits. The museum also includes rooms devoted to Eleanora Duse (1858–1924) and British traveller and writer Freya Stark (1893–1993), who re-treated to Asolo between Middle Eastern forays. Try to come on the second Sunday of the month, when an outdoor antiques mar-ket takes over the town.

BASSANO DEL GRAPPA
TOWN

Bassano del Grappa sits with charming simplicity on the banks of the River Brenta as it winds its way free from Alpine foot-hills. The town is famous above all for its namesake spirit, grappa – a fiery distilla-tion made from the discarded skins, pulp, seeds and stems from wine-making. At the **Poli Museo della Grappa** (☑0424 52 44 26; www.grappa.com; Via Gamba 6; ☺9am-7.30pm) **FREE** you can explore four centuries of pro-duction and enjoy a free tasting.

But there's more to Bassano than you can see in the bottom of a grappa glass. Its **Museo Civico** (☑0424 51 99 01; www.museibas-sano.it; Piazza Garibaldi 34; adult/reduced €4/3; ☺9am-7pm Tue-Sat, 10.30am-1pm & 3-6pm Sun) is beautifully housed around the cloisters of the **Convento di San Francesco**. Endowed in 1828 by the naturalist Giambattista Broc-chi, it has an extensive archaeological col-lection alongside 500 paintings, including masterpieces such as the 1545 *Flight into Egypt* from local son Jacopo Bassano.

Spanning the river is Palladio's photo-genic 1569 covered bridge, the **Ponte degli Alpini**. Fragile as the wooden structure seems, it is cleverly engineered to with-stand the rush of spring melt waters from Monte Grappa. It's always been critical in times of war: Napoleon bivouacked here for many months and in the Great War the Al-pine brigades adopted the bridge as their emblem. Hundreds of them died on the slopes of **Monte Grappa** (1775m), where Er-nest Hemingway drove his ambulance and an enormous tiered memorial now com-memorates the sacrifice of over 12,000 Ital-ian and 10,000 Austro-Hungarian soldiers.

CASTELFRANCO VENETO
TOWN

Giorgio Barbarelli da Castelfranco (aka Giorgione) was one of the great masters of the High Renaissance. Born in the pictur-

Azienda Agricola Campion (☑0423 98 04 32; www.campionspumanti.it; Via Campion 2, San Giovanni di Valdobbiadene; s €45, d €65-75; ☉tasting room 9am-noon & 3-7pm; P ✳ ☒) Why not quit worrying about the challenges of *prosecco* tasting and driving and instead bed down at this farmstay amid 14 hectares of vines in the heart of Valdobbiadene? Walk across the road for lunches at Da Ottavio, or take a dip in the pool in summer. The four charming rooms have been coverted from farm buildings and are renovated in a warm rustic style.

esque walled town of Castelfranco, he was a contemporary of Titian's but an early death in 1510 left an adoring public with just six acclaimed canvases. Luckily for Castelfranco, one of his surviving works, an altarpiece known simply as the *Castelfranco Madonna*, still hangs in the **Cappella Costanza** in the **Duomo** (Vicolo del Christo 10; ☉9am-noon Mon-Fri) FREE.

Like Titian, with whom he worked on the frescoes of the Fondaco dei Tedeschi in Venice, Giorgione is credited with revolutionising Renaissance painting, freeing it from its linear constraints and using a refined *chiaroscuro* technique called *sfumato* ('smokey') to blur hard lines and enhance the emotional quality. The *Castelfranco Madonna* is a perfect example: the light that suffuses the painting appears to have no clear source; is the sun rising, or setting, or is the scene illuminated from another unseen source as the figures of the St Francis and the armoured saint suggest? What's more, all three figures seem withdrawn and mysteriously preoccupied with events or emotions entirely disconnected from their physical setting. It is an intriguing composition, and profoundly moving.

✕ EATING

★**AGRITURISMO DA OTTAVIO** AGRITURISMO € (☑0423 98 11 13; Via Campion 2, San Giovanni di Valdobbiadene; meals €15-20; ☉noon-3pm Sat, Sun & holidays, closed Sep; ☝) ✎ *Prosecco* is traditionally paired with flavourful, oily appetisers like *soppressa* (fresh salami) and cheese, as the sparkling spumante cleans the palate and refreshes the mouth. At Da Ottavio you get a chance to sample it with food rooted in the same *terroir*, as everything on the table, *prosecco* included, is made on the spot by Graziano and Martina Spada.

VILLA CIPRIANI   MODERN ITALIAN €€€ (☑0423 52 34 11; www.villaciprianiasolo.com; Via Canova 298, Asolo; meals €60; ☉12.30-2.30pm & 8-10.30pm) The Ciprianis behind this Renaissance villa are the same as those in Venice, and they are just the latest in a long line of illustrious owners including the Guinnesses, Galantis and poet Robert Browning. Now you too can enjoy the perfumed rose garden and dine overlooking cypress-cloaked Asolo.

Verona

Explore

Shakespeare placed star-crossed lovers Romeo Montague and Juliet Capulet in Verona for good reason: romance, drama and fatal family feuding have been the city's hallmark for centuries. From the 3rd century BC Verona (population 263,950) was a Roman trade centre with ancient gates, a forum (now Piazza delle Erbe) and a grand Roman arena, which still serves as one of the world's great opera venues. In the Middle Ages the city flourished under the wrathful Scaligeri clan, who were as much energetic patrons of the arts as they were murderous tyrants. Their elaborate Gothic tombs, the **Arche Scaligere**, are just off **Piazza dei Signori**. To get around all the main sights in a day you'll need an early start and careful planning. Consider spending the night if you want to delve deeper – or explore Verona's remarkable wine country.

The Best...

➜ **Sight** Museo di Castelvecchio (p205)
➜ **Place to Eat** Locanda 4 Cuochi (p207)
➜ **Place to Drink** Osteria del Bugiardo (p208)

Shakespeare's Veneto

There is much debate about whether Shakespeare ever visited Italy, but his Italian plays are full of local knowledge. Venetian writer, architect and presenter Francesco da Mosto spoke to *Lonely Planet Traveller* magazine about the playwright's favourite Italian cities.

Verona

Verona was not thought of as a city of romance before *Romeo and Juliet* – in fact, not many people would have heard of it as it was very much in the shadow of Venice at that time. We don't know whether Romeo and Juliet existed, although Italian poet Dante did mention two feuding families, called the Montecchi and the Cappelletti. The famous balcony where Romeo is said to have declared his love to Juliet is close to Verona's main promenade – although since the balcony was apparently added to a suitably old house in 1936, it's doubtful it is the original! My favourite site in Verona is Juliet's tomb. People go there to pay tribute to Juliet and Shakespeare – even Dickens visited.

Padua

The University of Padua was one of the first in the world, and in Shakespeare's time, the city was very well known as a centre of learning throughout Europe – Galileo [of telescope fame] and Casanova [of sexual-conquest fame] are both alumni. Shakespeare used its reputation, rather than actual locations, as a backdrop to *The Taming of the Shrew* – apart from the university, he rarely mentions specific sites. The best way to experience Shakespeare's Padua is

1. Palazzo Ducale and Piazza San Marco (p61) **2.** Juliet's balcony, Casa di Giulietta, Verona (p206) **3.** Prato della Valle, Padua (p189)

by having a stroll around the university. It feels like a little world unto itself, detached from the rest of the city. There is a marvellous wooden anatomical amphitheatre in the Medical School that was built in the 16th century, where they dissected humans and animals for the students. The life of the university runs through the city. It's lovely to walk through the portico walkways that run under the houses, and into the Prato della Valle, one of the main city squares.

Venice

Shakespeare set *Othello* in Venice, and *The Merchant of Venice* mentions the Rialto Market area several times. He even talked about gondolas and 'the tranect', which could refer to the *traghetto* ferry, which transported people from Venice to the mainland. If he did visit, Shakespeare would have spent his time wandering the streets, eavesdropping on people's conversations and observing the goings-on in shops and at the market. A walk to the Rialto is certainly evocative of that time. The Palazzo Ducale, with its magnificent Gothic facades and huge council hall, is probably what Shakespeare had in mind as the setting for the final courtroom scene in *The Merchant of Venice*, while the two bronze figures on top of the Torre dell'Orologio clock tower in Piazza San Marco are known as 'i Mori', or 'the Moors', which is a key reference in *Othello*.

Verona

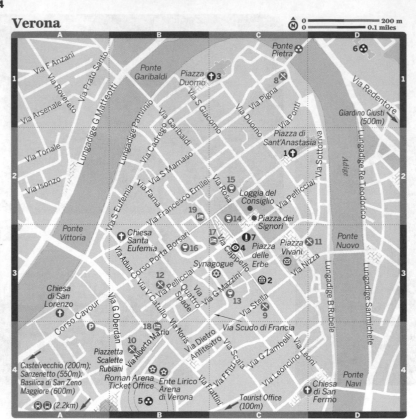

Top Tip

VeronaCard (www.veronacard.it; 2/5 days €15/20), available at tourist sights as well as tobacconists, is great value, providing access to virtually all major monuments and churches, plus unlimited use of local buses.

Getting There & Away

➡ **Train** There are at least three trains hourly to Venice (€7.50 to €22, 1¼ to 2½ hours). The station is about a 20-minute walk south of the historic centre. There is a taxi rank just in front of the station, and there are also frequent local bus connections to the centre.

➡ **Car** Verona is at the intersection of the A4 (Turin–Trieste) and A22 motorways.

Need to Know

➡ **Area code** 045

➡ **Location** 120km west of Venice

➡ **Tourist Office** (☏045 806 86 80; www.tourism.verona.it; Via degli Alpini 9; ☺9am-7pm Feb-Nov, 9am-1pm & 2-6pm Dec & Jan)

◉ SIGHTS

ROMAN ARENA   ARCHAEOLOGICAL SITE

(☏045 800 32 04; www.arena.it; Piazza Brà; opera tickets €21-220, tours adult/reduced €6/4.50, or with VeronaCard; ☺8.30am-7.30pm Tue-Sun, 1.30-7.30pm Mon; ⚘) This Roman-era arena, built of pink-tinged marble in the 1st century AD, survived a 12th-century earthquake to become Verona's legendary open-air opera house, with seating for 30,000 people. You can visit the arena year-round, though it's at its best during the June-to-August opera season. You'll find the ticket office (045 800 51 51) at Via Dietro Anfiteatro 6b.

Performances, of which there are around 50 during the season, feature all the clas-

Verona

⊙ **Sights**

⊗ **Eating**

⊙ **Drinking & Nightlife**

⊜ **Sleeping**

sics, particularly those of home-grown talent Giuseppe Verdi (*Aida, Nabucco* and *La Traviata* being perennial favourites). Some of the world's top names perform – Placido Domingo debuted here – so book online and book early for headline shows. In winter months, concerts are held at the adjacent 18th-century **Ente Lirico Arena**.

MUSEO DI CASTELVECCHIO MUSEUM

(☑045 806 26 11; Corso Castelvecchio 2; adult/reduced €6/4.50, or with VeronaCard; ⊙8.30am-7.30pm Tue-Sun, 1.30-7.30pm Mon; ⊕) Bristling with battlements along the River Adige, Castelvecchio was built in the 1350s by Cangrande II. The fortress was so severely damaged by Napoleon and then WWII bombings that many feared it was beyond repair. But instead of erasing the past with restorations, Carlo Scarpa reinvented the building, constructing bridges over exposed foundations, filling gaping holes with glass panels, and balancing a statue of Cangrande I above the courtyard on a concrete gangplank.

Scarpa's revived Castelvecchio makes a fitting home for Verona's largest museum, with a diverse collection of statuary, frescoes, jewellery, medieval artefacts and paintings by Pisanello, Giovanni Bellini, Tiepolo and Veronese. The museum also hosts interesting temporary exhibitions ranging from Old Master retrospectives to modernist arts and crafts.

BASILICA DI SAN ZENO MAGGIORE BASILICA

(www.chieseverona.it; Piazza San Zeno; adult/child €2.50/free, combined Verona church ticket €6 or VeronaCard; ⊙8.30am-6pm Tue-Sat, 12.30-6pm Sun Mar-Oct, 10am-1pm & 1.30-5pm Tue-Sat, 12.30-5pm Sun Nov-Feb) A masterpiece of Romanesque architecture, the striped brick and stone basilica was built in honour of the city's patron saint. Enter through the flower-filled cloister into the nave – a vast space lined with 12th- to 15th-century frescoes, including Mary Magdalene modestly covered in her curtain of golden hair. Painstaking restoration has revived Mantegna's 1457–59 *Majesty of the Virgin* altarpiece, painted with such astonishing perspective that you actually believe there are garlands of fresh fruit hanging behind the Madonna's throne.

Under the **rose window** depicting the Wheel of Fortune you'll find meticulously detailed 12th-century **bronze doors**, including a scene of an exorcism with a demon being yanked from a woman's mouth. An eerie **crypt** is located beneath the main altar, with faces carved into medieval capitals and St Zeno's corpse glowing in a transparent sarcophagus.

DUOMO CATHEDRAL

(☑045 59 28 13; www.chieseverona.it; Piazza Duomo; adult/reduced €2.50/2, or with VeronaCard; ⊙10am-5.30pm Mon-Sat, 1.30-5.30pm Sun Mar-Oct, 10am-1pm & 1.30-5pm Tue-Sat, 1.30-5pm Sun Nov-Feb) Verona's 12th-century cathedral is a striking, striped Romanesque building, with bug-eyed statues of Charlemagne's paladins Roland and Oliver, crafted by medieval master Nicolò, on the west porch. Nothing about this sober facade hints at the extravagant 16th- to 17th-century frescoed interior with angels aloft amid *trompe l'oeil* architecture. At the left end of the nave is the **Cartolari-Nichesola Chapel**, designed by Renaissance master Jacopo Sansovino and featuring a vibrant Titian *Assumption*.

BASILICA DI SANT'ANASTASIA BASILICA

(www.chieseverona.it; Piazza di Sant'Anastasia; adult/reduced €6/2, or entry with VeronaCard;

PONTE PIETRA

At the northern edge of the city centre, this bridge is a quiet but remarkable testament to the Italians' love of their artistic heritage. Two of the bridge's arches date from the Roman Republican era in the 1st century BC, while the other three were replaced in the 13th century. The ancient bridge remained largely intact until 1945, when retreating German troops blew it up. But locals fished the fragments out of the river, and painstakingly rebuilt the bridge stone by stone in the 1950s.

⊗9am-6pm Tue-Sat, 1-6pm Sun Mar-Oct, 1.30-5pm Tue-Sat, 1-5pm Sun Nov-Feb) Dating from the 13th to the 15th centuries, the Gothic Sant'Anastasia is Verona's largest church and a showcase for local art. The multitude of frescoes is overwhelming, but don't overlook Pisanello's storybook-quality fresco *St George Setting out to Free the Princess from the Dragon* in the **Pisanelli Chapel**, or the 1495 holy-water font featuring a hunchback carved by Paolo Veronese's father, Gabriele Caliari.

TEATRO ROMANO E MUSEO
ARCHEOLOGICO   ARCHAEOLOGICAL SITE
(⌂045 800 03 60; Regaste Redentore 2; adult/reduced €4.50/3, or with VeronaCard; ⊗8.30am-7.30pm Tue-Sun, 1.30-7.30pm Mon) Just north of the historic centre you'll find a **Roman theatre**. Built in the 1st century BC, it is cunningly carved into the hillside at a strategic spot overlooking a bend in the river. Take the lift at the back of the theatre to the former convent above, which houses an interesting collection of Greek and Roman artefacts.

GIARDINO GIUSTI   GARDEN
(⌂045 803 40 29; Via Giardino Giusti 2; adult/reduced €6/5; ⊗9am-8pm Apr-Sep, to 7pm Oct-Mar; ⊞) Across the river from the historic centre, these sculpted gardens, considered a masterpiece of Renaissance landscaping, are well worth seeking out. Named after the noble family that has tended them since opening them to the public in 1591, they have lost none of their charm. The vegetation is an Italianate mix of the manicured and natural, graced by soaring cypresses,

one of which the German poet Goethe immortalised in his travel writings.

According to local legend, lovers who manage to find each other in the little labyrinth on the right side of the garden are destined to stay together. On the back end of the garden, a short but steep climb rewards with sweeping views over the city.

CASA DI GIULIETTA   MUSEUM
(Juliet's House; ⌂045 803 43 03; Via Cappello 23; adult/reduced €6/4.50 or with VeronaCard; ⊗8.30am-7.30pm Tue-Sun, 1.30-7.30pm Mon) Never mind that Romeo and Juliet were completely fictional characters, and that there's hardly room for two on the narrow stone balcony: romantics flock to this 14th-century house to add their lovelorn pleas to the graffiti on the courtyard causeway.

PIAZZA DELLE ERBE &
PIAZZA DEI SIGNORI   HISTORICAL SITE
Originally a Roman forum, Piazza delle Erbe is ringed with buzzing cafes and some of Verona's most sumptuous buildings, including the elegantly baroque **Palazzo Maffei** (now a corporate headquarters) at its northern end.

Separating Piazza delle Erbe from **Piazza dei Signori** is the monumental gate known as **Arco della Costa**, hung with a whale's rib that, according to legend, will fall on the first just person to walk beneath it. So far, it remains intact, despite visits by popes and kings.

Dividing the two piazzas, the striped **Torre dei Lamberti** (⌂045 927 30 27; adult/reduced €6/4.50; ⊗8.30am-7.30pm) rises a neck-craning 85m. Begun in the 12th century and finished in 1463 – too late to notice invading Venetians – this watchtower still offers panoramic views of the city and nearby mountains, which are snowcapped in winter. A lift whisks you up two-thirds of the way.

✕ EATING

GELATERIA PONTE PIETRA   GELATO €
(⌂340 471 72 94; Via Ponte Pietra 23; ⊗2.30-7.30pm, to 10pm Jun-Aug, closed Nov-Feb) Impeccable gelato is made on the premises, with flavours like *bacio bianco* (white chocolate and hazelnut), candied orange with cinnamon, and *mille fiori* (cream with honey and bits of pollen gathered from local hillsides).

PIZZERIA DU DE COPE PIZZERIA €
(☎045 59 55 62; www.pizzeriadudecope.it; Galleria Pellicciai 10; pizzas €6-12; ☻noon-2pm & 7-11pm) This fashion-forward pizzeria manages to blend refinement with relaxed ease in its airy and vividly coloured dining space. You can peek over the counter and watch your pizza bubbling in the wood-fired oven, or ease up on the carbs with one of the high-quality salads.

★**LOCANDA 4 CUOCHI** MODERN ITALIAN €€
(☎045 803 03 11; www.locanda4cuochi.it; Via Alberto Mario 12; meals €30-40; ☻12.30-2.30pm & 7.30-10.30pm Wed-Sun, 7.30-10.30pm Tue) With its open kitchen and four hot-shot chefs at the stations, you're right to expect great things from the *locanda*. The menu is short and seemingly simple. Don't be fooled: some of the dishes are genuinely revelatory, such as the mushroom *velouté* (a velvety soup made from stock, egg yolks, cream and smoked potato) in a halo of golden olive oil, which packs such a flavour punch you'll wonder if you've ever truly tasted a mushroom before.

LA TAVERNA DI VIA STELLA VERONESE €€
(☎045 800 80 08; www.tavernadiviastella.com; Via Stella 5c; meals €25-30; ☻11.30am-2.30pm & 6.30-11pm Thu-Sun & Tue, 11.30am-2.30pm Mon) Brush past the strings of garlic and haunches of *prosciutto* dangling over the deli and make your way into a dining room, decorated Tiepolo-style (although with considerably less skill) with rustic murals of chivalric knights and maidens. This is the place you'll want to sample traditional Veronese dishes such as horse *pastissada* (stew), bigoli with duck *ragù* and DOP Lessinia cheeses from Monte Veronese.

★**PESCHERIA I MASENINI** SEAFOOD €€€
(☎045 929 80 15; www.imasenini.com; Piazzetta Pescheria 9; meals €50; ☻12.30-2pm & 7.30-10pm Wed-Sun, 7.30-10pm Tue) In a spot on the piazza where Verona's Roman fish market once held sway, Elio Rizzo is quietly serving up traditional Veronese dishes with a modern twist. Mullet tartare comes in a fresh tomato and basil puree, octopus is roasted with broccoli and anchovies, and scallops come gratinated with baked endives. With its black-and-white

---

SLEEPING IN VERONA

Cooperativa Albergatori Veronesi (☎045 800 98 44; www.veronabooking.com) offers a no-fee booking service for two-star hotels. For home-style stays outside the city centre, check **Verona Bed & Breakfast** (www.bedandbreakfastverona.com). Try to book well ahead if you plan to be here during the summer opera season.

Sanzenetto (☎392 982 59 86; www.sanzenetto.com; Vicolo Cieco Boscarello 3a; s €60-90, d €80-130; ▣☎) Sanzenetto's midcentury-modern style is a breath of fresh air in traditional Verona. Located down a quiet side street, beside the Adige River, this really is like living local. Chantal is happy to provide unusual tips on what to see and where to eat, but before you rush out make time for the splendid breakfast of fresh croissants, yoghurt, honey, cereals and cold cuts served on the best house china and silverware.

Anfiteatro B&B (☎347 248 84 62; www.anfiteatro-bedandbreakfast.com; Via Alberto Mario 5; s €60-90, d €80-130, tr €100-150) Opera divas and fashionistas rest up steps from the action in this 19th-century townhouse, one block from the Roman Arena and just off boutique-lined Via Mazzini. Spacious guestrooms have high wood-beamed ceilings, antique armoires for stashing purchases, and divans for swooning after shows.

Albergo Aurora (☎045 59 47 17; www.hotelaurora.biz; Piazza XIV Novembre 2; s €90-135, d €100-160; ▣) Right off bustling Piazza delle Erbe, yet cosy and blissfully quiet, this hotel has spacious, unfussy doubles, some with city views. There are cheaper single rooms with shared bathroom (€58 to €80). Head to the sunny terrace for drinks overlooking the Piazza.

Hotel Gabbia d'Oro (☎045 59 02 93; www.hotelgabbiadoro.it; Corso Porta Borsari 4a; d from €220; ▣▣@☎) One of the city's top addresses and also one of its most romantic, the Gabbia d'Oro features luxe rooms inside an 18th-century *palazzo* that manage to be both elegant and cosy. The rooftop terrace and central location are icing on the wedding cake.

bistro floor and stacked wine shelves, the restaurant is terribly romantic.

DRINKING

⭐ OSTERIA DEL BUGIARDO   WINE BAR
(⏻045 59 18 69; Corso Porta Borsari 17a; ⏲11am-11pm, to midnight Fri & Sat) On busy Corso Porta Borsari, traffic converges at Bugiardo for glasses of upstanding Valpolicella bottled specifically for the *osteria*. Polenta and *sopressa* make worthy bar snacks for the powerhouse Amarone.

ANTICA BOTTEGA DEL VINO   WINE BAR
(⏻045 800 45 35; www.bottegavini.it; Vicolo Scudo di Francia 3; 3 tasting plates €27; ⏲noon-11pm) Wine is the primary consideration at this historic *enoteca* with beautiful wood panelling and backlit bottles of Valpolicella vintages. Some of the best wines here are bottled specifically for the *bottega*. It sometimes closes in November and February, so call ahead.

CAFFÉ MONTE BALDO   WINE BAR
(⏻045 803 05 79; Via Rosa 12; cicheti €2-3, pasta & plates €5.50-8; ⏲10am-3pm & 5-10pm Tue-Sun) Packed to bursting come *aperitivo* hour, Monte Baldo combines old-fashioned charm (think wood-panelled rooms and a long marble counter) with a generous selection of snacks and well-priced wines by the glass. Choose from any number of bottles lined up on the counter and pile a plate high with *polpette* (meatballs) and marinated vegetables.

CAFFÉ FILIPPINI   BAR
(⏻045 800 45 49; Piazza delle Erbe 26; ⏲4pm-2am Thu-Tue, daily Jun-Aug) On the town's most bustling square, the hippest joint in town has been here since 1901, perfecting house speciality Filippini, a killer cocktail of vermouth, gin, lemon and ice.

Verona's Wine Country

Explore
Seventy three thousand hectares (186,100 acres) of the Veneto are planted with vines, with the most productive vineyards – Soave and Valpolicella – within easy reach of Verona. Northwest of Verona, Valpolicella is celebrated for Amarone – an intense red made from partially dried grapes, while Soave delivers its crisp namesake whites amid storybook medieval walls between Vicenza and Verona. You'll need wheels to visit far-flung vineyards. Most growing areas are also bike-friendly. Since vineyards are spread out, each region requires a full day for relaxed appreciation, including a long, vinous lunch. Italy's largest national wine fair, Vinitaly (p22), is held in Verona in early April and offers infinite sampling opportunities.

The Best...
→ **Sight** Castello di Soave (p209)
→ **Place to Eat** Trattoria Caprini (p210)
→ **Place to Drink** Enoteca Valpolicella (p210)

Top Tip
If you don't want to bother renting a car, **Pagus** (⏻045 751 44 28; www.pagusvalpolicella.net; Via Magellano 19, Verona) offers half- and full-day tours of Valpolicella and Soave, leaving regularly from Verona. Tours include unusual sites, impromptu country rambles, lunches in local restaurants and, of course, wine tastings. Tours can also be customised.

Getting There & Away
→ **Train** To get to Soave from Venice, take the train to San Bonifacio (90 minutes, €6.40, hourly), then catch the local ATV bus 30 (€1.80, 10 minutes, about twice hourly). Trains do not serve Valpolicella.
→ **Car** Your own wheels are your best option for visiting individual wineries. Valpolicella lies just past Verona's northwest suburbs, just off the E45. Soave lies just off the A4, which connects Verona and Mestre.

Need to Know
→ **Area Code** 045
→ **Location** Valpolicella (140km west of Venice); Soave (85km west of Venice)
→ **Tourist Offices Soave** (⏻045 768 06 48; www.prolocosoave.it; Via XXV Aprile 6, Soave); **Valpolicella** (⏻045 770 19 20; www.valpolicellaweb.it; Via Ingelheim 7, San Pietro in Cariano; ⏲9am-1pm Mon-Fri, to noon Sat)

SIGHTS & ACTIVITIES

Soave

Barely 20km from Verona, Soave is nestled in a landscape of gentle green hills and vineyards. The DOC quality-controlled zone includes the parishes of Soave, Castelcerino, Fittà, Castelletto and Costeggiola. Head up to Fittà on a sunny day and you'll have a splendid view of the Val d'Alpone that channels the mountain meltwaters down to Soave and, in the process, feeds its abundant crop of cherries.

Soave itself is a charming medieval town, mapped out along the Roman axis of Via Roma and Via Camuzzoni. Notable buildings line the route, culminating in the Venetian Gothic Palazzo Scaligeri, now the Town Hall. May, June and September are the liveliest times to visit, when the wine festival, cherry season and harvest are in full swing.

CASTELLO DI SOAVE HISTORIC BUILDING
(☑045 768 00 36; www.castellodisoave.it; admission €6; ☺9am-noon & 3-6.30pm Tue-Sun Apr-Oct, 9am-noon & 2-4pm Oct-Mar) Built on a medieval base by Verona's fratricidal Scaligeri family, the Castello complex encompasses an early-Renaissance villa, grassy courtyards, the remnants of a Romanesque church and the Mastio (the defensive tower apparently used as a dungeon): during restoration, a mound of human bones was unearthed here. Be sure to make your way to the upper ramparts for fine views of the town and surrounding countryside.

AZIENDA AGRICOLA COFFELE WINERY
(☑045 768 00 07; www.coffele.it; Via Roma 5, Soave; ☺9am-12.30pm & 2.30-6.30pm Mon-Sat & by appointment) Across from the old-town church, this family-run winery offers tastings of lemon-zesty DOC Soave Classico and nutty, faintly sweet bubbly DOCG (guaranteed quality) Recioto di Soave. The family also rents out rooms among vineyards a few kilometres from town in Castelcerino di Soave.

★SUAVIA WINERY
(☑045 767 50 89; www.suavia.it; Via Centro 14, Fittà; ☺9am-1pm & 2.30-6.30pm Mon-Fri, 9am-1pm Sat & by appointment; ℗) ✐ Soave is not known as a complex white, but this trailblazing winery, run by three of the Tessari daughters, is changing the equation. Using sun-ripe Garganega grapes the often light Soave is transformed into something altogether more complex in Le Rive, which suggests accents of licorice, aniseed and fennel. Don't miss DOC Monte Carbonare Soave Classico, with its mineral, ocean-breeze finish.

Valpolicella

The 'valley of many cellars', from which Valpolicella gets its name, has been in the business of wine production since the ancient Greeks introduced their *passito* technique (the use of partially dried grapes) to create the blockbuster flavours we still enjoy in the region's Amarone and Recioto wines.

Situated in the foothills of Monti Lessini, the valleys benefit from a happy microclimate created by the enormous body of Lake Garda to the west and cooling breezes from the Alps to the north. No wonder Veronese nobility got busy building showy weekend retreats here. Many of them, like the extraordinary **Villa della Torre** (www.villadellatorre.it; Fumane), still house noble wineries, while others like **Villa Spinosa** (☑045 750 00 93; www.villaspinosa.it; Via Colle Masua 12, Negrar; apt per 2/4/6 people €110/235/300; ℗) provide very comfortable accommodation.

Seven *comuni* compose the DOC quality-controlled area: Pescantina, San Pietro in Cariano, Negrar, Marano di Valpolicella, Fumane, Sant'Ambrogio di Valpolicella and Sant' Anna d'Alfaedo.

ALLEGRINI WINERY
(☑045 683 20 11; www.allegrini.it; Via Giare 9/11, Fumane; tours €12-60; ☺by appointment; ℗) This is one of the leading wineries of the Valpolicella region – the Allegrini family have been tending vines in Fumane, Sant'Ambrogio and San Pietro since the 16th century. Pride of place goes to the *cru* wines produced from Corvinia and Rondinella grapes grown on the La Grola hillside (La Poja, La Grola and Palazzo della Torre). Wine tastings in the 16th-century Villa della Torre are a fabulous experience.

FRATELLI VOGADORI WINERY
(☑328 941 72 28; www.amaronevalpolicella.org; Via Vigolo 16, Negrar; ☺by appointment; ℗) ✐ Producing just 10,000 bottles of Valpolicella,

Ripasso, Amarone and Recioto wines, the eponymous brothers *(fratelli)* of Vogadori are meticulous when it comes to organic, environmentally friendly production techniques. They've also started to reintroduce native, heirloom varieties such as Oseleta and Negrara. The result: the wonderfully full-bodied Amarone Riserva Forlago (2004) and the velvety, smooth 2007 Recioto della Valpolicella, which pairs wickedly with dark chocolate cake. Prices range from €15 to €30 per bottle.

PIEVE DI SAN GIORGIO CHURCH
(San Giorgio, Valpolicella; ⊙7am-6pm) FREE In this tiny hilltop village of San Giorgio a few kilometres northwest of San Pietro in Cariano, you'll find this fresco-filled, cloistered 8th-century Romanesque church. Not old enough for you? In the little garden to its left, you can also see a few fragments of an ancient Roman temple.

EATING

TRATTORIA CAPRINI TRATTORIA €€
(☑045 750 05 11; www.trattoriacaprini.it; Via Zanotti 9, Negrar; meals €25-30; ⊙noon-2.30pm & 7-10pm Thu-Mon) This family-run trattoria in the centre of Negrar serves heart-warming bowls of broth and plates of pasta. Highlights include the house *soppressa* (salami)

and the delicious *lasagnetta*, made with hand-rolled pasta and a *ragù* of beef, tomato, *porcini* and *finferli* mushrooms. Downstairs, beside the fire of the old *pistoria* (bakery), you can sample some 200 Valpolicella labels.

LOCANDA LO SCUDO MODERN ITALIAN €€
(☑045 768 07 66; www.loscudo.vr.it; Via Covergnino 9, Soave; meals €35-45; ⊙12.30-2.30pm & 7-10.30pm Tue-Sat Sep-Jul) Just outside the medieval walls of Soave, Lo Scudo is half country inn and half high-powered gastronomy. Arrive early and order fast – or miss out on daily fish specials or risotto made with Verona's zesty Monte Veronese cheese. Above the restaurant, the owners rent out four lovely rooms (singles/doubles €75/110) that continue the theme of countrified sophistication.

★ENOTECA DELLA VALPOLICELLA ITALIAN €€€
(☑045 683 91 46; www.enotecadellavalpolicella. it; Via Osan 47, Fumane; meals €25-35; ⊙noon-2.30pm & 7-10pm Tue-Sun) Foodies flock to the town of Fumane, just a few kilometres north of San Pietro in Cariano, where an ancient farmhouse has been converted to a rustically elegant restaurant. The chef keeps flavours pure – puree of asparagus, risotto with wild herbs, game with polenta – so as not to compete with 700 Italian wines on the menu.

Sleeping

Want to wake up in a palazzo to the sound of lagoon waters lapping at the fondamente (canal banks)? It's an unforgettable experience – and probably more affordable than you think. High-end hotels are no longer your only option. Many Venetians are opening historic homes as locande (guesthouses), B&Bs, affittacamere (rooms for rent) and holiday rental apartments.

More Options Than Ever

Venice still offers plenty of luxe hotels along the Grand Canal and Riva degli Schiavone, and there's also a growing inventory of boutique sleeps. But the real news is the concerted effort to make overnight stays affordable. In the last decade, the number of Venetian properties dedicated to tourist lodgings has nearly quintupled. At the same time, the internet has made it much easier for locals to rent out their homes (or extra rooms).

For budget travellers, Venice offers a range of hostels (called *foresterie*). Some bunks at Giudecca's revamped hostel even have canal views, while the frescoed Foresteria Valdese also offers private rooms at unbeatable prices. During summer, university housing also opens to tourists.

Location, Location, Location

Of course, it is always preferable to stay as close to key sights as possible – for example, near San Marco or anywhere within striking distance of the Grand Canal. However, a frequent and efficient *vaporetto* system makes navigating the city easy. Outlying areas – including other islands like Giudecca, Lido and Murano – are often cheaper, quieter and more authentically Venetian.

Season Matters

In low season – November, early December, and January to March (except around New Year, Carnevale and Easter) – you can expect discounts of 40% or more off peak rates. July and August also bring bargains, though usual-ly not quite as substantial. Even in high season, midweek rates tend to be lower than weekend ones. By contrast, expect to pay a hefty premium during Carnevale, New Year and Easter.

Rates cited here should be considered a guide, since hotels make constant adjustments according to season, day of the week and holidays of varying importance.

Amenities

In general, rooms tend to be small in Venice, and sometimes dark or awkwardly shaped as per the quirks of ancient *palazzi*. Unless otherwise stated in our reviews, guestrooms come with private bathroom, often with a shower rather than a bathtub. Business centres are rarely well equipped, even in swanky hotels, since the assumption is that you're here for pleasure. Only a few large hotels have a pool – mostly on the Lido. While increasingly available, wi-fi doesn't always penetrate thick stone walls and may only be available in common areas.

Buyer Beware

Not all hotels in Venice are grand: some are cramped, frayed and draughty, with lackadaisical service. Budget and midrange places around the train station tend to be especially drear – sometimes despite glowing online 'reviews'. Note also that many hotels boast of 'Venetian-style' rooms. Sometimes this implies real antiques and Murano chandeliers, but it can mean a kitsch version of baroque in rooms where the former charms have been remodelled out of existence.

NEED TO KNOW

Price Ranges
Price ranges are for standard double rooms with private bathroom.

€   less than €120
€€   €120–220
€€€   over €220

Reservations
➡ Book ahead at weekends and any time during high season.

➡ The best, and best-value, hotels are always in high demand; book well ahead.

➡ Check individual hotel websites for increasingly common online deals.

➡ Confirm arrival at least 72 hours in advance – some hotels may assume you've changed your plans.

Getting to Your Hotel
➡ Pack light to better negotiate twisting alleys, footbridges and narrow staircases.

➡ Try to arrive during daylight to avoid getting lost in night-time Venice.

➡ Get directions from your hotel, plus a detailed map.

➡ Though expensive, water taxis can be worth the price for night arrivals or if you're heavily laden.

Breakfast
Except in higher-end places, breakfast tends to be utilitarian. *Affittacamere* generally don't offer breakfast because of strict dining codes. However, you're never far from a great local cafe.

Lonely Planet's Top Choices

Ca' Zanardi (p219) Pristine 16th-century palace with original furnishings, canal views and drawing-room concerts.

Novecento (p215) Plush bohemian-chic getaway ideal for modern Marco Polos.

Palazzo Abadessa (p220) Frescoed, fabulous Venetian palace, ready for romance since 1540.

Oltre Il Giardino (p218) A stylish secret-garden hideaway in the heart of Venice.

Palazzo Schiavoni (p221) Eighteenth-century extravagance with sleek modern trimmings.

Palazzo Soderini (p221) Tranquil, all-white retreat with garden and lily pond.

B&B San Marco (p220) Home from home with bird's-eye view of terracotta rooftops and canals.

Le Garzette (p166) Country-house living with lagoon views and a farm-to-table kitchen.

Best by Budget

€
Gio & Gio (p214)
Foresteria Valdese (p220)
Allo Squero (p219)
Locanda Sant'Anna (p221)
Hotel Ai Do Mori (p214)
Ostello Venezia (p223)

€€
Ca' Zanardi (p219)
Novecento (p215)
Hotel Le Isole (p221)
Palazzo Schiavoni (p221)
Al Redentore di Venezia (p223)
Oltre Il Giardino (p218)

€€€
Gritti Palace (p215)
Aqua Palace (p222)
Palazzo Abadessa (p220)
Bauer Palladio Hotel & Spa (p223)

Best Design or Boutique Hotel
Aqua Palace (p222)
Domus Orsoni (p219)
Palazzo Soderini (p221)
Novecento (p215)
Hotel Palazzo Barbarigo (p219)

Most Romantic
Palazzo Abadessa (p220)
Bauer Palladio Hotel & Spa (p223)
Locanda Cipriani (p224)
Oltre Il Giardino (p218)
Palazzo Paruta (p214)

Best Heritage
Ca' Zanardi (p219)
Gritti Palace (p215)
Hotel Danieli (p222)
Ca' Angeli (p217)
Pensione Accademia Villa Maravege (p217)
Albergo Quattro Fontane (p223)

Best Views
Gritti Palace (p215)
Al Redentore di Venezia (p223)
Hotel Danieli (p222)
Ca' Angeli (p217)
La Calcina (p217)
Hotel Galleria (p216)

Where to Stay

Neighbourhood	For	Against
San Marco	Historic and design hotels in central location, optimal for sightseeing and shopping.	Rooms often small with little natural light; streets crowded and noisy in the morning; fewer good-value restaurant options.
Dorsoduro	Lively art and student scenes, with design hotels near museums and seaside getaways along Zattere.	Lively student scene can mean noise echoing from Campo Santa Margherita until 2am, especially on weekends.
San Polo & Santa Croce	Top value on spacious B&Bs and opulent boutique hotels with prime local dining, Rialto markets, drinking and shopping; convenient to train and bus.	Easy to get lost in maze of streets, and it may be a long walk to major sights and a *vaporetto* stop.
Cannaregio	Venice's best deals on B&Bs with character and hotels convenient to the train and car park, with canal-bank happy hours and restaurants frequented by locals.	Long walk or *vaporetto* ride to San Marco sightseeing; pedestrian traffic between train station and Rialto.
Castello	Calmer and fewer tourists as you move away from San Marco; good budget options.	The eastern fringes are quite far away from key sights and quiet at night.
Giudecca, Lido & the Southern Islands	Better value for money; beaches within walking distance in summer; fewer tourists.	Far from the action, especially at night; must rely on *vaporetti*.
Murano, Burano & the Northern Islands	Far from Venice crowds, excellent island-fresh cuisine.	Far from Venice; sporadic *vaporetti* after 5.30pm; very quiet in low season.

SLEEPING

🛏 Sestiere di San Marco

GIÒ & GIÒ
B&B €

(Map p308; ☎347 366 50 16; www.giogiovenice. com; Calle delle Ostreghe 2439; d incl breakfast €90-150; ✲🕸; 🚤Santa Maria del Giglio) Restrained baroque sounds like an oxymoron, but here you have it: burl-wood bedsteads, pearl-grey silk draperies, polished parquet floors and spotlit art. Packaged breakfasts are available in the shared kitchen. Ideally located near Piazza San Marco along a side canal, next to the Gritti Palace; angle for rooms overlooking the gondola stop, and wake to choruses of *Volare, oh-oh-oooooh!*

HOTEL AI DO MORI
HOTEL €

(Map p308; ☎041 520 48 17; www.hotelaidomori. com; Calle Larga San Marco 658; d €50-150; ✲🕸; 🚤San Zaccaria) Artist's garrets just off Piazza San Marco, each snug as an Arsenale ship's cabin. Book ahead to score upper-floor rooms with sloped wood-beamed ceilings, parquet floors, wall tapestries and close-up views of basilica domes and the clock tower's Do Mori (bell ringers) in action. Ask for No 11, with a private terrace – but pack light, because there's no lift.

LOCANDA CASA PETRARCA
B&B €

(Map p308; ☎041 520 04 30; www.casapetrarca. com; Calle Schiavine 4386; d incl breakfast €105-155, with shared bathroom €80-125; 🕸; 🚤Rialto) A budget option with heart and character, this family-run place offers seven unfussy, sparkling rooms in a historic brick apartment building, with breakfast serenades from passing gondolas. Five rooms have aircon and ensuite bathrooms; rooms facing the side canal are brighter and slightly bigger. Fair warning: the route to nearby Piazza San Marco is lined with tempting boutiques.

PALAZZO PARUTA
HOTEL €€

(Map p308; ☎041 241 08 35; www.palazzoparuta. com; Campo Sant'Angelo 3824; d incl breakfast €90-320; ✲🕸; 🚤Sant'Angelo) Kissing frogs won't get you princely palace getaways like this: lantern-lit courtyard staircases beckon to silken boudoir bedrooms with mirrored bedsteads and Carrara marble ensuite baths. Museum-worthy suites feature velvet-draped beds, stuccoed ceilings and parquet floors; ask for marble fireplaces and canal views. Breakfasts seduce gourmets with fresh-squeezed juices, award-winning local cheeses and cured meats, fresh pastries, pancakes and eggs.

Clever staff will organise water-taxi transfers, arrange tickets to exclusive events and map backstreet routes to your desired destinations – Museo Fortuny, Palazzo Grassi, the Accademia and La Fenice are under five minutes away on foot. Wheelchair-accessible rooms available.

HOTEL FLORA
HOTEL €€

(Map p308; ☎041 520 58 44; www.hotelflora.it; Calle Bergamaschi 2283a; d incl breakfast €100-358; ✲🕸; 🚤Santa Maria del Giglio) Down a lane from glitzy Calle Larga XXII Marzo, this ivy-covered retreat quietly outclasses brash designer neighbours with its delightful tearoom, breakfasts around the garden fountain and gym offering shiatsu massage. Guestrooms feature antique mirrors, fluffy duvets atop hand-carved beds, and tiled ensuite baths with apothecary-style amenities; damask-clad superior rooms overlook the garden. Strollers and kids' teatime complimentary; babysitting available.

BLOOM/7 CIELO
B&B €€

(Map p308; ☎340 149 8872; www.bloom-venice. com; Campiello Santo Stefano 3470; d incl breakfast €100-290; 🕸; 🚤Accademia) Fraternal-twin B&Bs occupy two upper floors of a historic home overlooking Santo Stefano right across the *calle.* Bloom offers glam-rock rooms in shocking scarlet, fuchsia and gold damask with leather bedsteads and full-frontal cathedral views. Downstairs 7 Cielo (Seventh Heaven) is artfully romantic, with exposed-brick walls and Murano glass mosaic bathrooms. Take breakfast on the sunny top-floor terrace.

LOCANDA ORSEOLO
B&B €€

(Map p308; ☎041 520 48 27; www.locandaorseolo.com; Corte Zorzi 1083; d incl breakfast €140-250; ✲@🕸; 🚤Vallaresso) Hide out behind Piazza San Marco: no one will know but the *gondolieri,* who regularly row past the lobby. Consistently warm greetings and cosy wood-trimmed rooms, some with vintage-kitsch Carnevale murals, make this an ideal launch pad. Upgrade to canal views, and don't try to resist owner Barbara's home-made crepes at breakfast. Babysitting and restaurant and concert bookings available.

CA' DEL NOBILE
HOTEL €€

(Map p308; ☎041 528 34 73; www.cadelnobile. com; Rio Terà delle Colonne 987; d €110-270; ✲🕸; 🚤San Marco) Move over, Casanova – Casa del Nobile makes romantic getaways behind

Piazza San Marco easy. The exposed-brick Casanova room has a canopied bed; cosy standards have wood-beamed ceilings and sleigh beds; deluxe rooms have room for daybeds and cribs. Mention you're celebrating your anniversary or wedding when booking, and strewn rose petals may await your arrival. Fresh breakfast pastries, but no views.

LOCANDA ART DECO
B&B €€

(Map p308; ☑041 277 05 58; www.locandaart deco.com; Calle delle Botteghe 2966; d incl breakfast €45-220; ✹☗; ⬇Accademia) Rakishly handsome, cream-coloured guestrooms with *terraza* marble floors, antique tables and comfy beds in wrought-iron bedframes. Wood-beamed lofts are romantic hideaways, if you don't mind low ceilings and stairs. Honeymooners may prefer the Locanda's apartments with hotel perks (kitchenettes, in-room breakfast, maid service). The B&B annexe is less charming, but cheaper. Ask staff about rides with Venice's pioneering woman gondolier.

HOTEL AL CODEGA
HOTEL €€

(Map p308; ☑041 241 46 21; www.hotelalcodega. com; Corte del Forno Vecchio 4435; d incl breakfast €103-276; ✹☗; ⬇Rialto) Unicorns are easier to find in Venice than a quiet, new, affordable, well-lit, family-run hotel five minutes' walk to Piazza San Marco – yet here you have it. Veer off boutique-lined Calle Goldoni, duck under the *sotoportego* (archway), and this flower-trimmed yellow inn greets you in the courtyard. Request sunny courtyard-facing rooms or the easy-access ground-floor Casanova room (there's no lift).

HOTEL NOEMI
B&B €€

(Map p308; ☑041 523 81 44; www.hotelnoemi. com; Calle dei Fabbri 909; d incl breakfast €80-250; ✹☗; ⬇San Zaccaria) The gilded baroque beds and Murano mood lighting in brocade-swagged guestrooms give stays here undeniable Venetian charm – but Noemi doesn't just get by on looks. Besides its prime location 50m behind Piazza San Marco, Noemi offers reserved garage space and 24-hour reception for late arrivals and early departures. Bathrooms are small, but the convivial breakfast salon is a perk.

★NOVECENTO
BOUTIQUE HOTEL €€

(Map p308; ☑041 241 37 65; www.novecento.biz; Calle del Dose 2683/84; d €140-300; ✹☗; ⬇Santa Maria del Giglio) World travellers put down roots in nine bohemian-chic rooms plush with Turkish kilim pillows, Fortuny draperies and 19th-century carved bedsteads piled with duvets. Linger over breakfasts in the garden under Indian parasols, go for a massage at sister property Hotel Flora, take a hotel-organised course in Venetian cooking or landscape drawing, or mingle with creative fellow travellers around the honesty bar.

AD PLACE VENICE
DESIGN HOTEL €€€

(Map p308; ☑041 241 23 24; www.adplacevenice. com; Fondamenta della Fenice 2557a; d incl breakfast €130-350; ✹☗; ⬇Santa Maria del Giglio) Like a diva at Teatro La Fenice across the canal, AD Place delivers shout-it-from-the-rooftops romance: patchwork theatre curtains line the lobby, a silver love-seat winks in the salon, and candy-striped guestrooms with tufted-velvet beds beckon upstairs. Let savvy staff arrange gondolas, art tours

SLEEPING

GRITTI PALACE RESTORATION

Guests at the **Gritti Palace** (Map p308; ☑041 79 46 11; www.hotelgrittipalacevenice.com; Campo di Santa Maria del Giglio 2467; d €425-700, ste from €1100; ✹☗; ⬇Santa Maria del Giglio) on the Grand Canal don't have to leave their balconies to go sightseeing: this landmark 1525 doge's palace reopened in 2013 after an extensive year-long restoration, from Rubelli silk damask lining top-floor suites and landmark Grand Canal rooms to underfloor heating beneath *terrazzo* marble floors in the Gritti Epicurean School and restaurant. Classic Venetian Rooms have also been touched up gently, with restored antique fainting couches, stucco ceilings, hand-painted vanities, and bathrooms sheathed in rare marble. Rooms and suites facing north and west toward Campo Santa Maria del Giglio lack Grand Canal views and southern light, but the level of luxury is consistent. Luxury hotel specialist Starwood manages operations to international standards, and chef Daniele Turco creates inspired Venetian trade-route cuisine for fabulous dockside meals.

and airport transfers, and don't skip breakfasts on the cushion-strewn terrace. Two-night stays required in high season.

🛏 Sestiere di Dorsoduro

HOTEL GALLERIA
INN €

(Map p312; ☑041 523 24 89; www.hotelgalleria.it; Campo della Carità 878a; d incl breakfast €110-220; 🖳Accademia) Smack on the Grand Canal alongside the Ponte dell'Accademia is this classic hotel in a converted 18th-century mansion. Book ahead, especially for rooms 7 and 9, small doubles overlooking the Grand Canal, and No 8, with Liberty furnishings and Grand Canal views. Most rooms share updated bathrooms; No 10 sleeps five, with an original frescoed ceiling and Grand Canal-facing windows.

CA' DELLA CORTE
B&B €

(Map p317; ☑041 715 877; www.cadellacorte.com; Campo Surian 3560, Santa Croce; d incl breakfast €80-170; ✖🛜; 🖳Piazzale Roma) Live like a Venetian in this 16th-century family home near Campo Santa Margherita, with a frescoed music salon, top-floor terrace overlooking Gothic palaces and breakfasts delivered to your room. Stay in snug wood-beamed garrets, chandelier-lit superior rooms or feng-shui eco-rooms. Sporty types, ask helpful staff to organise sailing, tennis, and horse-riding on the Lido; babysitting and shiatsu massage available.

B&B DORSODURO 461
B&B €

(Map p312; ☑041 582 61 72; www.dorsoduro461.com; Rio Terà San Vio 461; d €70-120; ✖🛜; 🖳Accademia) Get to know Venice from the inside out at Sylvia and Francesco's home-style B&B, around the corner from Peggy Guggenheim's place. Your hosts' shared love of books, antique restoration and design is obvious in the bookshelf-lined breakfast room and three well-curated guestrooms, with Kartell lamps perched atop 19th-century poker tables. English-speaking violin-maker Francesco cooks tasty pancakes and dishes excellent Venice tips.

LOCANDA CA' DEL BROCCHI
B&B €

(Map p312; ☑041 522 69 89; www.cadelbrocchi.it; Rio Terà San Vio 470; d incl breakfast €79-149; 🅿✖🛜; 🖳Accademia) A colourful character inhabiting a quiet side street in Dorsoduro's museum district, Ca' del Brocchi has small yet over-the-top baroque-styled rooms –

tasselled, gilt to the hilt and upholstery padded, with matching scrollwork wallpaper. Lower-level rooms have porthole-sized windows; better options have garden views, balconies and/or Jacuzzi tubs. Breakfasts are packaged, but guestroom mini-bars are handy. Babysitting and cradles are available for families.

B&B LEONARDO
B&B €

(Map p312; ☑347 680 58 71; www.bebleonardo.com; Calle delle Botteghe 3153; incl breakfast d €60-180, tr €80-250; ✖; 🖳Ca' Rezzonico) Take a break from baroque in this serene, simple retreat overlooking Ca' Rezzonico's formal garden. Three snug guestrooms are upstairs (no lift) and ship-shape, with televisions stashed in deco dressers and a wood-beamed triple lined with shelves. All have compact private bathrooms, though one is downstairs – light sleepers, bring earplugs for creaky floors. Rates rarely hit maximum; basic breakfast included.

SILK ROAD
HOSTEL €

(Map p312; ☑388 119 68 16; www.silkroadhostel.com; Zattere 1420e; dm/d €27/60; 🛜; 🖳San Basilio) Breathe easy along the Giudecca Canal in this new hassle-free hostel with unexpected perks, including laundry service, communal kitchen, wi-fi and, best of all: no curfew. The four-bed women's dorm has canal views; the other dorm is mixed gender, and there's one private room. The hostel is down the block from a supermarket, canalfront cafes and gelaterie, plus handy *vaporetto* stops.

LOCANDA SAN BARNABA
B&B €€

(Map p312; ☑041 241 12 33; www.locanda-san barnaba.com; Calle del Traghetto 2785-6; d incl breakfast €120-185; ✖; 🖳Ca' Rezzonico) The stage is set for intrigue at this 16th-century *palazzo*, with its frescoed grand salon, hidden courtyard garden and cupboards concealing a secret staircase. Ask for the romantic wood-beamed Poeta Fanatico room; Campiello, with skylight views of a neighbouring bell tower; or superior Il Cavaliere e la Dama, for 18th-century frescoed ceilings and balconies dangling over the canal.

LA CHICCA
B&B €€

(Map p312; ☑041 552 55 35; www.lachicca-venezia.com; Calle Franchi 644; d incl breakfast €60-200; ✖🛜; 🖳Accademia) Neatly wedged among Dorsoduro's trifecta of museums: Accademia, Peggy Guggenheim, Punta della Dogana. Yet all you'll hear at night in this family-run B&B is the lapping of the canal at the end of the *calle*. Venetian damask-clad, terrazzo-floored guestrooms are spacious and blessedly uncluttered after a museum binge; book ahead to nab one with a tub.

LA CALCINA
INN €€

(Map p312; ☑041 520 64 66; www.lacalcina.com; Fondamenta Zattere ai Gesuati 780; d incl breakfast €100-320; ❋❓; ⛴Zattere) Upgrade from ordinary seaside resorts to La Calcina, with breezy roof-garden breakfasts, canal-dock restaurant, and panoramas of Palladio's Redentore church across Giudecca Canal. Antique armoires, brocade bedspreads and ship-shape modern bathrooms come standard with airy, parquet-floored guestrooms. Book ahead for the waterfront rooms – especially No 2, where John Ruskin wrote his classic (though inexplicably Palladio-bashing) 1876 *The Stones of Venice*.

PALAZZO GUARDI
B&B €€

(Map p312; ☑041 296 0725; www.palazzoguardi venice.com; Calle del Pistor 995; d incl breakfast €92-149; ❋@❓; ⛴Accademia) Relive the Renaissance at this 16th-century palace, right around the corner from Accademia and Gia Schiavone – you're never more than a minute away from a Titian masterpiece or glass of Amarone. Baroque-style guestrooms with modern baths accommodate two to five guests, but only the suites and breakfast room have canal vistas worthy of a Guardi painting.

★PENSIONE ACCADEMIA VILLA MARAVEGE
INN €€

(Map p312; ☑041 521 01 88; www.pensioneac cademia.it; Fondamenta Bollani 1058; d €145-340; ❋❓; ⛴Accademia) Step through the ivy-covered gate of this 17th-century garden villa just off the Grand Canal, and you'll forget you're a block from the Accademia. All 27 guestrooms are recently restored and effortlessly elegant, with parquet floors, antique desks, creamy walls and snug, shiny modern bathrooms – but some offer four-poster beds, wood-beamed ceilings and glimpses of the canal.

Ask for Thelma, a superior double with its own patch of greenery, named after a regular who loved reading in the garden. Buffet breakfasts are served on the lawn in summer, sunsets are toasted with a complimentary drink at the bar, and garden swings for two promise romance under the stars. Handicap-accessible rooms and wheelchair use upon request; wi-fi cards and laundry service available for additional fee.

CA' PISANI
DESIGN HOTEL €€€

(Map p312; ☑041 240 14 11; www.capisanihotel.it; Rio Terà Antonio Foscarini 979a; d €140-351; ❋❓; ⛴Accademia) Sprawl out in style right behind the Accademia, and luxuriate in sleigh beds, Jacuzzi tubs and walk-in closets. Mood lighting and sound-proofed padded leather walls make downstairs deco rooms right for romance, while families appreciate top-floor rooms with sleeping lofts. Venetian winters require in-house Turkish steam baths, summers mean roof-terrace sunning, and patio breakfasts and wine-bar happy hours are ideal year-round.

🛏 Sestieri di San Polo & Santa Croce

AL GALLION
B&B €

(Map p314; ☑041 524 47 43; www.algallion.com; Calle Gallion 1126, Santa Croce; d incl breakfast €75-110; ⛴San Biasio) A couple of bridges away at train-station hotels, weary tourists wait at front desks – while in this 16th-century family home, you'll be chatting and sipping espresso in the living room. Whitewashed guestrooms are handsomely furnished with walnut desks, cheerful yellow bedspreads, terrazzo floors and host Daniela's family art collection. Breakfasts are homemade spreads; tasty, affordable restaurants abound nearby.

HOSTEL DOMUS CIVICA
HOSTEL €

(Map p317; ☑041 522 71 39; www.domuscivica. com; Campiello Ciovare Frari 3082, San Polo; s/d/ tr €36/62/93, student €29/50/75; ☉Jun-Sep; ❓; ⛴Piazzale Roma) A graceful 1918 building commandeered by Germans in WWII and used as a postwar refugee shelter is now a women's dorm that becomes a hostel in summer. Simple, clean dorm rooms are equipped with single beds, desks and sinks. Shared facilities include five bathrooms per floor, TV room, elevator, terraces and fee-based wi-fi access. Bring earplugs – hallways and nearby church bells reverberate. Midnight curfew.

CA' ANGELI
BOUTIQUE HOTEL €€

(Map p314; ☑041 523 24 80; www.caangeli.it; Calle del Traghetto de la Madonnetta 1434, San

Polo; d incl breakfast €70-215; 🌀🔊; 🚤San Silvestro) 🏊 Brothers Giorgio and Matteo inherited this Grand Canal palace and restored its Murano glass chandeliers, Louis XIV love-seat and namesake 16th-century angels. Guestrooms feature beamed ceilings, antique carpets and big bathrooms; some have Grand Canal or secluded courtyard views. Hearty breakfasts are made with organic products and served on antique china in the dining room, overlooking the Grand Canal.

AL PONTE MOCENIGO HOTEL €€
(Map p314; ☎041 524 47 97; www.alpontemo cenigo.com; Fondamenta Rimpetto Mocenigo 2063, Santa Croce; d €85-170; 🌀🔊; 🚤San Stae) A doge of a deal near the Grand Canal, steps from San Stae *vaporetto* stop, with prime dining nearby and in-house Turkish bath. Ten swanky guestrooms with Murano chandeliers illuminating high wood-beamed ceilings are often spacious enough for gymnastic routines, even ones with four-poster beds, minibars, gilt-edged armoires and salon seating. Ask for rooms overlooking Rio San Stae or the courtyard.

DOMINA HOME CA' ZUSTO BOUTIQUE HOTEL €€
(Map p314; ☎051 639 18 01; www.dominavacanze. it; Campo Rielo 1358, Santa Croce; d incl breakfast €110-210; 🌀🔊; 🚤Riva di Biasio) Gothic goes pop at this palace, where the stately Veneto-Byzantine exterior disguises a colourful wild streak. Designer Gianmarco Cavagnino winks at nearby Fondaco dei Turchi (Turkish trading house) and Fondazione Prada, with 22 mod-striped, harem-styled suites named after Turkish ladies. Pedestal tables flank baroque beds fit for pashas; amenities may include slippers, Jacuzzis and iPod docks. Breakfast and wi-fi in the '60s lounge.

HOTEL AL DUCA HOTEL €€
(Map p314; ☎041 812 30 69; www.alducadiven ezia.com; Fontego dei Turchi 1739, Santa Croce; d €80-220; 🌀@🔊; 🚤San Stae) Bedrooms swagged with red damask and black Murano chandeliers are Venetian bordello-chic, honouring the courtesans that once ruled nearby Rialto backstreets – but all-bronze guestrooms are serene Serenissima retreats. Get an insider's view of Venice at family-friendly kitchenette apartments, next-door Museo di Storia Naturale and nearby Campo San Giacomo dell'Orio happy hours. Reception is open 24 hours; baby-sitting, laundry and wheelchair-accessible guestrooms available.

CA DEI POLO B&B €€
(Map p317; ☎041 244 02 13; www.cadeipolo.com; Fondamenta dei Tolentini 203, Santa Croce; d incl breakfast €90-260; 🌀🔊; 🚤Piazzale Roma) A smart, stylish new option for quick getaways by car, bus, or train – but breakfasts on the canalfront terrace and sunset toasts on the roof deck are valid reasons to linger. Custom Murano art-glass chandeliers grace sprawling suites and superior rooms like extraterrestrial lilies, and the even smaller rooms have wood floors and design mag-worthy details, including bathrooms with excellent water pressure.

PENSIONE GUERRATO INN €€
(Map p314; ☎041 528 59 27; www.pensioneguerra to.it; Calle Drio la Scimia 240a, San Polo; d/tr/q incl breakfast €145/165/185; 🌀🔊; 🚤Rialto Mercato) In a 1227 landmark that was once a hostel for knights headed for the Third Crusade, updated guestrooms haven't lost their sense of history – some have frescoes or glimpses of the Grand Canal. A prime Rialto Market location amid gourmet *bacari* makes Pensione Guerrato the Holy Grail for visiting foodies, and newly restored apartments are equipped with kitchens. Wi-fi in lobby.

CAMPIELLO ZEN B&B €€
(Map p314; ☎041 71 03 65; www.campiellozen. com; Rio Terà 1285, Santa Croce; d incl breakfast €160-190; 🌀🔊; 🚤Riva de Biasio) Hotels would have you believe Venetians live a twee existence in fussy brocade-upholstered pink salons, but this B&B in a traditional family home has comfortable beds, handsome antique wardrobes, quirky wall niches and every modern convenience, especially in the bathrooms. The high-ceilinged upstairs suite accommodates a third bed (fee applies). Handy to train and *vaporetto*, but blissfully off the tourist track.

★ OLTRE IL GIARDINO BOUTIQUE HOTEL €€
(Map p314; ☎041 275 00 15; www.oltreilgiardino -venezia.com; Fondamenta Contarini, San Polo 2542; d incl breakfast €180-250; 🌀@; 🚤San Tomà) Live the design-magazine dream in this garden villa brimming with historic charm and modern comforts: marquetry composer's desks and flat-screen TVs, candelabras and minibars, 19th-century poker chairs and babysitting services. Light fills six high-ceilinged bedrooms, and though

sprawling Turquoise overlooks the canal and Green hides away in the walled garden, Grey has a sexy wrought-iron bedframe under a cathedral ceiling.

HOTEL PALAZZO
BARBARIGO
DESIGN HOTEL €€€

(Map p314; ☑041 740 172; www.palazzobarbarigo. com; Grand Canal 2765, San Polo ; d incl breakfast €240-380; ❄ @; ᵬSan Tomà) Not your grandmother's Grand Canal getaway, the Palazzo Barbarigo is Venice's splashiest design hotel. The traditional water-gate entryway has been turned into a slick watering hole, with a deco lounge and disco-inspired uplighting. The 18 guestrooms combine modern luxury and Venetian masquerade intrigue, with contemporary furnishings in sumptuous velvets with the occasional feathered lamp or fringed fainting couch.

Whether you opt for the junior suites overlooking the Grand Canal (go for triple-windowed Room 10) or standard rooms overlooking Rio di San Polo, expect compact, sleek bathrooms, positively royal breakfasts, and drinks on the balcony over the Grand Canal.

🛏 Sestiere di Cannaregio

★ALLO SQUERO
B&B €

(Map p318; ☑041 523 69 73; www.allosquero.it; Corte dello Squero 4692; d incl breakfast €80-130; ᵬ; ᵬFondamenta Nuove) Dock for the night at this historic gondola *squero* (shipyard), recently converted into a garden retreat. Gondolas passing along two canals can be spotted from modern, sunny upstairs guestrooms, with *terrazzo* marble floors and sleek mosaic-striped ensuite baths, some with tubs. Hosts Andrea and Hiroko offer Venice-insider tips over cappuccino and pastry breakfasts in the fragrant, wisteria-filled garden. Cots and cribs available.

CA' DOGARESSA
INN €

(Map p318; ☑041 275 9441; www.cadogaressa. com; Fondamenta di Cannaregio 1018; d incl breakfast €50-170; ❄ @; ᵬGuglie) Splashy new canalside inn with Venetian charm (princess beds, gilt mirrors, chandeliers) that won't drain vacation budgets. Roofterrace views and designer bathrooms are four star–worthy, and canalbank breakfasts best most B&Bs. Your Antenori family hosts offer major hotel-chain perks, including 24-hour reception, laptops for in-room use and

laundry service. The annexe is cheaper but smaller, with shared bathrooms.

RESIDENZA CA' RICCIO
B&B €

(Map p318; ☑041 528 23 34; www.cariccio.com; Campo dei Miracoli 5394a; d incl breakfast €90-160; ❄ @ᵬ; ᵬFondamenta Nuove) Down the street from Casanova's house is the Riccio family's lovingly restored 14th-century residence, a hidden yet convenient getaway between the Rialto bridge and Fondamenta Nuove *vaporetto* stop. Seven rooms over two top floors overlook the courtyard, with simple wrought-iron beds, wood-beamed ceilings, Murano glass lamps, terracotta-tiled floors and whitewashed walls. Restaurants are around the corner.

★CA' ZANARDI
BOUTIQUE HOTEL €€

(Map p318; ☑041 241 33 05; www.cazanardi.eu; Calle Zanardi 4132; d €130-300; ᵬ; ᵬMadonna dell'Orto) Pristine 16th-century Venetian palace, international contemporary art gallery, idyllic canalside garden retreat: since Ca' Zanardi is all these things, calling it home for the weekend is a distinct privilege. Those throne-like chairs, tapestries and mercury-glass mirrors aren't decor but the original furnishings kept in the family over four centuries; drawing-room concerts and gala ballroom masquerades are still held here.

Princess fantasies seem inevitable, with new management welcoming guests like long-lost royal relatives. Crystal chandeliers light the way to sunwashed guestrooms with museum-quality furnishings, views over the cloistered garden or canal, and vintage-tiled ensuite baths (ask for one with a bathtub). Breakfast is served on the arcaded patio or stuccoed breakfast salon, as befits visiting dignitaries such as yourself.

★DOMUS ORSONI
B&B €€

(Map p318; ☑041 275 95 38; www.domusorsoni. it; Corte Vedei 1045; d incl breakfast €100-250;

✳ @; 🜨Guglie) Surprise: along a tranquil Ghetto lane and behind a rosy, historic facade is Venice's most original artist's retreat. Continental breakfasts are served in the palm-shaded garden near the Orsoni mosaic works, located here since 1885 – hence the custom mosaics glittering across walls, bathrooms and tables. Find artistic bliss in five mosaic-splashed guestrooms, or join Venetian crowds mid-toast around the corner.

CA' POZZO INN €€

(Map p318; 🖉041 524 05 04; www.capozzoven ice.com; Sotoportego Ca' Pozzo 1279; d €90-190; ✳ @🜨; 🜨Guglie) Recover from Venice's sensory onslaught at this minimalist-chic hotel near the Ghetto. Sleek contemporary guestrooms feature platform beds, abstract artwork and cube-shaped bathroom fixtures; some have balconies, two accommodate disabled guests, and sprawling No 208 could house a Damien Hirst entourage. Laundry, concert-booking and ticket-printing services are available; check the website for photography expeditions led by National Geographic photographers. Two-night minimum stay April to June.

ALLA VITE DORATA B&B €€

(Map p318; 🖉041 241 30 18; www.allavitedorata. com; Rio Terà Barba Frutariol 4690b; d incl breakfast €75-180; ✳🜨; 🜨Ca' d'Oro) *Venexianárse* (become Venetian) at this family home recently converted to a B&B in a quiet, untouristy Cannaregio corner handy to Venetians' favourite restaurants and happy-hour hot spots. Romantics can upgrade to rooms with four-poster beds overlooking a canal, and one guestroom is disabled accessible. All rooms are effortlessly charming, with high wood-beamed ceilings, wrought-iron furnishings and colourful drapery.

RESIDENZA CANNAREGIO HOTEL €€

(Map p318; 🖉041 524 43 32; www.eurostarsresi denzacannaregio.com; Dei Reformati 3210a; d €55-240; ✳🜨; 🜨Tre Archi) A monastery gone mod, this former spiritual retreat is cleverly repurposed into a B&B with contemporary comforts. Original brickwork and exposed-beam ceilings are preserved, while low-slung leather chairs and floating steel stairwells add the cool factor. Spacious rooms have sleeping lofts and backlit bedsteads, and the canalside location is handy to the Ghetto and excellent dining. Laundry, cradles and babysitting available.

★ PALAZZO ABADESSA BOUTIQUE HOTEL €€€

(Map p318; 🖉041 241 37 84; www.abadessa.com; Calle Priuli 4011; d €125-375; ✳🜨; 🜨Ca' d'Oro) Evenings seem enchanted in this opulent 1540 Venetian *palazzo,* with staff fluffing pillows, plying guests with *prosecco,* arranging water taxis to the opera and plotting irresistible marriage proposals. Classic guestrooms feature kingly beds, silk damask-clad walls, Murano glass lamps and wood-beamed ceilings; go for baroque in frescoed superior rooms with 18th-century vanities and canal vistas. Breakfasts are served in the tree-shaded, lily-perfumed garden.

🛏 Sestiere di Castello

For luxury with lagoon views, grand hotels along the Riva degli Schiavoni have reeled in visitors for two centuries. Bargain hunters, take note: some Castello lodgings are closer to Piazza San Marco than ones with a San Marco address, often at a substantially lower price. For even better rates, walk another 15 minutes from the Piazza towards the Arsenale, where rates plummet up to 50% from central city rates.

★ B&B SAN MARCO B&B €

(Map p320; 🖉041 522 75 89; www.realvenice.it/ smarco; Fondamente San Giorgio 3385l; s €65-100, d €105-135; ✳; 🜨Pietà, Arsenale) One of the few genuine B&Bs in Venice. Alice and Marco welcome you warmly to their home overlooking Carpaccio's frescoed Scuola di San Giorgio Schiavoni. The 3rd-floor apartment (no elevator), with its parquet floors and large, bright windows, is furnished with family antiques and offers photogenic views over the terracotta rooftops and canals. Marco and Alice live upstairs, so they're always on hand with great recommendations.

FORESTERIA VALDESE HOSTEL €

(Palazzo Cavagnis; Map p320; 🖉041 528 67 97; www.foresteriavenezia.it; Castello 5170; dm €30-35, d €70-140, q €95-190; 🜨Ospedale, San Zaccaria) Holy hostel: this rambling palace retreat owned by the Waldensian church has 1st-floor guestrooms with 18th-century frescoes by Bevilacqua, and one floor up guestrooms have canal views. Dorm beds are available only for families or groups; book well ahead. Rates include breakfast.

ALLOGGI BARBARIA B&B €

(Map p320; ☑041 522 27 50; www.alloggibar
baria.it; Calle delle Cappuccine 6573; s €45-100,
d €55-130, q €110-170; ✳; ⊜Ospedale) Located
near the Fondamente Nuove, this *pensione*
isn't easy to find – but that's part of its
charm, and so are the intrepid fellow travellers you'll meet over breakfast on a shared
balcony. All six rooms are simple but tidy,
bright and airy, and rates rarely hit the
quoted maximums. Giorgio and Fausto
also maintain a great blog (see website for
details), which is worth browsing before
travelling.

LOCANDA SANT'ANNA B&B €

(Map p320; ☑041 528 64 66; www.locandasan
tanna.com; Corte del Bianco 269; s €35, d €90-
100; ✳ @; ⊜Giardini) Escape the madding
crowd on a quiet *campiello* (small square)
on the sleepy side of Castello. Antique
vanities, marquetry bedsteads and parquet
floors add character to spacious rooms,
some with views of Isola San Pietro. A little terrace is ideal for sunny days, and the
reading room makes a welcome retreat
when lagoon mists roll in. Prices drop by
50% in low season.

★PALAZZO SCHIAVONI APARTHOTEL €€

(Map p320; ☑041 241 12 75; www.palazzoschiavo
ni.com; Fondamente dei Furlani 3288; d €155-263,
2-person apt €170-295, 4-person apt €210-380;
✳ @; ⊜San Zaccaria, Arsenale) Lie beneath
your crown canopy and gaze at frescoed
ceilings in this 18th-century *palazzo*–
boutique hotel. The impeccable refurbishment retains many period features, while
paying close attention to guest comforts.
Rooms, reached via an elevator, are spacious and furnished with period reproductions, while apartments are kitted out
with designer kitchens and generous living
space. Perfect for families seeking a little
dolce vita on a reasonable budget.

PALAZZO SODERINI B&B €€

(Map p320; ☑041 296 08 23; www.palazzoso
derini.it; Campo di Bandiera e Mori 3611; d incl
breakfast €150-200; ✳ ?; ⊜Arsenale) Whether
you're coming from cutting-edge art at the
Biennale or baroque masterpieces at the
Palazzo Ducale, this tranquil all-white retreat with a lily pond in the garden is a welcome reprieve from the visual onslaught of
Venice. Minimalist decor emphasises spare
shapes and clean lines, with steel-edged
modern furniture and whitewashed walls.

The three rooms have all the mod cons:
TVs, wi-fi, minibars, air-con and heating.
Book well ahead.

HOTEL LE ISOLE BOUTIQUE HOTEL €€

(Map p320; ☑041 522 89 11; www.hotel-leisole.
it; Campo San Provolo 4661; d €130-250; ✳ @ ?;
⊜San Zaccaria) Barely a stone's throw from
San Marco and less than five minutes from
the San Zaccaria *vaporetto* stop, this small,
friendly hotel, opened in 2012, offers incredibly good value. Arranged around a
vine-clad central courtyard, rooms are un-
derstated and elegant with wooden floors,
Venetia Studium lamps, Fortuny-style fabrics, Sky TV and gleaming marble bathrooms. Breakfast is similarly generous: a
huge buffet loaded with cold cuts, fruit and
cakes, with eggs to order from the kitchen.

CA' DEI DOGI BOUTIQUE HOTEL €€

(Map p320; ☑041 241 37 51; www.cadeidogi.it;
Corte Santa Scolastica 4242; s €90, d €100-170;
✳ @; ⊜San Zaccaria) Even the nearby Bridge
of Sighs can't dampen the high spirits of the
sunny yellow Ca' Dei Dogi, with guestroom
windows sneaking peeks into the convent
cloisters next door. Streamlined, modern
rooms look like ships' cabins, with tilted
wood-beamed ceilings, dressers that look
like steamer trunks, and compact mosaic-
covered bathrooms – ask for the one with
the terrace and Jacuzzi (€210).

Friendly staff can arrange concerts, free
trips to Murano and sunset gondola rides.
Book well ahead.

CASA VERARDO HOTEL €€

(Map p320; ☑041 528 61 38; www.casaverardo.
it; Calle Castagna 4765; d €90-280, ste €150-
350; ✳ @; ⊜San Zaccaria) Take part in your
own period drama by checking into Casa
Verardo. This family-run hotel has just 23
rooms arranged around two spectacular
period salons. Take breakfast on the canalside terrace and on summer afternoons
seek refuge in the shade of the 16th-century
garden courtyard. Rooms vary considerably
in size, and room 305 is the only one with
a private terrace. Off-season rates are good
value for money.

HOTEL AL PIAVE HOTEL €€

(Map p320; ☑041 528 51 74; www.hotelalpiave.
com; Ruga Giuffa 4838; d incl breakfast €130-
200; ✳; ⊜San Zaccaria) Steps from Campo
Santa Maria di Formosa, this neat-as-a-
pin midrange option offers comfortably

equipped rooms with beautifully polished *terrazzo* (marble chips set in mortar) floors, and 'traditional' Venetian designs. Smallish digs and no views, but it's good value if comfort and location are your priority.

★AQUA PALACE   LUXURY HOTEL €€€

(Palazzo Scalfarotto; Map p320; ☑041 296 04 42; www.aquapalace.it; Calle de la Malvasia 5492; s €150-350, d €200-490; ❋@🛜; 🚇San Marco, San Zaccaria) With its exotic, spice-route vibe and burnished colour pallete of gold, bronze and old grey, the Aqua Palace is a heady mixture of modern amenities and Eastern romance. Suites 'interpret' the distant past of Marco Polo, and with only 25 of them you can expect aristocratic proportions, acres of weighty fabric, and bathrooms marbled within an inch of their lives. Complete with its own private gondola pier, this is the hotel for love birds.

IQS   DESIGN HOTEL €€€

(Map p320; ☑041 277 02 62; www.dd724.it; Campiello Querini Stampalia 4425; ste €259-625; ❋@🛜; 🚇San Zaccaria) Step out of your boat ahead of art-show aficionados and into the romantic lobby of iQS. These achingly cool suites are arranged around an ancient Gothic courtyard opposite the Querini Stampalia foundation, and are hung with modern art and furnished in B&B Italia style.

All four of them look out on the vivid teal waters of the Rio di Santa Maria Formosa, made even more luminous by the deliciously dark colour palate of the high-design interiors.

HOTEL DANIELI   HISTORIC HOTEL €€€

(Map p320; ☑041 522 64 80; www.danielihotel venice.com; Riva degli Schiavoni 4196; s €250, d €260-700; ❋@🛜; 🚇San Zaccaria) As eccentric and luxurious as Venice itself, the Danieli has attracted artistic bohemians,

LONGER-TERM RENTALS

For longer stays and groups of three or more, renting an apartment is an economical option that gives you the freedom to cook your own meals. Generally, flats are let by the week or month.

ApartmentsApart (www.apartmentsapart.com) Offers flats for rent by the day, starting at about €70.

Airbnb (www.airbnb.co.uk) Offers shared and private rooms, as well as apartments in all the main *sestieri*.

BB Planet (www.bbplanet.it) Smaller B&Bs and dozens of apartment rentals searchable by *sestiere*.

Bianco Holidays (www.apartmentinitaly.com) Well-priced apartment rentals starting at €110 a night. These aren't people's homes, so expect fewer frills and home comforts.

Guest in Italy (www.guestinitaly.com) Apartments and B&Bs ranging from €100 to €350 a night; you may have to fill out a booking form to see the prices on many places.

There are also several Venice-only dedicated websites:

Venetian Apartments (www.venice-rentals.com) Arranges accommodation in flats, often of a luxurious nature. Two- to four-person apartments start at around €895 per week.

Views on Venice (www.viewsonvenice.com) A collection of 70 apartments picked for their personality, character and view, of course. Rentals start around €1000 per week.

Venice Apartment Rental (www.veniceapartment.com) A broader selection of apartments for rent on a daily or weekly basis.

If you plan to stay for a month or more, you'll want to seek out longer-term rental, which you might find through **Craigslist Venice** (http://venice.it.craigslist.it) or word of mouth. If you don't mind sharing with students, check out the **Università Ca' Foscari noticeboards** (Calle Larga Foscari, San Polo), where you might find rooms in a shared apartment for about €300 to €600 a month (usually the low-end places are in mainland Mestre). To rent a studio for yourself, expect to pay €800 to €1200 per month.

minor royalty and their millionaire lovers for over a century. The hotel sprawls along the lagoon in three landmark buildings: the 14th-century *casa vecchia* (old house), built for Doge Enrico Dandolo, with frescoed, antique-filled rooms; the 18th-century, gilt-to-the-hilt *casa nuova* (new house); and the Danielino, a Fascist edifice with a modern-luxe interior redesign by Jacques Garcia.

In summer weather, breakfast is served on the rooftop terrace, with its extraordinary views of San Marco and the lagoon. This is also *the* best place in Venice for summer sundowners. However, at these prices the €15 daily surcharge for in-room wi-fi seems churlish.

🛏 Giudecca, Lido & the Southern Islands

Take a breather from the palatial grandeur of Venice at seaside art nouveau villas on the Lido or bargain lodging on Giudecca. If you want to stay on the Lido during the Venice International Film Festival in September, plan to make reservations months in advance and pay premium rates.

OSTELLO VENEZIA
HOSTEL €

(Map p323; ☑041 523 82 11; www.ostellovenezia. it; Fondamenta delle Zitelle 86, Giudecca; dm €21-33, s €39-60, d €65-95; ✳@🛜; 🚤Zitelle) After a swish new refurbishment by Generator Venice in 2012, Giudecca's hostel rocks a sharp, contemporary interior including a fabulous new bar-restaurant. To claim that perfect bunk by the window, you'll need to arrive promptly at the 3.30pm opening. Sheets, blanket and a pillow are provided in the bunk price; the buffet breakfast is an extra €3.50.

Check-in is from 3.30pm to 10pm; checkout is at 9.30am. There's no curfew. Reserve ahead for one of two viewless private rooms.

LE GARZETTE
FARMSTAY €€

(☑041 712 16 53; www.legarzette.it; Lungomare Alberoni 32; s €70-80, d €90-120; ⊗closed mid-Dec–mid-Jan; P✳; 🚤Lido) After a mouthwatering meal, retire to your comfy room for a nap on your 18th-century bed as herb-scented sea breezes waft through the window.

AL REDENTORE DI VENEZIA
APARTMENTS €€

(Map p323; ☑041 522 94 02; www.alredentoredi venezia.com; Fondamenta Ponte Lungo 234a, Giu-

decca; 2-person apt €70-190, 4-person apt €205-270; ✳🛜; 🚤Redentore) Within the shadow of Il Redentore, these fully serviced apartments offer divine views across the water to San Marco at less than half the price of the Bauer a few doors down. But don't think they've skimped on the details – from the travertine-marble lobby, up the ash-clad staircase to the anallergic pillows and high-end courtesy bath products, Al Redentore has thought of it all.

For the best views beneath ancient timber beams, book one of the top-floor apartments.

HOTEL PANORAMA
HOTEL €€

(Map p324; ☑041 276 04 86; www.hpanorama. com; Piazzale Santa Maria Elisabetta 1b, Lido; s €60-140, d €90-190, with lagoon views €120-220; P✳@🛜; 🚤Lido) Steps from the Lido *vaporetto* stop, this cheerful, lemon-yellow hotel offers airy rooms with huge windows, many of which look out onto the lagoon. Double-paned windows keep out noise from the busy waterfront, while Murano-glass light fixtures, a lagoon-facing terrace and great off-season deals complete the pleasant picture.

ALBERGO QUATTRO FONTANE
HOTEL €€€

(Map p324; ☑041 526 07 26; www.quattrofontane. com; Via Quattro Fontane 16, Lido; s €110-210, d €180-280, apt €350-430; ⊗Apr-Nov; P✳@🛜; 🚤Lido) Strange but true: this alpine chalet is just a stone's throw from Lido beaches, and its shaded gardens and tennis court swarm with festival buffs during the film festival. Celebrities are nothing new to this inn, with a chequered floor and a chequered past as a casino frequented by royalty in the 16th century, and a tavern beloved of Robert Browning and his 19th-century bohemian crowd.

Rooms are vast and unabashedly retro in the 1970s A-frame annexe; the original building offers tighter, more traditional quarters with charming wrought-iron beds. Bicycle rental, laundry and babysitting services available.

⭐BAUER PALLADIO HOTEL & SPA
LUXURY HOTEL €€€

(Map p323; ☑041 520 70 22; www.palladiohotel spa.com; Fondamenta della Croce 33, Giudecca; d from €720; ⊗closed mid-Nov–mid-Mar; ✳🛜; 🚤Zitelle) Splash out in a serene, Palladio-designed former cloister with San Marco views, private solar-powered boat service

SLEEPING

and a superb spa. These premises once housed nuns and orphans but now offer heavenly comfort in 37 rosy, serenely demure guestrooms, many with garden terraces or Giudecca Canal views. Head downstairs for local organic breakfast buffets and ecofriendly spa treatments. Check online for discounts.

⌂ Murano, Burano & the Northern Islands

IL LATO AZZURRO
INN €

(⌁041 523 06 42; www.latoazzurro.it; Via Forti 13, Sant'Erasmo; dm €25-40, s €50-90, d €70-115, q €120-190; @🖥; 🚍Sant'Erasmo Capannone) 🖉 Sleep among the artichokes on Venice's garden isle of Sant'Erasmo in a red-roofed country villa, 25 minutes by boat from central Venice. Spacious guestrooms with parquet floors and wrought-iron beds open onto a wraparound veranda. Meals are largely home-grown, organic and fair trade, bicycles are available, and the lagoon laps at the end of the lane – bite-prone guests should bring mosquito repellent.

The guesthouse supports a nonprofit cultural organisation, and guests are invited to participate in nature excursions, archaeological digs, theatre performances and cultural exchange programs.

★ LOCANDA CIPRIANI
B&B €€

(Map p326; ⌁041 73 01 50; www.locandacipriani. com; Piazza Santa Fosca 29, Torcello; per person €100-190, with half board €160-240; ⊘restaurant closed Tue & Jan; 🕸; 🚍Torcello) Not much has changed since this rustic wine shop was transformed into a country inn in 1934 by Harry's Bar founder Giuseppe Cipriani. The six spacious rooms are more like suites, with stocked libraries and easy chairs in lieu of TVs for a true literary retreat – and you're bound to find inspiration for your next novel in Hemingway's favourite room, Santa Fosca, with its balcony overlooking the garden and original creaky oak floors.

You won't see Ernest hauling in his hunting trophies or working on his manuscripts any more, but you can still enjoy wild duck by the *fogher* (fireplace) or Venice's finest peach bellini beneath the rose pergola.

VENISSA
INN €€

(Map p326; ⌁041 527 22 81; www.venissa.it; Fondamenta Santa Caterina 3, Mazzorbo; d €150-170; 🕸🖥; 🚍Mazzorbo) Gourmet getaways are made in the shade of the vineyards at Venissa, which offers some of the lagoon's finest, freshest dining as well as six large, strikingly contemporary rooms under the manor-house rafters. Breakfast – if that's what you can call the lavish gourmet affair – is extra, either prix fixe (€15) or à la carte.

MURANO PALACE
BOUTIQUE HOTEL €€

(Map p325; ⌁041 73 96 55; www.muranopalace. com; Fondamenta Ventrai 77, Murano; d €110-180; 🕸🖥; 🚍Murano Colonna) Come here for designer fabulousness at an outlet price. Jewel-toned colour schemes and (naturally) Murano glass chandeliers illuminate high-ceilinged, parquet-floored rooms, and there are free drinks and snacks in the minibar. Expect canal views and unparalleled art-glass shopping, but eerie calm once the shops close around 6pm. Ask the front desk about fishing excursions and Venetian rowing lessons.

Understand Venice & the Veneto

Venice Today

Look around: all those splendid palaces, paintings and churches were dreamed up by a handful of Venetians. In the city's 1000-year history, there have only been about three million Venetians who could claim grandparents from Venice. Luckily, Venice attracted global talents and international admirers. Resting on past glories would be easy and topping them seems impossible, but, as usual, Venetians are opting for the impossible.

Best on Film

Pane e Tulipani (Bread & Tulips) (2000) An AWOL housewife starts life anew in Venice.

Casanova (1976) Fellini's take on Venice's seducer with Donald Sutherland tops Lasse Halstrom's with Heath Ledger.

Don't Look Now (1973) A couple's demons follow them to Venice in Nicolas Roeg's taut thriller.

Casino Royale (2006) James Bond hits the Grand Canal (don't worry, that palace survived).

Best in Print

Watermark (1992) Nobel Laureate Joseph Brodsky's 17-year fascination with Venice spills onto every page.

Invisible Cities (1972) Italo Calvino imagines Marco Polo recounting his travels to Kublai Khan – yet every city he describes is Venice.

Stabat Mater (2009) Tiziano Scarpa won Italy's top literary prize for this tale based on the true story of Antonio Vivaldi's orphan-girl orchestra.

Shakespeare in Venice (2007) Venetian historian Alberto Toso Fei unravels local legends intertwined with Shakespearean dramas.

Changing Demographics

With 59,000 official residents outnumbered by visitors most days, Venetians may seem as rare as unicorns in their own city. The population has halved since 1848, and a quarter of the city's population is retired. But local universities attract over 26,000 students, keeping the city young and full of ideas.

Living by Its Wits

Since the fall of its shipping empire, Venice has lived by its wits. The city's extraordinary support for opera, orphan orchestras and theatre kept Monteverdi, Vivaldi and Goldoni gainfully employed, and established Venice as Europe's entertainment capital. Even in the dark days of the plague, Venetian artists Titian and Tintoretto filled the city with light and colour. Venice's Biennale and film festival keep inspiration coming to the city, and the Peggy Guggenheim Collection helped raise the city's spirits and broaden its horizons after WWII.

Today Venice's arts traditions are upheld by civic institutions such as La Fenice, Goldoni Theatre, the Biennale and a dozen world-class museums. Yet with Italy's ongoing recession straining resources, public and private arts gigs are tough to find. Mose barriers are intended to prevent flooding, but with billions of euros directed towards its establishment by 2014, it has drained funds that might have supported other programs essential to city life – including the arts.

This is where you enter the picture. Venice's admirers have been the heroes of its story many times, not only funding vital restorations after the devastating flood of 1966, but also filling its concert halls and galleries, keeping its signature arts and crafts traditions alive, and providing a steady stream of outside inspiration. So when Venetians thank you for visiting, they mean it.

A Few Words from Our Sponsor

As Venice thinks ahead to its next act, its spectacular past remains both a blessing and a burden. For decades, Venice's 'Special Law' allowed the city to keep a portion of its tax revenues to defray city upkeep. This revenue has been gradually eroded as Italy redirects funds to service its growing debt, which has reached 120% of GDP. International nonprofit organisations have generously donated funds to help keep Venice afloat – but often their grants are earmarked for preservation of Venice's heritage rather than projects essential to Venice's future, such as public works maintenance or support for its living legacy of artisans and musicians.

To raise restoration funds, Venice has recently relaxed historic-preservation rules, allowing anachronistic advertising banners on historic buildings undergoing corporate-sponsored restoration works. The Ponte dei Sospiri is only now rekindling its romance with Venetian gondoliers, who avoided it while it was draped in advertising during its three-year, €3-million restoration, cheekily dubbing it the 'Bridge of Signs'.

But there may be a new candidate for the nickname. After stones fell off the Rialto bridge, Venice's council invited bids to sponsor an essential €5-million Rialto restoration; Italian fashion company Diesel won. Sighs of relief and audible groans were heard across Venice, anticipating advertising on the Renaissance landmark from the company behind the 'Be Stupid' campaign.

Alongside the Rialto, another Grand Canal landmark is under debate. The 16th-century Fontego dei Tedeschi that recently served as Venice's post office was bought for €53 million in 2008 by Veneto-based clothing retailer Benneton, which intends to turn it into a mega-store. Benneton also promised €6 million for 'public benefit', and plans to include a local artisan showcase and auditorium in the building. Though remaining fragments of the building's original frescoes by Giorgione and Titian have long been relocated at Ca' d'Oro, and its 1930s concrete restoration was admittedly grim, Italy's Culture Ministry baulked at altering Venice's Grand Canal frontage. Architect Rem Koolhaas modified the contested roof-terrace details in 2012, but Benneton must still clear heritage rules, and contend with protest banners near the Rialto reading: 'Our town is not Bennetown'.

There is an alternative to corporate sponsors: you. To cover €20 million in urgent maintenance projects, Venice has raised public transportation costs, and introduced a hotel and B&B tax in 2011. Visitors don't seem to mind: Venice tourism rose in 2012. So come to Venice, stay awhile, and help make vinyl advertising banners obsolete with Malefatte, the prison co-operative that upcycles them into handbags.

if Venice were 100 people

53 would be adults
26 would be pensioners
14 would be children
7 would be university students

ethnicity
(% of population)

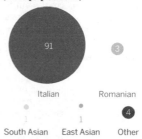

91 Italian
3 Romanian
1 South Asian
1 East Asian
4 Other

population per sq km

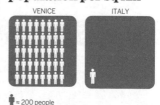

VENICE   ITALY

≈ 200 people

History

Not content with conquering the known world with its naval fleets, Venice dispatched intrepid explorers like Marco Polo to expand its trade horizons. When its maritime empire passed its high-water mark, Venice refused to concede defeat on the world stage. Instead the city itself became a stage, attracting global audiences with its vivid painting, baroque music, modern opera, independent thinkers, and parties without parallel. In its audacious 1000-year history, Venice has not only risen above sea level, but repeatedly risen to the occasion.

John Julius Norwich's *History of Venice* (1981) is an engrossing, epic account of the city's maritime empire, if a bit long on naval battles and short on recent history.

From Swamp to Empire

A malarial swamp seems like a strange place to found an empire, unless you consider the circumstances: from the 5th to the 8th century, Huns, Goths and sundry other barbarians repeatedly sacked Roman Veneto towns along the Adriatic, and made murky wetlands off the coast seem comparatively hospitable. Celtic Veneti had lived in the area relatively peacefully since 1500 BC, had been Roman citizens since 49 BC, and were not in the habit of war. When Alaric led a Visigoth invasion through the province of Venetia in 402, many Veneti fled to marshy islands in the lagoon that stretches along the province's Adriatic coast. Some Veneti tentatively returned to the mainland when the Visigoths left, but after Attila, king of the Huns, attacked in 452, many refugees took up permanent residence on the islands.

The nascent island communities elected tribunes and in 466 met in Grado, south of Aquileia, forming a loose federation. When Emperor Justinian claimed Italy's northeast coast for the Holy Roman Empire in 540, Venetia (roughly today's Veneto region) sent elected representatives to local Byzantine government in Ravenna, which reported to a central authority in Constantinople (now called Istanbul). But when warring French Lombards swept eastward across the Po plains in 568, Veneti refugees headed for the islands in unprecedented numbers, and the marsh began to look like a city. Thousands settled on the commercial centre of Torcello; others headed to the now submerged island of

TIMELINE	c 1500 BC	7th–9th Century AD	AD 726
	Celtic Veneti tribes, possibly from Anatolia (in present-day Turkey), arrive in northeast Italy to inhabit the region now known as the Veneto.	Glass-making furnaces on Torcello get fired up, creating the cathedral's Byzantine glass-mosaic masterpieces.	Orso Ipato is the first elected Venetian doge. The Byzantines consider the election an act of rebellion, and are not devastated by Ipato's assassination in 737, even if they're not behind it.

Malamocco, bucolic Chioggia, and the fishing and local trading centre of Rivoalto (colloquially known as Rialto).

Crafty Venetian settlers soon rose above their swampy circumstances, residing on land lifted above tides with wooden pylons driven into some 30m (100ft) of soft silt. When the Byzantine grip slipped, Venice seized the moment: in 726 the people of Venice elected Orso Ipato as their *dux* (Latin for leader), or doge (duke) in the Venetian dialect, the first of 118 elected Venetian dogi that would lead the city for more than a thousand years. Like some of his successors, Orso tried to turn his appointment into a hereditary monarchy. He was assassinated for overstepping his bounds; some later dogi with aspirations to absolute power were merely blinded. At first, no one held the doge's hot seat for long: Orso's successor, Teodato, managed to transfer the ducal seat to Malamocco in 742 before being deposed. Gradually the office of the doge was understood as an elected office, kept in check by two councillors and the Arengo (a popular assembly).

The Lombards had failed to conquer the lagoon, but the Franks were determined to succeed. When they invaded, the Franks were surprised by resistance led by Agnello Partecipazio from Rivoalto, a shallow area of the lagoon inaccessible to most seafaring vessels – only locals knew how to navigate the maze of deep-water channels criss-crossing the lagoon. Partecipazio was elected doge in 809, and the cluster of islets around Rivoalto became the focus of community development. Land was drained, canals were cleared, and Partecipazio built a fortress on the eventual site of the Palazzo Ducale. The duchy launched commercial and naval fleets that would become the envy of the Adriatic, with Venetian ships trading from Croatia to Egypt.

The Stolen Saint

Venice had all the makings of an independent trading centre – ports, a defensible position against Charlemagne and the Huns, leadership to settle inevitable trade disputes – but no glorious shrine to mark the city's place on the world map. So Venice did what any ambitious, God-fearing medieval city would do: it procured a patron saint. Under Byzantine rule, St Theodore (San Teodoro) had been the patron saint. But according to local legend, the evangelist St Mark (San Marco) had visited the lagoon islands and been told by an angel that his body would rest there – and some Venetian merchants decided to realise this prophecy.

In AD 828, Venetian smugglers stole St Mark's body from its resting place in Alexandria (Egypt), apparently hiding the holy corpse in a load of pork to deter inspection by Muslim customs officials. Venice summoned the best artisans from Byzantium and beyond to enshrine these

810	828	957	1094
The seat of the Venetian empire is moved from the hamlet of Malamocco on the Lido to the bustling market centre of Rivoalto, known today as the Rialto.	According to legend, the corpse of St Mark the Evangelist is smuggled from Alexandria (Egypt) to Venice in a shipment of pork. St Mark is adopted as the patron saint of Venice.	Holy Roman Emperor Otto the Great recognises key trading rights for Venice, cutting the Eastern Byzantine Christian empire out of Venice's increasingly lucrative deals.	Basilica di San Marco is consecrated. The doge's spectacular Chiesa d'Oro (Church of Gold) stands for the glory of Venice, St Mark and a brain trust of Mediterranean artisans.

relics in an official ducal church that would impress visitors with the power and glory of Venice. The usual medieval construction setbacks of riots and fires thrice destroyed exterior mosaics and weakened the underlying structure, and St Mark's bones were misplaced twice in the mayhem. With Basilica di San Marco under construction, the winged lion of St Mark was officially adopted as the emblem of the Venetian empire, symbolically setting Venice apart from Constantinople and Rome.

War & Spoils

Once terra firma was established, Venice set about shoring up its business interests. When consummate diplomat Pietro Orseolo was elected doge in 991, he positioned Venice as a neutral party between the western Holy Roman Empire and eastern territories controlled by Constantinople, and won the medieval equivalent of most-favoured-nation status from both competing empires.

Even at the outset of the Crusades, Venice maintained its strategic neutrality, continuing to trade with Muslim leaders from Syria to Spain while its port served as the launching pad for crusaders bent on wresting the Holy Land from Muslim control. With rivals Genoa and Pisa vying for lucrative contracts to equip crusaders, Venice established the world's first assembly lines in the Arsenale, capable of turning out a warship a day. Officially, La Serenissima ('The Most Serene'; the Venetian Republic) remained above the fray, joining crusading naval operations only sporadically – and almost always in return for trade concessions.

Constantinople knew who was supplying the crusaders' ships, and in the wake of the First Crusade in 1095, Venice's relations with Byzantium were strained. Byzantine emperor Manuele Comnenus played on Venetian–Genoese rivalries, staging an 1171 assault on Constantinople's Genoese colony and blaming it on Constantinople's Venetian residents, who were promptly clapped into irons. Venice sent a fleet to the rescue, but the crew contracted plague from stowaway rats, and the ships limped home without having fired a shot.

Meanwhile, Venice was under threat by land from Holy Roman Emperor Frederick Barbarossa's plans to force Italy and the Pope to recognise his authority. Back in 1154, Barbarossa's strategy must have seemed like an easy win: divide and conquer competing Italian city-states frequently on the outs with the papacy. But after several strikes, Barbarossa found northern Italy a tough territory to control. When his army was struck by plague in 1167, Barbarossa was forced to withdraw to Pavia – only to discover that 15 Italian city-states, including Venice,

Top Five Landmarks of Multicultural Venice

Ghetto
(Cannaregio)

....

Museo delle Icone
(Castello)

....

Scuola di San Giorgio degli Schiavoni (Castello)

....

Fondaco dei Turchi
(Santa Croce)

....

Palazzo Zenobio
(Dorsoduro)

1167	1171	1172	1203–04
About 200,000 Venetians occupy their own quarter in Constantinople, subject to their own laws, and make a nuisance of themselves.	After attacking Genoese in Constantinople and pointing the finger at Venice, Byzantium orders the arrest of all Venetians. A noticeable chill sets in over the Adriatic.	Venice establishes an elected Maggior Consiglio (Great Council). Though citizenry makes up 80% of the population, nobles are elected councillors.	Doge Dandolo promises to transport Frankish crusaders to the Holy Land but heads to Constantinople; his forces massacre and pillage, then return to Venice with booty.

PIRATE BRIDES

Today the only pirates you're likely to spot in Venice are the ones selling knock-off Prada handbags on the Ponte dell'Accademia, but for centuries pirate ships prowled the waters around the Lido. In AD 944, a bevy of wealthy Venetian brides sparkling with golden dowries were sailing off into the sunset to weddings on the Lido when their boat was intercepted by pirates. The women were whisked off to a nearby harbour at Caorle, but Venetians in hot pursuit discovered the lair, slaughtered the pirates and delivered the rattled brides to their weddings. The event was long commemorated with the annual Festa delle Marie (Feast of the Marys), in which Venice's 12 wealthiest families presented money for dowries to 12 poor but beautiful young women. Today the 'Marys' are remembered during Carnevale with a procession and beauty pageant crowning the most beautiful of the 12 honorary Marys.

had formed the Lombard League against him. Barbarossa met with spectacular defeat, and when things couldn't get any worse, he was excommunicated. Venice quickly recognised that it could only handle one holy war at a time, and through nimble diplomatic manoeuvres, convinced Pope Alexander III and the repentant emperor to make peace in Venice in 1177.

The Dodgy Doge

For fast talking, even the shrewdest Venetian merchant couldn't top Doge Enrico Dandolo. The doddering nonagenarian doge who'd lost his sight years before might have seemed like an easy mark to Franks seeking Venice's support in the Fourth Crusade. But Doge Dandolo drove a hard bargain: Venice would provide a fleet to carry 30,000 Crusaders, but not for less than 84,000 silver marks – approximately double the yearly income of the king of England at the time.

Only one-third of the proposed Frankish forces turned up in Venice the following year, and their leaders couldn't pay. But Venice had the ships ready, and figured it had kept its side of the bargain. To cover the balance due, Doge Dandolo suggested that the crusaders might help Venice out with a few tasks on the way to Palestine. This included invading Dalmatia and a detour to Constantinople in 1203 that would last a year, while Venetian and Frankish forces thoroughly pillaged the place.

Finally Doge Dandolo claimed that Constantinople had been suitably claimed for Christendom – never mind that it already was under Christian rule. At age 96, the doge declared himself 'Lord of a Quarter and a Half-Quarter of the Roman Empire' of Byzantium. This title con-

1271	1297	1309	1310
Traders Nicolò and Matteo Polo set sail for Xanadu, the court of Kublai Khan, with Nicolò's 20-year-old son, Marco. The Polos make a fortune in the jewellery business in Asia.	Venice ends constitutional monarchy, allowing only those from noble families to participate in the Assembly – until it runs low on funds, and allows merchants to buy noble titles.	For openly defying Rome's orders, Venice is excommunicated from the Church for the first time. Through its wealth and negotiation skills, Venice convinces Rome to relent.	With rebellion afoot, a temporary security force called the Consiglio dei Dieci (Council of Ten) is convened; it lasts almost five centuries, effectively running Venice for two.

veniently granted Venice three-eighths of the spoils, including the monumental gilt-bronze horses in Basilica di San Marco. Venetian ships opted to head home loaded with booty instead of onward to Christian duty, leaving the Franks to straggle onwards to the Crusades. With its control of the Adriatic secured, Venice began sending ships directly to the Holy Land – only this time, they were in the tourism business, ferrying pilgrims to and from holy sites.

In *The Wings of the Dove* (1902), a dapper con man and sickly heiress meet in Venice, with predictable consequences – but Henry James' gorgeous storytelling makes for riveting reading.

Venice Versus Genoa

The puppet emperor Doge Dandolo put on the throne in Constantinople didn't last long: the Genoese conspired with the Byzantines to overthrow the pro-Venetian regime. Having taken Constantinople for all it was worth, Venice set its sights on distant shores. Through the overland trip of native son Marco Polo to China in 1271–91, Venetian trade routes extended all the way to China. Rival Genoa's routes to the New World were proving slower to yield returns, and the impatient empire cast an envious eye on Venice's spice and silk-trade routes.

In 1372 Genoa and Venice finally came to blows over an incident in Cyprus, initiating eight years of maritime warfare that took a toll on Venice. To make matters worse, plague decimated Venice in the 1370s. Genoa's allies Padua and Hungary took the opportunity to seize Venetian territories on the mainland, and in 1379 a Genoese fleet appeared off the Lido. Venetian commander Carlo Zeno's war fleet had been sent out to patrol the Mediterranean, leaving the city outflanked and outnumbered.

But the Genoese made a strategic mistake: instead of invading, Genoa attempted to starve out the city. With stores of grain saved for just such an occasion, Venice worked day and night to build new ships and defences around the islands. Mustering all of Venice's might, Venetian commander Vittore Pisani mounted a counter-attack on the Genoese fleet – but his forces were inadequate. All hope seemed lost for Venice, until ships flying the lion of St Mark banner appeared on the horizon: Carlo Zeno had returned. Venice ousted the Genoese, exerting control over the Adriatic and a backyard that stretched from Dalmatia (Croatia) to Bergamo (northern Italy).

Rats & Redemption

As it was a maritime empire, ships came and went through Venice's ports daily, carrying salt, silks, spices and an unintentional import: rats infested with fleas carrying bubonic plague. In 1348 the city was still recovering from an earthquake that had destroyed houses and drained the Grand Canal, when the plague struck. Soon as many as 600 people

1348–49	1386	1403	1444
A horrific bout of the Black Death hits Venice, killing some 60% of the population. Venetian doctors observe that the worst-hit areas are by Dorsoduro's docks, where rats arrive.	A Jewish cemetery is established on the Lido, with land granted by the state. The cemetery remains in use until its abandonment with Mussolini's racial laws in 1938.	The world's first quarantine stations are established with proceeds from Venice's salt monopoly, saving lives by limiting contact with the bubonic plague.	The second Rialto bridge collapses under spectators watching a wedding flotilla. After 148 years and huge cost overruns, Antonio da Ponte provides a spectacular stone replacement.

were dying every day, and undertakers' barges raised the rueful cry: *'Corpi morti! Corpi morti!'* (Bring out your dead!) Within a year, more than 50,000 Venetians died.

No one was sure how the disease had spread, but Venice took the unprecedented step of appointing three public health officials to manage the crisis. Observing that outbreaks seemed to coincide with incoming shipments, Venice decided in 1403 to intercept all incoming ships arriving from infected areas on Isola di Lazzaretto Nuovo. Before any ship was allowed to enter the city, it was required to undergo inspection, and its passengers had to wait for a *quarantena* (40-day period) while Venetian doctors monitored them for signs of plague. This was the world's first organised quarantine station, setting a precedent that saved untold lives from plague and other infectious diseases since.

While the plague struck Italy's mainland as many as 50 more times before 1500, the outbreaks often seemed to miraculously bypass Venice. The city's faithful chalked up their salvation to divine intervention, and built the spectacular churches of Il Redentore and Basilica di Santa Maria della Salute as monumental thanks.

Traders & Traitors

Like its signature Basilica di San Marco, the Venetian empire was dazzlingly cosmopolitan. Venice turned arrivals from every nation and creed into trading partners with a common credo: as long as everyone was making money, cultural boundaries need not apply. Armenians, Turks, Greeks and Germans became neighbours along the Grand Canal, and Jewish and Muslim refugees and other groups widely persecuted in Europe settled into established communities in Venice.

Commerce provided a common bond. At the height of Venice's maritime prowess, 300 shipbuilding companies in the Arsenale had 16,000 employees. By the mid-15th century, Venice's maritime ventures had left the city swathed in golden mosaics, rustling silks and incense to cover mucky summer smells that were the downsides of a lagoon empire. In case of trade disputes or feuds among neighbours, La Serenissima retained its calm through a complex political system of checks, balances and elections, with the doge as the executive presiding over council matters.

Yet inside the red-velvet cloak of its ruling elite, Venice was hiding an iron hand. Venice's shadowy secret service, the Consiglio dei Dieci (Council of Ten), thwarted conspiracies by deploying Venetian James Bonds throughout Venice and major European capitals. Venice had no qualms about spying on its own citizens to ensure a balance of power, and trials, torture and executions were carried out in secret. Still,

Top Five for Byzantine Splendour

Basilica di San Marco (San Marco)

Museo di Torcello (Torcello)

Chiesa di San Zaccaria (Castello)

Chiesa dei SS Maria e Donato (Murano)

Chiesa di San Giacomo dell'Orio (Santa Croce)

1470	1492	1494
Cyprus is the latest of Venice's conquests, which stretch across the mainland to Bergamo, through the Aegean to Crete, and to Middle East trading outposts in Jaffa, Beirut and Alexandria.	Genoese Cristoforo Colombo's voyage kicks off the age of discovery and Venice's long slide into obsolescence, as the Portuguese and Spanish bypass its customs controls.	Aldo Manuzio founds Aldine Press, introducing mass-market paperbacks, including Dante's *Divine Comedy*. By 1500, one in six books published in Europe is printed in Venice.

KIMBERLEY COOLE / GETTY IMAGES ©

Rialto bridge (p107)

compared with its neighbours at the time, Venice remained a haven of tolerance.

Occasionally, the Council made examples of lawbreakers. Denunciations of wrongdoers were nailed to the door of the Palazzo Ducale and published by Venice's presses – and when that failed to convey the message, the Council of Ten ordered the bludgeoning or decapitation of those found guilty of crimes against the doge. Severed heads were placed atop columns outside the Palazzo Ducale and sundry parts distributed for display in the *sestieri* (neighbourhoods) for exactly three nights and four days, until they started to smell.

Friendly Foes

Never mind that Venice sacked Constantinople, or that Constantinople sided with Genoa against Venice: warfare wasn't enough to deter the two maritime powers from doing brisk business with one another for centuries. When Constantinople fell to Ottoman rule in 1453, business carried on as usual. The rival powers understood one another very well; the Venetian language was widely spoken across the eastern Mediterranean.

There were some awkward moments in diplomatic relations, however. Both sides periodically took prisoners of war, and seldom released them. Prisoners were routinely forced into servitude and/or religious conversion. In 1428 Venice established a special prison in Dorsoduro to convert Muslim Turkish women prisoners to Christianity. Ottomans tended to hold Venetians for ransom, though it wasn't always an especially profitable gambit. Though Venice officially installed collection boxes in churches in 1586 to raise funds for POW ransom, they remained mostly empty.

Director Luchino Visconti takes on Nobel Prize winner Thomas Mann's story of a Mahler-esque composer, an infatuation and a deadly outbreak in *Death in Venice* (1971).

Prisoners & Princesses

After Suleiman the Magnificent took over Cyprus in 1571, Venice sensed its maritime power slipping, and allied with the papal states, Spain and even arch-rival Genoa to keep the Ottoman sultan at bay. The same year a huge allied fleet (much of it provided by Venice) routed the Turks off Lepanto (Greece) and Sebastiano Venier and his Venetian fleet sailed home with 100 Turkish women as war trophies.

Legend has it that when Turkish troops took over the island of Paros, the POWs included Cecilia Venier-Baffo, who was apparently the illegitimate daughter of Venice's noble Venier family, a niece of the doge, and possibly the cousin of Sebastiano (of Lepanto fame). Cecilia became the favourite wife of Sultan Salim II in Constantinople, and when he died in 1574 she took control as Sultana Nurbani (Princess of Light).

1498	1499	1508	1516
Portuguese explorer Vasco da Gama sails around the Cape of Good Hope, and the boom in trans-Atlantic trade shuts out many Venetian merchants.	To ensure Venice doesn't lose valuable time, a clockwatcher moves into the Torre dell'Orlogio – and stays there for 500 years.	The Holy Roman Empire, papal states, Spain and France form the League of Cambrai against Venice – but with Venice cutting side deals, ensuing war doesn't change the map much.	A proclamation declares that Jewish residents of Venice are to live in a designated zone called the Ghetto, with access to the area closed at midnight by guards.

The regent of Sultan Murad III, she was a faithful pen pal of Queen Elizabeth I of Britain and Catherine de Medici of France. According to historian Alberto Toso Fei, the Sultana's policies were so favourable to Venetian interests that the Venetian senate set aside special funds to fulfil her wishes for Venetian specialities, from lapdogs to golden cushions. Genoa wasn't pleased by her favouritism, and in 1582 she was poisoned to death by what appears to have been Genoese assassins.

The Age of Decadence

While Italy's city-states continued to plot against one another, they were increasingly eclipsed by marriages cementing alliances among France, Henry VIII's England and the Habsburg Empire. As it lost ground to these European nation-states and the seas to pirates and Ottomans, Venice took a different tack, and began conquering Europe by charm.

Sensations & Scandals

Venice's star attractions were its parties, music, women and art. Nunneries in Venice held soirées to rival those in its *ridotti* (casinos), and Carnevale lasted up to three months. Claudio Monteverdi was hired as choir director of San Marco in 1613, introducing multi-part harmonies and historical operas with crowd-pleasing tragicomic scenes. Monteverdi's modern opera caught on: by the end of the 17th century, Venice's season included as many as 30 operas, including 10 brand-new operas composed for Venetian venues.

New orchestras required musicians, but Venice came up with a ready workforce: orphan girls. Circumstances had conspired to produce an unprecedented number of Venetian orphans: on the one hand were plague and snake-oil cures, and on the other were scandalous masquerade parties and flourishing prostitution. Funds poured in from anonymous donors to support *ospedaletti* (orphanages), and the great baroque composers Antonio Vivaldi and Domenico Cimarosa were hired to lead orphan orchestras. The Venetian state took on the care and musical training of the city's orphan girls, who earned their keep by performing at public functions and *ospedaletti* fundraising galas. Visiting diplomats treated to orphan concerts were well advised to tip the orphan performers: you never knew whose illegitimate daughter you might be insulting otherwise.

Socialites began gifting snuffboxes and portraits painted by Venetian artists as fashionable tokens of their esteem, and salon habitués across Europe became accustomed to mythological and biblical themes painted in luminous Venetian colours, with the unmistakable city on the water as a backdrop. On baroque church ceilings across Venice, fres-

PARTIES

Venetian party planners outdid themselves with the 1574 reception for King Henry III of France. The king's barge was greeted with glass-blowers performing on rafts, bevvies of Venetian beauties dressed in white, a 1200-course meal, and decorations provided by an all-star committee of Palladio, Veronese and Tintoretto.

1564	1571	1575-6	1609
When noblewoman Bianca Cappello runs off with a Florentine clerk, she is sentenced to death for treason – but once she becomes the Grand Duchess of Tuscany, all is forgiven.	Venice and the Holy League of Catholic states defeat Ottoman forces at the naval Battle of Lepanto, thanks in part to a technical advantage: cannons and guns versus archers.	Plague claims many lives, including Titian's. Quarantine aids Venice's recovery; a new painting cycle by Tintoretto is dedicated to San Rocco, patron saint of the plague-stricken.	Venice passes a law defining penalties for casino employees caught cheating: cutting the ears and nose, plus 10 to 20 years of incarceration.

VENICE'S 'HONEST COURTESANS'

High praise, high pay and even high honours: Venice's *cortigiane oneste* were no ordinary strumpets. An 'honest courtesan' earned the title not by offering a fair price, but by providing added value with style, education and wit that reflected well on her patrons. They were not always beautiful or young, but *cortigiane oneste* were well educated, dazzling their admirers with poetry, music, philosophical insights and apt social critiques. In the 16th century, some Venetian families of limited means spared no expense on their daughters' educations: beyond an advantageous marriage or career, educated women who become *cortigiane oneste* could command prices 60 times those of the average *cortigiana di lume* ('courtesan of the lamp' – streetwalker).

Far from hiding their trade, a catalogue of 210 of Venice's *piu honorate cortigiane* (most honoured courtesans) was published in 1565, listing contact information and going rates, payable directly to the courtesan's servant, her mother or, occasionally, her husband. A *cortigiana onesta* might circulate in Venetian society as the known mistress of one or more admirers, who compensated her for her company rather than services rendered, and with an allowance rather than pay per hour – though on rare occasions, an exceptionally clever Petrarchan sonnet might win her favours. Syphilis was an occupational hazard, and special hospices were founded for infirm courtesans.

One of the better-paid courtesans was Veronica Franco (1546–91), the daughter of a *cortigiana onesta*. She married a wealthy doctor and had a child as a teenager, but by 20 left her stormy marriage to become a courtesan. By age 30, Franco had patrons including Henry III of France, and she'd published an acclaimed volume of her poetry. When an outbreak of the plague forced Franco to flee the city in 1575, her home was looted. She returned to the city two years later to provide for her six children and orphaned relatives, only to face Inquisition accusations of witchcraft. Franco defended herself successfully, and went on to publish 50 of her letters (including two sonnets to Henry III) in 1580. She petitioned the city to establish a charity for courtesans and their children, but she died before her vision could be realised.

coed angels play heavenly music on lutes and trumpets – instruments officially banned from churches by Rome. Venetian art became incredibly daring, with Titian and Veronese bringing voluptuous red colours and sly social commentary to familiar religious subjects.

Pulling Rank: The Pope & the Doge

Rome repeatedly censured Venice for depicting holy subjects in an earthy, Venetian light, and for playing toe-tapping tunes in churches, but such censorship was largely ignored within Venice. According to late-16th-century gossip, Cardinal Camillo Borghese had a beef with the

1630	1669	1678	1703–40
The plague kills a third of Venice's population within 16 months. With few leaders surviving, Venice allows wealthy Venetians to buy their way into the Golden Book of nobles.	The Venetian colony of Crete is lost to the Ottoman Turks, yet the two powers continue to trade with one another – despite repeated objections from Rome.	Venetian scholar Eleonora Lucrezia Cornaro Piscopia is the first woman to receive a university degree in Europe, earning her doctorate in philosophy at the University of Padua.	Antonio Vivaldi is musical director at La Pietà, composing many concertos for orchestras of orphan girls. He is fired in 1709 but swiftly recalled, to Venice's immense credit.

Venetian ambassador to Rome, Leonardo Donà, ever since the two exchanged heated words in the Roman halls of power. The cardinal hissed that, were he pope, he'd excommunicate the entire Venetian populace. 'And I would thumb my nose at the excommunication', retorted Donà.

As fate would have it, by 1606 cardinal and ambassador were promoted to Pope Paul V and doge, respectively. Rome had never appreciated Venice's insistence on reserving a degree of control over Church matters, and when Venice claimed that zoning laws required its approval of church expansion plans within the city, Pope Paul V issued a papal bull excommunicating Venice. As promised, Doge Donà defied the bull, ordering all churches to remain open on Venetian territory. Any church that obeyed the bull would have its doors permanently closed, property seized and clergy exiled from Venice.

Venetian-born monk and philosopher Paolo Sarpi convincingly argued Venice's case, claiming Venice's right to self-determination came directly from God, not through Rome. Before the excommunication could cause further loss of Church property in Venice, or other Catholic territories became convinced by Sarpi's argument, Pope Paul V rescinded his bull.

But the power struggle didn't stop there. After Rome issued its umpteenth official reprimand of Venice, the Venetian state decided to do some paperwork of its own. Venice conducted an official 1767 audit of 11 million golden ducats in revenues rendered to Rome in the previous decade, and decided to cut its losses: 127 Veneto monasteries and convents were closed, cutting the local clerical population in half and redirecting millions of ducats to Venice's coffers.

**Top Five
Hallmarks
of Venetian
Decadence**

....

Carnevale

....

*Ca' Rezzonico
(Dorsoduro)*

....

*Ponte delle Tette
(San Polo)*

....

*Palazzo Mocenigo
(Santa Croce)*

....

*Palazzo Fortuny
(San Marco)*

Red Lights, White Widows & Grey Areas

While Roman clerics furiously scribbled their disapproval, Venetian trends stealthily took over drawing rooms across the continent, and Grand Canal *palazzi* (palaces) and Veneto villas lining the Riviera Brenta became playgrounds for Europe's upper crust.

Venetian women's lavish finery, staggering platform shoes up to 50cm high and masculine quiff hairdos scandalised visiting European nobility, until Venice felt obliged to enact sumptuary laws preventing women from wearing manly hairstyles and blinding displays of jewels on dipping décolletages. Venetian noblewomen complained to the doge and the Pope, and the restrictions were soon dropped.

With maritime trade revenues dipping and the value of the Venetian ducat slipping in the 16th century, Venice's fleshpots brought in far too much valuable foreign currency to be outlawed. Instead, Venice opted for regulation and taxation. Rather than baring all in the rough-and-ready streets around the Rialto, prostitutes could only display their

1718	1797	1807
Venice and Austria sign the Treaty of Passarowitz with the Ottoman Empire, splitting prime coastal territory and leaving Venice with nominal control and some Ionian islands.	The segregation of Jewish Venetians comes to an end and the gates of the Ghetto are opened, just as Napoleon arrives in the city.	Napoleon suppresses religious orders to quell dissent. Upon Independence, some churches are reconsecrated – but many aren't, serving instead as archives or tourist attractions.

The Ghetto (p124)

wares from the waist up in windows, or sit bare-legged on windowsills. Venice decreed that to distinguish themselves from noblewomen who increasingly dressed like them, ladies of the night should ride in gondolas with red lights. By the end of the 16th century, the town was flush with some 12,000 registered prostitutes, creating a literal red-light district. Today red beacons mostly signal construction, but you can enjoy decadent dinners at Antiche Carampane (Old Streetwalkers) near Ponte delle Tette (Tits Bridge).

PRINCE OF PLEASURE

Never was a hedonist born at a better time and in a more appropriate place: 18th-century Venice had retired from the arduous business of running a maritime empire, and was well into its new career as the pleasure capital of Europe when Giacomo Casanova (1725–98) arrived on the scene. He was abandoned as a young boy, and became a gambler and rake on the make while studying law in Padua. He graduated by age 17 to take up a position with the Church in Venice, but adventuring soon became Casanova's primary career, with minor sidelines in penning love letters for cardinals, looking good in military uniform, and playing violin badly in an orchestra of drunkards. His charm won him warm welcomes into the homes of wealthy patrons – and the beds of their wives, lovers and daughters.

Venice was a licentious place, but some political limits still applied. Though Casanova's escapades may have been dangerous to marriages, his dalliances with Freemasonry and banned books were considered nothing less than a threat to the state. After an evening foursome with the French ambassador and a couple of nuns, Casanova was arrested on the nebulous charge of 'outrages against religion' and dragged to the Piombi, the Palazzo Ducale's dreaded attic prison. Sentenced to five years in a sweltering, flea-infested cell, Casanova complained bitterly, and carved an escape hatch through the wooden floor – but just when he was ready to make his getaway, a sympathetic warden had him moved to a more comfortable cell. Casanova soon devised plan B: he escaped through the roof of his new cell, entered the palace, and casually breezed past the guards in the morning.

Casanova fled Venice to make his fortune in Paris and serve briefly as a French spy. But his extracurricular habits caused him no end of trouble: he went broke in Germany, survived a duel in Poland, fathered and abandoned several children (possibly including a child by one of his daughters), and contracted venereal diseases in England (despite occasional use of a linen condom prototype). Late in life, he returned to Venice as a celebrity, and served the government as a spy – but he was exiled for publishing a satire of the nobility. He wound up as a librarian in an isolated castle in Bohemia, where boredom drove him to finally write his memoirs. In the end, he concluded, 'I can say I have lived'.

1814	1836	
Austria takes Venice as a war trophy and imposes order with thousands of troops, a house-numbering system and heavy taxes that push Venice to the brink of starvation.	Fire guts Venice's legendary public opera house, but a new version soon rises from the ashes. When La Fenice (The Phoenix) burns again in 1996, an exact replica is rebuilt.	

Teatro La Fenice (p66)

Beyond red lights ringing the Rialto, 16th- to 18th-century visitors encountered broad grey areas in Venetian social mores. Far from being shunned by polite society, Venice's 'honest courtesans' became widely admired as poets, musicians and taste makers. As free-spirited, financially independent Venetian women took lovers and accepted lavish gifts from admirers in the 16th to 18th centuries, there became a certain fluidity surrounding the definition of a *cortigiana* (courtesan). With their husbands at sea for months or years, Venice's 'white widows' took young, handsome *cicisbei* (manservants) to tend their needs. Not coincidentally, Venetian ladies occasionally fell into religious fervours entailing a trimester-long seclusion.

During winter masquerades and Carnevale, Venice's nobility regularly escaped the tedium of salons and official duties under masks and cloaks, generating enough gossip to last until the summer social season in Riviera Brenta villas provided fresh scandal. Some Venetians dropped the mask of propriety altogether, openly cohabitating with lovers year-round and acknowledging illegitimate heirs in their wills. By the 18th century, less than 40% of Venetian nobles bothered with the formality of marriage, and the regularity of Venetian annulments scandalised even visiting French courtiers.

From Colonisation to Revolution

When Napoleon arrived in 1797, Venice had been reduced by plague and circumstances from 175,000 to fewer than 100,000 people, and their reputation as fierce partiers did nothing to prevent the French and Austrians from handing the city back and forth as a war trophy. Venice declared its neutrality in the war between France and Austria, but that didn't stop Napoleon. Venetian warships managed to deter one French ship by the Lido, but when Napoleon made it clear he intended to destroy the city if it resisted, the Maggior Consiglio (Grand Council) decreed the end of the Republic. The doge reportedly doffed the signature cap of his office with a sigh, saying, 'I won't be needing this any more'. Rioting citizens were incensed by such cowardice, but French forces soon ended the insurrection, and began systematically plundering the city.

Though Napoleon only controlled Venice sporadically for a total of about 11 years, the impact of his reign is still visible. Napoleon grabbed any Venetian art masterpiece that wasn't nailed down, and displaced religious orders to make room for museums and trophy galleries in the Gallerie dell'Accademia and Museo Correr. Napoleon's city planners lifted remaining restrictions on the Jewish Ghetto, filled in canals and widened city streets to facilitate movement of troops and loot; his

1840	1846	1848	1866
At La Serenissima's height, Venice's fabled Golden Book of nobles included more than 1200 families – but by 1840, all but 200 were destitute and subsisting on charity.	The first train crosses to the mainland. The feat is bittersweet: churches were demolished for the station, trains brought occupying Austrian troops, and Venetians footed the bill.	Daniele Manin leads an anti-Austrian rebellion and declares Venice a republic for 17 months. Austrians retake the city in 1849, and Venice remains under Austrian control for 17 years.	Venice and the Veneto join the new Kingdom of Italy. The unification of Italy is complete when Rome is made the capital in 1870.

decorators established a style of gaudy gold cornices and whimsical grotesques. Napoleon lost control of Venice in 1814, and two years later one-quarter of Venice's population was destitute.

But Austria had grand plans for Venice, and expected impoverished Venetians to foot the bill. They were obliged to house Austrian soldiers, who spent off-duty hours carousing with bullfights, beer and their new happy-hour invention, the *spritz* (a *prosecco*-and-bitters cocktail). Finding their way back home afterwards was a challenge in Venetian *calli* (alleyways), so the Austrians implemented a street-numbering system. To bring in reinforcements and supplies, they dredged and deepened entrances to the lagoon for ease of shipping access and began a train bridge in 1841 – all with Venetian labour and special Venetian taxes. To make way for the new train station in 1846, *scuole* (religious confraternities) and a palace were demolished.

With no say in the Austrian puppet government running Venice, many Venetians voted with their feet: under the Austrians, the population fell from 138,000 to 99,000. When a young lawyer named Daniele Manin suggested reforms to Venice's puppet government in 1848, he was tossed into prison – sparking a popular uprising against the Austrians that would last 17 months. Austria responded by bombarding and blockading the city. In July, Austria began a 24-day artillery bombardment, raining some 23,000 shells down on the city and its increasingly famished and cholera-stricken populace, until Manin finally managed to negotiate a surrender to Austria with a guarantee of no reprisals. Yet the indignity of Austria's suppression continued to fester, and when presented with the option in 1866, the people of Venice and the Veneto voted to join the new independent kingdom of Italy under King Vittorio Emanuele II.

Life During Wartime

One of Italy's most beloved graphic novels, *Corto Maltese in Fables of Venice* (originally published in 1967) follows Hugo Pratt's cosmopolitan sea captain as he cracks the mysteries of the *calli* (alleyways).

Glamorous Venice gradually took on a workaday aspect in the 19th century, with factories springing up on Giudecca and around Mestre and Padua, and textile industries setting up shop around Vicenza and Treviso. As an increasingly strategic industrial area, Venice began to seem like a port worth reclaiming. But when Austro-Hungarian forces advanced on Venice, they were confronted by Italy's naval marines. Two days after Italy declared war on Austria in 1915, air raids on the city began, and would continue intermittently throughout WWI until 1918. Venice was lucky: the bombardments caused little damage or loss of life.

When Mussolini rose to power after WWI, he was determined to turn the Veneto into a modern industrial powerhouse and a model Fas-

1918	1933	1943	1948
Austro-Hungarian planes drop almost 300 bombs on Venice in WWI, but their aim is off, resulting in mercifully little loss of life or damage.	Mussolini opens the Ponte della Libertà (Freedom Bridge) from Mestre to Venice. The 3.85km-long, two-lane highway remains the only access to Venice by car.	From the Ghetto, 256 Jewish Venetians are rounded up and deported to concentration camps. A memorial in Campo del Ghetto commemorates those lost in the camps.	Peggy Guggenheim arrives with major modernists, renewing interest in Italian art, reclaiming Futurism from the Fascists and championing Venetian abstract expressionism.

cist society – despite Venice's famously laissez-faire outlook. Mussolini constructed a roadway from the mainland to Venice, literally bringing the free-wheeling city into line with the rest of Italy. While Italy's largest Fascist rallies were held in the boulevards of Padua, with up to

VENETIANS WHO CHANGED HISTORY

Doge Marin Falier (1285–1355)

Claim to fame The hot-headed doge was in power for eight months. After a Venetian courtier apparently made a joke at his expense, the doge plotted to overthrow Venice's noble council. Details leaked out and he was arrested and beheaded within the hour.

Legacy In the Palazzo Ducale's Sala del Maggior Consiglio, Doge Falier's portrait is blacked out, and his sarcophagus was emptied and used as a washbasin in Venice's public hospital. The thwarted coup justified consolidation of power by Venice's security service, the Consiglio dei Dieci, which encouraged Venetians to spy on their neighbours.

Paolo Sarpi (1552–1623)

Claim to fame When the Pope excommunicated the republic of Venice in 1606 for ignoring Rome's rulings, Servite monk Paolo Sarpi defended Venice's 'God-given' right to govern its people. Under Sarpi's direction, Venice ordered churches to ignore the excommunication, and Venetian religious orders that failed to hold Mass were closed and had their property seized. The excommunication was lifted a year later.

Legacy Six months after Rome recanted, five would-be assassins stabbed Sarpi in Campo Santa Fosca and fled to papal territories. Sarpi survived, writing legal and scientific tracts for 13 more years. Venice raised a monument in Sarpi's honour on the site of the attempted assassination in Cannaregio.

Daniele Manin (1804–57)

Claim to fame After suggesting reforms to Austrian rulers, this young Venetian lawyer was arrested for treason. On 22 March 1848, fellow Venetians rescued him from jail to lead an insurrection. Manin was declared president of Venice, and for 17 months the republic survived Austrian bombardment, starvation and cholera. Manin negotiated favourable terms for surrender, with amnesty granted to all Venetians except himself.

Legacy Manin was exiled to France, where he agitated for an independent Italy. Manin did not live to see his dream fulfilled, but in 1868 his remains were returned to Venice for a state funeral. Today, Via Lunga XXII Marzo (22 March St) commemorates the Venice uprising.

1955	1966	2003	2006
Venice opens Italy's first museum of Jewish history, the Museo Ebraico, in the historic Ghetto. The museum opens the Ghetto's synagogues and Lido cemetery to visitors.	Record floods cause widespread damage and unleash debate on measures to protect Venice. Its admirers around the world rally to save the city, and rescue its treasures from lagoon muck.	After decades of debate, Berlusconi launches the construction of Modulo Sperimentale Elettromeccanico (Mose) to prevent disastrous flooding from rising sea levels.	With support from the city, François Pinault moves his world-class contemporary-art collection to Giorgio Masari's 1749 Palazzo Grassi, redesigned by Tadao Ando.

300,000 participants, Italian Resistance leaders met in Padua's parks to plot uprisings throughout northern Italy. When Mussolini's grip on the region began to weaken, partisans joined Allied troops to wrest the Veneto from Fascist control.

Venice emerged relatively unscathed from Allied bombing campaigns that targeted mainland industrial sites, and was liberated by New Zealand troops in 1945 – but the mass deportation of Venice's historic Jewish population in 1943 shook Venice to its very moorings. When the Veneto began to rebound after the war, many Venetians left for the mainland, Milan and other postwar economic centres. The legendary lagoon city seemed mired in the mud, unable to reconcile its recent history with its past grandeur, and unsure of its future.

Keeping Venice Afloat

When a devastating flood hit the city in 1966, a world of admirers rushed to Venice's rescue. Fifty organisations worldwide rallied to preserve the city, raising €50 million to complete 1500 restoration projects over 40 years. For its exceptional cultural contributions, Venice and its lagoon have been named a Unesco World Heritage site.

While the city is actively seeking sustainable solutions to rising water levels, Venice can also seem inundated by a wave of admirers at high noon in high season, when an average of two cruise ships a day release thousands of passengers for mad dashes on Piazza San Marco. Venetian protestors took to the Giudecca Canal in rowboats in September 2012, symbolically blocking the entry of ships they claim put undue environmental stress on the city.

But when it comes to responsible, intrepid travellers, Venice wants to see more of you, not less. The more time you spend here – staying in Venice's neighbourhoods, supporting Venetian artisans and musicians, trading Venetian toasts over happy hour – the more you become part of Venice's long and exceptionally colourful history of international exchange.

2008	2009	2012	2013
The first new bridge across the Grand Canal since before WWII, Ponte di Calatrava opens amid controversy over its modernity, cost and wheelchair accessibility.	Tadao Ando reinvents abandoned Punta della Dogana customs houses as a museum showcasing French billionaire Pinault's provocative art-installation collection.	Italy's Culture Ministry blocks a Rem Koolhaas–designed roof terrace for conversion of Benneton's Fontego dei Tedeschi into a department store.	International readers and 50 Venetian authors rally in Libreria Marciana to preserve Venetian bookstores as global literary culture hubs.

Architecture

Lulls in Venetian happy-hour conversation are easily resolved with one innocent question: so what is Venetian architecture? Everyone has a pet period in Venice's chequered architectural history, and hardly anyone agrees which is Venice's defining moment. Ruskin waxed rhapsodic about Venetian Gothic and detested Palladio; Palladians rebuffed baroque; fans of regal rococo were scandalised by the Lido's louche Liberty (Italian art nouveau); and pretty much everyone was horrified by the inclinations of industry to strip Venice of all ornamentation. Now that the latest architectural trend is creative repurposing, it's all making a comeback.

Engineering Marvels

Over the centuries, Venetian architecture has evolved into such a dazzling composite of materials, styles and influences that you might overlook its singular defining feature: it floats. Thousands of wood pylons sunk into lagoon mud support stone foundations, built up with elegant brickwork and rustic ceiling beams, low *sotoportegi* (passageways) and lofty loggias, grand water gates and hidden *cortile* (courtyards). Instead of disguising or wallpapering over these essential Venetian structural elements, modern architects have begun highlighting them. With this approach, the Fondazione Giorgio Cini converted a naval academy into a gallery, Tadao Ando turned Punta della Dogana customs houses into a contemporary-art showplace, and Renzo Piano transformed historic Maggazini del Sale (salt warehouses) into a rotating gallery space for Fondazione Emilio Vedova. With original load-bearing supports and brickwork exposed to public admiration, Venice's new-old architecture seems more fresh and vital than ever.

More than 1000 years of architectural history arc covered on the short trip down the Grand Canal, lined with 200 palaces that range from Venetian Gothic with Moorish flourishes (the Ca' d'Oro) to postmodern neo-classical (Palazzo Grassi).

Veneto-Byzantine

If Venice seems to have unfair aesthetic advantages, it did have an early start: cosmopolitan flair has made Venetian architecture a standout since the 7th century. While Venice proper was still a motley, muddy outpost of refugee settlements, the nearby island of Torcello was a booming Byzantine trade hub of 20,000 to 30,000 people. At its spiritual centre was the Basilica di Santa Maria Assunta, which from afar looks like a Byzantine-style basilica on loan from Ravenna. But look closely: those 7th- to 9th-century apses have Romanesque arches, and the iconostasis separating the central nave from the presbytery is straight out of an Eastern Orthodox church. Back in Torcello's heyday, traders from France, Greece or Turkey could have stepped off their boats and into this church, and all felt at home.

But to signal to visitors that they had arrived in a powerful trading centre, Santa Maria Assunta glitters with 12th- to 13th-century golden mosaics. Recent excavations reveal Torcello glassworks dating from the 7th century, and those furnaces would have been kept glowing through the night to produce the thousands of tiny glass tesserae (tiles) needed to create the mesmerising Madonna hovering over the altar – not to mention the rather alarmingly detailed Last Judgment mosaic, with hellfire licking at the dancing feet of the damned.

TOP FIVE CONTROVERSIAL BRIDGES

Ponte di Calatrava Officially known as Ponte della Costituzione (Constitution Bridge), Spanish architect Santiago Calatrava's modern bridge between Piazzale Roma and Ferrovia was commissioned for €4 million in 1999, and for a decade was variously denounced as unnecessary, inappropriate and wheelchair-inaccessible. Though the bridge cost more than triple the original estimate, it also received private backing by companies headquartered at the foot of the bridge – so some Venetians refer to it as 'Benetton Bridge'. Foot traffic is noticeably diverting over this minimalist arc of steel, glass and stone. Wheelchair access has been added, but with a projected 15-minute wait and crossing time, the *vaporetto* (water bus) seems comparatively efficient.

Ponte di Rialto The main bridge across the Grand Canal was disaster-prone for centuries: the original 1255 wooden structure burned during a 1310 revolt, and its replacement collapsed under spectators watching a 1444 wedding parade. The state couldn't gather funds for a 1551 stone bridge project pitched for by Palladio, Sansovino and Michelangelo, and the task fell to Antonio da Ponte in 1588. Cost over-runs were enormous: as the stonework settled, the bridge cracked, and legend has it that only a deal with the Devil allowed da Ponte to finish by 1592. Architect Vincenzo Scamozzi sniffed that the structure was doomed, but da Ponte's bridge has remained a diabolically clever masterpiece of engineering – at least until chunks of bridge pylons abruptly dropped into the canal in 2011. Fashion company Diesel recently won a €5-million restoration bid, which may include advertising banners on the bridge's construction scaffolding. Some Venetians are relieved by the Rialto restoration; others consider it a new deal with the Devil.

Ponte dei Pugni (Bridge of the Fists) Turf battles were regularly fought on this pugnacious Dorsoduro bridge between residents of Venice's north end, the Nicolotti, and its south end, the Castellani. Deadly brawls evolved into full-contact boxing matches, with starting footholds marked in the corners of the bridge (which was restored in 2005). It was all fun and games even after someone's eye was put out; bouts ended with fighters bloodied, bruised and bobbing in the canal. King Henry III of France apparently enjoyed the spectacle, but escalation into deadly knife fights in 1705 ended the practice. Today Venetians compete for neighbourhood bragging rights with regattas instead.

Ponte delle Tette 'Tits Bridge' got its name in the late 15th century, when neighbourhood prostitutes were encouraged to display their wares in the windows of buildings above the bridge instead of taking their marketing campaigns to the streets. According to local lore (and rather bizarre logic), this display was intended to curb a dramatic increase in sodomy. The bridge leads to Rio Terà delle Carampane, named after a noble family's house (Ca' Rampani) that became a notorious hang-out for local streetwalkers (dubbed *carampane*).

Ponte dei Sospiri Built by Antonio Contino in 1600 and given its 'Bridge of Sighs' nickname by Lord Byron, the bridge connects the upper storeys of the Palazzo Ducale and Prigioni Nuove (New Prisons). According to Byron's conceit, doomed prisoners would sigh at their last glimpse of lovely Venice through the bridge's windows – but as you'll notice on Palazzo Ducale tours, the lagoon is scarcely visible through the stonework-screened windows. Legend has it that couples kissing under the bridge will remain in love forever, but no doubt Venice's prisoners took a less romantic view of the construction.

Breakout Byzantine Style

When Venice made its definitive break with the Byzantine empire in the 9th century, it needed a landmark to set the city apart, and a platform to launch its golden age of maritime commerce. Basilica di San Marco captures Venice's grand designs in five vast gold mosaic domes, refracting stray sunbeams like an indoor fireworks display. Even today, the sight elicits audible gasps from crowds of international admirers. The basilica began with a triple nave in the 9th century, but after a fire two wings were added to form a Greek cross, in an idea borrowed from the Church of the Holy Apostles in Constantinople. The finest artisans from around the Mediterranean were brought in to raise the basilica's dazzle factor to mind-boggling, from 11th- to 13th-century marble relief masterpieces over the Romanesque entry arches to the intricate Islamic geometry of 12th- to 13th-century inlaid semiprecious stone floors.

Since the basilica was the official chapel of the doge, every time Venice conquered new territory by commerce or force, the basilica displayed the doge's share of the loot – hence the walls of polychrome marble pilfered from Egypt, and 2nd-century Roman bronze horses looted from Constantinople's hippodrome in 1204. The basilica's ornament shifted over the centuries from Gothic to Renaissance, but the message to visiting dignitaries remained the same: the glory above may be God's, but the power below rested with the doge.

Romanesque

Romanesque was all the rage across Western Europe in the 9th century, from the Lombard plains to Tuscany, southern France to northeast Spain and, later, Germany and England. While the materials ranged from basic brick to elaborate marble, Romanesque rounded archways, barrel-vaulted ceilings, triple naves and calming cloisters came to define medieval church architecture. This austere, classical style was a deliberate reference to the Roman empire and early martyrs who sacrificed all for the Church, reminding the faithful of their own duty through the Crusades. But in case the architecture failed to send the message, sculptural reliefs were added, heralding heroism on entry portals – and putting the fear of the devil into unbelievers, with angels and demons carved into stone capitals in creepy crypts.

Venice's new-old architecture is more fresh and vital than ever.

As Venice became a maritime empire in the 13th century, many of the city's smaller Byzantine and early Romanesque buildings were swept away to make room for International Gothic grandeur. The finest examples of Romanesque in the Veneto – and possibly in northern Italy – are Verona's vast 12th- to 14th-century Basilica di San Zeno Maggiore and Padua's frescoed jewel of a Romanesque Baptistry. Within Venice, you can admire Romanesque simplicity in Chiesa di San Giacomo dell'Orio.

Venetian Gothic

Soaring spires and flying buttresses rose above Paris in the 12th century, making the rest of Europe suddenly seem small and squat by comparison. Soon every European capital was trying to top Paris with Gothic marvels of their own, featuring deceptively delicate ribbed cross-vaulting that distributed the weight of stone walls and allowed openings for vast stained-glass windows.

Europe's medieval superpowers used this grand international style to showcase their splendour and status. Venice one-upped its neighbours not with height but by inventing its own version of Gothic. Venice had been trading across the Mediterranean with partners from Lebanon to North Africa for centuries, and the constant exchange of building materials, engineering innovations and aesthetic ideals led to a creative cross-pollination in Western and Middle Eastern architecture. Instead of framing windows with the ordinary ogive (pointed) arch common to France and Germany, Venice added an elegantly tapered, Moorish flourish to its arches, with a trilobate (three-lobed) shape that became a signature of Venetian Gothic at Ca' d'Oro.

Brick Gothic

While Tuscany, like France and Germany, used marble for Gothic cathedrals, Venice showcased a more austere, cerebral style with clever brickwork and a Latin cross plan at I Frari, completed in 1443 after a century's work, and Zanipolo, consecrated in 1430. The more fanciful brick Madonna dell'Orto was built on 10th-century foundations, but its facade was lightened up with lacy white porphyry ornament in 1460–64. This white stone framing red brick may have Middle Eastern origins: the style is pronounced in Yemen, where Venice's Marco Polo established trade relations in the 13th century.

Wagering which of Venice's brick *campanile* (bell towers) will next fall victim to shifting *barene* (mud banks) is a morbid Venetian pastime – but don't bet on the leaning tower of San Giorgio dei Greci, which has slouched ever since 1592. San Marco's *campanile* stood ramrod-straight until its 1902 collapse.

Secular Gothic

Gothic architecture was so complicated and expensive that it was usually reserved for cathedrals in wealthy parishes – but Venice decided that if it was good enough for God, then it was good enough for the doge. A rare and extravagant secular Gothic construction, the Palazzo Ducale was built in grand Venetian Gothic style beginning in 1340, with refinements and extensions continuing through the 15th century. The palace was just finished when a fire swept through the building in 1577, leaving Venice with a tricky choice: rebuild in the original *gotico fiorito* (flamboyant Gothic) style, or go with the trendy new Renaissance style proposed by Palladio and his peers. The choice was Gothic, but instead of brick, the facade was a puzzlework of white Istrian stone and pink Veronese marble with a lofty, lacy white loggia facing the Grand Canal. In 1853, critic and unabashed Gothic architecture partisan John Ruskin called the Palazzo Ducale the 'central building of the world'.

While the doge's palace is a show-stopper, many Venetian nobles weren't living too shabbily themselves by the 14th century. Even stripped of its original gilding, the Ca' d'Oro is a Grand Canal highlight. The typical Venetian noble family's *palazzo* (palace) had a water gate that gave access from boats to a courtyard or ground floor, with the grand reception hall usually on the *piano nobile* ('noble' or 1st floor). The *piano nobile* was built to impress, with light streaming through double-height loggia windows and balustraded balconies. The 2nd floor might also feature an elegant arcade topped with Venetian Gothic marble arches and trefoils, with crenellation crowning the roofline like a tiara.

Renaissance

For centuries Gothic cathedrals soared to the skies, pointing the eye and aspirations heavenward – but as the Renaissance ushered in an era of reason and humanism, architecture became more grounded and rational. Venice wasn't immediately sold on this radical new Tuscan world view, but the revival of classical ideals was soon popularised by Padua University and Venetian publishing houses.

TOP FIVE DIVINE ARCHITECTURAL EXPERIENCES

Basilica di San Marco Domes glimmer with golden mosaics.

Chiesa di San Giorgio Maggiore Palladio's expansive, effortlessly uplifting interiors.

Scuola Grande dei Carmini Longhena's stairway to heaven.

Chiesa di Santa Maria dei Miracoli The little Renaissance miracle in polychrome marble.

Schola Spagnola (Spanish Synagogue) Lofty, elliptical women's gallery with operatic drama.

With the study of classical philosophy came a fresh appreciation for strict classical order, harmonious geometry and human-scale proportions. A prime early example in Venice is the 1489 Chiesa di Santa Maria dei Miracoli, a small church and great achievement by sculptor-architect Pietro Lombardo (1435–1515) with his sons Tullio and Antonio. The exterior is clad in veined multicolour marbles apparently 'borrowed' from Basilica di San Marco's slag-heap, kept in check by a steady rhythm of Corinthian pilasters. The stark marble interiors set off a joyous profusion of finely worked sculpture, and the coffered ceiling is filled in with portraits of saints in contemporary Venetian dress. This is ecclesiastical architecture come down to earth, intimate and approachable.

Sansovino's Humanist Architecture

Born in Florence and well versed in classical architecture in Rome, Jacopo Sansovino (1486–1570) was a champion of the Renaissance as Venice's *proto* (official city architect). His best works reveal not just a shift in aesthetics but a sea change in thinking. While the Gothic ideal was a staggeringly tall spire topped by a cross, his Libreria Nazionale Marciana is an ideal Renaissance landmark: a low, flat-roofed monument to learning, showcasing statues of great men. Great men are also the theme of Sansovino's Scala dei Giganti in the Palazzo Ducale, a staircase reserved for Venetian dignitaries and an unmistakable metaphorical reminder that in order to ascend to the heights of power, one must stand on the shoulders of giants.

Instead of striving for the skies, Renaissance architecture reached for the horizon. Sansovino changed the skyline of Venice with his work on 15 buildings, including the serenely splendid Chiesa di San Francesco della Vigna, completed with a colonnaded facade by Palladio and sculptural flourishes by Pietro and Tullio Lombardo. But, thankfully, one of Sansovino's most ambitious projects never came to fruition: his plan to turn Piazza San Marco into a Roman forum.

Renaissance Palaces

As the Renaissance swept into Venice, the changes became noticeable along the Grand Canal: pointed Gothic arcades relaxed into rounded archways, repeated geometric forms and serene order replaced Gothic trefoils, and palaces became anchored by bevelled blocks of rough-hewn, rusticated marble. One Renaissance trendsetter was Bergamo-born Mauro Codussi (c 1440–1504), whose pleasing classical vocabulary applied equally to churches, the 15th-century Torre dell'Orologio and several Grand Canal palaces, including Palazzo Vendramin-Calergi, better known today as Casinó di Venezia.

Michele Sanmicheli (1484–1559) was from Verona but, like Sansovino, he worked in Rome, fleeing its sacking in 1527. The Venetian Republic kept him busy engineering defence works for the city, including Le Vignole's Forte Sant'Andrea, also known as the Castello da Mar (Sea Castle). Even Sanmicheli's private commissions have an imposing imperial Roman grandeur; the Grand Canal's Palazzo Grimani (built 1557–59) incorporates a triumphal arch on the ground floor, and feels more suited to its current use as the city's appeal court than a 16th-century pleasure palace. Sanmicheli is also occasionally credited with the other Renaissance Palazzo Grimani in Castello, along with Sansovino – but Venetian Renaissance man Giovanni Grimani seems to have mostly designed his own home as a suitably classical showcase for his collection of ancient Roman statuary, now in the Museo Correr.

Venetians avoid walking between the San Marco quay pillars, where criminals were once executed. According to legend, anyone wandering between these pillars will meet an untimely demise – doomed Marin Falier was beheaded eight months after supposedly passing between them to accept the post of doge.

MARK SADLIER / ALAMY ©

1. Chiesa di Santa Maria dei Miracoli (p130) **2.** Palazzo Ducale (p61) **3.** Basilica di San Marco (p58) **4.** Basilica di Santa Maria della Salute (p88)

Architectural Marvels

➡ **Basilica di San Marco** (p58) Only if angels and pirates founded an architecture firm could there ever be another building like Venice's cathedral. Saints tip-toe across gold mosaics inside bubble domes, gilded horses pilfered from Constantinople gallop off the loggia, and priceless marbles lining the walls and floors are on exceedingly long-term loan from Syria and Egypt. Awed glee ensues.

➡ **Basilica di Santa Maria della Salute** (p88) The sublime white dome defies gravity, but thousands of wooden poles underfoot are doing the heavy lifting. Posts sunk deep into lagoon mud create an ingenious foundation for Baldassare Longhena's white Istrian stone masterpiece, influenced by mystical cabbala designs and rumoured to have curative powers.

➡ **Palazzo Ducale** (p61) Town halls don't get grander than this pink palace. Other medieval cities reserved Gothic graces for cathedrals, but Venice went all out to impress visiting dignitaries and potential business partners with pink Veronese marble and gilt staircases – you'd never guess there were spies and prisoners hidden upstairs.

➡ **Biennale Pavilions** (p142) International relations never looked better than in Venice's Giardini Pubblici, where Biennale pavilions are purpose-built to reflect national architectural identities from Hungary (futuristic folklore hut) to Korea (creative industrial complex). Venetian modernist Carlo Scarpa steals the show with his cricket-shaped ticket booth.

➡ **Chiesa di Santa Maria dei Miracoli** (p130) Small with outsized swagger, this corner church is a masterpiece of Renaissance repurposing. Pietro Lombardo and sons worked wonders from San Marco's marble slag-heap, creating a gleaming, aquarium-like space where carved mermaids and miracle-working Madonnas seem right at home.

Palladio

As the baroque began to graft flourishes and curlicues onto basic Renaissance shapes, Padua-born Andrea Palladio (1508–80) carefully stripped them away, and in doing so laid the basis for modern architecture. His facades are an open-book study of classical architecture, with rigorously elemental geometry – a triangular pediment supported by round columns atop a rectangle of stairs – that lends an irresistible logic to the stunning exteriors of San Giorgio Maggiore and Redentore.

Critic John Ruskin detested Renaissance architecture in general and Palladio in particular, and ranted about San Giorgio Maggiore in his three-volume book *The Stones of Venice* (1851–53): 'It is impossible to conceive a design more gross, more barbarous, more childish in conception, more servile in plagiarism, more insipid in result, more contemptible under every point of rational regard...The interior of the church is like a large assembly room, and would have been undeserving of a moment's attention, but that it contains some most precious pictures.' But don't take his word for it: Palladio's blinding white Istrian facades may seem stoic from afar, but up close they become relatable, with billowing ceilings and an easy grace that anticipated baroque and high modernism.

Top Five Palladio Landmarks

Chiesa di San Giorgio Maggiore (Isola di San Giorgio Maggiore)
....
La Malcontenta (Riviera Brenta)
....
La Rotunda (Vicenza)
....
Villa di Masèr (north of Vicenza)
....
Teatro Olimpico (Vicenza)

Baroque & Neoclassical

In other parts of Europe, baroque architecture seemed lightweight: an assemblage of frills and thrills, with no underlying Renaissance reason or gravitas. But baroque's buoyant spirits made perfect sense along the Grand Canal, where white-stone party palaces with tiers of ornament looked like floating wedding cakes. Baldassare Longhena (1598–1682) stepped into the role of the city's official architect at a moment when the city was breathing a sigh of relief at surviving the Black Death, and he provided the architectural antidote to Venice's dark days with the buoyant white bubble-dome of Basilica di Santa Maria della Salute.

Architectural historians chalk up Longhena's unusual octagon-base dome to the influence of Roman shrines and cabbala diagrams, and the church's geometric stone floors are said to have mystical healing powers. Santa Maria della Salute's exterior decoration evokes pagan triumphal arches, with statues posing triumphantly on the facade and reclining over the main entrance. The building has inspired landscape artists from Turner to Monet, leading baroque-baiting Ruskin to concede that 'an architect trained in the worst schools, and utterly devoid of all meaning or purpose in his work may yet have such natural gift of massing and grouping as will render all his structures effective when seen from a distance'.

Ruskin deemed Longhena's fanciful facade of hulking sculptures at the Ospedaletto 'monstrous'; baroque fans will think otherwise. Another Longhena-designed marvel is Ca' Rezzonico, featuring sunny salons with spectacular Tiepolo ceilings. For its soaring grandeur and mystical geometry, the interior of the Ghetto's Schola Spagnola is also often attributed to Longhena.

Neoclassicism

Venice didn't lose track of Renaissance harmonies completely under all that ornament, and in the 18th century, muscular neoclassicism came into vogue. Inspired by Palladio, Giorgio Massari (c 1686–1766) created the Chiesa dei Gesuati as high theatre, setting the stage for Tiepolo's trompe l'œil ceilings. He built the gracious Palazzo Grassi with salons around a balustraded central light well, and brought to completion Longhena's Ca' Rezzonico on the Grand Canal.

Napoleon burst into Venice like a bully in 1797, ready to rearrange its face. The emperor's first order of architectural business was demolishing Sansovino's Chiesa di Geminiano to construct a monument in his own glory: the Ala Napoleonica (now Museo Correr) by Giovanni Antonio Selva (1753–1819). Napoleon had an entire district with four churches bulldozed to make way for the Giardini Pubblici and Via Garibaldi in Castello. Though Napoleon ruled Venice for only 11 years, French boulevards appeared where there were once churches across the city. Among others, Sant'Angelo, San Basilio, Santa Croce, Santa Maria Nova, Santa Marina, San Mattio, San Paterniano, San Severo, San Stin, Santa Ternita and San Vito disappeared under Napoleon.

The 20th Century

After Giudecca's baroque buildings were torn down for factories and the Ferrovia (train station) was built, the city took decades to recover from the shock. Venice reverted to 19th-century *venezianitá*, the tendency to tack on exaggerated Venetian elements from a range of periods – a Gothic trefoil arch here, a baroque cupola there. Rather than harmonising these disparate architectural elements, interiors were swagged in silk damask and moodlit with Murano chandeliers. The resulting hodge-podge seemed to signal the end of Venice's architectural glory days.

Lido Liberty

But after nearly a century dominated by French and Austrian influence, Venice let loose on the Lido with the bohemian decadence of *stile liberty* (Liberty style, or Italian art nouveau). Ironwork vegetation wound around balconies of seaside villas and wild fantasy took root at grand hotels, including Giovanni Sardi's 1898–1908 Byzantine-Moorish Excelsior and Guido Sullam's Hungaria Palace Hotel. Eclectic references to Japanese art, organic patterns from nature and past Venetian styles give Lido buildings cosmopolitan flair with *stile liberty* tiles, stained glass, ironwork and murals.

Fascist Monuments

In the 1930s the Fascists arrived to lay down the law on the Lido, applying a strict, functional neoclassicism even to entertainment venues such as the 1937–38 Palazzo della Mostra del Cinema and former Casinò (now undergoing redevelopment). Fascist architecture makes occasional awkward appearances in central Venice too, notably the Hotel Bauer and the extension to the Hotel Danieli, which represent an architectural oxymoron: the strict Fascist luxury-deco hotel.

Scarpa's High Modernism

The Biennale introduced new international architecture to Venice, but high modernism remained mostly an imported style until it was championed by Venice's own Carlo Scarpa (1906–78). Instead of creating seamless modern surfaces, Scarpa frequently exposed underlying structural elements and added unexpectedly poetic twists. At Negozio Olivetti, mosaic and water channels mimic *acque alte* across the floor, a floating staircase makes ascent seem effortless, and internal balconies jut out midair like diving boards into the infinite. Scarpa's concrete-slab Venezuela Pavilion was ahead of its time by a full half-century, and inevitably steals the show at Biennales. High modernist architecture aficionados make pilgrimages outside Venice to see Scarpa's Brioni Tomb near Asolo, and Castelvecchio in Verona. Scarpa's smaller works

Venice's first bridge to the mainland was built by the Austrians at Venetian taxpayers' expense in 1841–46, enabling troop and supplies transport by railway. The bridge spans 1.7 miles of lagoon waters and is propped up by 222 arches. Explosives were originally planted under the piers to be detonated in case of emergency, but these are said to have been quietly removed in later restorations.

ARCHITECTURE THE 20TH CENTURY

can be spotted all over Venice: the cricket-shaped former ticket booth at the Biennale, the entry and gardens of Palazzo Querini Stampalia and spare restorations to the doorway of the Accademia.

Contemporary Venice: Works in Progress

Modernism was not without its critics, especially among Venice's preservationists. But when a disastrous flood hit Venice in 1966, architecture aficionados around the globe put aside their differences, and aided Venetians in bailing out *palazzi* and reinforcing foundations across the city. With the support of Unesco and funding from 24 affiliated organisations worldwide, Venice has completed 1500 restoration projects in 40 years.

Today the city is open to a broader range of styles, though some controversies remain. Among the projects that never left the drawing board are a 1953 design for student housing on the Grand Canal by Frank Lloyd Wright, Le Corbusier's 1964 plans for a hospital in Cannaregio, and Luis Kahn's 1968 Palazzo dei Congressi project for the Giardini Pubblici. Plans to transform Venice's rather drab Marco Polo Airport with Frank Gehry's €80-million Venice Gateway complex remain stalled, and the Italian Culture Ministry requires revisions to Rem Koolhaas' 2012 designs transforming Fontego dei Tedeschi into a Benetton megastore on the Grand Canal. Controversy continues to rage over the costly 2010 Ponte di Calatrava and 2003 reconstruction of Teatro La Fenice, which is a €90-million replica of the 19th-century opera house, instead of the modernised version proposed by Gae Aulenti. Yet there's more modern architecture here than you might think: one-third of all buildings in Venice have been raised since 1919.

The Ando Effect

A surprising number of avant-garde projects have been recently realised in Venice, despite strict building codes and the challenges of construction with materials transported by boat, lifted by crane and hauled by handcart. With support from the city and financing from his own deep pockets, French billionaire art collector François Pinault hired Japanese minimalist architect Tadao Ando to repurpose two historic buildings into showcases for his contemporary-art collection. Instead of undermining their originality, Ando's careful repurposing revealed the muscular strength of Giorgio Masari's 1749 neoclassical Palazzo Grassi and Venice's abandoned c 1675 Punta della Dogana customs houses, relaunched as an art museum in 2009. Around the corner from Punta della Dogana, Pritzker Prize–winning architect Renzo Piano reinvented the Magazzini del Sale as a showcase for modern art with Fondazione Vedova. The transformation is only fitting: Venice's salt monopoly was once its dearest treasure, but now its ideas are its greatest asset.

Giudecca's Creative Comeback

MIT-trained Italian architect Cino Zucci kicked off the creative revival of Giudecca in 1995 with his conversion of 19th-century brick factories and waterfront warehouses into art spaces and studio lofts. A triangular bunker-warehouse for bombs during WWII has been reincarnated as Teatro Junghans, inaugurated in 2005 as Venice's hot spot for experimental theatre. Giudecca's transformation calls for a toast at the Skyline Rooftop Bar, atop the swanky hotel that was once Ernest Wullekopf's 1896 Molino Stucky flour mill.

Next to bridges, Venice's most common architectural features are its *poggi* (well-heads). Before Venice's aqueduct was constructed, more than 6000 wells collected and filtered rainwater for public use. Even today, overflow happy-hour crowds at neighbourhood *bacari* (bars) gossip around 600 ancient watering holes that still remain.

POGGI

TOP FIVE MODERN-ARCHITECTURE LANDMARKS

Biennale pavilions High-modernist pavilion architecture often steals the show at art siennales.

Punta della Dogana Customs houses are creatively repurposed as a contemporary-art showcase by Tadao Ando.

Negozio Olivetti Forward-thinking Carlo Scarpa transformed a dusty souvenir shop into a showcase for high technology c 1958.

Fondazione Giorgio Cini Former naval academy rocks the boat as an avant-garde art gallery.

Palazzo Grassi Tadao Ando's minimalism rescues Massari's palace from neoclassical ornament overload.

Watch This Space

New architecture projects are cropping up in unlikely places around Venice's lagoon. On the cemetery island of San Michele, David Chipperfield Architects are building extensions to echo the firm's sombre, minimalist Courtyard of the Four Evangelists. The evolution of Venice's historic Arsenale shipyards continues, with medieval assembly-line sheds serving as pre-industrial-chic galleries during the Biennale. Ca' Pisani's glam-rock-deco interiors kicked off a historic-design-hotel trend, including Domina Home Ca' Zusto's mod-harem redesign of a medieval palace, Gritti Palace's historically hip 2013 relaunch, and Alvin Grassi's deco-luxe redesign for the Grand Canal's Palazzo Barbarigo. Fondazione Giorgio Cini is continuing to reinvent Isola di San Giorgio Maggiore as a global cultural centre, with a new maze dedicated to Argentine writer Jorge Luis Borges behind the Palladian cloisters, and a former dormitory transformed into a humanities library to complement Baldassare Longhena's original 17th-century science library. In Venetian architecture, the distant past is once again cutting edge.

The Arts

By the 13th century, Venice had already accomplished the impossible: building a maritime empire on a shallow lagoon, with trading-houses and palaces rising majestically from mud banks. But its dominance didn't last. Plague repeatedly decimated the city in the 14th century, new trade routes to the New World bypassed Venice and its tax collectors, and the Ottoman Empire dominated the Adriatic by the middle of the 15th century. Yet when Venice could no longer prevail by wealth or force, it triumphed with new forms of art, music, theatre and poetry.

Visual Arts

Turbaned figures appear across Venice on the corners of Campo dei Mori, on jewels at Sigfrido Cipolato, and propping up I Frari funerary monuments. Misleadingly referred to as 'Mori' (Moors), some represent Venetians from Greek Morea, others Turkish pirates, and others enslaved West Africans who once rowed merchant ships across the Mediterranean.

The sheer number of masterpieces packed into Venice might make you wonder if there's something in the water here, but the reason may be more simple: historically, Venice tended not to starve its artists. Multiyear commissions from wealthy private patrons, the city and the Church gave them some sense of security. Artists were granted extraordinary opportunities to create new artwork without interference, with the city frequently declining to enforce the Inquisition's censorship edicts. Instead of dying young, destitute and out of favour, painters such as Titian and Giovanni Bellini survived into their 80s to produce late, great works. The side-by-side innovations of emerging and mature artists created schools of painting so distinct, they still set Venice apart from the rest of Italy – and the world.

Early Venetian Painting

Once you've seen the mosaics at Basilica di San Marco and Santa Maria Assunta in Torcello, you'll recognise key aspects of early Venetian painting: larger-than-life religious figures with wide eyes and serene expressions float on gold backgrounds and hover inches above Gothic thrones. Byzantine influence can be seen in the *Madonna and Child with Two Votaries* painted c 1325 by Paolo Veneziano (c 1300–62) in the Gallerie dell'Accademia: like stage hands parting theatre curtains, two angels pull back the edges of a starry red cloak to reveal a hulking Madonna, golden baby Jesus, and two tiny patrons.

By the early 15th century, Venetian painters were breaking with Byzantine convention. *Madonna with Child* (c 1455) by Jacopo Bellini (c 1396–1470) in the Accademia is an image any parent might relate to: bright-eyed baby Jesus reaches one sandalled foot over the edge of the balcony, while an apparently sleep-deprived Mary patiently pulls him away from the ledge. Padua's Andrea Mantegna (1431–1506) took Renaissance perspective to extremes, showing bystanders in his biblical scenes reacting to unfolding miracles and martyrdoms with shock, awe, anger, even inappropriate laughter.

Tuscan painter Gentile da Fabriano was in Venice as he was beginning his transition to Renaissance realism, and apparently influenced the young Murano-born painter Antonio Vivarini (c 1415–80), whose *Passion* polyptych in Ca' d'Oro shows tremendous pathos. Antonio's brother, Bartolomeo Vivarini (c 1432–99), created a delightful altarpiece in I Frari showing a baby Jesus wriggling out of the arms of the Madonna, squarely seated on her marble Renaissance throne.

Venice's Red-Hot Renaissance

Jacopo Bellini's sons used a new medium that would revolutionise Venetian painting: oil paints. The 1500 *Miracle of the Cross at the Bridge of San Lorenzo* by Gentile Bellini (1429–1507) at the Accademia shows the religious figure not high on a throne or adrift in the heavens, but floating in the Grand Canal, with crowds of bystanders stopped in their tracks in astonishment. Giovanni Bellini (c 1430–1516) takes an entirely different approach to his Accademia *Annunciation,* using glowing reds and oranges to focus attention on the solitary figure of the kneeling Madonna awed by an angel arriving in a swish of rumpled drapery.

From Venice's guild of house painters emerged some of art history's greatest names, starting with Giovanni Bellini's apt pupils: Giorgione (1477–1510) and Titian (c 1488–1576). The two worked together on the frescoes that once covered the Fondaco dei Tedeschi (only a few fragments remain in the Ca' d'Oro), with teenage Titian following Giorgione's lead. Giorgione was a Renaissance man who wrote poetry and music, is credited with inventing the easel, and preferred to paint from inspiration without sketching out his subject first, as in his enigmatic, Leonardo da Vinci-style 1508 *La Tempesta* (The Storm) at Gallerie dell'Accademia.

When Giorgione died at 33, probably of the plague, Titian finished some of his works – but young Titian soon set himself apart with brushstrokes that brought his subjects to life, while taking on a life of their own. At Basilica di Santa Maria della Salute, you'll notice Titian started out a measured, methodical painter in his 1510 *St Marco Enthroned.* After seeing Michelangelo's expressive *Last Judgment,* Titian let it rip: in his final 1576 *Pietà* he smeared paint onto canvas with his bare hands.

But even for a man of many masterpieces, Titian's 1518 *Assunta* (Ascension) at I Frari is a radiant altarpiece that mysteriously lights up the cavernous room. Vittore Carpaccio (1460–1526) rivalled Titian's reds with his own sanguine hues – hence the dish of bloody beef cheekily named in his honour by Harry's Bar – but it was Titian's *Assunta* that cemented Venice's reputation for glowing, glorious colour.

Not Minding Their Manners: Venice's Mannerists

Although art history tends to insist on a division of labour between Venice and Florence – Venice had the colour, Florence the ideas – the Venetian School had plenty of ideas that repeatedly got it into trouble. Titian was a hard act to follow, but there's no denying the impact of Venice's Jacopo Robusti, aka Tintoretto (1518–94) and Paolo Cagliari from Verona, known as Veronese (1528–88).

A crash course in Tintoretto begins at Chiesa della Madonna dell'Orto, his parish church and the serene brick backdrop for his

---

VENETIAN PAINTINGS THAT CHANGED PAINTING

➡ *Feast in the House of Levi* (Veronese, Gallerie dell'Accademia)

➡ *Assunta* (Titian, I Frari)

➡ *St Mark in Glory* (Tintoretto, Scuola Grande di San Rocco)

➡ *La Tempesta* (Giorgione, Gallerie dell'Accademia)

➡ *Madonna with Child Between Saints Caterina and Maddalena* (Giovanni Bellini, Gallerie dell'Accademia)

action-packed 1546 *Last Judgment*. True-blue Venetian that he is, Tintoretto shows the final purge as a teal tidal wave, which lost souls are vainly trying to hold back, like human Mose barriers. A dive-bombing angel swoops in to save one last person – a riveting image Tintoretto reprised in the upper floor of the Scuola Grande di San Rocco. Tintoretto spent some 15 years creating works for San Rocco, and his biblical scenes read like a modern graphic novel. Tintoretto sometimes used special effects to get his point across, enhancing his colours with a widely available local material: finely crushed glass.

Veronese's colours have a luminosity entirely their own, earning him Palazzo Ducale commissions and room to run riot inside Chiesa di San Sebastian – but his choice of subjects got him into trouble. When Veronese was commissioned to paint the *Last Supper* (in Gallerie dell'Accademia) his masterpiece ended up looking suspiciously like a Venetian party, with apostles in Venetian dress mingling freely with Turkish merchants, Jewish guests, serving wenches, begging lapdogs and (most shocking of all) Protestant Germans. When the Inquisition demanded he change the painting, Veronese refused to remove the offending Germans and altered scarcely a stroke of paint, simply changing the title to *Feast in the House of Levi*. In an early victory for freedom of expression, Venice stood by the decision.

The next generation of Mannerists included Palma il Giovane (1544–1628), who finished Titian's *Pietá* after the master's death and fused Titian's early naturalism with Tintoretto's drama. Another Titian acolyte who adopted Tintoretto's dramatic lighting was Jacopo da Ponte from Bassano del Grappa, called Bassano (1517–92). Bassano's work is so high contrast and high drama, at first glance you might wonder how black-velvet paintings wound up in Gallerie dell'Accademia, Chiesa di San Giorgio Maggiore and Bassano del Grappa's Museo Civico.

Going for Baroque

By the 18th century, Venice had endured plague and seen its ambitions for world domination dashed – but the city repeatedly made light of its dire situation in tragicomic art. Pietro Longhi (1701–85) dispensed with lofty subject matter and painted wickedly witty Venetian social satires, while Giambattista Tiepolo (1696–1770) turned religious themes into a premise for dizzying ceilings with rococo sunbursts. Ca' Rezzonico became a show place for both their talents, with an entire salon of Pietro Longhi's drawing-room scenarios and Giambattista Tiepolo's trompe l'œil ceiling masterpieces.

Instead of popes on thrones, portraitist Rosalba Carriera (1675–1757) captured her socialite sitters on snuffboxes, and painted in a medium she pioneered: pastels. Her portraits at Ca' Rezzonico walk a fine line between Tiepolo's flattery and Longhi's satire, revealing her sitters' every twinkle and wrinkle.

As the 18th-century party wound down, the Mannerists' brooding theatricality merged with Tiepolo's pastel beauty in works by Tiepolo's son, Giandomenico Tiepolo (1727–1804). His 1747–49 *Stations of the Cross* in Chiesa di San Polo takes a dim view of humanity in light colours, illuminating the jeering faces of Jesus' tormentors. Giandomenico used a lighter touch working alongside his father on the frescoes at Villa Valmarana 'ai Nani' (p194) outside Vicenza, covering the walls with Chinese motifs, rural scenes and carnival characters.

The Vedutisti

Many Venetian artists turned their attention from the heavens to the local landscape in the 18th century, notably Antonio Canal, aka Canaletto

Winged lions carved onto Venetian facades symbolise St Mark, Venice's patron saint, but some served sinister functions. In the 1500s, the Consiglio dei Dieci (Council of Ten) established *bocca dei leoni* (lion's mouths), stone lions' heads with slots for inserting anonymous denunciations of neighbours for crimes raging from cursing to conspiracy.

TOP FIVE ARTISTS IN RESIDENCE

Albrecht Dürer (1471–1528) left his native Nuremberg for Venice in 1494, hoping to see Venetian experiments in perspective and colour that were the talk of Europe. Giovanni Bellini took him under his wing, and once Dürer returned to Germany in 1495, he began his evolution from Gothic painter into Renaissance artist. When Dürer returned to Venice in 1505, he was feted as a visionary.

William Turner (1775–1851) was drawn to Venice three times (in 1819, 1833 and 1840), fascinated by the former merchant empire that, like his native England, had once commanded the sea. Turner's hazy portraits of the city are studies in light at different times of day; as he explained to art critic John Ruskin, 'atmosphere is my style'. Ruskin applauded the effort, but in London many critics loathed Turner's work.

James Whistler (1834–1903) arrived in Venice in 1879, bankrupt and exhausted after a failed libel case brought against John Ruskin. The American painter rediscovered his verve and brush in prolific paintings of the lagoon city, returning to London in 1880 with a formidable portfolio that re-established his reputation.

John Singer Sargent (1856–1925) was a lifelong admirer of Venice; the American visited at a young age and became a part-time resident from 1880 to 1913. Sargent's intimate knowledge of the city shows in his paintings, which capture new angles on familiar panoramas and illuminate neglected monuments.

Claude Monet (1840–1926) turned up in Venice in 1908, and immediately found Impressionist inspiration in architecture that seemed to dissolve into lagoon mists and shimmering waters.

(1697-1768). He became the leading figure of the *vedutisti* (landscape artists) with minutely detailed *vedute* (views) of Venice that leave admiring viewers with vicarious hand cramps. You might be struck how closely Canalettos resemble photographs – and, in fact, Canaletto created his works with the aid of a forerunner to the photographic camera, the *camera oscura* (camera obscura). Light entered this instrument and reflected the image onto a sheet of glass, which Canaletto then traced. After he had the outlines down, he filled in exact details, from lagoon algae to hats on passers-by.

Vedute sold well to Venice visitors as a kind of rich man's postcards. Canaletto was backed by the English collector John Smith, who introduced the artist to such a vast English clientele that only a few of his paintings can be seen in Venice today, in the Gallerie dell'Accademia and Ca' Rezzonico.

Canaletto's nephew Bernardo Bellotto (1721–80) also adopted the *camera oscura* in his painting process, though his expressionistic landscapes use strong *chiaroscuro* (shadow and light contrasts). His paintings hang in the Accademia alongside *San Marco Basin with San Giorgio and Giudecca* by Francesco Guardi (1712–93), whose Impressionistic approach shows Venice's glories reflected in the lagoon. Among the last great *vedutisti* was Venetian Impressionist Emma Ciardi (1879-1933), who captured Venetian mysteries unfolding amid shimmering early-morning mists in luminous landscapes at Ca' Rezzonico and Ca' Pesaro.

Top Five for Modernism

Peggy Guggen-heim Collection (Dorsoduro)

Ca' Pesaro (Santa Croce)

Fondazione Prada (Santa Croce)

Fondazione Giorgio Cini (Isola di San Giorgio Maggiore)

Museo Fortuny (San Marco)

Lucky Stiffs: Venetian Funerary Sculpture

Bookending Venice's accomplishments in painting are its masterpieces in sculpture. Venice kept its sculptors busy, with 200 churches needing altars, fire-prone Palazzo Ducale requiring near-constant rebuilding for 300 years, and especially tombs for nobles with political careers cut short by age, plague and intrigue. The tomb of Doge Marco Corner in

VENICE VIEWS INDOORS

➡ *Procession in San Marco* (1496, Gentile Bellini; Gallerie dell'Accademia)

➡ *Rio dei Mendicanti* (1723–24, Canaletto; Ca' Rezzonico)

➡ *Piazza San Marco, Mass after the Victory* (1918, Emma Ciardi; Museo Correr)

➡ *The San Marco Basin with San Giorgio and Giudecca* (1770–74, Francesco Guardi; Gallerie dell'Accademia)

➡ *Rio dei Mendicanti with the Scuola di San Marco* (1738–40, Bernardo Bellotto; Gallerie dell'Accademia)

Zanipolo by Pisa's Nino Pisano (c 1300–68) is a sprawling wall monument with a massive, snoozing doge that somewhat exaggerated his career: Corner was doge for under three years.

Venice's Pietro Lombardo (1435–1515) and his sons Tullio (1460–1532) and Antonio (1458–1516) kept busy sculpting heroic, classical monuments to short-lived dogi: doge for a year Nicolo Marcello (1473–74), Pietro Mocenigo (1474–76) and Andrea Vendramin (1476–78). This last gilded marble monument was probably completed under Tullio, who literally cut corners: he sculpted the figures in half relief, and chopped away part of Pisano's Corner tomb to make room for Vendramin. Tullio's strong suit was the ideal beauty of his faces, as you can see in his bust of a young male saint at Chiesa di Santo Stefano.

Antonio Canova (1757–1822) is the most prominent sculptor to emerge from the Veneto, and his pyramid tomb intended for Titian at I Frari would become his own funerary masterpiece. Mourners hang their heads and clutch one another, scarcely aware that their diaphanous garments are slipping off; even the great winged lion of St Mark is curled up in grief. Don't let his glistening Orpheus and Eurydice in Museo Correr fool you: Canova's seamless perfection in glistening marble was achieved through rough drafts modelled in gypsum, displayed at his studio outside Asolo, the Gipsoteca Canoviana.

Not Strictly Academic: Venetian Modernism

The arrival of Napoleon in 1797 was a disaster for Venice and its art. During his Kingdom of Italy (1806–14), Napoleon and his forces knocked down churches and systematically plundered Venice and the region of artistic treasures. Some works have been restored to Venice, including the bronze horses of Basilica di San Marco that probably belong in Istanbul, since Venice pilfered them from Constantinople. Yet even under 19th-century occupation, Venice remained a highlight of the Grand Tour, and painters who flocked to the city created memorable Venice cityscapes.

After joining the newly unified Italy in 1866, Venice's signature artistic contribution to the new nation was Francesco Hayez (1791–1882). The Venetian painter paid his dues with society portraits but is best remembered for Romanticism and frank sexuality, beginning with *Rinaldo and Armida* (1814) in the Gallerie dell'Accademia.

Never shy about self-promotion, Venice held its first Biennale in 1895 to reassert its role as global taste maker and provide an essential corrective to the brutality of the Industrial Revolution. A garden pavilion showcased a self-promoting, studiously inoffensive take on Italian art – principally lovely ladies, pretty flowers, and lovely ladies wearing pretty flowers. Other nations were granted pavilions in 1907, but the Biennale retained strict control, and had a Picasso removed from the Spanish pavilion in 1910 so as not to shock the public with modernity.

A backlash to Venetian conservatism arose from the ranks of Venetian painters experimenting in modern styles. Shows of young artists backed by the Duchess Felicita Bevilaqua La Masa found a permanent home in 1902, when the Duchess gifted Ca' Pesaro to the city as a modern-art museum. A leader of the Ca' Pesaro crowd was Gino Rossi (1884–1947), whose brilliant blues and potent symbolism bring to mind Gauguin, Matisse and the Fauvists, and whose later work shifted toward Cubism. Often called the Venetian Van Gogh, Rossi spent many years in psychiatric institutions, where he died. Sculptor Arturo Martini (1889–1947) contributed works to Ca' Pesaro ranging from the rough-edged terracotta *Prostitute* (c 1913) to his radically streamlined 1919 gesso bust.

Future Perfect: From Futurism to Fluidity

In 1910, Filippo Tommaso Marinetti (1876–1944) threw packets of his manifesto from Torre dell'Orologio promoting a new vision for the arts: futurism. In the days of the doge, Marinetti would have been accused of heresy for his declaration that Venice (a 'magnificent sore of the past') should be wiped out and replaced with a new industrial city. The futurists embraced industry and technology with their machine-inspired, streamlined look – a style that Mussolini co-opted in the 1930s for his vision of a monolithic, modern Italy. Futurism was conflated with Mussolini's brutal imposition of artificial order until championed in Venice by a heroine of the avant-garde and refugee from the Nazis: American expat art collector Peggy Guggenheim, who recognised in futurism the fluidity and flux of modern life.

Artistic dissidents also opposed Mussolini's square-jawed, iron-willed aesthetics. Emilio Vedova (1919–2006) joined the *Corrente* movement of artists, which openly opposed Fascist trends in a magazine shut down by the Fascists in 1940. After WWII, Vedova veered towards abstraction, and his larger works are now in regular robot-assisted rotation at the Magazzini del Sale. Giovanni Pontini (1915–70) was a worker who painted as a hobby until 1947, when he discovered Kokoshka, van Gogh and Roualt, who inspired his empathetic paintings of fishermen at the Peggy Guggenheim Collection.

Venetian Giuseppe Santomaso (1907–90) painted his way out of constrictive Fascism with lyrical, unbounded abstract landscapes in deep teals and brilliant blues. Rigidity and liquidity became the twin fascinations of another avant-garde Italian artist, Unesco-acclaimed, Bologna-born and Venice-trained video artist Fabrizio Plessi (b 1940), from his 1970s *Arte Povera* (Poor Art) experiments in humble materials to multimedia installations featuring Venice's essential medium: water.

The fluidity that characterises Venice and its art continues into the 21st century, with new art galleries in San Marco and Giudecca showing a range of landscapes, abstraction, video and installation art. Yet of all the laws posted at Venetian *vaporetto* stops – including admonitions against strutting about town bare-breasted – the one most strictly observed by Venetians is against graffiti. Since solvents to remove graffiti damage Venice's brick foundations and pollute its waters, Venetians save graffiti art for indoor spaces like Osteria all'Alba, and appreciate visitors who take photos or paint pictures instead of defacing ancient walls. When (not if) artistic inspiration strikes, canvases are readily available at Arcobaleno for you to jump-start the next Venetian art movement.

Music

Over the centuries, Venetian musicians developed a reputation for playing music as though their lives depended on it, which at times wasn't far from the truth. In its trade-empire heyday, La Serenissima had official musicians, including the distinguished directorship of Flemish Adrian

THE ARTS MUSIC

Top Five for Contemporary Art

Venice Biennale

Punta della Dogana (Dorsoduro)

Palazzo Grassi (San Marco)

Caterina Tognon Arte Contemporanea (San Marco)

Fondazione Prada (Santa Croce)

Top Five Arts Workshops

Venice Biennale hands-on workshops

Writing at Libreria Marco Polo

Masquerade acting at Teatro Junghans

Life drawing at Novecento

Photography at Ca' Pozzo

Venice in Art

Water may be the first thing you notice about Venice when you arrive, but as you get closer, you'll discover that this city is actually saturated with art. Canals are just brief interruptions between artworks in this Unesco World Heritage Site, with more art treasures than any other city.

Art Heists, Foiled

Until Napoleon grabbed every Venetian painting that he fancied, most remained in the churches and palaces for which they were painted. But lavishly painted ceilings weren't so easy to detach, and can still be seen their original settings at Chiesa di San Sebastiano, Ca' Rezzonico, Palazzo Ducale and Scuola Grande dei Carmini. Tintoretto's looming masterpieces were left in place at Scuola Grande di San Rocco and Chiesa della Madonna dell'Orto, where a more portable Bellini was stolen as recently as 1993. Though some of Napoleon's favourite souvenirs remain in the Louvre – including Paolo Veronese's *Wedding at Cana*, ripped from San Giorgio Maggiore's monastery wall and shipped to Paris in pieces – stolen artwork returned after Napoleon's fall forms the basis of collections at Museo Correr, Accademia and Ca' d'Oro.

Mosaics

All that glitters is probably mosaic in Venice, where the art of making tiny glass *tesserae* (tiles) into wall-sized artworks dates from the lagoon's Byzantine heyday. The medieval lagoon capital of Torcello perfected mosaic technique, with cathedral mosaics showing the Madonna staring down

1. Giambattista Tiepolo fresco in Ca' Rezzonico (p90) **2.** Tintoretto's *Crucifixion* in the Scuola Grande di San Rocco (p101) **3.** Mosaic detail, Basilica di San Marco (p58)

blue devils tipping the scales of Final Judgment. But Torcello was soon upstaged by the Basilica di San Marco's 8500 sq metres of golden mosaics. Even the basilica was impressed with itself: the church is depicted at least nine times in its own mosaics. To appreciate the effort involved, technical explanations accompany stunning mosaic fragments at the basilica, the Museo di Torcello and Murano's Museo del Vetro.

Frescoes

Things are perpetually looking up in Venice, thanks to the prolific maestro of ceiling frescoes, Giambattista Tiepolo. The sun seems to shine right through the roof of Chiesa dei Gesuati and Ca' Rezzonico in his staggering ceilings, where angels perch on rose-gold clouds. Tiepolo and his son Domenico frescoed Villa Valmarana 'ai Nani' outside Vicenza from floor to ceiling, turning salons into a woodland wonderland, *commedia dell'arte* circus and chinoiserie curiosity cabinet. Without the Inquisition looking over his shoulder to censor his paintings, Paolo Veronese frescoed Palladio's Villa di Masèr with a lighthearted touch, painting a *trompe-l'oeil* painter's ladder in the living room and a self-portrait exchanging conspiratorial glances with his favourite niece in adjoining salons. But for frescoes that are both heavenly and down to earth, head to Padua to encounter colourful, relatable saints in Giotto's 1303–05 Cappella degli Scrovegni Renaissance masterpiece.

GIANANTONIO DE VINCENZO: MUSICIAN

Beyond Baroque

Vivaldi is like masquerade masks in Venice: it's everywhere, you can't miss it. When you encounter different music, stop and listen: this is how culture evolves, by paying attention to unexpected sensations. Otherwise, we're stuck with whatever's on TV.

Dinner & a Show

Restaurants close early, but you can find cicheti (Venetian tapas) before and after concerts. I'll grab panini and natural-process prosecco at Al Mercà before shows, or hit the cicheti bar at Al Pesador or Ai Postali afterwards.

Venetian Jazz

The creak of a gondola oar in the oarlock, followed by the rush of swirling water: those are the quiet, rhythmic sounds you can actually hear in Venice, because there is no aggressive traffic noise. Saturdays at Rialto Market you'll hear an improvised call-and-response between vendors and shoppers – it's Venice's own jazz.

Giannantonio De Vincenzo is a musician and composer

Willaert (1490–1562) for 35 years at Capella Ducale. But when the city fell on hard times in the 17th to 18th centuries, it discovered its musical calling.

With shrinking trade revenues, the state took the quixotic step of underwriting musical education for orphan girls, and the investment yielded unfathomable returns. Among the *maestri* hired to conduct orphan orchestras was Antonio Vivaldi (1678–1741), whose 30-year tenure yielded hundreds of concertos and popularised Venetian baroque music across Europe. Visitors spread word of extraordinary performances by orphan girls, and the city became a magnet for novelty-seeking moneyed socialites. Modern visitors to Venice can still see music and opera performed in the same venues as in Vivaldi's day – *palazzi* (palaces), churches and *ospedaletti* (orphanages) such as La Pietà, where Vivaldi worked – and sometimes on 18th-century instruments.

Opera

Today's televised talent searches can't compare to Venice's ability to discover talents like Claudio Monteverdi (1567–1643), who was named the musical director of the Basilica di San Marco and went on to launch modern opera. Today, opera reverberates inside La Fenice and across town in churches, concert halls and *palazzi* – but until 1637 you would have been able to hear opera only by invitation. Opera and most chamber music were the preserve of the nobility, performed in private salons.

Then Venice threw open the doors of the first public opera houses. Between 1637 and 1700, some 358 operas were staged in 16 theatres to meet the musical demands of a population of 140,000. Monteverdi wrote two stand-out operas, *Il Ritorno di Ulisse al suo Paese* (The Return of Ulysses) and *L'Incoronazione di Poppea* (The Coronation of Poppea), with an astonishing range of plot and subplot, strong characterisation and powerful music. Critical response couldn't have been better: he was buried with honours in I Frari.

A singer at the Basilica di San Marco under Monteverdi, Pier Francesco Cavalli (1602–76) became the outstanding 17th-century Italian opera composer, with 42 operas. With his frequent collaborator Carlo Goldoni and Baldassare Galuppi (1706–84), he added musical hooks to *opera buffa* (comic opera) favourites like *Il Filosofo di Campagna* (The Country Philosopher).

Classical

Get ready to baroque-and-roll: Venetian classical musicians are leading a revival of 'early music' from medieval through to Renaissance and baroque periods, with historically accurate arrangements played *con brio* (with verve) on period instruments. Venetian baroque was the rebel music of its day, openly defying edicts from Rome deciding which instruments could accompany sermons and what kinds of rhythms and melodies were suitable for moral uplift. Venetians kept right on playing stringed instruments in churches, singing along to bawdy *opera buffa* and writing compositions that were both soulful and sensual.

Modern misconceptions about baroque being a nice soundtrack to accompany wedding ceremonies are smashed by baroque 'early music' ensembles. Among Vivaldi's repertoire of some 500 concertos is his ever-popular *Four Seasons*, instantly recognisable from hotel lobbies and ringtones – but you haven't heard summer-lightning strike and spring flood the room until you've heard it played *con brio* by Interpreti Veneziani (p78).

The pleasure palace of Palazzetto Bru Zane is now restored to its original function: concerts to flirt at and swoon over, with winking approval from Sebastiano Ricci's frolicking, frescoed angels. Venetian venues make all the difference: any classical performance in the grand salon of Palazzo Querini Stampalia or Tiepolo-frescoed Ca' Rezzonico will transport you to the 18th century in one movement, and catapult you into the 21st with the next. Seek out programs featuring Venetian baroque composer Tomaso Albinoni (1671–1750), especially the exquisite *Sinfonie e Concerti a 5*. For a more avant-garde take on classical music, look for works by Bruno Maderna (1920–73) or Luigi Nono (1924–90).

Leggera & Jazz

Most of the music you'll hear booming out of water taxis and *bacari* (bars) is *musica leggera* ('light' or pop music). This term covers Italian rock, jazz, folk and hip-hop talents, plus perniciously catchy dance tunes and pop ballads. The San Remo Music Festival (televised on RAI 1) annually honours Italy's best songs and mercifully weeds out the worst early on, unlike the wildly popular Italian version of *X Factor*. In summer, beach-front battles of the bands on the Lido and free concerts on Lido di Jesolo by the likes of Franz Ferdinand will keep you guessing what's next.

Besides Italian and international radio-ready fare and the odd reality-show winner, Venice has an indie music scene performing jazz, reggae and ska. Venice Jazz Club features tribute nights year-round, and during July's Venice Jazz Festival, you may luck into a performance by Venetian saxophonist and composer Giannantonio De Vincenzo or Venetian trumpeter-musicologist Massimo Donà. With a natural affinity for island music, Venice grooves to Italian-accented reggae and ska – especially at free summer beach concerts on the Lido, and retro reggae-on-vinyl DJ nights at Torino@Notte.

Literature

In a surprising 15th-century plot twist, shipping magnate Venice became a publishing empire. Johannes Gutenberg cranked out his first Bible with a movable-type press in 1455, and Venice became an early adopter of this cutting-edge technology, turning out the earliest printed Qur'an. Venetian printing presses were in operation by the 1470s, with

THE ARTS LITERATURE

Top Five for Jazz

Venice Jazz Festival

Venice Jazz Club

I Figli delle Stelle

Osteria Da Filo

Ai Postali

lawyers settling copyright claims soon thereafter. Venetian publishers printed not just religious texts but histories, poetry, textbooks, plays, musical scores and manifestos.

Early Renaissance author Pietro Bembo (1470–1547) was a librarian, historian, diplomat and poet who defined the concept of platonic love and solidified Italian grammar in his *Rime* (Rhymes). Bembo collaborated with Aldo Manuzio on an invention that revolutionised reading and democratised learning: the Aldine Press, which introduced italics and paperbacks, including Dante's *La Divina Commedia* (The Divine Comedy). By 1500, nearly one in six books published in Europe was printed in Venice.

In trying to describe the Inferno to contemporary readers circa 1307, Dante compared it to Venice's Arsenale, with its stinking vats of tar, sparks flying from hammers and infernal clamour of 16,000 labourers working nonstop on its legendary ship-assembly lines.

Poetry

Duels, politics and romance seemed impossible in Venice without poetry. Shakespeare has competition for technical prowess from Veneto's Petrarch (aka Francesco Petrarca; 1304–74), who added wow to Italian woo with his eponymous sonnets. Writing in Italian and Latin, Petrarch applied a strict structure of rhythm (14 lines, with two quatrains to describe a desire and a sestet to attain it) and rhyme (no more than five rhymes per sonnet) to romance the idealised Laura. He might have tried chocolates instead: Laura never returned the sentiment.

Posthumously, Petrarch became idolised by Rilke, Byron, Mozart and Venice's *cortigiane oneste* (well-educated 'honest courtesans'). Tullia d'Aragona (1510–56) wrote sharp-witted Petrarchan sonnets that wooed men senseless: noblemen divulged state secrets, kings risked their thrones to beg her hand in marriage, and much ink was spilled in panegyric praise of her hooked nose.

Written with wit and recited with passion, poetry might get you a free date with a high-end courtesan, killed or elected in Venice. Leonardo Giustinian (1388–1446) was a member of the Consiglio dei Dieci (Council of Ten) who spent time off from spying on his neighbours writing poetry in elegant Venetian-inflected Italian, including *Canzonette* (Songs) and *Strambotti* (Ditties). Giorgio Baffo (1694–1768) was a friend of Casanova's whose risqué odes to the posterior might have affected his political career elsewhere – but in Venice, he became a state senator. To experience his bawdy poetry, head to Taverna da Baffo, where his ribald rhymes may be chanted by night's end.

One of Italy's greatest poets, Ugo Foscolo (1778–1827) studied in Padua and arrived in Venice as a teenager amid political upheavals. Young Foscolo threw in his literary lot with Napoleon in a 1797 ode to the general, hoping he would revive the Venetian Republic, and even joined the French army. But Napoleon considered him a dangerous mind, and Foscolo ended his days in exile in London.

Memoirs

Life on the lagoon has always been stranger than fiction, and Venetian memoirists were early bestsellers. Venice-born Marco Polo (1254–1324) captured his adventures across central Asia and China in memoirs entitled *Il Milione* (c 1299), as told to Rustichello da Pisa. The book achieved bestseller status even before the invention of the printing press, each volume copied by hand. Some details were apparently embellished along the way, but his tales of Kublai Khan's court remain riveting. In a more recent traveller's account, *Venezia, la Città Ritrovata* (Venice Rediscovered; 1998), Paolo Barbaro (b 1922) captures his reverse culture shock upon returning to the lagoon city.

Memoirs with sex and scandal sold well in Venice. 'Honest courtesan' Veronica Franco (1546–91) kissed and told in her bestselling memoir, but for sheer *braggadocio* it's hard to top the memoirs of Casanova

(1725–98). Francesco Gritti (1740–1811) parodied the decadent Venetian aristocracy in vicious, delicious *Poesie in Dialetto Veneziano* (Poetry in the Venetian Dialect) and satirised the Venetian fashion for memoirs with his exaggerated *My Story: The Memoirs of Signor Tommasino Written by Him, a Narcotic Work by Dr Pifpuf.*

Modern Fiction

Venetian authors have remained at the forefront of modern Italian fiction. The enduring quality of Camillo Boito's 1883 short story *Senso* (Sense), a twisted tale of love and betrayal in Austrian-occupied Venice, made it a prime subject for director Luchino Visconti in 1954. Mysterious Venice proved the ideal setting for Venice's resident expat American mystery novelist Donna Leon, whose inspector Guido Brunetti uncovers the shadowy subcultures of Venice, from island fishing communities *(A Sea of Troubles)* to environmental protesters *(Through a Glass Darkly)*. But the pride of Venice's literary scene is Tiziano Scarpa (b 1963), who earned the 2009 Strega Prize, Italy's top literary honour, for *Stabat Mater,* the story of an orphaned Venetian girl learning to play violin under Antonio Vivaldi.

Film

Back in the 1980s, a Venice film archive found that the city had appeared in one form or another in 380,000 films – feature films, shorts, documentaries, and other works archived and screened at the city's Casa del Cinema. But Venice's photogenic looks have proved a mixed

Eighteenth-century Venetian grande dame Isabella Teotochi Albrizzi was practically wedded to her literary salon: when her husband received a post abroad, she got her marriage annulled to remain in Venice and continue her discussions of poetry with the patronage of a new husband, her *cicisbeo* (manservant-lover) in devoted attendance.

VENICE'S BESTSELLING WOMEN WRITERS

At a time when women were scarcely in print elsewhere in Europe, Venetian women became prolific and bestselling published authors in subjects ranging from mathematics to politics. Over 100 Venetian women authors from the 15th to 18th centuries remain in circulation today. Among the luminaries of their era:

Writer Sara Copia Sullam (1592–1641) A leading Jewish intellectual of Venice's Accademia degli Incogniti literary salon, Sullam was admired for her poetry and spirited correspondence with a monk from Modena. A critic accused her of denying the immortality of the soul, a heresy punishable by death under the Inquisition. Sullam responded with a treatise on immortality written in two days; her manifesto became a bestseller. Sullam's writings remain in publication as key works of early modern Italian literature.

Philosopher Isotta Nogarola (c 1418–66) The Verona-born teen prodigy corresponded with Renaissance philosophers and was widely published in Rome and Venice. An anonymous critic published attacks against her in 1439, claiming 'an eloquent woman is never chaste' and accusing her of incest. But she continued her correspondence with leading humanists and, with Venetian diplomat Ludovico Foscarini, published an influential early feminist tract: a 1453 dialogue asserting that since Eve and Adam were jointly responsible for expulsion from Paradise, women and men must be equals.

Musician and poet Gaspara Stampa (1523–54) A true Renaissance intellectual, Gaspara Stampa was a renowned lute player, literary-salon organiser, and author of published Petrarchan sonnets openly dedicated to her many lovers. Historians debate her livelihood before she became a successful author; some claim she was a courtesan.

Dr Eleonora Lucrezia Cornaro Piscopia (1646–84) Another prodigy, she became the first female university doctoral graduate in Europe in 1678 at the University of Padua, where a statue of her now stands. Her prolific contributions to the intellectual life of Venice are commemorated with a plaque inside Venice's city hall.

blessing. This city is too distinctive to fade into the background, so the city tends to upstage even the most photogenic co-stars (which only partly excuses 2010's *The Tourist*).

Since Casanova's escapades and a couple of Shakespearean dramas unfolded in Venice, the lagoon city was a natural choice of location for movie versions of these tales. In the Casanova category, two excellent accounts are Alexandre Volkoff's 1927 *Casanova* and Federico Fellini's 1976 *Casanova*, starring Donald Sutherland. Oliver Parker directed a 1995 version of *Othello*, but the definitive version remains Orson Welles' 1952 *Othello*, shot partly in Venice, but mostly on location in Morocco. Later adaptations of silver-screen classics haven't lived up to the original, including Michael Radford's 1994 *The Merchant of Venice* starring Al Pacino as Shylock, and Swedish director Lasse Hallström's 2005 *Casanova*, with a nonsensical plot but a charmingly rakish Heath Ledger in the title role.

After WWII, Hollywood came to Venice in search of romance, and the city delivered as the backdrop for Katherine Hepburn's midlife Italian love affair in David Lean's 1955 *Summertime*. Of all his films, Lean claimed this was his favourite, above *Lawrence of Arabia* and *Doctor Zhivago*. Locals confirm that yes, Signora Hepburn did fall into that canal, and no, she wasn't happy about it. Gorgeous Venice set pieces compensated for some dubious singing in Woody Allen's musical romantic comedy *Everyone Says I Love You* (1996). But the most winsome Venetian romance is Silvio Soldini's *Pane e Tulipani* (Bread and Tulips; 1999), a tale of an Italian housewife who restarts her life as a woman of mystery in Venice, trying to dodge the detective novel–reading plumber hot on her trail.

More often than not, romance seems to go horribly wrong in films set in Venice. It turns to obsession in *Morte a Venezia* (Death in Venice), Luchino Visconti's 1971 adaptation of the Thomas Mann novel, and again in *The Comfort of Strangers* (1990), featuring Natasha Richardson and Rupert Everett inexplicably following Christopher Walken into shadowy Venetian alleyways. A better adaptation of a lesser novel, *The Wings of the Dove* (1997) was based on the Henry James novel and mostly shot in the UK, though you can scarcely notice behind Helena Bonham-Carter's hair.

Venice has done its best to shock moviegoers over the years, as with Nicolas Roeg's riveting *Don't Look Now* (1973) starring Donald Sutherland, Julie Christie, and Venice at its most ominous and depraved. *Dangerous Beauty* (1998) is raunchier but sillier, a missed opportunity to show 16th-century Venice through the eyes of a courtesan.

Always ready for action, Venice made appearances in *Indiana Jones and the Last Crusade* (1989) and *Casino Royale* (2006), whose Grand Canal finale was shot in Venice with some help from CGI – don't worry, no Gothic architecture was harmed in the making of that blockbuster. To see the latest big film to make a splash in Venice, don't miss the Venice International Film Festival.

Venice's first movie role dates from the earliest days of cinema, as the subject of the 1897 short film *A Panoramic View of Venice*. But since Venice was complicated and expensive for location shooting, silver-screen classics set in Venice, such as the Astaire-Rogers vehicle *Top Hat*, were shot in Hollywood backlots.

Theatre & Performing Arts

Venice is a theatre, and whenever you arrive, you're just in time for a show. Sit on any *campo* (square), and the *commedia dell'arte* (archetypal comedy) and *opera buffa* commence, with stock characters improvising variations on familiar themes: graduating university students lurching towards another round of toasts, kids crying over gelato fallen into canals, neighbours hanging out laundry gossiping indiscreetly across the *calle*. Once you've visited Venice, you'll have a whole new appreciation for its theatrical innovations.

HISTORIC PERFORMANCE VENUES

Teatro La Fenice Opera in a blaze of glory.

Palazzetto Bru Zane Leading interpreters of Romantic music raise the frescoed roof.

Interpreti Veneziani Baroque among masterpieces in Chiesa di San Vidal.

Pietà The Venetian baroque composer Vivaldi's work played at the orphanage where he was musical director.

Scuola di San Giovanni Evangelista Arias in Venice's frescoed halls of power.

Commedia dell'Arte

During Carnevale, *commedia dell'arte* conventions take over, and all of Venice acts out with masks, extravagant costumes and exaggerated gestures. It may seem fantastical today, but for centuries this was Italy's dominant form of theatre. Scholars attribute some of Molière's running gags and Shakespeare's romantic plots to the influence of *commedia dell'arte* – although Shakespeare would have been shocked to note that in Italy, women's parts were typically played by women. But after a couple of centuries of *commedia dell'arte*, 18th-century Venice began to tire of bawdy slapstick. Sophisticated improvisations had been reduced to farce, robbing the theatre of its subversive zing.

Comedy & Opera Buffa

Enter Carlo Goldoni (1707–93), a former doctor's apprentice, occasional lawyer, and whipsmart librettist who wrote some serious tragic opera. But of his 160 plays and 80 or so libretti, he remains best loved for *opera buffa*, unmasked social satires that remain ripe and delicious: battles of the sexes, self-important socialites getting their comeuppance, and the impossibility of pleasing one's boss.

Goldoni was light-hearted but by no means a lightweight; his comic genius and deft wordplay would permanently change Italian theatre. His *Pamela* (1750) was the first play to dispense with masks altogether, and his characters didn't fall into good or evil archetypes: everyone was flawed, often hilariously so. Some of his most winsome roles were reserved for women and *castrati* (male soprano countertenors), from his early 1735 adaptation of Apostolo Zeno's *Griselda* (based on Bocaccio's *Decameron*, with a score by Vivaldi) to his celebrated 1763 *Le Donne Vendicate* (Revenge of the Women). Princess Cecilia Mahony Giustiniani commissioned this latter work, in which two women show a preening chauvinist the error of his ways with light swordplay and lethal wordplay.

But one Venetian dramatist was not amused. Carlo Gozzi (1720–1806) believed that Goldoni's comedies of middle-class manners were prosaic, and staged a searing 1761 parody of Goldoni – driving Goldoni to France in disgust, never to return to Venice. Gozzi went on to minor success with his fairy-tale scenarios, one of which would inspire the Puccini opera *Turandot*. But Gozzi's fantasias had little staying power, and eventually he turned to...comedy.

Meanwhile, Goldoni fell on hard times in France, after a pension granted to him by King Louis XVI was revoked by the Revolution. He died impoverished, though at his French colleagues' insistence, the French state granted his pension to his widow. But Goldoni got the last laugh: while Gozzi's works are rarely staged, Goldoni regularly gets top billing along with Shakespeare at the city's main theatre, Teatro Goldoni.

While the Venice Biennale and International Film Festival are now major draws for international celebrities, spring and autumn theatre programs hosted by the Venice Biennale remain experimental, drawing on Venice's 400-year tradition of risk-taking theatre.

Contemporary Performing Arts

The modern performing-arts scene is not all Goldoni and Shakespeare reruns. Avant-garde troupes and experimental theatres such as Teatro Junghans, Teatro Fondamenta Nuove and Laboratorio Occupato Morion bring new plays, performance art and choreography to Venetian stages. Elements of *commedia dell'arte* ballet periodically enjoy revivals on the contemporary dance scene, and contemporary dance is highlighted at Fondazione Giorgio Cini and during the Biennale International Festival of Contemporary Dance in June.

Life as a Venetian

Despite what you may have heard, Venice isn't sinking – it's breaking new ground. With the world's most artistic masterpieces per square kilometre, you'd think the city would take it easy, maybe rest on its laurels. But between billionaire benefactors and cutting-edge biennales, Venice's palazzi (palaces) are overflowing with new eyebrow-raising contemporary art and architecture. In narrow calli (alleyways), you'll glimpse artisans hammering out shoes crested like lagoon birds, cooks whipping up four-star dishes on single-burner hotplates, and musicians lugging 18th-century cellos to baroque concerts played with punk-rock bravado. Your timing couldn't be better: the people who made walking on water look easy are already well into their next act.

Fellow Travellers

Don't go expecting to have the city to yourself. Even in the foot-stomping chill of January, Venice has its admirers. The upside is that you'll keep fascinating company here. More accessible than ever and surprisingly affordable given its singularity, Venice remains a self-selecting city: it takes a certain imagination to forgo the convenience of cars and highways for slow boats and crooked *calli*. Your fellow travellers probably share your passions for art, music, history, architecture, food and drink, since Venice really isn't big on business conventions, nightclubs or extreme sports (unless you include glass-shopping in Murano). Except for couples canoodling on gondolas and secluded corners of the *campo*, this is a highly sociable city, so don't be shy about sharing a table or striking up conversation.

Mingling After Hours

Venetians don't always have time to join the conversation during their workdays, but stick around and you'll see a different city. Venice is best when caught between acts, after the day-trippers rush off to beat afternoon traffic, and before cruise ships dump dazed newcomers off in Piazza San Marco with three hours to see all of Venice before lunch. Those visitors may never get to see Venice in its precious downtime, when mosaic artisans converge at the bar for tesserae shoptalk and jokes over a *spritz* (*prosecco*-bitters cocktail).

The most sensitive happy-hour subject is still Mose (Modulo Sperimentale Elettromeccanico), the controversial flood-barrier system currently under construction. But the combined effects of industrial pollution and global warming are also taken very seriously in this fragile lagoon ecosystem, and any effort you make to help mitigate the impact of travel – stay longer, eat and drink local specialities, support local artisans, tidy up after yourself – makes you a most welcome guest. Share your appreciation with Venetians, and they'll return the sentiment. 'There's only one Venice', explains one host as he pours another glass of fizzy Veneto *prosecco* well past the mark for *un ombra* (half-glass). 'We might as well enjoy it.'

Even in high season, Venice never hits maximum capacity. At its population peak c 1563, Venice accommodated 170,000 residents. Today, on its busiest summer days, the city accommodates around 120,000 residents and visitors combined: comparatively uncrowded, by historical standards.

VENETIAN ROAD RULES

Even though there are no cars in Venice, some pedestrian traffic rules apply:

Walk single file and keep right along narrow streets to let people pass in either direction, and make way for anyone who says *permesso* (excuse me) – usually a local rushing to or from work or school.

Pull over to the side if you want to check out a shop window or snap a photo, but don't linger for long: this is the pedestrian equivalent of double-parking your car.

Keep moving on smaller bridges, where stalled shutterbugs can cause traffic jams. But feel free to snap away on the Rialto and Accademia bridges – everyone loves photographing these Grand Canal views, including locals.

Offer to lend a hand if you see someone struggling with a stroller or heavy bag on a bridge, and you may earn a grateful *grazie!*

A Day in the Life

At some point in your trip to Venice, you might notice a rental sign on a palace door that starts you daydreaming. If you were to wake up tomorrow as a Venetian, how might your day be different? By cross-referencing demographic statistics with interviews with Venetians, an answer can be approximated. But there's only one scientific way to find out: check out your rental options and cancel that return flight. You wouldn't be alone – nearly 10% of Venice's current residents were born outside Italy.

Morning

You might wake up feeling wiser, or at least older: the average age is four years older than in most Italian cities, at 47. Don't count on the usual urban street noise to wake you from your slumber, because there aren't technically any streets here. Instead of honks and squealing brakes, you may hear gondoliers warming up their vocal chords before work and Venetian dogs padding across marble footbridges. If you're in a rush to get to work, you may have to take the long way around – on your usual route, you're duty-bound to stop and say hello to so many neighbours and colleagues that you're bound to arrive 15 minutes late ('on Venetian time').

No matter which way you take, you are likely to get stopped by a tourist asking for directions. You politely oblige, but you privately wish visitors would consult a map or follow yellow signs posted around town pointing towards San Marco, Accademia and Ferrovia. If each day tripper asked one local for directions to San Marco, every Venetian would hear the question repeated some 350 times a year. Besides, you'd appreciate someone showing some personal interest in your thoughts instead, and asking a more interesting question – your current favourite Veneto wine, say, or your opinion about who should win the Golden Lion at this year's Venice Film Festival.

Since this is Venice, statistically you probably work in a service-related field, or you might be one of Venice's 2000 union-certified master artisans – but since this city is a costly place to live, you may have a couple of different jobs to pay the rent. On a coffee break, you once again debate with neighbours about the merits of moving to mainland Mestre for the lower cost of living and broader choices of amenities, including schools and hospitals. But you dread the commute, and can't quite convince yourself that the mainland conveniences of cars and malls compensate for the sense of wonder Venice provides. Like most Venetians, you hit the mainland for sales around the holidays, and hurry back via train and *vaporetto*, hauling shopping bags across bridges and along canals, eager to reach your modest apartment in your glorious city.

Afternoon

Even if work is busy, you can't put off your break for a quick lunch at a backstreet *bacaro* (bar) for too long – otherwise, you'll be jostling for elbow room at the counter with sculptors, harpsichordists, sushi chefs and dreamers passing as accountants. Judging by the crowd, a newcomer to town might think the Art Biennale must be happening – but no, it's just an average Wednesday in Venice. At your neighbourhood *bacaro*, the server whom you've known since school days immediately recognises you're in a rush,

> *Share your appreciation with Venetians, and they'll return the sentiment.*

and prepares an extra-heaped plate of *risotto di seppie* (squid risotto) on the double while *forestieri* (mainlanders) wait. Being Venetian may seem like an uphill struggle some days, but it does have its perks.

Towards the end of the workday, you coordinate with friends to meet for a drink; there's no particular hurry to get home. Like most Italians, you may have lived with family members until well into your adulthood: but unlike other Italians, more than half of Venetians live alone. There are statistically more women then men in Venice, which makes for a somewhat skewed dating scene. But with as many visitors every day to Venice as there are Venetians, there are fresh possibilities perpetually on the horizon. Though you dodge crowds in major thoroughfares by taking winding *calli* (backstreets), you might chat, joke and flirt with visitors who linger over happy hour, kicking off promptly at 6pm.

Evening

So what if the siren just blasted out the signal for *acque alte*? Neither rain nor high tides can dampen high spirits at Venice's happy hour, when even the most orthodox fashionistas gamely pull on *stivali di gomma* (rubber boots), and slosh out to the bar to get first dibs on *cicheti* (Venetian tapas). At happy hour, you'll have the usual: *prosecco, crostini* (open-face sandwiches) and a side of controversy. Did you hear about wheelchair-access issues on the Ponte di Calatrava, possible publicity on the Ponte di Rialto, the disappearance of funds for building a new Palazzo del Cinema, and art installations causing uproars at the latest Biennale and Punta della Dogana shows? Get your opinions and wisecracks ready, because diplomatic deferral is not an option –

NOALTRÌ VERSUS VOALTRÌ (US VERSUS THEM)

The usual outside-insider dynamic doesn't quite wash in cosmopolitan Venice, whose excellent taste in imports ranges from Byzantine mosaics to the Venice Film Festival. Bringing a world-class art collection with you is one way to fit in, as Peggy Guggenheim and François Pinault (founder of Palazzo Grassi and Punta Dogana) discovered. But you don't have to be a mogul to *Venexianárse*, or 'become Venetian'. Of the 20 million visitors each year, only some three million stay overnight, and staying in a locally run B&B is a chance to experience Venice among Venetians. You can eat like a Venetian, attempt a few words of Venet, or learn a Venetian craft. But the surest way to win over Venetians is to express curiosity about them and their city – so few rushed day trippers stop to make polite conversation that the attempt is received with surprise and appreciation. As you'll find out, those other 17 million visitors are missing out on excellent company.

VENEXIANÁRSE (BECOME VENETIAN)

Banter like a local Pick up a few choice phrases in Venet, or take a weekend intensive Italian-language course at Istituto Venezia (www.istitutovenezia.com; from €500).

Take to the water Learn to row standing like *gondolieri* do with Row Venice (p174), or sail away into the blue lagoon with sailing classes at Vento di Venezia (p178).

Start a Venetian art movement Ca' Pozzo (p220) offers photography expeditions with a local National Geographic photographer, and Novecento (p215) hosts plein-air drawing classes.

Cook authentic cicheti Novecento (p215) cooking classes cover the basics, and Gritti Palace (p215) offers advanced lessons at its in-house cooking school.

Drink like a lagoon fish Sip your way to aficionado status with wine-tasting classes from Venetian Vine (p133), self-guided tastings at I Rusteghi (p76), and events at Vinitaly (p22) or ViniVeri (p40).

Masquerade like you mean it Devise your own mask for Carnevale – or for back at the office, when the boss is looking for you – at Ca' Macana (p25), or create your own costume and learn *commedia dell'arte* acting at Teatro Junghans (p167).

and joking is expected here in the home of Goldoni and *opera di buffa* (comic opera).

Glancing at your watch, you might decide to attend a friend's invitation to a recital or debut. If you accepted every invitation you received to a theatre performance, book reading, jazz concert or art opening by a relative, neighbour or friend-of-a-friend, your social calendar would be as packed as Carnevale year-round. But some events you just can't skip – if Venice's history is any indication, you never know which show could be the one people will be talking about for decades or even centuries to come. Besides, that way you won't have to take the long way around to work tomorrow, to avoid inevitable delays from apologies and belated congratulations in the *calle*. Tomorrow you're on call to assist in Venice's encore performance, for a whole new audience of visitors – but tonight there's time for one last toast, to *la bea vita di Venezia* (Venice's beautiful life).

The Fragile Lagoon

White ibis perch on rock outcroppings, piles of lagoon crab are hauled into the Pescaria, and waters change like mood rings from teal blue to oxidised silver: life on the lagoon is extraordinary, and extraordinarily fragile. Gazing across these waters to the distant Adriatic horizon, the lagoon appears to be an extension of the sea. But with its delicate balance of salty and fresh water, barene (mud banks) and grassy marshes, the lagoon supports a unique aquaculture.

Rivers & Tides

The lagoon is a great shallow dish, where ocean tides meet freshwater streams from alpine rivers. The salty-sweet lagoon is protected by a slender 50km arc of islands, halting the Adriatic's advances. Between Punta Sabbioni and Chioggia, three *bocche di porto* (port entrances) allow the Adriatic entry into the lagoon. When sirocco winds push ocean waves toward the Venetian gulf, or *seiche* (long waves) gently unroll along the Adriatic coast, *acque alte* ensue. These seasonal tides help wash the lagoon clean of extra silt and maintain the salty-sweet balance of its waters.

Rising Waters

You may have heard that Venice is sinking, but that's not quite accurate. The city is partly built on wooden foundations sunk deep into lagoon silt, and it's held up miraculously well for centuries. Well-drilling by coastal industries resulted in subsidence, but drilling has been halted since the 1960s.

However, the dredging of deeper channels to accommodate supertankers and cruise ships allows more water to rush in from the sea during *acque alte*, posing danger to the city. Back in 1900, Piazza San Marco flooded about 10 times a year; now it's closer to 60. Engineers estimate that, with technological advances, Venice may be able to withstand a 26cm to 60cm rise in water levels in the 21st century – great news, except that an intergovernmental panel on climate change recently forecast increases as high as 88cm. In 2011, Unesco expressed concern about the impact of climate change in the Unesco-protected Venice lagoon.

You probably won't be sloshing through seawater while you're in Venice – though 2012 had two high tides, extremely high tides usually happen once every three to five years – but rising tides threaten Venice all the same. The lagoon's salt content is increasing, endangering sea life and corroding stone foundations. To keep Venice above water, the city has been raising the banks to 120cm above normal tide level, especially in low-lying San Marco.

Mose

The hot topic of the last 30 years in Venice is a mobile flood barrier project known as Mose (Modulo Sperimentale Elettromeccanico – Experimental Electromechanical Module). With a planned completion date of 2014, these inflatable barriers 30m high and 20m wide are intended to seal the three entrances to Venice's lagoon whenever the sea approaches dangerous levels. Ever since the great flood of 1966, many Unesco-affiliated

Venice's plague quarantine island of Lazaretto Nuovo serves a new decontamination function: Venetian marshland grasses found effective in absorbing industrial pollutants are currently being propagated outside the quarantine-barrack walls.

organisations have been urgently concerned about this jewel box of a city containing the world's great art treasures, and Mose proponents say the city must be saved at any cost.

But what are the costs, exactly? Current estimates top €5 billion for what is described even by its supporters as only a partial solution, since flooding is also caused by excessive rain, run-off and swollen inland rivers. As many Venetians point out, the city is their home, not just a treasure chest, and any stopgap measure must be considered for its public impact. Would flood barriers fill the lagoon with stagnant water, creating public health risks and driving away tourists? Could Mose change local aquaculture, and end fishing on the lagoon? Will it delay solutions to underlying problems, in addition to diverting funds essential for city maintenance? Debates continue as Mose's completion date nears, despite nine court appeals to halt its construction.

> *Seasonal tides help wash the lagoon clean of extra silt and maintain the salty-sweet balance of its waters.*

Lagoon Conservation

High waters aren't the only concern. Venice's foundations are taking a pounding as never before, with new stresses from wakes of speeding motorboats and industrial pollutants. When pollution and silt fill in shallow areas, algae takes over, threatening building foundations and choking out other marine life. Since 1930 an estimated 20% of bird life has disappeared, 80% of lagoon flora is gone, and lagoon water transparency has dropped 60%. The birds perched on canal posts, the plentiful crabs, the gleaming teal waters: all the distinctive features of Venice's Unesco World Heritage–listed lagoon are at risk.

Venetians have made remarkable progress in preserving lagoon life. Industrial waste from mainland Porto Marghera has been curbed over the years, and water is cleaner today than in the 1980s. Plans are under way to convert inland industrial complexes into hi-tech parks, sustainable fisheries and wetland preserves.

Responsible Tourism

In the wake of Tuscany's 2012 *Costa Concordia* shipwreck, Unesco expressed concern about the impact of cruise ships on Venice and

---

THE TIDE IS HIGH

Sirens on a winter's afternoon don't send Venetians into a panic – though they might sport rubber boots at happy hour. The alarm from 16 sirens throughout the city is a warning that *acque alte* (high tide) is expected to reach the city within two to four hours. Venetians aren't often surprised: most monitor Venice's Centro Maree 48-hour tidal forecast at at www.comune.venezia.it for winter-spring high-tide warnings.

Acque alte sirens aren't heard that often. Water levels only reach 110cm above normal lagoon levels four to six times a year, usually between November and April. When alarms sound, it's not an emergency situation but a temporary tide that principally affects low-lying areas. Within five hours, the tide usually ebbs, and you can hear tidal waters gurgling into the city's drains like a giant bathtub.

➡ **One even tone** (up to 110cm above normal): barely warrants a pause in happy-hour conversation.

➡ **Two rising tones** (up to 120cm): you might need *stivali di gomma* (rubber boots).

➡ **Three rising tones** (around 130cm): check Centro Maree online to see where *passarelle* (gangplank walkways) are in use.

➡ **Four rising tones** (140cm and up): shopkeepers close up early, sliding flood barriers across their doorsteps.

its Unesco-protected lagoon. Italy's Port Authority has proposed re-routing cruise ships to Venice via Porta Marghera, bypassing Giudecca Canal, at an estimated cost of €123 million – a bargain, considering cruise lines pay Italy €40 million annually for docking privileges. But critics like Venice's No Grandi Navi (No Big Ships) committee oppose cruise-ship entry for introducing pollution to the lagoon, including canal bank–corroding sulphur. Alternative seaward ports have been proposed at Malamocco.

Meanwhile, responsible tourists are taking action. The conservation measures many visitors already take – eating sustainably sourced local food, conserving water, using products free of industrial chemicals – are offsetting their impact on lagoon. To change Venice travel patterns for the greener, consider supporting Venetian businesses that are known to be environmentally savvy (marked with a leaf symbol in this book).

Canalside dining

Survival Guide

Transport

ARRIVING IN VENICE

Most people arrive in Venice by train, though for better or worse an increasing number are arriving by plane and cruise ship. There is a long-distance bus service to the city itself and it is also possible to drive to Venice, though you have to park at the end of the city and then walk or take a *vaporetto* (small passenger ferry).

Flights from London or Madrid to Venice take about 2½ hours; from New York nine hours; from Paris two hours; and from most other destinations in Europe between one and two hours.

Trains from Paris to Venice take about 13 hours; from London 17 hours; from Berlin 16 hours; from Frankfurt 11 hours; from Milan three hours; and from Rome four hours.

Flights, tours and rail tickets can be booked online at lonelyplanet.com.

Train

Prompt, affordable, scenic and environmentally savvy, trains (www.trenitalia.it) are the preferred transport option to and from Venice. Trains run frequently to Venice's Stazione Santa Lucia (appearing on signs as Ferrovia within Venice). There is direct, intercity service to most major Italian cities, as well as major points in France, Germany, Austria, Switzerland, Slovenia and Croatia.

Local trains that link Venice to the Veneto are frequent, reliable and remarkably inexpensive, including Padua (Padova; €3.50, 30 to 50 minutes, three to four per hour), Verona (€7.40, 1¾ hours, three to four per hour) and points in between. Faster intercity trains also serve these Veneto destinations, but the time saved may not be worth the 200% surcharge.

Train Stations

VENICE

When getting train tickets, be sure to specify **Venezia Santa Lucia** (VSL), for the station in central Venice, as opposed to Venezia Mestre. The station has a rail-travel **information office** (☉7am-9pm) opposite the APT office and a **deposito bagagli** (left luggage office; ☎041 78 55 31; Venezia Santa Lucia; per piece 1st 5hr €5, next 6hr €0.70, thereafter per hr €0.30; ☉6am-11pm) opposite platform 1.

MESTRE

On the mainland (which is a 10-minute train ride from Santa Lucia), **Venezia Mestre** station offers rail information, a hotel-booking office and a **deposito bagagli** (☎041 78 44 46; Venezia Mestre; per piece 1st 5hr €5, next 6hr €0.70, thereafter per hr €0.30; ☉7am-11pm). While many trains head

---

USEFUL VAPORETTO ROUTES

Whether you're arriving in Venice by train, bus, boat or car you'll find the following *vaporetti* connect Santa Lucia train station and Piazzale Roma (the bus terminus and shuttle drop for cruise ships and car passengers) with all parts of Venice:

Line 1 Plies the Grand Canal to San Marco and Lido every 10 minutes.

Line 2 Follows the same route as Line 1, with fewer stops, returning via Giudecca.

Lines 41, 42 Circles the outside of Venice's perimeter in both directions.

Lines 51, 52 Follows the same route as 41 and 42 but with fewer stops and adds in Lido.

Line N All-night local service for Giudecca, the Grand Canal, San Marco and Lido (11.30pm to 4am about every 40 minutes).

There is also a handy water-taxi stand at Piazzale Roma if you are heavily laden.

CLIMATE CHANGE & TRAVEL

Every form of transport that relies on carbon-based fuel generates CO_2, the main cause of human-induced climate change. Modern travel is dependent on aeroplanes, which might use less fuel per kilometre per person than most cars but travel much greater distances. The altitude at which aircraft emit gases (including CO_2) and particles also contributes to their climate change impact. Many websites offer 'carbon calculators' that allow people to estimate the carbon emissions generated by their journey and, for those who wish to do so, to offset the impact of the greenhouse gases emitted with contributions to portfolios of climate-friendly initiatives throughout the world. Lonely Planet offsets the carbon footprint of all staff and author travel.

all the way to Santa Lucia, some itineraries may require a change here.

To/From Venezia Santa Lucia

Vaporetti connect Santa Lucia train station with all parts of Venice. See p278 for the most useful routes. There is also a handy water-taxi stand just out front if you are heavily laden.

Tickets

Train tickets can be purchased at self-serve ticketing machines in the station, online at www.trenitalia.it, in the UK at **Rail Europe** (www. raileurope.co.uk) or through travel agents.

Validate your ticket in the orange machines on station platforms before boarding your train. Failure to do so can result in embarrassment and a hefty on-the-spot fine when the inspector checks tickets on the train.

Air

Most flights to Venice fly in to **Marco Polo airport** (☑041 260 92 60; www.veniceairport. it; Viale Galileo Galilei 30/1, Tessera), 12km outside Venice, east of Mestre. Ryanair and some other budget airlines also use **Treviso Airport** (TSF; ☑0422 31 51 11; www.trevisoairport.it; Via Noalese 63), 5km southwest of Treviso and a 30km, one-hour drive from Venice.

Low-cost airlines are a benefit to travellers but a

burden on the environment and Venice's air quality; to travel with a cleaner conscience, consider a carbon-offset program.

To/From the Airport
MARCO POLO AIRPORT
There is a range of options for getting from the airport to the heart of Venice, including buses, water taxis and reliable passenger ferry links.

Azienda Trasporti Veneto Orientale (ATVO; ☑0421 59 46 71; www.atvo. it) runs buses to the airport from Piazzale Roma (€6, 30 minutes, every 30 minutes from 8am to midnight).

Azienda del Consorzio Trasporti Veneziano (☑041 24 24; www.actv.it) runs bus 5 between Marco Polo airport and Piazzale Roma (€6, about one hour, four per hour).

A taxi ride to Venice's Piazzale Roma costs €30 to €40, but Alilaguna boats are likely to get you much closer to your final destination at least as fast.

Alilaguna (☑041 240 17 01; www.alilaguna.com; Marco Polo airport) operates four water-taxi lines that link the airport with various parts of Venice at a cost of €15. Lines include the following:

Linea Blu (Blue Line) Stops at Lido, San Marco, Stazione Marittima and points in between.

Linea Rossa (Red Line) Stops at Murano and Lido.

Linea Arancia (Orange Line) Stops at Stazione Santa Lucia, Rialto and San Marco via the Grand Canal.

Linea Gialla (Yellow Line) Stops at Murano and Fondamento Nuovo.

TREVISO AIRPORT
Public-transport options to and from Treviso airport to Venice include the following:

Barzi Bus Service (☑0422 68 60 83; www.bar ziservice.com) provides the most direct service to Piazzale Roma in Venice (€7, 40 minutes, one to two per hour

WATER TAXIS

Private water taxis are available for hire in the arrivals hall at Marco Polo. They can also be booked online at discounted prices through www.venicelink.com. There are options for private and shared taxis at a cost of €110 one way for a private transfer and €32 per person in a shared taxi. Boats seat a maximum of eight people and accommodate up to 10 bags. Those opting for a shared taxi should be aware that the service has set drop-off points in Venice; only private transfers will take you directly to your hotel.

from 8am to 10.30pm). Buy tickets on the bus or at its desk in the arrivals hall. Tickets purchased on Ryanair are not valid.

Azienda Trasporti Veneto Orientale (ATVO; ☑0422 31 53 81; www.atvo. it) also offers a service to Mestre and Piazzale Roma in Venice (€7, 70 minutes, one to two per hour from 5.30am to 11.30pm), but it takes a more circuitous route.

ACTT (☑0422 32 71; www.actt.it) line 6 connects Treviso airport with Treviso train station (€1.20 or €2.50 if purchased on the bus, 20 minutes, two to three an hour from 6am to 10.30pm).

Taxis from Treviso airport to Venice cost upwards of €70.

Bus

Urban, regional and long-distance buses all arrive in Venice's Piazzale Roma, from where *vaporetti* connect with the rest of the city. Service includes:

Eurolines (☑041 538 21 18; www.eurolines.com) Operates a wide range of international routes.

ACTV (Azienda del Consorzio Trasporti Veneziano; ☑041 24 24; www.actv.it) Runs buses to Mestre and surrounding areas.

ATVO (Azienda Trasporti Veneto Orientale; ☑041 520 55 30) Operates buses from Piazzale Roma to destinations all over the eastern Veneto, including airport connections.

Car & Motorcycle

To get to Venice by car or motorcycle, take the often congested Trieste–Turin A4, which passes through Mestre. From Mestre, take the 'Venezia' exit. Once over Ponte della Libertà from Mestre, cars must be left at the car park at Piazzale Roma or Tronchetto.

Car ferry 17 also transports vehicles from Tronchetto to the Lido.

If you are determined to drive, be warned: visitors who drive across the bridge into Venice pay a hefty price in parking fees, and traffic backs up at weekends.

Getting from Tronchetto to Piazzale Roma

If you park on Tronchetto, the new monorail known as the People Mover will whisk you from Tronchetto to Piazzale Roma. For onward travel from Piazzale Roma see p278.

Parking

You'll find car parks in Piazzale Roma or on Isola del Tronchetto. Prices in Venice start at €21 per day. At peak times, lots become completely full. However, you can book a parking place ahead of time at www.venicecon nected.com.

To avoid these hassles (and to make the most of the cheaper car parks) consider parking in Mestre, and take the bus or train into Venice instead. Remember to take anything that looks even remotely valuable out of your car, since thieves prowl local car parks.

For a range of parking options in Venice and Mestre, including prices and directions, head to www. asmvenezia.it.

Garage Europa Mestre (☑041 95 92 02; www.gara geeuropamestre.com; Corso del Popolo 55, Mestre; 1st day €14, each additional day €12; ☺8am-10pm) Has 300 spaces; ACTV bus 4 to/from Venice stops right outside the garage, or it's a 10-minute walk to the Mestre train station.

ASM Autoremissa Comunale (☑041 272 73 07; www. asmvenezia.it; Piazzale Roma; compact car in low/peak period per day €24/26, car

DRIVING DISTANCES TO VENICE

Berlin 1135km
Florence 260km
Frankfurt 940km
Geneva 579km
London 1515km
Madrid 1820km
Milan 279km
Paris 1112km
Prague 798km
Rome 529km
Vienna 610km

over 185cm €27/29; ☺24hr) Has 2182 spaces; the largest lot in Piazzale Roma; discounts available with online reservations; free six-hour parking for people with disabilities.

Garage San Marco (☑041 523 22 13; www.garagesan marco.it; Piazzale Roma 467f; per 12/24hr €26/30, overnight 5pm-4am €15; ☺24hr) Has 900 spaces; guests of certain hotels get discounts.

Parking Sant'Andrea (☑041 272 73 04; www.asm venezia.it; Piazzale Roma; per 2hr or part thereof €6; ☺24hr) Has 100 spaces; best for short-term parking.

Interparking (Tronchetto Car Park; ☑041 520 75 55; www.veniceparking.it; Isola del Tronchetto; per 2/24hr €6/21; ☺24hr) Has 3864 spaces; the largest lot with the cheapest 24-hour rate; *vaporetti* connect directly with Piazza San Marco, while the People Mover provides connections to Piazzale Roma and the cruise terminal.

Boat

Venice has regular ferry connections with Greece, Croatia and Slovenia. However, remember that long-haul ferries and cruise ships have an outsize environmental impact on tiny Venice and its fragile lagoon aquaculture.

Consider the lower-impact train instead – Venice will be grateful.

Anek (www.anek.gr) runs four ferries week between Venice and Greece with boats docking at Igoumenitsa, Corfu and Patras.

Venezia Lines (☑385 524 228 96; www.venezialines.com) runs high-speed boats to and from Croatia and Slovenia in summer.

To/From Stazione Marittima

Cruise ships usually provide free shuttles that connect the Stazione Marittima with Piazzale Roma. From Piazzale Roma, *vaporetti* head out to all parts of Venice (see p278).

GETTING AROUND VENICE

Vaporetto

The city's main mode of public transport is the *vaporetto*. **ACTV** (☑041 24 24; www. actv.it) runs public transport in the Comune di Venezia (the municipality), covering mainland buses and all the waterborne public transport around Venice. Although the service is efficient and generally punctual, it has suffered some recent cuts, which means that at peak times boats on main lines get full fast. One-way tickets cost €7.

Some lines make only limited stops, especially from 8am to 10am and 6pm to 8pm, so check boat signage. If in doubt, ask the person charged with letting people on and off the boat.

Interisland ferry services to Murano, Torcello, the Lido and other lagoon islands are usually provided on larger *motonave* (big interisland *vaporetti*). One-way tickets on these slower services cost €4.

Vaporetto stops can be confusing, so check the signs at the landing dock to make sure you're at the right stop for the direction you want. At major stops like Ferrovia, Piazzale Roma, San Marco and Zattere, there are often two separate docks for the same *vaporetto* line, heading in opposite directions.

The cluster of stops near Piazza San Marco are especially tricky. If your boat doesn't stop right in front of Piazza San Marco, don't panic: it will probably stop at San Zaccaria, just past the Palazzo Ducale.

Tickets

Tickets for *vaporetti* can be purchased from the **HelloVenezia** (☑041 24 24; www.hellovenezia.com) ticket booths at most landing stations, and free timetables and route maps are available at many of these ticket booths.

Instead of spending €7 for a one-way ticket, consider a Tourist Travel Card – a timed pass for unlimited travel within a set period beginning when you first validate your ticket in the yellow machine located at ferry stations. Swipe your card every time you board, even if you have already validated it upon your initial ride. If you're caught without a valid ticket, you'll be required to pay a €60 fine.

People aged 14 to 29 can get a three-day ticket for €18 with the Tourist Travel Card.

Routes

From Piazzale Roma or the train station, *vaporetto* 1 zigzags up the Grand Canal to San Marco and onward to the Lido. If you're not in a rush, it's a great introduction to Venice. *Vaporetto* 17 carries vehicles from Tronchetto, near Piazzale Roma, to the Lido.

Frequency varies greatly according to line and time of day. *Vaporetto* 1 runs every 10 minutes throughout most of the day, while lines such as the 41 and 42 only run every 20 minutes. Services

---

to Burano and Torcello are less frequent. Night services can be as much as one hour apart. Some lines stop running by around 9pm, so check timetables.

Keep in mind that routes, route numbers and schedules can change, and not all routes go both ways. Here are the key *vaporetto* lines and major stops, subject to seasonal changes:

No 1 Runs Piazzale Roma–Ferrovia–Grand Canal (all stops)–Lido and back (runs 5am to 11.30pm, every 10 minutes from 7am to 10pm).

No 2 Circular line: runs San Zaccaria–Redentore–Zattere–Trochetto–Ferrovia–Rialto–Accademia–San Marco.

No 5 Runs San Zaccaria–Murano and back.

No 8 Runs Giudecca–Zattere–Redentore–Giardini–Lido.

No 13 Runs Fondamente Nuove–Murano–Vignole–

The Tourist Travel Card *vaporetto* pass allows for unlimited travel within the following time blocks:

12 hours €18
24 hours €20
36 hours €25
48 hours €30
72 hours €35
1 week €50

Sant'Erasmo–Treporti and back.

No 17 Car ferry: runs Tronchetto–Lido and back.

No 18 Runs Murano–Sant'Erasmo–Lido and back (summer only).

No 20 Runs San Zaccaria–San Servolo–San Lazzaro degli Armeni and back.

No 41 Circular line: runs Murano–Fondamente Nuove–Ferrovia–Piazzale Roma–Redentore–San Zaccaria–Fondamente Nuove–San Michele–Murano (6am to 10pm, every 20 minutes).

No 42 Circular line in reverse direction to No 41 (6.30am to 8.30pm, every 20 minutes).

No 51 Circular line: runs Lido–Fondamente Nuove–Riva de Biasio–Ferrovia–Piazzale Roma–Zattere–San Zaccaria–Giardini–Lido.

No 52 Circular line in reverse direction to No 51.

No 61 Circular line, limited stops, weekdays only: runs Piazzale Roma–Santa Marta–San Basilio–Zattere–Giardini–Sant'Elena–Lido.

No 62 Circular line, limited stops, weekdays only in reverse direction to No 61.

DM (Diretto Murano) Runs Tronchetto–Piazzale Roma–Ferrovia–Murano and back.

N All-stops night circuit, including Giudecca, Grand Canal, San Marco, Piazzale Roma and the train station (11.30pm to 4am, every 40 minutes).

N (NMU) A second night service from Fondamente Nuove to Murano (all stops).

N (NLN) A third night run offering sporadic service between Fondamente Nuove and Burano, Mazzorbo, Torcello and Treporti.

T Runs Torcello–Burano and back (7am to 8.30pm, every 30 minutes).

Vaporetto dell'Arte

New in 2012, the **Vaporetto dell'Arte** (☑041 24 24; www.vaporettoarte.com; ⊙every 30min 9am-7pm) provides a luxurious hop-on, hop-off ride down the Grand Canal. Unlike the public *vaporetti*, which can be jam-packed, the Vaporetto dell'Arte offers seating in plush red armchairs complete with seat-back monitors screening multilingual information about the attractions en route. Most people don't bother with these, as the view out the windows is far more arresting.

To get the best value from the service, buy the ticket in conjunction with your Tourist Travel Card, when the +ARTE add-on will only set you back €10. What's more, the ticket will then be valid for the same length of time as your Tourist Travel Card.

Gondola

A gondola ride offers a view of Venice that is anything but pedestrian, with glimpses through water gates into *palazzi* courtyards. Official daytime rates are €80 for 40 minutes (it's €100 from 7pm to 8am), not including songs (negotiated separately) or tips. Additional time is charged in 20-minute increments (day/night €40/50). You may negotiate a price break in overcast weather or around midday, when other travellers get hot and hungry. Agree on a price, time limit and singing in advance to avoid unexpected surcharges.

Gondolas cluster at *stazi* (stops) along the Grand Canal, at the Ferrovia stop at the **Venezia Santa Lucia station** (☑041 71 85 43), the **Rialto** (☑041 522 49 04) and near major monuments (such as I Frari, Ponte Sospiri and Accademia), but you can also book a **pick-up** (041 528 50 75) at a canal near you.

Water Taxi

Licensed **water taxis** (Consorzio Motoscafi Venezia; ☑041 240 67 11, 24hr 041 522 23 03; www.motoscafivenezia.it) are a costly way to get around Venice, though they may prove handy when you're late for the opera or have lots of luggage. Prices can be metered or negotiated in advance. Official rates start at €8.90 plus €1.80 per minute, €6 extra if they're called to your hotel. There are additional fees for night trips (10pm to 7am), luggage and for each extra passenger above the first five. Even if you're in a hurry, don't encourage your taxi driver to speed through Venice – this kicks up *motoschiaffi* (motorboat wakes) that expose Venice's ancient foundations to degradation and rot. Make sure your water taxi has the yellow strip with the licence number displayed. Illegal water-taxi drivers have been a special problem on the Isola del Tronchetto.

ETIQUETTE

Vaporetti can get crowded, and visitors anxious about missing their stops tend to cluster near exits. If you're standing near an exit, it is common practice to get off and let passengers behind you disembark before you get back on. Passengers with disabilities are first to embark or disembark, and offers of assistance are welcome. On smaller boats, leave luggage in designated areas or risk local ire.

Bicycle

Cycling is banned in central Venice. On the larger islands of Lido and Pellestrina, cycling is a pleasant way to get around and to reach distant beaches. Bicycle-hire places are clustered around the Lido *vaporetto* stop, including **Lido on Bike** (☑041 526 80 19; www.lidoonbike.it; Gran Viale 21b; bikes per 90min/day €5/9; ☺9am-7pm Apr-Sep). Take some ID.

To sort out a set of wheels for a day-trip excursion contact **Veloce** (☑346 84 71 14; www.rentalbikeitaly.com; Via Gramsci 85, Mira; touring/mountain bike per day €20/25; ☺8am-8pm), which offers a handy drop-off and pick-up service from train stations and hotels.

Boat

Aspiring sea captains can take on Venetian water traffic in a rented boat from **Brussa** (☑041 71 57 87; www.brussaisboat.it; Fondamenta Labia 331, Cannaregio; ☺7.30am-5.30pm Mon-Fri, to 12.30pm Sat). You can hire a 7m boat (including fuel) that can carry up to six

CHEAP THRILLS ON THE GRAND CANAL: TRAGHETTI

A *traghetto* is the gondola service locals use to cross the Grand Canal between its widely spaced bridges. *Traghetti* rides cost just €0.50 and typically operate from 9am to 6pm, although some routes finish by noon. For major *traghetto* crossings, consult the main map section, though note that service can be spotty at times at all crossings, so be sure to have a back-up plan.

people for an hour (€32.50) or a day (€181.50), or make arrangements for longer periods. You don't need a licence, but you will be taken on a test run to see if you can manoeuvre and park; be sure to ask them to point out the four boat-petrol stations around Venice on a map.

Car

Obviously you can't drive in Venice proper, but Lido and Pellestrina allow cars, and they can be the most efficient way of seeing far-flung sites across the Veneto. The car-rental companies Avis, Europcar and Hertz all have offices both on Piazzale Roma and at Marco Polo airport. Several companies

operate in or near Mestre train station as well.

Avis (☑041 523 73 77; www.avis.co.uk; Piazzale Roma 496g)

Europcar (☑041 523 86 16; www.europcar.co.uk; Piazzale Roma 496h)

Hertz (☑041 528 40 91; www.hertz.co.uk; Piazzale Roma 496)

Monorail

Designed by the architect Francesco Cocco, Venice's **People Mover monorail** (APM; www.apmvenezia.com; per ride €1; ☺7am-11pm Mon-Sat, 8am-9pm Sun) connects the car parks on Tronchetto with the Stazione Maritima and Piazzale Roma.

Directory A–Z

Customs Regulations

Duty-free sales within the EU no longer exist, but goods are sold free of value-added tax (VAT) in European airports. Visitors coming into Italy from non-EU countries can import duty-free: 1L of spirits (or 4L of wine), 200 cigarettes and any other goods up to a total of €430 for air and sea travellers (€300 for all other travellers). Anything over this limit must be declared on arrival and the appropriate duty paid.

For info on VAT refunds see p287.

Discount Cards & Passes

An **International Student Identity Card** (ISIC; www.isic. org) can get you discounted admission prices at some sights (such as the Scuola Grande di San Rocco) and help with cheap flights out of Italy, but ISIC benefits are limited in Venice.

Chorus Pass

The association of Venice churches offers a **Chorus Pass** (☑041 275 04 62; www. chorusvenezia.org; adult/re-duced/child €10/7/free) for single entry to 16 historic Venice churches any time within one year, including I Frari, Chiesa di Santa Maria dei Miracoli, Chiesa di San Sebastiano and Chiesa di Madonna dell'Orto. Otherwise, admission to these individual churches costs €3. Passes are for sale at church ticket booths; proceeds from the pass support restoration and maintenance of churches throughout Venice.

Civic Museum Passes

Available from the APT tour-ist office, the **Civic Museum Pass** (☑041 240 5211; www.vis itmuve.it; adult/child €20/14) is valid for six months and covers single entry to 11 civic muse-ums, including Palazzo Ducale, Ca' Rezzonico, Ca' Pesaro,

---

PRACTICALITIES

➡ The metric system is used for weights and measures.

➡ Since 2005, smoking in all closed public spaces (from bars to elevators, offices, trains and hotel rooms) has been banned.

➡ The Veneto's major newspaper is *Il Gazzettino* (www.gazzettino.it). Each city has its own edition with specific local content. *La Nuova Venezia* (www.nuovavenezia.it) is Ven-ice's own city paper and is a good source of information on local events. Of the nation-als, *Corriere della Sera* (www.corriere.it) is the most widely read, followed closely by the centre-left *La Reppublica* (www.repubblica.it).

➡ State-owned RAI-1, RAI-2 and RAI-3 (www.rai.it) broadcast all over the country. Venice Classic Radio (www.veniceclassicradio.eu) mines the city's rich archive of classi-cal, baroque and chamber music, Padua's Megamix FM (www.megamix.fm) appeals to student listeners with a dance and pop repertoire (much of it in English), and Vicenza's Golden Radio Italia (www.goldenradio.it) offers two internet channels, one featuring the top 40 and the other dedicated to the best of the '80s!

➡ Turn on the box to watch the state-run RAI-1, RAI-2 and RAI-3 (www.rai.it) and the main commercial channels (mostly run by Silvio Berlusconi's Mediaset company): Ca-nale 5 (www.canale5.mediaset.it), Italia 1 (www.italia1.mediaset.it), Rete 4 (www.rete4. mediaset.it) and LA 7 (www.la7.it).

Palazzo Mocenigo, Museo Correr, Museo del Vetro (Glass Museum) on Murano and the Museo del Merletto (Lace Museum) on Burano. Short-term visitors may prefer the **Museum Card** (adult/child €16/8), which covers four museums around Piazza San Marco (Palazzo Ducale, Museo Correr and the attached Museo Archeologico Nazionale and Biblioteca Nazionale Marciana).

Other Combined Museum Tickets

For art aficionados planning to visit the Gallerie dell'Accademia and Palazzo Grimani, consider the **combined ticket** (adult/child €14/11). The combined ticket is good for three months but may not be available during special exhibitions.

A combined ticket to the Palazzo Grassi and Punta della Dogana costs €20, for a saving of €10 on adult admission.

Venice Card

The **Venice card** (✆041 24 24; www.venicecard.com; adult/junior €39.90/29.90; ☺call centre 8am-7.30pm) is the most extensive (and expensive) discount card for the city, with an adult card for the over-30s, and a junior version for those aged between six and 29 years. Valid for seven days, it allows free entrance to the Palazzo Ducale, 10 civic museums, 16 Chorus churches, the Querini Stampalia Foundation and the Jewish Museum, as well as two free toilet passes. In addition, discounted rates are offered at a number of other museums such as the Palazzo Fortuny and the Peggy Guggenheim Collection, as well as at shops and cafes that display the Venice card sign.

A reduced version, called the **San Marco Venice card** (✆041 24 24; www.venicecard.com; €24.90), is also available, offering a more limited range of discounts and perks.

Rolling Venice Card

Visitors aged 14 to 29 years should pick up the €4 Rolling Venice card (from tourist offices and most ACTV public-transport ticket points), entitling purchase of a 72-hour public-transit pass (€18) and discounts on museums, monuments and cultural-event access, food, accommodation and entertainment.

Electricity

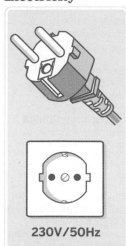

230V/50Hz

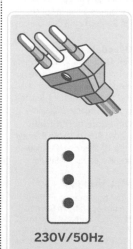

230V/50Hz

Emergency

Ambulance (✆118)
Police Station (✆113, 112) Castello (✆041 271 5511; www.poliziadistato.it; Fondamenta di San Lorenzo 505); Piazza San Marco (Piazza San Marco 63)

Gay & Lesbian Travellers

Homosexuality is legal in Italy and generally well tolerated in Venice and the Veneto. At the same time, federal officials, including former prime minister Berlusconi, have made openly disparaging remarks about homosexuality. **ArciGay** (www.arcigay.it), the national gay, lesbian, bisexual and transgender organisation, has information on the GLBT scene in Italy. The useful website www.gay.it (in Italian) lists gay and lesbian events across the country, but options in Venice are slim. Head to Padua for a wider range of gay-friendly nightlife and the nearest GLBT organisation, **ArciGay Tralaltro** (✆049 876 24 58; www.tralaltro.it; Corso Garibaldi 41).

Internet Access

If you plan to carry your notebook or palmtop computer, consider bringing a grounded power strip – it will allow you to plug in more appliances and protect your computer from the power fluctuations that can occur in Venice's older buildings.

Internet Cafes

There are internet cafes throughout Venice, though their numbers are slowly dwindling. Connections are generally fast, but prices are high: expect to pay €4 to €6 per hour.

Wi-Fi

Wi-fi access is widely available in midrange and top-

CITYWIDE WI-FI ACCESS

Since 2009, Venice has had a **citywide wi-fi access plan** (www.veniceconnected.com; per day/72hr/week €8/20/30), providing access at 20 to 100 megabits per second – free to residents and €8 per day for visitors. In reality, the quality of connection varies dramatically depending on time of day and location: the signals have trouble penetrating thick old stone walls. Note that you can get a discount of about 30% if you sign up online in advance, but it is probably best to find out first if it will actually work where you need it to.

To purchase a connection once in Venice, select one of the //venice>connected network connections in among the available wi-fi networks and then open a browser window, which should take you straight to the welcome page, where you can purchase a plan that works immediately.

end accommodation, and increasingly even in budget sleeps – plus some cafes and restaurants, though less than in other parts of Europe. Another option is to buy a PCMCIA card pack with one of the Italian mobile-phone operators, which gives wireless access through the mobile telephone network. These are usually prepaid services that you can top up as you go.

Medical Services

All foreigners have the same right as Italians to free emergency medical treatment in a public hospital in Venice. However, other medical care is not necessarily covered.

EU, Switzerland, Norway and Iceland Citizens are entitled to the full range of health-care services in public hospitals free of charge upon presentation of a European Health Insurance Card (EHIC).

Australia Thanks to a reciprocal arrangement with Italy, Australian citizens are entitled to free public health care – carry your Medicare card.

New Zealand, the USA and Canada Citizens of these and other countries have to pay for anything other than emergency

treatment. Most travel-insurance policies include medical coverage.

Emergency Clinics

Opening hours of medical services vary, though most are open 8am to 12.30pm Monday to Friday, and some open for a couple of hours on weekday afternoons and Saturday morning.

Guardia Medica (☑041 238 5648) This service of nighttime call-out doctors in Venice operates from 8pm to 8am on weekdays and from 10am the day before a holiday (including Sunday) until 8am the day after.

Ospedale Civile (☑041 529 41 11; Campo SS Giovanni e Paolo 6777) Venice's main hospital; for emergency care and dental treatment, ask for *pronto soccorso* (casualty).

Ospedale dell'Angelo (☑041 965 71 11; Via Paccagnella 11, Mestre) Vast modern hospital on the mainland.

Pharmacies

Most pharmacies in Venice are open from 9am to 12.30pm and 3.30pm to 7.30pm, and are closed on Saturday afternoon and Sunday. Information on rotating late-night pharmacies is

posted in pharmacy windows and listed in the free magazine *Un Ospite di Venezia* as well as on its website (www.unospitedivenezia.it) under 'Night Chemists'.

Money

As in 12 other EU nations (Austria, Belgium, Finland, France, Germany, Greece, Ireland, Luxembourg, the Netherlands, Portugal, Slovenia and Spain), the currency in Italy is the euro. Each participating state decorates the reverse side of the coins with its own designs, but all euro coins can be used anywhere that accepts euros.

Euro notes come in denominations of €500, €200, €100, €50, €20, €10 and €5, in different colours and sizes. Euro coins are in denominations of €2, €1, 50c, 20c, 10c, 5c, 2c and 1c.

ATMs

There are ATMs that accept international ATM cards throughout the city, with many near San Marco, Ponte di Rialto and the train station. ATMs are the most convenient and cost-effective way to access cash in Venice.

Changing Money

You can exchange money in banks, at post offices or in bureaus de change. See www.xe.com for the most current exchange rates. The post office and banks are reliable, but always ask about commissions. Also, keep a sharp eye on commissions at bureaus de change, which sometimes exceed 10% on travellers cheques.

Travelex Marco Polo Airport (☑041 541 68 33; ⊙7.30am-9.30pm); Piazza San Marco (☑041 528 73 58; Piazza San Marco 142; ⊙9am-7pm Mon-Fri, 9am-6pm Sat, 9.20am-6pm Sun); Riva del Ferro (☑041 528 73 58; Riva del Ferro 5126; ⊙9.30am-

6.45pm Mon-Sat, to 5pm Sun)
To reclaim VAT from purchases
over €200, bring completed
forms and local receipts to the
Piazza San Marco branch.

Credit Cards

Major cards such as Visa and
MasterCard are accepted
throughout Italy. Some banks
may allow you to obtain cash
advances over the counter
with MasterCard or Visa, but
be aware that this is a lengthy
process. Check charges
with your bank beforehand
to avoid any nasty surprises
later. American Express and
Diners Club are also accepted, though not as widely.

Note also that most banks
now build a fee of around
2.75% into every foreign
transaction. In addition, ATM
withdrawals attract a fee,
which can range from a flat
fee to 1.5% of the withdraw-
al, or both.

Tipping

A 10% tip is customary at
restaurants where a service
charge is not included, and
you can leave small change
at cafes and bars. Tipping
water-taxi drivers is not common practice; hotel porters
are tipped €1 per bag.

Opening Hours

The hours listed here are
a general guide; individual
establishments can vary,
sometimes widely. Also note
that hours at shops, bars and
restaurants can be some-
what flexible in Venice, as
they are in the rest of Italy.

Banks 8.30am to 1.30pm and
3.30pm to 5.30pm Monday
to Friday, though hours vary;
some open Saturday mornings.

Restaurants Noon to 2.30pm
and 7pm to 10pm.

Shops 10am to 1pm and
3.30pm to 7pm (or 4pm to
7.30pm) Monday to Saturday.

Supermarkets 9am to 7.30pm
Monday to Saturday.

Post

There are a couple of post
offices in every Venetian
sestiere, with addresses and
hours online at www.poste.it.
Convenient offices:

Post Office (Calle San
Salvador 5106, San Marco;
⊙8.30am-7.10pm Mon-Fri, to
12.35pm Sat) The main post
office branch in the historic
centre with the longest opening
hours.

Post Office (Calle Larga de
l'Ascension 1241; ⊙8.25am-
1.25pm Mon-Fri, to 12.35pm
Sat) Conveniently located
branch, just behind Piazza San
Marco.

Public Holidays

For Venetians, as for most
Italians, the main holiday
periods are summer (July
and especially August), the
Christmas–New Year period
and Easter. Restaurants,
shops and most other activity also grind to a halt around
Ferragosto (Feast of the
Assumption; 15 August).

Capodanno/Anno Nuovo
(New Year's Day) 1 January

Epifania/Befana (Epiphany)
6 January

Lunedì dell'Angelo (Good
Friday) March/April

Pasquetta/Lunedì dell'Angelo
(Easter Monday) March/April

Giorno della Liberazione
(Liberation Day) 25 April

Festa del Lavoro (Labour Day)
1 May

Festa della Repubblica
(Republic Day) 2 June

Ferragosto (Feast of the Assumption) 15 August

Ognissanti (All Saints' Day)
1 November

Immaculata Concezione
(Feast of the Immaculate
Conception) 8 December

Natale (Christmas Day)
25 December

Festa di Santo Stefano (Boxing Day) 26 December

Taxes & Refunds

VAT (value-added tax) of
around 20%, known as
Imposta di Valore Aggiunto
(IVA), is slapped onto just
about everything in Italy. If
you are a non-EU resident
and spend more than €155 in
a single transaction on selected purchases, you can claim
a refund when you leave, or
sometimes at the time of
purchase. The refund only applies to purchases from affiliated retail outlets that display
a 'tax free for tourists' (or
similar) sign. For more info
visit www.taxrefund.it.

Telephone

National and international
numbers can be requested
at ☑1254 or online at 1254.
virgilio.it.

Domestic Calls

Italian telephone area codes
all begin with 0 and consist
of up to four digits. The area
code is an integral part of the
telephone number and must
always be dialled. When calling Venice land lines, even
from within the city, you
must dial the 041 city code.

Mobile phone numbers
begin with a three-digit prefix
such as 330. Toll-free (free-
phone) numbers are known
as *numeri verdi* and usually
start with 840, 841, 848,
892, 899, 163, 166 or 199.

International Calls

The cheapest options for
calling internationally are
free or low-cost computer
programs such as Skype,
cut-rate call centres or international dialling cards, which
are sold at newsstands and
tabacchi. All of these offer
cheaper calls than the Telecom payphones.

If you're calling an international number from an Italian

phone, you must dial 00 to get an international line, then the relevant country and city codes, followed by the telephone number.

To call Venice from abroad, call the international access number for Italy (011 in the United States, 00 from most other countries), Italy's country code 39, then the Venice area code 041, followed by the telephone number.

Mobile Phones

Italy uses GSM 900/1800, so GSM and tri-band mobile phones can be used in Venice with the purchase of a local SIM card. Buy these at Vodafone and Telecom Italia Mobile (TIM) outlets across the city. However, be sure to check with your provider before you leave home, as some phones may be code blocked. Prepaid plans are fairly reasonable, and most offer the option to have internet access for an additional fee.

US mobile phones generally work on a frequency of 1900MHz, so your US handset will have to be tri-band to be usable in Italy.

Pay-as-you-go SIM cards are readily available at telephone and electronics stores. Once you're set up with an Italian SIM card, you can easily purchase recharge cards at many tobacconists and newsstands. Of the main mobile phone companies TIM and Vodafone have the best coverage in Venice.

You'll need your passport to open any kind of mobile phone account, prepaid or otherwise.

Phonecards

You can buy phonecards (€3, €5 or €10) at post offices, tobacconists and newsstands, and from vending machines in Telecom offices. Snap off the perforated corner before using it. Phonecards have an expiry date – usually 31 December or 30 June, depending on when you purchase it.

Stick to Telecom phone-cards rather than the over-priced 'international calling cards' available in vending machines in Marco Polo airport, which can charge as much as €1 per minute for local calls.

PUBLIC PHONES

Many orange Telecom payphones only accept carte/schede telefoniche (phonecards), though there are payphones that accept coins around the Santa Lucia train station, Piazzale Roma, Campo Santa Margherita and Piazza San Marco. There's also a bank of telephones near the post office on Calle Galeazza.

Time

Italy (and hence Venice) is one hour ahead of GMT/ UTC during winter and two hours ahead during the daylight-saving period, which runs from the last Sunday in March to the last Sunday in October. Besides the UK, Ireland and Portugal, most other Western European countries are on the same time as Italy year-round; New York (Eastern Time) is six hours behind Italy. To compare Venice with other time zones, see www.world timezone.com. Note that times are often listed using a 24-hour clock (ie 2pm is written as 14 hours).

Toilets

Most bars and cafes reserve the restroom for paying customers only, so sudden urges at awkward moments call for a drink-buying detour – but be sure the place actually has a toilet before plunking down your cash. Look before you sit: even in women's bathrooms, some toilets don't have seats, and sometimes there is no toilet at all – just a hole with footrests. Public toilets (€1.50) are scattered

around Venice near tourist attractions (look for the 'WC Toilette' signs), and are usually open from 7am to 7pm (sometimes closing earlier in winter).

Tourist Information

The useful monthly booklet **Un Ospite di Venezia** (A Guest in Venice; www.unospi tedivenezia.it), published by a group of Venetian hoteliers, is distributed in many hotels and can also be viewed online. In tourist offices, ask for La Rivista di Venezia, a bimonthly free magazine with articles in Italian and English, with a handy Shows & Events listings insert. Another useful listings freebie in Italian and English is **Venezia da Vivere** (www.veneziadavivere.com), which you can check out online. You may find it in printed form in bars and shops. The Veneto section of **Corriera della Sera** (www.corriere.it) is also useful for current and upcoming events.

Tourist Offices

Azienda di Promozione Turistica (Azienda di Promozione Turistica; ☑041 529 87 11; www.turismovenezia.it) has several branches that can provide information on sights, suggested itineraries, day trips from Venice, transport, special events, shows and temporary exhibitions. Official APT outlets providing tourist information include the following – all open daily:

Marco Polo Airport (arrivals hall; ☺9am-8pm)

Piazzale Roma (ground fl, multistorey car park; ☺9.30am-2.30pm; ⊠Santa Chiara)

Piazza San Marco (Piazza San Marco 71f; ☺9am-7pm; ⊠San Marco)

Stazione di Santa Lucia (☺9am-7pm Nov-Mar, 1.30-7pm Apr-Oct; ⊠Ferrovia Santa

Lucia) In the summer months (April to October) an information kiosk sets up in front of the station and is open from 9am to 2.30pm.

Travellers with Disabilities

With all the foot bridges, stairs, and scant guard railings along canals, Venice might not seem like the easiest place to visit for travellers with disabilities. But the city has been making a more conscientious effort lately to provide access to key monuments, especially after the considerable embarrassment of paying millions for the Calatrava bridge without considering its wheelchair accessibility.

In its favour, Venice is a compact city and the public *vaporetti* (water buses) are efficient and relatively easy to access. Water bus is also the most effective way to access sites while avoiding some of those 435 bridges. Planning ahead is the key.

The most accessible tourist office is the one located just off Piazza San Marco. A **disabled assistance office** (⊗7am-9pm) is also located in front of platform 4 at Venice's Santa Lucia station.

Of the other islands, Murano, Burano, the Lido and Torcello are all fairly easy to access, although the Comune has recently removed the stairlifts on Murano and Burano, as they aren't currently able to offer the support needed (previously the keys had to be obtained from the tourist office in order to operate them).

Maps

A printable 'Accessible Venice' map is available on the **Comune di Venezia** (www.comune.venezia.it) website, buried under the 'Your Life' header on the right of the navigation bar. The map delimits the area around each water-bus stop that can be accessed without crossing a bridge. In addition, the website provides information on accessible attractions, including 12 'barrier-free' itineraries, which can also be downloaded. The maps are also available from the APT tourist offices.

Public Transport

Vaporetti have access for wheelchairs, offering an easy way to get around town. Passengers in wheelchairs travel for just €1.30 on the *vaporetto*; a companion travels free.

Virtually all local buses connecting Venice with mainland destinations are also wheelchair accessible.

Organisations

Accessible Italy (☑378 94 11 11; www.accessibleitaly.com) Specialises in holiday services for the disabled, with proceeds helping pay for accessibility improvements sorely needed throughout Italy.

Città Per Tutti (☑041 274 81 44, 041 965 54 40; www.comune.venezia.it/informa handicap; Ca' Farsetti 4136, San Marco) This city program is devoted to improving disabled access in Venice and can provide the latest information about access issues around the city.

Visas

Citizens of EU countries, Iceland, Norway and Switzerland do not need a visa to visit Italy. Nationals of some other countries, including Australia, Brazil, Canada, Israel, Japan, New Zealand and the USA, do not require visas for tourist visits of up to 90 days. For more information and a list of countries whose citizens require a visa, check the website of the **Italian foreign ministry** (www.esteri.it).

The standard tourist visa issued by Italian consulates is the Schengen visa, valid for up to 90 days. This visa is valid for travel in Italy and in several other European countries with which Italy has a reciprocal visa agreement (see www.eurovisa.info for the full list). These visas are not renewable inside Italy.

Permits

EU citizens do not need permits to live, work or start a business in Italy, but they are advised to register with a *questura* (police station) if they take up residence. Non-EU citizens coming to Venice for work or long-term study require study and work visas, which you must apply for in your country of residence.

Women Travellers

Of the major travel destinations in Italy, Venice is among the safest for women, given the low rate of violent crime of any kind in Venice proper. Chief annoyances would be getting chatted up by other travellers in Piazza San Marco or on the more popular Lido beaches, usually easily quashed with a *'Non mi interessa'* (I'm not interested) or that universally crushing response, the exasperated eye roll.

Centro Anti-Violenza (Anti-Violence Centre; ☑toll-free in case of emergency 1522 041 269 06 10; Viale G Garibaldi 155a, Villa Franchin, Mestre; ⊗9am-6pm Mon-Thu) is a violence-prevention organisation that includes a women's centre offering legal advice, counselling and support to women who have been assaulted, regardless of nationality. All services are free. Take bus 2 from Piazzale Roma.

Language

Standard Italian is spoken throughout Italy, but regional dialects are an important part of identity in many parts of the country, and this also goes for Venice where you'll no doubt hear some Venetian (also known as Venet) spoken or pick up on the local lilt standard Italian is often spoken with. This said, you'll have no trouble being understood – and your efforts will be much appreciated – if you stick to standard Italian, which we've also used in this chapter.

Italian pronunciation is straightforward as most sounds are also found in English.

Note that ai is pronounced as in 'aisle', ay as in 'say', ow as in 'how', dz as the 'ds' in 'lids', and that r is a strong, rolled sound. Keep in mind that Italian consonants can have a stronger, emphatic pronunciation – if the consonant is written as a double letter, it should be pronounced a little stronger, eg *sonno son*·no (sleep) and *sono so*·no (I am). If you read our coloured pronunciation guides as if they were English (with the stressed syllables in italics), you'll be understood.

BASICS

Italian has two words for 'you' – use the polite form *Lei* lay if you're talking to strangers, officials or people older than you. With people familiar to you or younger than you, you can use the informal form *tu* too.

In Italian, all nouns and adjectives are either masculine or feminine, and so are the articles *il/la* eel/la (the) and *un/una* oon/oo·na (a) that go with the nouns.

WANT MORE?

For in-depth language information and handy phrases, check out Lonely Planet's *Italian phrasebook*. You'll find it at **shop.lonelyplanet.com**, or you can buy Lonely Planet's iPhone phrasebooks at the Apple App Store.

In this chapter the polite/informal and masculine/feminine options are included where necessary, separated with a slash and indicated with 'pol/inf' and 'm/f'.

Hello.	*Buongiorno.*	bwon·*jor*·no
Goodbye.	*Arrivederci.*	a·ree·ve·*der*·chee
Yes./No.	*Sì./No.*	see/no
Excuse me.	*Mi scusi.* (pol)	mee skoo·zee
	Scusami. (inf)	skoo·za·mee
Sorry.	*Mi dispiace.*	mee dees·*pya*·che
Please.	*Per favore.*	per fa·vo·re
Thank you.	*Grazie.*	*gra*·tsye
You're welcome.	*Prego.*	*pre*·go

How are you?
Come sta/stai? (pol/inf)   ko·me sta/stai

Fine. And you?
Bene. E Lei/tu? (pol/inf)   be·ne e lay/too

What's your name?
Come si chiama? pol   ko·me see *kya*·ma
Come ti chiami? inf   ko·me tee *kya*·mee

My name is ...
Mi chiamo ...   mee *kya*·mo ...

Do you speak English?
Parla/Parli   *par*·la/*par*·lee
inglese? (pol/inf)   een·*gle*·ze

I don't understand.
Non capisco.   non ka·*pee*·sko

ACCOMMODATION

I'd like to book a room, please.
Vorrei prenotare una   vo·*ray* pre·no·*ta*·re oo·na
camera, per favore.   ka·me·ra per fa·vo·re

Is breakfast included?
La colazione è   la ko·la·*tsyo*·ne e
compresa?   kom·*pre*·sa

How much is it per ...?	*Quanto costa per ...?*	kwan·to kos·ta per ...
night	*una notte*	oo·na no·te
person	*persona*	per·so·na

air-con	aria condizionata	a·rya kon·dee·tsyo·na·ta
bathroom	bagno	ba·nyo
campsite	campeggio	kam·pe·jo
double room	camera doppia con letto matrimoniale	ka·me·ra do·pya kon le·to ma·tree·mo·nya·le
guesthouse	pensione	pen·syo·ne
hotel	albergo	al·ber·go
single room	camera singola	ka·me·ra seen·go·la
youth hostel	ostello della gioventù	os·te·lo de·la jo·ven·too
window	finestra	fee·nes·tra

DIRECTIONS

Where's ...?
Dov'è ...?   do·ve ...

What's the address?
Qual'è l'indirizzo?   kwa·le leen·dee·ree·tso

Could you please write it down?
Può scriverlo,   pwo skree·ver·lo
per favore?   per fa·vo·re

Can you show me (on the map)?
Può mostrarmi   pwo mos·trar·mee
(sulla pianta)?   (soo·la pyan·ta)

at the corner	all'angolo	a·lan·go·lo
behind	dietro	dye·tro
far	lontano	lon·ta·no
in front of	davanti a	da·van·tee a
left	a sinistra	a see·nee·stra
near	vicino	vee·chee·no
next to	accanto a	a·kan·to a
opposite	di fronte a	dee fron·te a
right	a destra	a de·stra
straight ahead	sempre diritto	sem·pre dee·ree·to

EATING & DRINKING

I'd like to reserve a table.
Vorrei prenotare   vo·ray pre·no·ta·re
un tavolo.   oon ta·vo·lo

What would you recommend?
Cosa mi consiglia?   ko·za mee kon·see·lya

What's in that dish?
Quali ingredienti   kwa·li een·gre·dyen·tee
ci sono in   chee so·no een
questo piatto?   kwe·sto pya·to

What's the local speciality?
Qual'è la specialità   kwa·le la spe·cha·lee·ta
di questa regione?   dee kwe·sta re·jo·ne

That was delicious!
Era squisito!   e·ra skwee·zee·to

Cheers!
Salute!   sa·loo·te

Please bring the bill.
Mi porta il conto,   mee por·ta eel kon·to
per favore?   per fa·vo·re

I don't eat ...	Non mangio ...	non man·jo ...
eggs	uova	wo·va
fish	pesce	pe·she
nuts	noci	no·chee
(red) meat	carne (rossa)	kar·ne (ro·sa)

Key Words

bar	locale	lo·ka·le
bottle	bottiglia	bo·tee·lya
breakfast	prima colazione	pree·ma ko·la·tsyo·ne
cafe	bar	bar
cold	freddo	fre·do
dinner	cena	che·na

drink list	lista delle bevande	lee·sta de·le be·van·de
fork	forchetta	for·ke·ta
glass	bicchiere	bee·kye·re
grocery store	alimentari	a·lee·men·ta·ree
hot	caldo	kal·do
knife	coltello	kol·te·lo
lunch	pranzo	pran·dzo
market	mercato	mer·ka·to
menu	menù	me·noo
plate	piatto	pya·to
restaurant	ristorante	ree·sto·ran·te
spicy	piccante	pee·kan·te
spoon	cucchiaio	koo·kya·yo
vegetarian (food)	vegetariano	ve·je·ta·rya·no
with	con	kon
without	senza	sen·tsa

Meat & Fish

beef	manzo	man·dzo
chicken	pollo	po·lo
duck	anatra	a·na·tra
fish	pesce	pe·she
herring	aringa	a·reen·ga
lamb	agnello	a·nye·lo
lobster	aragosta	a·ra·gos·ta
meat	carne	kar·ne
mussels	cozze	ko·tse
oysters	ostriche	o·stree·ke
pork	maiale	ma·ya·le
prawn	gambero	gam·be·ro
salmon	salmone	sal·mo·ne
scallops	capasante	ka·pa·san·te
seafood	frutti di mare	froo·tee dee ma·re
shrimp	gambero	gam·be·ro
squid	calamari	ka·la·ma·ree
trout	trota	tro·ta
tuna	tonno	to·no
turkey	tacchino	ta·kee·no
veal	vitello	vee·te·lo

Fruit & Vegetables

apple	mela	me·la
beans	fagioli	fa·jo·lee
cabbage	cavolo	ka·vo·lo
capsicum	peperone	pe·pe·ro·ne
carrot	carota	ka·ro·ta
cauliflower	cavolfiore	ka·vol·fyo·re
cucumber	cetriolo	che·tree·o·lo
fruit	frutta	froo·ta
grapes	uva	oo·va
lemon	limone	lee·mo·ne
lentils	lenticchie	len·tee·kye
mushroom	funghi	foon·gee
nuts	noci	no·chee
onions	cipolle	chee·po·le
orange	arancia	a·ran·cha
peach	pesca	pe·ska
peas	piselli	pee·ze·lee
pineapple	ananas	a·na·nas
plum	prugna	proo·nya
potatoes	patate	pa·ta·te
spinach	spinaci	spee·na·chee
tomatoes	pomodori	po·mo·do·ree
vegetables	verdura	ver·doo·ra

Other

bread	pane	pa·ne
butter	burro	boo·ro
cheese	formaggio	for·ma·jo
eggs	uova	wo·va
honey	miele	mye·le
ice	ghiaccio	gya·cho
jam	marmellata	mar·me·la·ta
noodles	pasta	pas·ta
oil	olio	o·lyo
pepper	pepe	pe·pe
rice	riso	ree·zo
salt	sale	sa·le
soup	minestra	mee·nes·tra
soy sauce	salsa di soia	sal·sa dee so·ya
sugar	zucchero	tsoo·ke·ro
vinegar	aceto	a·che·to

Drinks

beer	birra	bee·ra
coffee	caffè	ka·fe
(orange) juice	succo (d'arancia)	soo·ko (da·ran·cha)
milk	latte	la·te
red wine	vino rosso	vee·no ro·so

soft drink	bibita	bee·bee·ta
tea	tè	te
(mineral) water	acqua (minerale)	a·kwa (mee·ne·ra·le)
white wine	vino bianco	vee·no byan·ko

EMERGENCIES

Help!
Aiuto!   a·yoo·to

Leave me alone!
Lasciami in pace!   la·sha·mee een pa·che

I'm lost.
Mi sono perso/a. (m/f)   mee so·no per·so/a

Call the police!
Chiami la polizia!   kya·mee la po·lee·tsee·a

Call a doctor!
Chiami un medico!   kya·mee oon me·dee·ko

Where are the toilets?
Dove sono i gabinetti?   do·ve so·no ee ga·bee·ne·tee

I'm sick.
Mi sento male.   mee sen·to ma·le

SHOPPING & SERVICES

I'd like to buy ...
Vorrei comprare ...   vo·ray kom·pra·re ...

I'm just looking.
Sto solo guardando.   sto so·lo gwar·dan·do

Numbers

1	uno	oo·no
2	due	doo·e
3	tre	tre
4	quattro	kwa·tro
5	cinque	cheen·kwe
6	sei	say
7	sette	se·te
8	otto	o·to
9	nove	no·ve
10	dieci	dye·chee
20	venti	ven·tee
30	trenta	tren·ta
40	quaranta	kwa·ran·ta
50	cinquanta	cheen·kwan·ta
60	sessanta	se·san·ta
70	settanta	se·tan·ta
80	ottanta	o·tan·ta
90	novanta	no·van·ta
100	cento	chen·to
1000	mille	mee·le

Signs

Entrata/Ingresso	Entrance
Uscita	Exit
Aperto	Open
Chiuso	Closed
Informazioni	Information
Proibito/Vietato	Prohibited
Gabinetti/Servizi	Toilets
Uomini	Men
Donne	Women

Can I look at it?
Posso dare un'occhiata?   po·so da·re oo·no·kya·ta

How much is this?
Quanto costa questo?   kwan·to kos·ta kwe·sto

It's too expensive.
È troppo caro/a. (m/f)   e tro·po ka·ro/a

Can you lower the price?
Può farmi lo sconto?   pwo far·mee lo skon·to

There's a mistake in the bill.
C'è un errore nel conto.   che oo·ne·ro·re nel kon·to

ATM	Bancomat	ban·ko·mat
post office	ufficio postale	oo·fee·cho pos·ta·le
tourist office	ufficio del turismo	oo·fee·cho del too·reez·mo

TIME & DATES

What time is it?	Che ora è?	ke o·ra e
It's one o'clock.	È l'una.	e loo·na
It's (two) o'clock.	Sono le (due).	so·no le (doo·e)
Half past (one).	(L'una) e mezza.	(loo·na) e me·dza

in the morning	di mattina	dee ma·tee·na
in the afternoon	di pomeriggio	dee po·me·ree·jo
in the evening	di sera	dee se·ra

yesterday	ieri	ye·ree
today	oggi	o·jee
tomorrow	domani	do·ma·nee

Monday	lunedì	loo·ne·dee
Tuesday	martedì	mar·te·dee
Wednesday	mercoledì	mer·ko·le·dee
Thursday	giovedì	jo·ve·dee
Friday	venerdì	ve·ner·dee
Saturday	sabato	sa·ba·to
Sunday	domenica	do·me·nee·ka

January	gennaio	je·na·yo
February	febbraio	fe·bra·yo
March	marzo	mar·tso
April	aprile	a·pree·le
May	maggio	ma·jo
June	giugno	joo·nyo
July	luglio	loo·lyo
August	agosto	a·gos·to
September	settembre	se·tem·bre
October	ottobre	o·to·bre
November	novembre	no·vem·bre
December	dicembre	dee·chem·bre

TRANSPORT

At what time does the ... leave/arrive?	A che ora parte/ arriva ...?	a ke o·ra par·te/ a·ree·va ...
boat	la nave	la na·ve
bus	l'autobus	low·to·boos
city ferry	il vaporetto	eel va·po·re·to
ferry	il traghetto	eel tra·ge·to
plane	l'aereo	la·e·re·o
train	il treno	eel tre·no

bus stop	fermata dell'autobus	fer·ma·ta del ow·to·boos
one-way	di sola andata	dee so·la an·da·ta
platform	binario	bee·na·ryo
return	di andata e ritorno	dee an·da·ta e ree·tor·no
ticket	biglietto	bee·lye·to
ticket office	biglietteria	bee·lye·te·ree·a
timetable	orario	o·ra·ryo
train station	stazione ferroviaria	sta·tsyo·ne fe·ro·vyar·ya

Does it stop at ...?
Si ferma a ...?   see fer·ma a ...

Please tell me when we get to ...
Mi dica per favore   mee dee·ka per fa·vo·re
quando arriviamo a ...   kwan·do a·ree·vya·mo a ...

I want to get off here.
Voglio scendere qui.   vo·lyo shen·de·re kwee

I'd like to hire a/an ...	Vorrei noleggiare un/una ... (m/f)	vo·ray no·le·ja·re oon/oo·na ...
bicycle	bicicletta (f)	bee·chee·kle·ta
car	macchina (f)	ma·kee·na
motorbike	moto (f)	mo·to

bicycle pump	pompa della bicicletta	pom·pa de·la bee·chee·kle·ta
helmet	casco	kas·ko
mechanic	meccanico	me·ka·nee·ko
petrol/gas	benzina	ben·dzee·na
service station	stazione di servizio	sta·tsyo·ne dee ser·vee·tsyo

Is this the road to ...?
Questa strada porta a ...? kwe·sta stra·da por·ta a ...

(How long) Can I park here?
(Per quanto tempo)   (per kwan·to tem·po)
Posso parcheggiare qui?   po·so par·ke·ja·re kwee

I have a flat tyre.
Ho una gomma bucata.   o oo·na go·ma boo·ka·ta

I've run out of petrol.
Ho esaurito la   o e·zow·ree·to la
benzina.   ben·dzee·na

VENETIAN BASICS

A few choice words in Venetian (or Venet as it is also known) will endear you to your hosts, especially at happy hour. To keep up with the *bacaro* banter, try mixing them with your Italian:

Yes, sir!	Siorsi!
Oh, no!	Simènteve!
You bet!	Figuràrse!
How lucky!	Bénpo!
Perfect.	In bròca.
Welcome!	Benvegnù!
Cheers!	Sanacapàna!
Watch out!	Òcio!

cheap wine	brunbrùn
glass of wine	ombra (lit: a shade)
happy hour	giro di ombra (lit: round of shade)
to become Venetian	Venexianàrse
Venetian	venexiano/a (m/f)
you guys	voàltri

GLOSSARY

alla busara Venetian prawn sauce

anatra wild lagoon duck

baccala mantecato creamed cod

bigoli Venetian whole-wheat pasta

branzino sea bass

bruscandoli wild hop buds

canoce mantis prawn

capasanta/canastrelo large/small scallops

carpaccio finely sliced raw beef

castraure baby artichokes from St Erasmo Island

cicheti Venetian taps

contorni vegetable dishes

crostini open-faced sandwiches

crudi Venetian sushi

curasan croissant

dolci sweets

dolci tipici venexiani typical Venetian sweets

fatto in casa house-made

fegato alla veneziana liver lightly pan-roasted in strips with browned onion and a splash of red wine

filetto di San Pietro fish with artichokes or radicchio trevisano

fritole sweet fritters

fritto misto e pattatine lightly fried lagoon seafood and potatoes

frittura seafood fry

gnochetti mini-gnocchi

granseola spider crab

krapfen doughnuts

latte di soia soy milk

lingue di suocere biscuit; 'mother-in-law's tongues'

macchiatone espresso liberally 'stained' with milk

margherite ripiene all'astice com sugo di pesce ravioli stuffed with lobster in fish sauce

moeche soft-shell crabs

moscardini baby octopus

mozzarella di bufala fresh buffalo-milk mozzarella

orechiette 'little ear' pasta

pan dei dogi 'doges' bread'; hazelnut-studded biscuits

panino sandwich

pastine pastry

peoci mussels

pizza margherita pizza with basil mozzarella and tomato

pizzette mini pizzas

polpette meatballs

radicchio trevisano feathery red radicchio

risotto di pesce fish risotto

saor Venice's tangy marinade

sarde sardines

sarde in saor sardines fried in tangy onion marinade with pine nuts and sultanas

senza limone without lemon

seppie cuttlefish

seppie in nero squid in its own ink

sfogio sole

sopressa Venetian soft salami

sopressa crostini soft salami on toast

sorbetto sorbet

spaghetti alla búsera spaghetti with shrimp sauce

surgelati frozen

tramezzini sandwiches on soft bread often with mayo-based condiments

verdure vegetables

zaletti cornmeal biscuits with sultanas

zuppa di pesce thick seafood soup

Behind the Scenes

SEND US YOUR FEEDBACK

Things change – prices go up, schedules change, good places go bad and bad places go bankrupt. So if you find things better or worse, recently opened or long since closed, or you just want to tell us what you loved or loathed about this book, please get in touch and help make the next edition even more accurate and useful. We love to hear from travellers – your comments keep us on our toes and our well-travelled team reads every word. Although we can't reply individually to postal submissions, we always guarantee that your feedback goes straight to the appropriate authors, in time for the next edition. Each person who sends us information is thanked in the next edition – the most useful submissions are rewarded with a selection of digital PDF chapters.

Visit **lonelyplanet.com/contact** to submit your updates and suggestions or to ask for help. Our award-winning website also features inspirational travel stories, news and discussions.

Note: We may edit, reproduce and incorporate your comments in Lonely Planet products such as guidebooks, websites and digital products, so let us know if you don't want your comments reproduced or your name acknowledged. For a copy of our privacy policy visit lonelyplanet.com/privacy.

OUR READERS

Many thanks to the travellers who used the last edition and wrote to us with helpful hints, useful advice and interesting anecdotes:

Peter Attwood, John Cloidt, Kim Klaka, Brian Knox, Elina Kuzjukevica, Keith Nicholson, Brenda Parker, Stephen Saslav, Emma Stocks, Victor Turner, David White

AUTHOR THANKS

Alison Bing

Mille grazie e tanti baci alla mia famiglia a Roma and stateside, the Bings, Ferrys and Marinuccis; to my *bravissima* co-author and *carissima* fellow traveller Paula Hardy; to editorial mastermind Joe Bindloss and editor Sarah Bailey, who upholds Venetian publishing excellence; and *prosecco* toasts to Venezia intelligentsia Cristina Bottero, Alberto Toso Fei, Francesca Forni, Rosanna Corrò, Giantantonio De Vincenzo, Giovanni d'Este, Francesco e Matteo Pinto, Jane and Luigi Caporal. *Ma sopra tutto:* to Marco Flavio Marinucci, for making *la bea vita* possible, even outside Venice.

Paula Hardy

Thank you to the wonderfully warm Venetians for sharing the best of their island home: Susan Steer for the stories behind the mosaics; Cristina Toffolo, Toni Tombola and Paolo du Rossi for lagoon secrets; Luigi Camozzo and Amy West for Murano insights; Tobia Morro and Adelia for Castello tips; and Mario Piccinin, Silvia Spera, Ivan Geronazzo, Graziano and Martina Spada and Roberto Frozza for great memories in the Veneto. *Brava,* too, to everinspiring coordinator Alison Bing, and thanks to Joe Bindloss for steering a steady course.

ACKNOWLEDGMENTS

Climate map data adapted from Peel MC, Finlayson BL & McMahon TA (2007) 'Updated World Map of the Köppen-Geiger Climate Classification', Hydrology and Earth System Sciences, 11, 163344.

Illustrations pp68-9 by Javier Martinez Zarracina.

Cover photograph: Basilica di Santa Maria della Salute, Sestiere di Dorsoduro. Harald Sund / Getty Images ©

THIS BOOK

This 8th edition of Lonely Planet's *Venice & the Veneto* guidebook was researched and written by Alison Bing and Paula Hardy. The previous two editions were written by Alison Bing and Robert Landon. This guidebook was commissioned in Lonely Planet's London office, and produced by the following:

Commissioning Editors Joe Bindloss, Helena Smith

Coordinating Editors Sarah Bailey, Kate James
Coordinating Cartographers Eve Kelly, Jacqueline Nguyen
Coordinating Layout Designer Wibowo Rusli
Managing Editor Annelies Mertens
Senior Editors Andi Jones, Catherine Naghten
Managing Cartographers Anita Bahn, Anthony Phelan
Managing Layout Designer Jane Hart
Assisting Editor Sam Trafford

Cover Research Naomi Parker
Internal Image Research Rebecca Skinner
Language Content Branislava Vladisavljevic
Thanks to Sasha Baskett, Laura Crawford, Ryan Evans, Larissa Frost, Genesys India, Jouve India, Laura Jane, Wayne Murphy, Karyn Noble, Trent Paton, Adrian Persoglia, Martine Power, Kerrianne Southway, Laura Stansfeld, Samantha Tyson, Gerard Walker

See also separate subindexes for:

✗ EATING P301

🍷 DRINKING & NIGHTLIFE P302

☆ ENTERTAINMENT P302

🛍 SHOPPING P302

🏃 SPORTS & ACTIVITIES P303

🛏 SLEEPING P303

Index

INDEX SPORTS & ACTIVITIES

Venice Maps

Map Legend

Sights
- Beach
- Buddhist
- Castle
- Christian
- Hindu
- Islamic
- Jewish
- Monument
- Museum/Gallery
- Ruin
- Winery/Vineyard
- Zoo
- Other Sight

Eating
- Eating

Drinking & Nightlife
- Drinking & Nightlife
- Cafe

Entertainment
- Entertainment

Shopping
- Shopping

Sleeping
- Sleeping
- Camping

Sports & Activities
- Diving/Snorkelling
- Canoeing/Kayaking
- Skiing
- Surfing
- Swimming/Pool
- Walking
- Windsurfing
- Other Sports & Activities

Information
- Post Office
- Tourist Information

Transport
- Airport
- Border Crossing
- Bus
- Cable Car/Funicular
- Cycling
- Ferry
- Monorail
- Parking
- S-Bahn
- Taxi
- Train/Railway
- Tram
- Tube Station
- U-Bahn
- Underground Train Station
- Other Transport

Routes
- Tollway
- Freeway
- Primary
- Secondary
- Tertiary
- Lane
- Unsealed Road
- Plaza/Mall
- Steps
- Tunnel
- Pedestrian Overpass
- Walking Tour
- Walking Tour Detour
- Path

Boundaries
- International
- State/Province
- Disputed
- Regional/Suburb
- Marine Park
- Cliff
- Wall

Geographic
- Hut/Shelter
- Lighthouse
- Lookout
- Mountain/Volcano
- Oasis
- Park
- Pass
- Picnic Area
- Waterfall

Hydrography
- River/Creek
- Intermittent River
- Swamp/Mangrove
- Reef
- Canal
- Water
- Dry/Salt/Intermittent Lake
- Glacier

Areas
- Beach/Desert
- Cemetery (Christian)
- Cemetery (Other)
- Park/Forest
- Sportsground
- Sight (Building)
- Top Sight (Building)

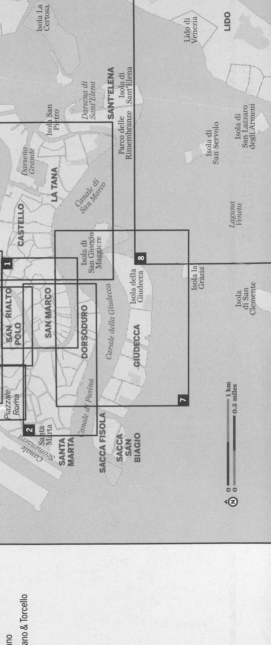

MAP INDEX

1 Sestiere di San Marco
2 Sestiere di Dorsoduro
3 Sestieri di San Polo & Santa Croce
4 West of Santa Croce
5 Sestiere di Cannaregio
6 Sestiere di Castello
7 Giudecca
8 Lido di Venezia
9 Murano
10 Burano & Torcello

Key on p310

SESTIERE DI SAN MARCO

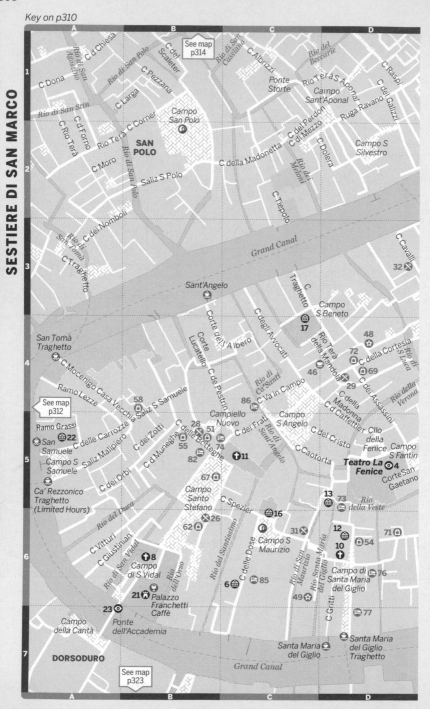

See map p314

See map p312

See map p323

A B C D

1

2

3

4

5

6

7

C.Dona
Rio di San Agostin
C d Chiesa
Rio di San Polo
C. Pezzana
C del Scaleter
Rio di San Cassiano
C Albrizzi
Rio del Beccarie
C.Raspi
C. del Galizzi

C Rio Terà
C Rio Terà
C d Forno
Rio Terà San Stin
C Larga
C Corner
Rio Terà C Corner
SAN POLO
Campo San Polo
Ponte Storte
Rio Terà S Aponal
Campo Sant'Aponal
Ruga Ravano

C. Moro
Rio di San Polo
Saliz S Polo
C della Madonetta
C del Perdon
C di Mezzo
C Dolera
Rio dei Meloni
Campo S Silvestro

C del Nomboli
Rio di San Tomà
C.Traghetto
C.Tiepolo
Grand Canal

San Tomà Traghetto
Sant'Angelo
Corte dell'Albero
C degli Avvocati
Traghetto
Campo S Beneto
17
C Cavalli
32

Ramo Lezze
C Mocenigo Casa Vecchia
Corte Lucatello
C de Pestrin
Rio di Ca'Sant'
C Va in Campo
46
Rio Terà della Mandola
72
48
C della Cortesia
Rio della Verona
69
29
C della Madonna
C del Assassini
C d Caffettier

Ramo Grassi
San Samuele
22
C delle Carrozze
Saliz S Samuele
58
86
Campiello Nuovo
28
51
74
55
82
C dei Zotti
C delle Botteghe
C dei Frati
Rio di Sant'Angelo
Campo S Angelo
C del Cristo
Cllo della Fenice
Campo S Fantin
Teatro La Fenice
4
CorteSan Gaetano

Campo S Samuele
Ca' Rezzonico Traghetto (Limited Hours)
Saliz Malipiero
C d Muneghe
67
11
C Caotorta
13
73
Rio della Veste

C dei Orbi
Rio del Duca
Campo Santo Stefano
C Spezier
16
31
12
10
54
71

C Vitturi
C Giustinian
62
26
Rio del Santissimo
C delle Dose
Campo S Maurizio
Rio di San Maurizio
Campo di Santa Maria del Giglio
76

8
Campo di S Vidal
Rio dell'Orso
Rio di San Vidal
6
85
49
77
C Gritti
Rio Santa Maria del Giglio

21
Palazzo Franchetti Caffè
23
Ponte dell'Accademia
Santa Maria del Giglio
Santa Maria del Giglio Traghetto

Campo della Carità
DORSODURO
Grand Canal

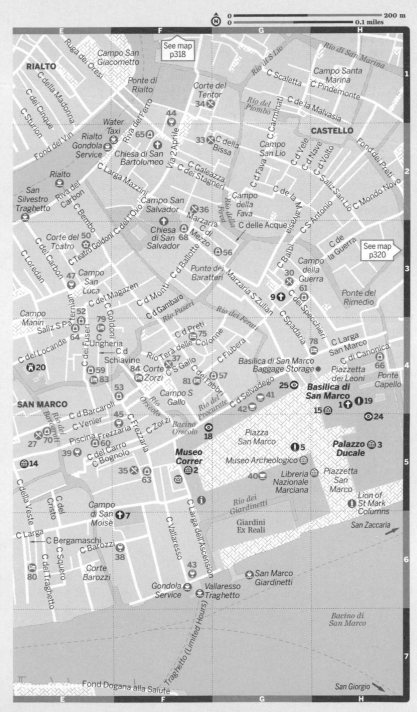

SESTIERE DI SAN MARCO *Map on p308*

SESTIERE DI SAN MARCO

SESTIERE DI DORSODURO

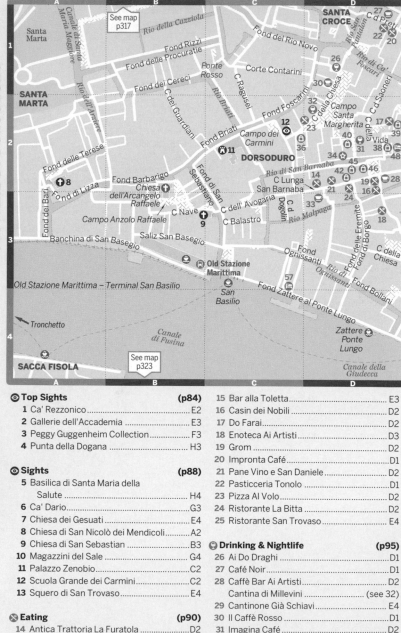

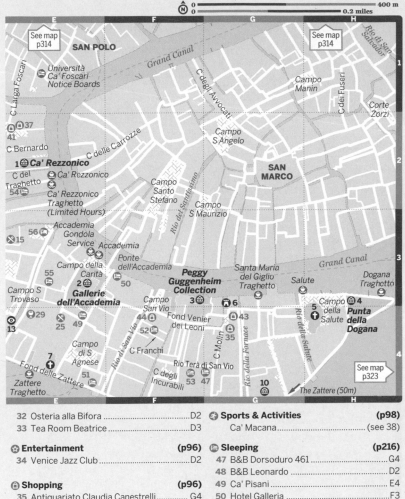

SESTIERI DI SAN POLO & SANTA CROCE

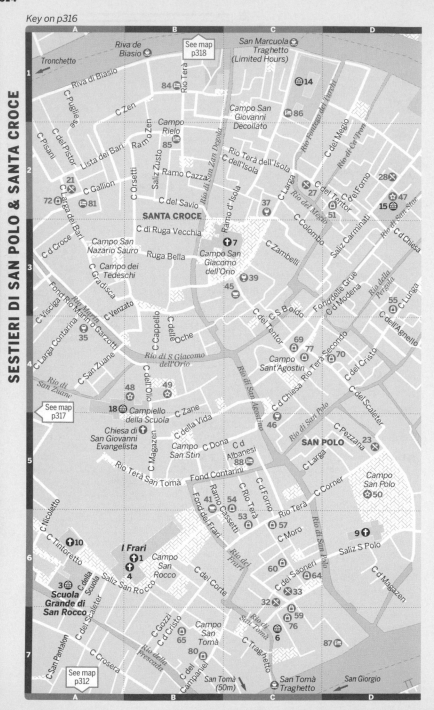

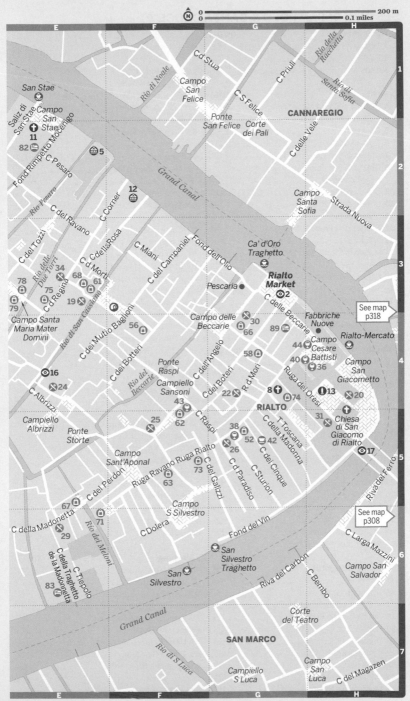

SESTIERI DI SAN POLO & SANTA CROCE *Map on p314*

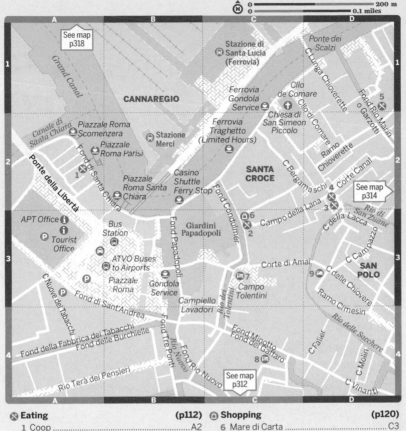

✖ Eating	(p112)
1 Coop	A2
2 Fritto e Frutta	C3
3 La Rivetta	D2
4 Pasticceria Trevisan	D2
5 Tearoom Caffè Orientale	D1

🛍 Shopping	(p120)
6 Mare di Carta	C3

🛏 Sleeping	(p217)
7 Ca dei Polo	C3
8 Ca' della Corte	C4
9 Hostel Domus Civica	D3

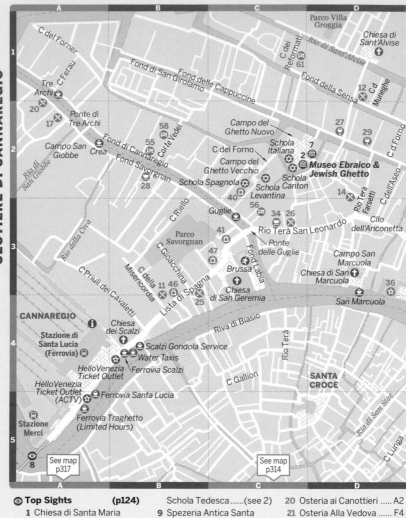

31 Cantina Vecia
   Carbonera E3
32 Il Santo Bevitore E3
33 Osteria Ai Osti F4
34 Torrefazione Marchi C3
35 Un Mondo Di Vino G5

🟢 **Entertainment**   **(p134)**
36 Casinò Di Venezia D3
37 Cinema Giorgione
   Movie D'essai G4
38 Paradiso Perduto E2
39 Teatro Fondamenta
   Nuove G2

🟢 **Shopping**   **(p135)**
40 Antichità al Ghetto C2
41 Brands C3
42 Carta & Design E3
43 De Rossi G5
44 Dolceamaro G5
45 Gianni Basso H4
46 Gibigiana B3
47 Giunti Al Punto C3
48 Libreria
   Internazionale
   Marco Polo G5
49 Mercantino dei
   Miracoli H5
50 Paolo Olbi H5

51 Spilli Lab & Shop H5
52 Vladì Shoes E3

🟢 **Sleeping**   **(p219)**
53 Alla Vite Dorata G4
54 Allo Squero G4
55 Ca' Dogaressa B2
56 Ca' Pozzo C3
57 Ca' Zanardi G3
58 Domus Orsoni B2
59 Palazzo Abadessa F4
60 Residenza Ca' Riccio H5
61 Residenza
   Cannaregio C1

Key on p322

SESTIERE DI CASTELLO

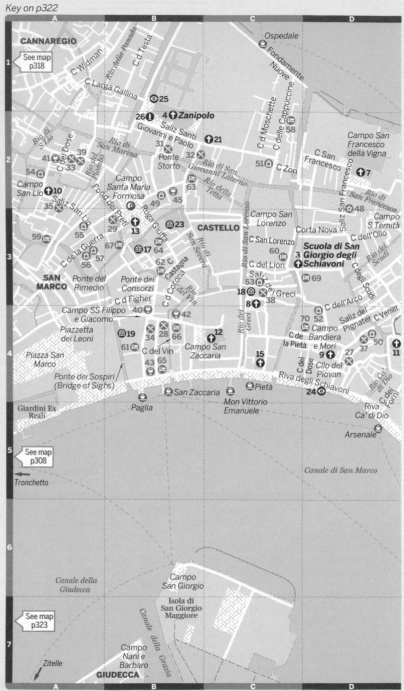

CANNAREGIO

See map p318

C Widman

Rio della Panada

C d Testa

Ospedale

Fondamente Nuove

C Larga Gallina

25

C d Moschette

C delle Cappuccine

58

26

4 **Zanipolo**

Saliz Santi Giovanni e Paolo

31

21

Campo San Francesco della Vigna

7

Rio di S Lio

C del Dose

39

41

33

Rio del Piombo

Rio di San Marina

32

Ponte Storto

Rio di San Giovanni Laterano

51

C Zon

C San Francesco

Saliz San Francesco

Rio di San Francesco

48

Campo S Ternità

C dell'Olio

54

Campo San Lio

10

35

Saliz San Lio

Campo Santa Maria Formosa

Fond dei Preti

Ruga Giuffa

49

45

63

Rio della Tetta

Campo San Lorenzo

Corta Nova

C San Lorenzo

60

Scuola di San Giorgio degli Schiavoni

3

C degli Scudi

Rio degli Scudi

59

55

29

13

64

23

CASTELLO

Rio di San Lorenzo

C de la Guerra

67

57

56

17

62 C Castagna

C Corona

Rio del Vin

C del Lion

69

SAN MARCO

Ponte del Rimedio

Ponte dei Consorzi

Sali del Greci

53

18

38

Ponte dei Consorzi

C d Figher

Campo SS Filippo e Giacomo

40

42

8

70

52

C dell'Arco

Saliz del Pignater

C Venier

Piazzetta dei Leoni

19

61

34

28

66

12

Campo San Zaccaria

C de la Pietà

Campo Bandiera e Mori

9

27

37

50

11

Piazza San Marco

C del Vin

43

65

15

C del Dose

Cllo del Piovan

Rio Ca' di Dio

C del Forni

Ponte dei Sospiri (Bridge of Sighs)

San Zaccaria

Pietà

24

Riva degli Schiavoni

Giardini Ex Reali

Paglia

Mon Vittorio Emanuele

Riva Ca' di Dio

Arsenale

See map p308

Tronchetto

Canale di San Marco

Canale della Giudecca

Campo San Giorgio

See map p323

Isola di San Giorgio Maggiore

Zitelle

Campo Nani e Barbaro

GIUDECCA

Canale della Grazia

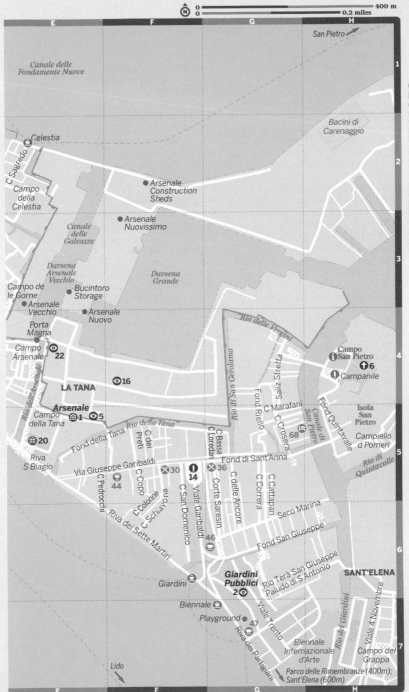

0
0
400 m
0.2 miles

San Pietro

Canale delle
Fondamente Nuove

Bacini di
Carenaggio

Celestia

C Sagredo

Campo
della
Celestia

Arsenale
Construction
Sheds

Arsenale
Nuovissimo

Canale
delle
Galeazze

Darsena
Arsenale
Vecchio

Darsena
Grande

Campo de
le Gorne

Bucintoro
Storage

Arsenale
Vecchio

Arsenale
Nuovo

Porta
Magna

Rio delle Vergini

Campo
San Pietro

Campo
Arsenale

22

6

Campanile

LA TANA

16

Rio di San Gerolamo

Saliz Stretta

Fond Riello

C Marafani

C Crosera

Canale di San Pietro

Fond Quintavale

Isola
San
Pietro

Arsenale

1

5

Campo
della Tana

20

Fond della Tana

Rio della Tana

C dei
Preti

C Bassa

C Loredan

Fond di Sant'Anna

68

Campiello
d'Pomeri

Rio di
Quintavalle

Riva
S Biagio

Via Giuseppe Garibaldi

C Pedrocchi

44

C Copo

C Colonne

C Schiavon

Viale Garibaldi

C San Domenico

30

14

36

Corte Saresin

C delle Ancore

C Correra

C Cattapan

Seco Marina

Riva dei Sette Martiri

46

Fond San Giuseppe

Rio Terà San Giuseppe

Paludo di S Antonio

SANT'ELENA

Giardini

Giardini
Pubblici

2

Biennale

Playground

47

Viale Trento

Riva dei Partigiani

Biennale
Internazionale
d'Arte

Rio dei Giardini

Viale 4 Novembre

Viale del Grappa

Campo del
Grappa

Lido

Parco delle Rimembranze (400m);
Sant'Elena (600m)

E
F
G
H

SESTIERE DI CASTELLO *Map on p320*

GIUDECCA

See map p312

See map p308

See map p320

See map p324

500 m
0.25 miles

◎ Top Sights (p160)
1 Chiesa di San Giorgio Maggiore........E2
2 Fondazione Giorgio Cini.....................E2

◎ Sights (p161)
3 Casa dei Tre Oci................................D2
4 Chiesa del Santissimo Redentore.....C3
5 Chiesa delle Zitelle..........................D2
6 Chiesa di Sant'Eufemia....................A2
7 Fortuny Tessuti Artistici...................A2
8 Giudecca 795.....................................A2

⊗ Eating (p165)
9 Al Pontil Dea Giudecca.....................C3
10 Harry's Dolci....................................A2
11 I Figli delle Stelle.............................B2
12 Mistrà...D3
13 Thursday Organic Market.................A3

⊖ Drinking & Nightlife (p167)
14 Skyline Rooftop Bar.........................A2

⊗ Entertainment (p167)
15 Teatro Junghans...............................B3

⊟ Sleeping (p223)
16 Al Redentore di Venezia...................C3
17 Bauer Palladio Hotel & Spa.............D2
18 Ostello Venezia................................D3

LIDO DI VENEZIA

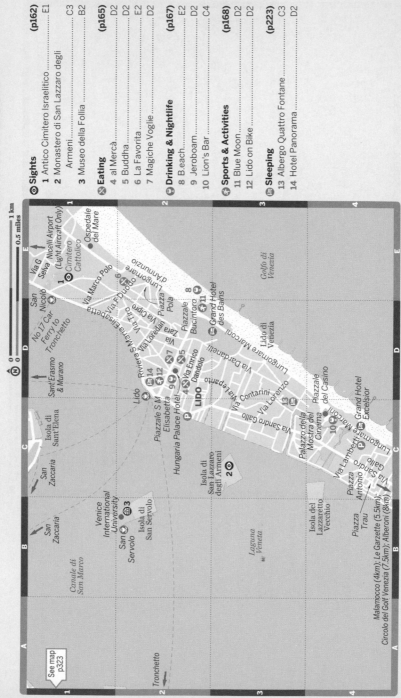

MURANO

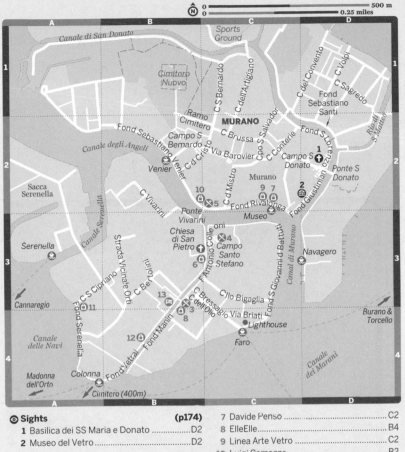

BURANO & TORCELLO

Our Story

A beat-up old car, a few dollars in the pocket and a sense of adventure. In 1972 that's all Tony and Maureen Wheeler needed for the trip of a lifetime – across Europe and Asia overland to Australia. It took several months, and at the end – broke but inspired – they sat at their kitchen table writing and stapling together their first travel guide, *Across Asia on the Cheap*. Within a week they'd sold 1500 copies. Lonely Planet was born.

Today, Lonely Planet has offices in Melbourne, London, Oakland and Delhi, with more than 600 staff and writers. We share Tony's belief that 'a great guidebook should do three things: inform, educate and amuse'.

Our Writers

Alison Bing

Coordinating Author; Plan Your Trip; Sestiere di San Marco; Sestiere di Dorsoduro; Sestieri di San Polo & Santa Croce; Sestiere di Cannaregio; Understand Venice & the Veneto When she's not scribbling notes in church pews or methodically eating her way across Venice's *sestieri* (neighbourhoods), Alison contributes to Lonely Planet's *USA, Morocco, San Francisco, Marrakesh, California* and *Discover Italy* guides, as well as food, art and architecture magazines. Alison holds a bachelor's degree in art history and a master's degree from the Fletcher School of Law and Diplomacy, a joint program of Tufts and Harvard Universities – perfectly respectable diplomatic credentials she regularly undermines with opinionated culture commentary for newspapers, magazines, TV and radio. Currently she divides her time between San Francisco and an Etruscan hilltop town in central Italy with partner Marco Flavio Marinucci, and tweets her finds at @AlisonBing. Alison also contributed to the Sleeping chapter of this guide.

Paula Hardy

Sestiere di Castello; Giudecca, Lido & the Southern Islands; Murano, Burano & the Northern Islands; Day Trips from Venice; Survival Guide From the slopes of Valpolicella to the curing houses of Valdobbiadene and the *spritz*-fuelled bars and *bacari* of Padua and Castello, Paula has been contributing to Lonely Planet's Italian guides for over 10 years, including guides to Milan, the Italian Lakes, Puglia, Sicily and Sardinia. When she's not scooting around the *bel paese*, she writes for a variety of travel publications and websites. You can find her tweeting from the lakes and mountains at @paula6hardy. Paula also contributed to the Sleeping chapter of this guide.

Published by Lonely Planet Publications Pty Ltd
ABN 36 005 607 983
8th edition – Nov 2013
ISBN 978 1 74220 872 5
© Lonely Planet 2013   Photographs © as indicated 2013
10 9 8 7 6 5 4 3 2 1
Printed in China